CALLAHAN LIBRARY
ST. JOSEPH'S COLLEGE
25 Audubon Avenue
Patchogue, NY 11772-2399

Creating Literacy Communities in the Middle School

Creating Literacy Communities in the Middle School

Leigh Van Horn

Christopher-Gordon Publishers, Inc.
Norwood, Massachusetts

Copyright Acknowledgments

Every effort has been made to contact copyright holders for permission to reproduce borrowed material where necessary. We apologize for any oversights and would be happy to rectify them in future printings.

Copyright © 2001 Christopher-Gordon Publishers, Inc.

Excerpt from "Sharing literature, sharing selves" by Leigh Van Horn, May, 2000, from *Journal of Adolescent and Adult Literacy, 43*(8), pp. 752–763. Copyright © 2000 by the International Reading Association. Reprinted with permission.

"Reading and writing essays about objects of personal significance" by Leigh Van Horn, January, 2001, from *Language Arts 78*, (3), pp. 273–378. Copyright © 2001 by the National Council of Teachers of English. Reprinted with permission of NCTE.

Excerpts from "Tickets to the theatre: Opening the curtain on a dialogue with words" by J. Parker-Webster and L. Van Horn, 2000, from *Voices from the Middle 7* (4), pp. 9–17. Copyright © 2000 by the National Council of Teachers of English. Reprinted with permission of NCTE.

All student work reprinted with permission.

All rights reserved. Except for review purposes, no part of this material protected by this copyright notice may be reproduced or utilized in any form or by any means, electronic or mechanical, including photocopying, recording, or any information and retrieval system, without the express written permission of the publisher or copyright holder.

Christopher-Gordon Publishers, Inc.
1502 Providence Highway, Suite 12
Norwood, MA 02062
800-934-8322

Printed in the United States of America

10 9 8 7 6 5 4 3 2 1   05 04 03 02 01

Library of Congress Catalog Card Number: 2001095883

ISBN: 1-929024-42-8

DEDICATION

To Jerry

Who is always
all that I hope for
and more.

Contents

Acknowledgments xiii

Introduction xv

Chapter 1: The Literacy Community 1
The Power of Belonging to a Group 1
A Picture of the School and the Students 7
Inside the Classroom 8
   Making Personal Literacy Public 9
   Organizing Our Community 9
   Seating In Our Community. 11
Developing a Literacy Community 12
   Reading, Writing, and Response. 13
   Defining Reading. 15
   Our History as Readers and Writers 16
Sustaining the Literacy Community 17
   The Learning Experience 19
   Learning From One Another 19
   Honoring the Products of Learning 22
   Commitment to the Literacy Community 23
Expanding Our View of the Literacy Community 26
   A New View of the Community 27
   Are We Doing it Right? 30
   The Community of Literary Texts 30
   The Community of Authors 31
   Sharing the Thoughts of Our Community 32
Evaluation/Assessment 33
Summary 34

Chapter 2: Defining Ourselves—Revealing the Literacies Inside Us 37
The Power of the Individual 37
   School Literacy Experiences 38
   Making Connections With Text 40
Constructing Life Maps 42
Reader of the Day 44
   Introducing Reader of the Day 46
   Who is Reading? 47
   What is Valued? 49
   What is Required of the Readers? 53
   Conduct for Readers and Listeners 54

    Choice of Texts 56
    Collaborative Curriculum 60
    Increased Awareness 61
    Merging of Personal and Academic Literacy 62
Defining Ourselves Through Objects of Personal Significance 63
    Collecting Tickets and Objects 64
    Creating the Museum of Objects and Ideas 65
    Reaction to the Museum of Objects and Ideas 67
    Extending the Exploration 67
    Prior Experiences With the Personal Essay 69
    Reading in Search of a Model 70
    Rereading to Analyze the Essay 71
    First Steps: Talking and Listening 72
    Writing Our Own Essays About Objects 73
    Further Exploration 76
    Thinking About the Experience 77
Defining Ourselves Through Poetry 77
    Introducing the Idea 78
    Students Writing About Themselves 80
Evaluation/Assessment 83
Summary 85

CHAPTER 3: TRANSACTING WITH TEXT 89
Questioning the Text 89
    Student Involvement 92
Reading Together 93
Thinking Together 94
Looking at the Process 95
Taking a Closer Look 99
The Students' Perspectives 109
    Their Initial Feelings 109
    Ownership of Ideas 112
    The Process and What it Means to Students 113
    Evaluation of the Process 114
Moving to Silent, Independent Reading 118
    Introducing the Books and the Process 119
    Difficulties and Transformations 120
    Writing Notes to One Another 123
Reading and Thinking on Our Own 126
Evaluation/Assessment 128
Summary 129

CHAPTER 4: THE POWER OF TALK 133
Developing Ideas About Talk 133

Opening Conversations 136
Balance of Power in Conversations 144
Talking in Small Groups 150
Evaluation/Assessment 161
Summary 162

CHAPTER 5: LIVING THE MEANINGS THROUGH PERFORMANCE 165
Developing Ideas About Performance 165
Was It Always Like This? 167
Choral Reading 168
The Van Gogh Café 169
Character Interrogation 174
The Poetry Café 178
    Compare and Contrast 179
    Performing Poetry 180
The Radio Play 182
    Listening to Learn. 183
    Practicing and Further Planning 184
    Commercial Break 184
    Connections 185
A Shakespearean Play 185
    Why *Macbeth*? 186
    Setting the Stage 186
    Preparing for Production 187
    Filming the Play 188
    Taking a Bow 189
    The Curtain Closes 189
Evaluation/Assessment 190
Summary 191

CHAPTER 6: THE POWER OF WRITING 193
Developing Our Writing Power 193
Responding to Photographs 196
Re-envisioning *The Van Gogh Café* 200
Canyons 205
    Making Connections 205
    Creating Journals 207
    Finding Poetry in the Prose 209
    Writing to the Author 213
The Outsiders 214
    Outsiders and Friends 214
    Considering the Setting 219
The Mystery 221
    The Elements of Mystery 221

	A Detective's Notebook	227
Macbeth: A Myriad of Meanings		232
	Finding Poetry in the Play	233
	Conclusions About *Macbeth*	236
Evaluation/Assessment		240
Summary		242

CHAPTER 7: THE POWER OF VISUAL REPRESENTATION ... 245

Reading, Writing, and Works of Art		245
	Beginning by Remembering	246
	Constructing a Collage	250
	Creating a Wallet	251
	Creating Paper Characters	255
Visual Representations of a Theme		256
	Creating Ransom Note Mystery Poems	256
	Spelling Out *The Giver*	257
	Piecing Together a Survival Quilt	258
Evaluation/Assessment		260
Conclusion		261

Appendix A:	Course Syllabus	263
Appendix B:	Meeting Objectives Checklist	269
Appendix C:	Museum of Objects and Ideas Planning Sheet	270
Appendix D:	Museum of Objects and Ideas Rubric	272
Appendix E:	Essay About Object of Personal Significance Rubric	273
Appendix F:	"I Am" Poem Planning Sheet	275
Appendix G:	Questions, Comments, and Observations—*Double Trouble Squared*	276
Appendix H:	Questions, Comments, and Observations—*Canyons*	281
Appendix I:	Questions, Comments and Observations—*The Outsiders*	288
Appendix J:	Questions, Comments, and Observations—*The Giver*	292
Appendix K:	Transcript of Discussion of *The Outsiders*	299
Appendix L:	Evaluation Sheet—Mystery Suspense Theater Radio Show	307
Appendix M:	Commercial for Mystery Suspense Theater Radio Show Planning Sheet	308
Appendix N:	Survival Across Time Project Planning Sheet	310
Appendix O:	Response Options/Specifications Planning Sheet	312
Appendix P:	Paper Bag Mystery Planning Sheet	314
Appendix Q:	You Are The Detective!!! Planning Sheet	316
Appendix R:	Detective Notebook Rubric	317

Appendix S:	Character Sketch in a Wallet Planning Sheet	318
Appendix T:	Letter to the Owner of Your Wallet Rubric	319
Appendix U:	Paper Characters and Character Profile Planning Sheet	320

REFERENCES 323

LITERATURE USED 326

INDEX 329

ABOUT THE AUTHOR 337

Acknowledgments

Our Voices, Our Meanings is a book about defining, establishing, and sustaining a literacy community in a 7th-grade reading classroom. It has long been a dream of mine to tell the story of the remarkable individuals who have shared this classroom with me. My deepest thanks go to my students who have enthusiastically joined me in this effort to go beyond the texts, to reflect, and to come to new understandings as we search for ways to make meaning and to make learning meaningful. This book would never have been possible without their willingness to think deeply and to share their insight with me. It is through my students that I have learned what it is to be a teacher.

I must also thank the parents of these children and the teachers, administrators, and staff of the school and the school district for their belief in me and for their support and encouragement. It is a joy to work with people who have so obviously dedicated their lives to children and to education.

My life and work have also been enriched through my membership in a larger literacy community which includes educators who live and work in the city where I live. These are the people who have been my teachers and whose words and ways of working have inspired me. I thank Kylene Beers, Phil Carspecken, Margaret Hill, Be Be Hood, Lee Mountain, Leslie Patterson, Barbara Samuels, Pat Smith, my fellows in the Greater Houston Area Writing Project and the Greater Houston Area Reading Council, and the faculty of the Department of Urban Education at the University of Houston—Downtown.

Finally, I want to thank the people at Christopher-Gordon who have made this book possible. Sue Canavan's dedication to this project has remained constant. From the moment of her first telephone call to me after she had read the opening chapters and through all of her calls, letters, and e-mail messages afterward, she has made me feel the importance of what we were doing together. I am also grateful to Kathryn Liston and Laurie Maker who have patiently answered all of my questions about the technical aspects and production of the book and who have helped to bring the voices of myself and my students into print.

INTRODUCTION

As teachers we are always learning. We learn by listening to and reading the words of other teachers and those of our students. We peruse professional journals and texts about language and literacy, walk the hallways of our schools, peeking into classrooms, share wonderings and discoveries at conferences, and talk to teachers and students engaged in literacy. Listening, reading, and talking leads to further wondering.

Cochran-Smith and Lytle (1993) describe teachers who examine their practices as those who "pose problems, identify discrepancies between their theories and their practices, challenge common routines, and attempt to make visible much of what is taken for granted about teaching and learning" (p. 19). This book reflects my own efforts *and* those of my students to address these issues as we examine our literacy community, our meaning making, and the power structures within our community.

Each year, in the opening days of school as I watch and listen to my students, I wonder at the diversity in their approaches to reading and to their construction of meaning. Some students read curled up contently on the floor or under the table, devouring the words as others sit tensely at their desks gazing around the room or at the clock, counting the pages they have flipped past. When we talk about the meaning of reading, some say that reading means finishing the number of pages you are supposed to read. When I probe further, asking about the meaning we might discover when we think about what we read, some reveal that they think about what they are reading and compare it to their own experiences. Others state that reading for meaning is reading to find the answers to the teacher's questions.

For four years my students and I examined our literacy practices as we developed a community of learners who read, questioned, talked, performed, wrote, and visually represented our meaning making and our lives together. Within the pages of this book you will read excerpts from the writings, discussions, and interviews of students from all of the classes I taught during this time. In the last year I chose a single class group that I determined to be the most representative and invited these students to go further with me in our examination of literacy practices. During one-on-one interviews, these students examined transcripts and tapes of our classroom discussions about literature as well as lists of our questions, comments, and observations about texts, talking with me about their processes and perceptions.

In the beginning of this examination I had a plan. I would observe my students and collect information in the form of checklists, anecdotal notes, journals, audio and visual tapes of classroom experiences and discussions, and copies of the students' written responses to literature. I believed that I alone would look at these artifacts of literacy, piecing together the elements of our literacy community and my students' meaning making processes. This is a true reflection of how it all began.

In the beginning, I did not plan to collect notes from my students, slips of paper thrust into my hands or placed upon my desk—paper worn thin as it was folded and unfolded and read again and again. I did not plan for my students to sit beside me and look at lists of their questions, comments, and observations about literature; to tell me how it is for them to do this thing, what it means to them, and what they think of when they reread what they have written. I did not plan for my students to read the transcripts of our conversations about literature and to talk with me about how they did this, what they fear, why it is important to them, and why it makes them feel important.

I did not plan to hear the voices of my students ringing in my ears or to feel them with me each and every day as I continued to think and to write. And yet, they were with me; and they *are* with me. It is not only my voice that you will read, it is our voices. Theirs are the voices at the center telling me, telling us, what we can do as teachers.

As my students accept and expand upon invitations to think about themselves and their literacy experiences, they exercise distinct and insightful voices. Anthony, for example, defines meaning making as a process of discovery in which we develop our own potential as we interpret and respond to literature. He writes,

> Real knowledge is what we learn in here. We learn how to understand literature and respond and interpret it. We learn how to express our feelings about what we've read. We learn how to communicate with each other and to build upon each other's ideas. And all of us develop to a certain degree our inner genius. By saying "genius" I do not so much mean being able to score high on an I.Q. test or get all A's. I mean finding the inner talents we all possess and building upon them. I mean growing and finding your dreams. I mean discovering yourself.

The voices of these adolescents and those of other adolescents may reveal much to us about the impact and the influence of our ways of doing school. Although I am not suggesting that we as teachers simply ask our students what they want to do in school and how they want to "do" school, I am suggesting that we may learn a great deal about ourselves and our students if we place them in the center of our practice. We might consider whether our students understand the what and the why of the classroom experience. We might talk to our students, asking them to reflect upon and to evaluate their experiences in our classrooms. We might ask them, "Why do you think we do this? Does this work for you? What could we do differently?" My own experiences have shown me that as I make notes about what students are saying and doing, tape record classroom interactions and discussions, engage students in explicit discussion of strategies, and invite them to collaborate with me on both curriculum and evaluation/assessment, they are both motivated and empowered as they begin to see themselves as participants in a study of our literacy practices.

Through ongoing exchanges in which we think and talk about what stands in the way of our learning and why we do the things we do, we and our students may be able to refine, customize, or transform the learning experience. This idea is expressed most powerfully by Maxine Greene (1988), who in writing about the transformations that occur through continued teaching and learning states that "we may be able to empower the young to create and re-create a common world, and, in cherishing it, in renewing it, discover what it signifies to be free" (p. 23).

Part I of this book (chapters 1–4) provides an introduction to our classroom. As you read, you will develop a view of the theories underpinning our practices as we define, develop, and sustain our literacy community, as we consider our life and literacy histories reflecting on what it is we know and how we come to know what we know. You will join us as we engage in questioning, commenting, observing, and talking about texts, and then as we reflect upon these processes.

Part II of this book (chapters 5–7) provides a practical view of the ways that our examination of community, meaning making, and the power structures within this classroom are reflected in the students' performance, writing, and visual representation of texts, and how these aspects of literacy contribute to further meaning making. Using my journals, audio and visual tapes, and excerpts from the students' products, I have attempted to reconstruct these experiences and present a picture that will enable you to "see" how we approach and work through each of these aspects of meaning making. In each section of these chapters you will read specific descriptions of what we do and what we think, as well as excerpts of the products of our experiences. In both parts of the book, where appropriate, I have included brief descriptions of the ways that we evaluate and assess our learning at the end of the chapter.

As you read, you may have questions about how this program fits into a prescribed curriculum. In this particular district, teams of teachers from various campuses and representing each grade level come together several times a year to evaluate and update our curriculum. Together we create lists of possible texts and descriptions of learning experiences and products based upon the elements of our standardized test (Texas Assessment of Academic Skills, TAAS) and our English Language Arts and Reading performance standards (Texas Essential Knowledge and Skills, TEKS).

To read more about the standardized test and the performance standards you may want to visit these websites: http://www/tea.state.tx.us/student.assessment/ and http://www.tea.state.tx.us/teks/. I have designed this program to incorporate the objectives of our academic skills for reading which are determining the meaning of words; identifying supporting ideas; summarizing; perceiving relationships and recognizing outcomes; analyzing information in order to make inferences and generalizations; and recognizing points of view, propaganda, and/or statements of fact and opinion in a variety of texts. Within a framework of texts and learning experiences designed to meet the interests and needs of my students I have also included opportunities for the students to develop their processes of reading, writing, listening, speaking, viewing, and visually representing their meaning making as described in the performance standards.

In general, my own process has been to design curriculum centered on a particular novel, genre, or theme, and then to address the skills and standards of performance through our reading and response to the texts. As the students engage in literacy activities, they have authentic opportunities to learn about and to practice the processes of successful readers and writers within the context of the learning experience. I have found this way of working, rather than the overt teaching of skills out of context, to be both motivating and productive. In order to "prove" to myself that our ways of working enable my students to perform well on the required standardized test in our state, I have made it a practice to analyze the individual results of the testing of each student at the beginning and end of the year and to compare the results of my students with the results of other students. The results of these analyses have reassured me that the students not only perform well on the standardized reading test for the 7th grade, but that a number of them exceed their previous performances on the test.

Teaching and learning are creative, collaborative activities. With this in mind, I have made it a practice to "field test" and adapt my readings of reading/language arts research to my own classroom. As my students and I engage in these learning experiences we stop at various points to reflect, evaluate, and recreate the process to fit our particular needs. At the beginning of each year, I provide my students with a syllabus or outline of the year which includes titles of texts and possible responses (see appendix A). As the year unfolds, we may find that our interests or needs lead us in other directions. Through our collaboration, we will make changes in this outline. At the end of the year I ask my students to write to me about what they enjoyed the most, what worked for them, what did not work, and to offer their recommendations to me about what to include and what to eliminate in the plans for the following year. Their evaluations and my own records of what I see and hear as we work together help me to react to their immediate needs and to refine my plans for the future.

As I said at the beginning of this introduction, we as teachers, are always listening, reading, talking, wondering, and learning as we interact with one another and with our students. As you read the words that follow I hope that you will listen, read, talk, and wonder with us and that you will learn something that renews and supports what you are already doing or something that reveals new possibilities for your own literacy communities.

1

THE LITERACY COMMUNITY

THE POWER OF BELONGING TO A GROUP

> While Don was reading I was watching you. Your face caught my eye. I saw you looking at him and you looked so proud. Then when Brian patted him on the back you smiled. But it wasn't a regular smile, it was one of those smiles like if you're watching your child walk or ride a bike for the first time. It's a proud smile.... As this whole situation was going on I had a smile on my face too. But it wasn't like your smile. This was a wow smile. I was thinking, wow, this is such a special moment for her.... Just watching you and Don made me want to cry. But I didn't, I just smiled.
>
> — Brandi

Beginnings, first impressions, I recall our coming to know one another as readers and writers, and as people; as I think about our literacy community and what it has come to mean, how it enables us to begin and sustain our search for meaning, and how this often leads to our empowerment, I wonder how best to open the story. Should I begin with possible definitions of the literacy community itself, or should I describe our own beginnings? While weighing the possibilities I came across the note above, handed to me by Brandi on her way out the door after class one day in mid-April of our year together. It occurs to me that I can start in the middle.

I remember this moment well. Don had always made us laugh. It wasn't unusual for him to come to class dragging a slightly worn Kermit the Frog puppet by the hand. In fact, Don would sometimes use Kermit to tell us what he really wanted to say. Today, Don was reading aloud the words he had written defining an outsider. As he read,

> I think an outsider is a person that does not blend with other people. Sometimes they will not be welcomed to certain groups, and other times they could walk right in and no one would notice,

Brian patted him on the back, as if to encourage him or to tell him that he understood. I smiled proudly, thinking about what Don had written as well as Brian's reaction to him and what he had written. It seemed to me that Don was "riding a bike for the first time," showing us another side of himself, and that Brian was encouraging that revelation.

As I think further about Don's statement defining an outsider and of his actions in the classroom, I come to a deeper understanding of the meaning of his statement. The first part of his statement reveals Don's own desire to be accepted as a part of the group. He seems to be telling us that there are times when he feels alone or like an outsider. Don realizes that school is a place where there are groups of friends, and that some people do not belong to or will not be invited to become members of such groups—that some people might be left alone. As he shares his thoughts with us, Don acknowledges a belief that there is power in belonging to a group. It is as if, through his written response, he is telling us that people should accept others as they are and that it is wrong to ignore or exclude others from membership in a group. The second part of his statement reveals Don's own desire to be noticed or appreciated and his recognition that school is a place where a person can go unnoticed or unrecognized.

As I consider the possible meanings of Don's statement about outsiders and reread Brandi's note about those moments, it occurs to me that these are claims and actions that reflect the possibilities entailed in a literacy community. Simply put, we experience a heightened awareness of ourselves and others as readers, writers, and as people. We notice things about one another, we accept that which is about each of us, and we encourage one another to continue.

Comments made in one-on-one interviews with the students reflect the importance of awareness and acceptance in our classroom community. Gina tells me she thinks that people here listen to what she has to say. When I ask her why she thinks that may happen, she replies, "Well before . . . I didn't, um. I was like, not exactly an outsider, but I was like, like, no one really knew me before." It appears that as we come to know one another we are better prepared to listen to one another. Nettie, when asked about how communities are formed and sustained, reflects on the importance of listening to others, saying, "I think *listen*, you know listening to what people have to say and not just ignoring them." Again, listening is a feature of our attending to or knowing others.

The Literacy Community

Burton speaks about the risk involved with allowing other people to know us; the risk that is inherent in a community where people read, write, think, speak, and listen to one another. He says, "But you know, if everybody knows you, you know at least a few people are not going to like you. And if a few people already don't like you when you're not like even popular, imagine how many people are not going to like you when you are popular and everyone knows you." Burton seems to believe that to become known by a larger group of people is to enlarge the risk of not being "liked" or accepted by those people. As we begin to engage in literacy events with one another, we acknowledge the risk involved and the expectation that awareness may lead to acceptance. Our community will be defined through our words, actions, and interactions.

We might think of a literacy community as a context for educational interactions.

> Griffin, Belyaeva, and Soldatova and the Velikhov-Hamburg collective (1993) describe the way this occurs, writing that " . . . context is also dynamic, fluid, and complex, not established beforehand like the backdrop prepared for a stage play; a context emerges being constituted in large measure by words used by the context participants and their other actions" (p. 121).

The creation of a literacy community is not something that is completed in the first few weeks of school; the "backdrop" may be provided, but the players must enter the stage or the world and come to understand both the purpose of that world and those who exist within the world. The creation of a literacy community is an ongoing effort which, in order to be empowering, must be at the same time responsive to the needs of its members and reflective of the words and actions of its members.

In a collection of essays on education Frank Smith (1988) compares the literacy community or "club" to what he calls the spoken language club in which membership enables us to establish ourselves in language and literacy.

> In describing what occurs in the literacy club, Frank Smith (1988) writes, "In particular, members occupy themselves with whatever activities the club has formed itself to promote, constantly demonstrating the value and utility of these activities to the new members, helping them to participate when they want but never forcing their involvement and never ostracizing them for not having the understanding or the expertise of more practiced members. Differences in ability and in specific interests are taken for granted" (pp. 2–3).

The author A. C. Purves (1984) refers to the connection between community and engagement with literature specifically, stating, "Communities are in part held together by shared experiences, shared perceptions, and shared language. . . . literature provides a major vehicle for creating communities" (p. 18). As we attempt to create and nurture a literacy community we build upon shared experiences, perceptions, and language. At the same time, a critical aspect of this way of envisioning a literacy community is the acknowledgement of our differences.

> Judith Langer (1995) refers to the acknowledgement of differences as the acknowledgement of shared elements within a framework of difference and states that through the dialogue of interpretation we realize the interwoven nature of the community while at the same time "the participants, and thus the community itself, are open to difference, empathy, awareness, and change" (p. 54).

In the classroom, Anita clarifies her thoughts about the acceptance of people who may be different from ourselves, saying, "it doesn't matter what you look like, it depends on who you are and how you react. I mean color and the flesh is what we use to keep ourselves together, that's nothing. I mean most of what we have is our brain. That's what we use." Her words reflect a claim that people should be defined by their thoughts, words, and actions, rather than by how they appear on the surface.

It is unlikely that the members of a school or classroom community will come together having identical life experiences, interests, abilities, goals, or ways of knowing. Envisioning a community in this way allows us to address those differences and to make them a part of the learning experience, using them to diversify our activities and to add to our own knowledge. The implication is that we may learn from one another.

I remember meeting Frank Smith at a social gathering during a conference in which he was the keynote speaker. I told him about some of the things my students were writing and saying about literature and their own literacy experiences, he remarked upon the "courage" of the students. I was taken aback for a moment, not having considered their actions and accomplishments in this light. In thinking further I told him that I believed they might derive their courage from one another, from the encouragement and support they receive within the literacy community as they come to know and to appreciate their diversity as well as what they have in common.

> Maxine Greene notes the nature of a community to actively create itself and to evolve, as she writes, "In thinking of community we need to emphasize the process words: making, creating, weaving,

saying and the like" (1995, p. 38). She compares the concept of community to that of freedom in that both are achieved as individuals are allowed to discover what they have in common and as they come to imagine their own possibilities as well as that of the group. Greene states that "In contexts of this kind, open contexts where persons attend to one another with interest, regard, and care there is a place for the appearance of freedom, the achievement of freedom by people in search of themselves" (1988, p. xi). She defines a free act as one that occurs as an individual seeks to express herself as a solitary person acting within a social world where there are "shared meanings and social realities" (1988, p. 70).

For the students in my classroom, the social world or social reality may be defined in terms of family or familial trust and attachment. During one-on-one interviews conducted with students at the closing of the academic year, repeated references are made to the word "family" in relation to this classroom and to the literacy community we have created and nurtured. Sandy talks about family in terms of our awareness of one another:

> When we're sitting in here together it makes me feel happy 'cause I feel like we're one big family and we're all, 'cause we all like ... sometimes I'll listen to a person read and I'll look around at other people, looking at what they're feeling. 'Cause kind of you can tell by the person's actions how they're feeling. And you can just tell by somebody's face—what their expressions are.

A sense of family also emerges through our growing trust in one another. Shelby and others describe this as our coming to know that we can share personal thoughts and feelings without fear of ridicule, explaining:

> Well, it's just like we grow together. It's like when we're in here, all the time it's like, I don't know, it's kind of like a family. You wouldn't go, you wouldn't try to hurt that person.

Further in our conversation I ask her directly, "If our class is like a family, how did that happen?" She tells me,

> After the first few weeks of school you knew the people in here and you knew how they were and you knew they wouldn't do bad stuff once they really got to know each other.

The students develop a sense of trust and family through their ongoing interactions with one another. As they engage in literacy events, they test this idea of trust; and then, when confident about their place in the community and the reaction or acceptance of others, they rename and transform the community. The community becomes a place which is "like a family."

This sense of the community as a place which is "like a family" may lead to feelings of academic freedom. At the end of the year when I ask the students to reflect on the experience as a whole, the word or concept of freedom is frequently mentioned. Sandy states, "When I'm in this class I feel free." She uses the metaphor of breaking down a wall and being allowed to cross the wall and experience the outside world to express her idea of the freedom she feels. Jake refers to freedom as stemming from the acceptance of diverse ideas, stating, "You don't have to be worried about saying the wrong thing, because there's nothing wrong, because that's your idea." As Burton states it, "we just go free and see what we're thinking about and how we're thinking."

Our choice in what we say or do or in how we act is grounded in our awareness and understanding that this context or world may be acted upon in ways which foster a transformation of self and/or our world. The capacity to act or to transform self and/or world can be equated with power or empowerment. Power may also be seen as a form of agency which is defined as "the capacity, condition, or state of acting or of exerting power" (Merriam-Webster's Collegiate Dictionary, 10th ed). Wertsch, Tulviste, and Hagstrom (1993) outline a sociocultural approach to agency which argues that human agency (humans as active and purposeful agents) extends "beyond the skin" of individuals, and is often a product of the interactions within groups (p. 337). In other words, individuals who use language to communicate within a socially created context or community may develop a sense of agency or power.

D. Bloome (1986) notes the critical connection between language and the development of a community stating,

> Since reading and writing are inherently social processes, one way to think about literacy is in terms of community building. As people use language they signal their membership and participation in a community.... people are expected to use language, including reading and writing, in ways consistent with that community. To do otherwise would signal that one was not a member of that community (pp. 71–72).

A Picture of the School and the Students

How does it all begin? How do we come to honor both our diversity and our commonality? How can communication and community provide a sense of freedom and power? These thoughts are uppermost in my mind as I stand "duty" on the circular driveway of our middle school, watching those who may become my students on the first day of school. The middle school (hereinafter referred to by the pseudonym of Westbrook) is perched alongside a five lane highway which cuts through the center of this suburb of a large metropolitan area. The students of Westbrook are primarily from lower middle- to middle-income households. The students come from diverse ethnic backgrounds including Anglo American, Latin American, Asian American, African American, and Middle Eastern. The facility itself is relatively new. Westbrook is in its seventh year of existence. At the central core of the main building are the commons (a combination cafeteria and gathering area), the library, and computer labs. Running on two sides of the central core are wide hallways. Branching off from the two main hallways are short hallways which house four classrooms each. Westbrook is a middle school for grades 6, 7, and 8.

Out on the driveway where I stand duty, the right, front door of an old Chevy Malibu screeches as it opens, and a roar of rap music emerges from the car as a young boy driven to school by his older brother steps out onto the pavement. Behind the Chevy is an old, dented truck, its bed consumed by a wire cage containing a goat. The small boy inside jumps down and turns with a solemn grin, to give his mother a parting salute. A van pulls up and I step out to help as the boy inside struggles to shoulder his backpack and open the door. From inside his father calls to me, "We were almost late. We always stop to have breakfast together on the first day of school." In the next car, a somewhat harried looking mother searches through her handbag for several dollars which she thrusts into the hand of her daughter who leans over and kisses her. As the girl steps from the car I hear her saying, "I love you mom." One after another, they disembark on this first day of school. As I watch them I think for a moment about their lives outside the classroom and all the experiences they will bring with them as they enter this school. My hope for them at this moment, and for every moment that follows, is that school will matter, that it will be meaningful, and that they will remember these days as ones in which they began to realize the full potential of their learning and becoming. With this in mind, I open the side door and proceed to my classroom, surrounded and moved forward by a teeming mass of students clutching schedules in hand, their expressions alternating between detached coolness, expectant curiosity, and outright fear.

My classroom is at the far end of the building. A walk down the wide hallway reveals hand made signs advertising various school clubs such as the Writers' Guild and Student Council hanging on the walls. Soon these hallways will be filled with examples of student work, a reflection of all that is happening in the school. Outside of room 157 is a sign which reads "Mrs. Van Horn, 7th Grade Reading."

Inside the Classroom

As I take my students on a "visual tour" of the classroom, explicitly inviting them to consider the room as their office or home and to write and post informal notes to me and to their fellow students, I begin to introduce the idea of the formation of the community through the creation of the physical context. We will attempt to organize our community in such a way that we may all move about independently; that we may be aware of current, ongoing, and future activities; and that a part of us remains in the room in the form of files that will become the students' portfolios. Shelves and cabinets hold the supplies that we may need as well as artifacts of past and present literacy communities. Further organization occurs as the students are invited to write to me about where and with whom they would like to be seated.

On the first days of my 7th-grade reading class I look upon a blur of hundreds of faces, reading aloud names which mean nothing to me now, but which will become everything to me in the time to come. They are silent and expectant in these first few days, waiting to know me and to know what will be expected of them. In my first few years of teaching I made the assumption that students would be familiar with collaborative learning and variations of the workshop approach to reading and writing. I assumed that they would feel comfortable in moving about the room to get what they needed to work. After being interrupted countless times during conferences with students and other activities to give my permission for a student to sharpen his pencil or to get another sheet of paper, I realized that it was necessary to extend an explicit invitation to them to consider this room as their office or home. If I wanted the students to be independent I would have to make it clear to them. The visual tour of the room on the first day is my initial step toward encouraging their independence. They will have to be reminded in the weeks and months to come that this is their place and that they have the right to move about and to get what they need in order to do what we are doing.

Student statements about the classroom reflect an awareness of the context itself as an aspect of community. Bet says, "I mean here in this big classroom with all of our stuff everywhere, and I mean everyone feels at home." Gina also makes a connection between the classroom and home, stating, "It's almost like home." The physical context of the room builds community by providing a place where students feel comfortable and a place where they are surrounded by examples of their own thinking and that of others.

Making Personal Literacy Public

The tour begins just inside the door where there is a large sheet of paper covered with yellow Post-it notes. Written at the top of the paper is the word "Notes." This is a note board on which the students and I can write to one another. They may leave notes to their friends who have the class during other periods of the day or they may write to me. I like to use the notes myself. There is always a crowd around the note board at the beginning and end of class with students checking to see if anyone has written to them or leaving a note for someone to discover. Sometimes a parent who is visiting the school will leave a note for his or her child. At the end of the second week of class as I read the notes posted on the board, I can not help but think that they reveal our first attempts to get to know one other, to talk about what we like, to plan, and to share a bit of humor.

I see the note board as a venue for extending and legitimizing our personal literacies. In my personal and professional life I write notes. My students write notes. The note board is a means of allowing our communications to become public. As the year progresses we will use the note board to congratulate one another, to make plans, to ask questions, and to comment on books and movies or to announce the beginning or ending of relationships. We may even reach out to one another, seeking new friends as did Jim who wrote asking if anyone would e-mail him at home. Jim, who related more to his teachers than to his peers, was fascinated by the potential of electronic communications. Through the note board he made connections with others who found it easier to talk "on-line."

Organizing Our Community

Next to our note board is a table. At the right end of this table is a rack filled with folders for independent activities and hall passes. In front of the rack is a sign-out book in which students may sign out to go to the restroom, nurse, lockers, and so forth. Above the table is a small bulletin board titled "Remember." Sports schedules, calendars, and advertisements for activities at the local book store are stapled to the bulletin board.

As we continue on our visual tour, stretching across the front of the classroom to the picture window at the far end is a blackboard. Activities for the day are posted here. The wall across from the door has a picture window on the right side which looks out onto a stretch of grass bordered by a thick growth of trees and underbrush which surround the nearby homes. On the far left side of the wall are two, four drawer file cabinets. These cabinets contain hanging files for each student filed alphabetically by class period. Each class has a drawer. Here the students will file their written responses to reading as well as presentation materials and products created in response to reading. These will be bound at the end of the year and each student will leave the 7th grade with a portfolio book of his or her work. I have found that keeping the files here in the room serves several purposes. First, the students have what they need with them. They no longer have to search through burgeoning binders or crammed lockers or even under their beds at home for a work in progress or completed work. Second, having their own file in the classroom gives the students a further sense that this is their place—a place to work and to think. In the first few years that I tried this approach, I put their work into the files myself. Comments such as "What file?" and "I have a file?" helped me realize that in doing this for them, I was the only one who was benefiting from the experience. Now, when I hear the students saying "I need to put this in my file," "Wow, look how big my file is getting," and "I can't believe how much I've changed this year," I see that the keeping of our files provides us with both a sense of belonging and a means of evaluating ourselves. For some students like Anthony, the creation of the portfolio book will be the beginning of a lifetime of collecting the artifacts of his existence. The following is a letter from Anthony's portfolio:

> This book is very special to me, and it contains nearly all the work that I have done this year, or at least the work I felt merited a place in these pages. I envision that in fifty years I will have a shelf full of portfolios, and this will be the one that started it all. Thus, this book holds a special place in my heart.

At the back of the classroom is another large blackboard. This one has a large sheet of white paper titled "Reader of the Day" on the right side. Student names and titles of readings will be recorded here. Index cards containing literary terms and definitions are attached to the blackboard with magnetic strips. These terms will be moved to the front board and manipulated and discussed by the students as they correspond to the themes of study. At the far left of the back wall is another large sheet of red paper headed with the words "I Love Reading." This is my own personal board on which I put notes and letters from students and friends. My desk is in front of this bulletin board. I never sit at the desk; it is just a place to stack things that need to go home or things I need to look at during my conference period.

Running on the same wall as the door to the classroom is a pale blue laminated work station consisting of a counter top with shelves above and below and a two door standing cabinet. Upper shelves contain class sets of novels and paper back books which the students may borrow. There is a set of dictionaries on one shelf. One shelf contains stuffed animals and statues received as gifts from students. The counter contains items we may need for our work or for inspiration. At the far right are framed drawings and letters from students. Sometimes students may ask what I would like for a Christmas or end of the year present. I always tell them that the best gift is one that comes from the heart and is a reflection of themselves. Of particular note is a framed drawing of a sports car with the words "Sheer Perfection" written in Vietnamese. This was a gift from Tran who struggled at first, lamenting "Is that all we're going to do in here? Read, read, read, and talk about books?" He is now in high school and sent this gift to me through his sister, Rose, along with a book of poems he had written about our class and his feelings about reading and writing. Beside this is a drawing of me in a kilt, holding a sword and shield, entitled "The Scottish Mrs. Van Horn." This was made by Ryan in honor of our study of *Macbeth*. There are poems by Ashley, Diane, and Sabrina about reading and our class. These gifts and the photographs of students, past and present, remind me of important moments in my life as a teacher. Further down the counter is a collection of scrapbooks, one for each year, containing photographs of the students engaged in classroom and school activities. These remind us all of why we are here. We enjoy looking at them and remembering the things we have done together. Sometimes we include artifacts of our experiences, such as the crumpled tissue inserted in a scrapbook by a group of girls who couldn't stop crying as we read *Journey* (MacLachlan, 1991). Beside the scrapbooks is a collection of specialized dictionaries—rhyming, synonyms, antonyms, idioms, and so forth. Next to these is a glass box I made while in art school and enamored with the work of Joseph Cornell. Sections of the box represent the four elements—earth, air, fire, and water. Next to this is a fish bowl containing word tickets (roll tickets with words cut out of magazines and newspapers glued to them). Beside this are a collection of tools; pencil sharpener, pencils, pens, scissors, glue, tape, stapler, and hole punch. The shelves below the counter are labeled with class period numbers. Each class has its own shelf on which are kept Reader/Writer logs and projects in progress. There are also several shelves which contain different types of paper we might use and magazines for clipping or reading. Finally, there is the two door cabinet which contains books and supplies not currently in use. The doors of the cabinet are covered with lists of the award winning books for this year and past years.

Seating In Our Community.

In the classroom there are 32 desks arranged in pairs facing the front of the room. They may be rearranged easily into groups of four to six or other configurations depending upon the activity in progress. There are also seven free standing chairs and a small table in the room for student conferences or discussion groups. Several weeks after the beginning of the year, the students are asked to write a note to me listing three people they would like to sit with in the classroom. I read over the notes and arrange the seating so that they are sitting near people with whom they feel comfortable. Some students may prefer to sit alone or at some particular location in the classroom. I think it is particularly important that we begin the year this way.

I began to see this through my own documentation of classroom proceedings. As I study my notations about where students are seated and what is occurring, I find that students are more likely to engage in literacy events when they are sitting with their friends. Some cluster in front of the window, others under the front table, or in a circle at the front of the room. Still others sit in the space behind my desk or in the back of the room near the file cabinets.

Burton illustrates the thinking about seating with his reflections on how his class became a group:

> At first when we came in here we didn't really know each other. I wasn't really friends with nobody in here. And then like me and Jarod started to hang out, you know over there (nods to where he usually sits) and then me and Bet and Jake. And everybody started building a little foundation.... cause, you know how Jess and Shelby got to be best friends in here. 'Cause everybody started bunching up and then everybody is friends in this class.

Burton's words and my own observations about the increased level of participation when students are sitting with friends suggest the importance of providing students with a place in which they feel safe or cared for by others before we ask them to engage in risk taking. The seating arrangement may be changed once every 6 weeks if the students in the class want to make such a change. Due to the fact that there are numerous opportunities to interact with others in the classroom during reading, discussion, and the arrangement of group activities and presentations, the assigned seats may be used less frequently than would be expected. Nevertheless, they provide a stable base from which to proceed.

DEVELOPING A LITERACY COMMUNITY

We develop ideas about the membership and the means of a literacy community as we begin to address the activities and concerns on which our efforts will be focused. We talk about what we will be doing—reading and responding to texts. Students begin to think about the meaning of reading itself, as they collaboratively create their own definitions of reading. As their definitions of the process are shared, we become aware that our ideas about reading are diverse. This realization is compounded as students respond to surveys about reading and writing and as their responses are shared with the group and displayed in the classroom. Through these experiences, we recognize the activities and concerns of the literacy community. Thus, we construct both tacit and explicit understandings of how our community might empower us as we engage with texts and with one another; as we read and write questions, comments, and observations about text; and as we talk about text and interact with one another. Central ideas which emerge as we think about the membership and the meaning of a literacy community are that we will read, write, and talk together; that our personal experiences matter; and that the differences in our views which emerge may be a reflection of the diversity of our past experiences. These ideas will be explained and exemplified as our story unfolds.

Reading, Writing, and Response

As the first day tour continues, I attempt to describe the activities in which we will be engaged and my own love of reading and writing. While involved in a spirited discussion of our all time favorite books with a few students who have overcome their first day shyness, I am interrupted by Tom, sitting in a front row seat, who exclaims exasperatedly, "What's everybody so excited about? Are we going to be talking about reading and books like this every day? Whew!" A few weeks later, Tom writes an emotional response to a book he is reading about drawing in his Reader/Writer log:

> Jose M. Parramou had this paragraph how I feel about draw. This is what he wrote, "The art is a grand tour that the love and memory of landscape was born a landscape painting from an artist." That's how I think when I draw or color. My brain is drawing and keeping memories, but in my heart I feel joy and love. I don't know why I feel that way. It feels like when I am drawing, I'm a real artist or a different person. Sometimes I just draw something sad and I cry in my heart, but after I finish I don't feel anything. I think that I am really into drawing and I wish everybody could feel like me or think like me.

As I read this, I am stunned by the depth of Tom's thinking; this from a boy who seemed interested only in skating; a boy who had come to class for several weeks now, slouching in a front row seat, doodling on scraps of paper. As I read Tom's description of his feelings as he draws and his involvement with drawing, I see a parallel to aesthetic reading as defined by Louise Rosenblatt. Rosenblatt (1978) describes aesthetic reading as reading in which "the reader's attention is centered directly on what he is living through during his relationship with that particular text" (p. 25).

As Tom writes of the interaction between what his brain is thinking as he draws and what he is feeling, he describes a transaction through the act of drawing. The act of reading involves a personal investment or involvement with the text. Readers may become involved with a work of fiction as they relate to or "become" a character. As Tom writes he describes that investment or involvement with the act of drawing as it might also be described in relation to the act of reading. Tom's reflections represent the empowerment that emerges when students are invited to respond to text in a way that is personally meaningful to them. I might have asked Tom to respond to a specific prompt; however, at this time I asked him to tell me what he felt about what he was reading and how it related to his life and interests outside this classroom.

> Frank Smith (1988) describes a community of learners speaking, thinking, reading, and writing together as a literacy club. According to Smith, members of the club are concerned with "each other's interests and welfare" and occupy themselves in literacy events while they acknowledge and accept the diversity of the members of the club and attempt to invite participation by nonmembers (p. 2).

Why is it that some readers become deeply involved with what they are reading—questioning, arguing about, and contemplating the text—while others simply read what is printed? Reading what Tom has written, "I wish everybody could feel like me or think like me," reminds me of myself as a member of the literacy club, calling out to others to join me in the ultimate experience.

> Judith Langer (1995) writes of a literary community which she describes as "a place where students interact within a social context forming individual responses to literature which are further developed through their interactions with others and their participation in class activities" (p. 53).

> Bill Searcy (1988) states that we become members of the literacy club when we are unconditionally accepted as language users by whatever means we choose to use written language and that this acceptance enables us to use all that we know about books, language, and print to build meaning.

The central question of my opening days with these students is how to go about the process of establishing a learning community and, subsequently, how to invite those who are not already members to join the literacy club. My invitations are not always accepted in the way that I envision. One year on the first day of school I made a statement that I was looking forward to a great year and that I hoped we would all become friends and enjoy this experience of reading, talking, and writing together. Rob, in the front row, responded to my invitation with a deprecating remark, saying, "Who could *ever* be friends with a teacher?" When I asked students to think about themselves as readers and writers and to write down their goals for the year, Jesse wrote, "I have never liked to read, maybe this can be one of *your* goals this year—to get me to read." Sometimes a student will let me know that my initial efforts have been well received, as evidenced by this note thrust into my hand several days into the new year:

Dear Mrs. Van Horn,

Conceter this a yellow postet just to big to be put in a little piece of paper.

When I walked into your classroom on the first day of school and saw your enthusiasm when you talked to us I didn't know what to think. Because you almost never see a teacher like you. Normally the teachers tell you what kind of work you will do in the whole year. But you talked to us about all of the fun we will have this year. Reading class has never been one of my favorite classes. I like reading books that I can relate to and get the story in my mind. But this year I have a hunch that this will be one of my favorite class of the year. I don't think that there a lot of teachers in the world like you and I don't think that they love what they do for a living. I think that when you teach you dig down deep inside you.

Michael

Defining Reading.

I am digging down deep inside of myself. I want to show them the potential of looking beyond the surface. We can learn as we take a deeper look at things we might have taken for granted. For example, we can assume that all of us have the same ideas about reading and what we will be doing in this class or we can make an attempt to define reading and arrive at some new understandings on which to build. On the first day of school I give my students sheets of bulletin board paper and markers. Their task is to form small groups and create a chart which defines reading. Questions to be considered are: What does reading look like, sound like, feel like, taste like, smell like? There is some initial laughter, just as there was in the graduate reading class where I was asked to consider this same question with my fellow reading teachers. The laughter is there because at first the question seems almost as simple as what is eating or breathing? Reading is something we just do; many of us have not stopped to consider how we might describe the process. As they talk and write, some of the students express feelings of joy, sadness, and wonder with statements such as "Reading is like breathing. . . . you do it all the time," "Reading feels like tears gliding down my face," "Reading sounds like a door opening to another world," or "Reading is a haunting feeling of déjà vu when though I may not have ever actually lived it, I have read, and therefore know that experience." Others see reading in a different light, writing that "Reading looks like little black dots on paper," "Reading feels like pages turning," and "Reading smells like worksheets." These definitions of reading fall into two distinct categories. The first four statements represent an experiential or subjective way of viewing reading. Students who make such statements show evidence of having moved beyond a literal interpretation of texts and the act of reading. For them, reading may be seen as an extension of self which encompasses sights, sounds, feelings, and prior experiences. The last three statements represent an objective view of reading. Reading is a physical, literal act and presence—one which is made up of text, pages, and worksheets, rather than emotional connection and thought.

As we hang our definitions on the walls, we talk about how each one of us comes to this room with a different view of reading. None of these views are incorrect; they reflect the diversity of our past experiences. I show them some quotes from other readers and writers. Frank Zappa once wrote that "All my best memories never happened." When we look at this I ask them what he means. Christine says, "Books, he's talking about books. Like your favorite stories—they didn't *really* happen but they're in your memories like they did!" "Ohhhhh." There are a few moments of thoughtful silence during which I assume hopefully that each of us is reflecting upon favorite books which are firmly established in our respective memories. As we read other quotations posted on the walls from people such as Eudora Welty, Joan Didion, and Gertrude Stein, one student asks "Who are these people, were they in your class last year?" "No," I laugh. "These are readers and writers who write books, novels and books about reading and writing."

Our History as Readers and Writers

This discussion provides an opportunity for me to present the students with surveys on reading and writing, based upon those created by Nancie Atwell (1987). I ask them, "How would you like to tell me what you think about reading and writing, about your own experiences?" My question is greeted with a mixture of groans and giggles, expressions of concern and resignation. As the students respond in writing to questions such as "Why do people read?" and "What does someone have to do in order to become a good reader?" and "Why do people write?" and "What do you think a good writer needs to do in order to write well?" they begin to write the history of their personal literacy.

That night, while reading their responses to the surveys it occurs to me that I might have an opportunity to demonstrate "a community of learners" or a "community of readers and writers" through the words of the students themselves. No, the quotes on the wall had not been the thoughts of students "in my class last year." But, what if they were the thoughts of the students in my class this year? I grab a pad of paper and begin writing down some responses which strike me as interesting. Amber writes, "I gather ideas from reading." Rita writes, "Every night I read for one hour by my iguana's light that stays on all night." Justin responds to the question about what a writer needs, answering that "A writer needs "a lot of ideas, paper, and a typewriter." Sharon writes that "People write because they've had a great thought and they want people to know it," and Lee writes that he thinks "a good writer needs to have a good brain." Within the next few days I process a statement from each of the students and hang them on the walls, several feet from the ceiling, forming a border of thoughts from readers and writers about reading and writing. The effect of these statements will be felt in many ways throughout the year.

Students peruse the words of their fellow learners before, during, and after class. These initial thoughts provoke further thinking. "Show it to her," I hear Lauren whisper to Brian one morning before class. Brian hands me a piece of paper, saying, "I had a thought last night that you might want to put up." On the paper he has written, "Talking everybody can understand and hear, but writing only a few can read, and it makes different pictures to different people." Seeing the thoughts of himself and others placed in a position of importance has empowered Brian. His statement shows that he is considering his own membership in the literacy club and reflecting on our initial discussion of interactions with text in which we concluded that our prior experiences and ways of reading might lead us to unique interpretations of text. Brian's actions are a reflection of the interaction and sense of community that begins to develop when invitations are issued and contributions are accepted.

Sustaining the Literacy Community

If we consider a literacy community in terms of it being a base or a platform, a social context from which the meaning making and the power of the group emerges, then the community must be envisioned not as a concept which is established in the first weeks of an academic year but as a process which is always evolving. Efforts must be made to sustain and nurture the community as it evolves. As teachers, our own enthusiasm for what we do and for what our students do can be a driving force in the community. Conversations with my students have shown me that they interpret a teacher's enthusiasm as a form of respect for learning and doing and for the individuals engaged in the process of learning and doing. This is an aspect of teacher behavior that they consider relevant to their own growth and participation in school and/or in literacy experiences.

My classroom is not a quiet classroom. In fact, it often takes a few minutes for us to get settled in at the beginning of the period. Students stop me in the doorway or follow me around the room asking questions about what we are going to be doing, recommending books, or sharing something they have written. They do the same with one another. I have a harmonica (passed on to me by my husband from his days in the Navy), and when I am ready to start class or signal a change in activities I play a few notes on it to get the students' attention. The students laugh and ask me to play the blues or suggest I might need some lessons. There is an atmosphere of respect here. We are engaged in establishing a literacy community. Students are asked to share ideas and thoughts about what we are reading, to participate in discussions, to contribute suggestions about responses to reading, and to share their outside reading and writing with others. This is not always easy for them.

As I consider my own role in fostering the development of our community I am reminded of the words of Burton as he talked to me about our class:

Burton: There's no limit because you like everybody. We can say what we want because everybody thinks so differently and we still try to evaluate whatever they're saying. There's no rules. . . . well, I think everybody has some rules in their brains, like stuff to do, but I mean there's no limit. 'Cause we're always doing stuff, exceeding the limit we thought we could do, you know. We can tell by your face when you think something is really good or when it's so-so.

Van Horn: The way I'm looking at you?

Burton: Yeah, and everybody. Everybody can notice that, you know.

Van Horn: So, how does that make you feel when you see me look excited?

Burton: I mean it makes everybody feel good. It's like we did a good job. Like we're the best.

Van Horn: Then you feel you can exceed your expectations?

Burton: Yeah! That's what I meant.

Thinking about my conversation with Burton provokes a flow of wonderings. There must be more to my role in developing and sustaining the community than my outward expressions of enthusiasm. The word "respect" is one that is frequently used by my students as they describe aspects of teacher behavior they consider important to their own growth. How is it that we show our students that we have respect for them? It occurs to me that respect is reflected in various ways—our willingness to participate in the learning experience as we work alongside our students, the emphasis we place on learning from one another, the way that we honor the products of our learning, and in the way that we care for one another.

The Learning Experience

As we participate in the learning experience alongside our students, our respect for the process is reflected through our own actions. As a child I remember reading and then silently writing answers to the questions at the end of the story, hoping that my answers would be the ones that the teacher expected to see—the "right" answers. I learned a great deal from my own school experiences, but I sometimes had the feeling that my teachers already knew what I should be thinking and were simply waiting for me to arrive at the correct conclusion. Worse yet, there were times when I felt that they would never want to do the things they asked us to do, that these were only activities that students had to do in order to make a good grade. As educators, we come to this process of learning with a different knowledge base and expectations from those of our students; and, yet, we may experience similar emotions as we interact with one another in reading, writing, and talking about literature. When my students read, I read with them attempting to model the thoughts that are going through my head as I read. In answer to their frequent questions, "Mrs. Van Horn, have you read this before?" or "Do you know what's going to happen?" I tell them that I have read the literature but that each time I read it I learn something new, both from my own reading and from listening to their reactions and responses. When my students write, I write with them. This helps me gauge both the difficulty and duration of the activity. When we pause to share our thoughts about what we are writing I can give concrete examples from my own work in progress. This often leads others to talk about their processes. In this way we learn from one another. I may not complete my writing due to conferencing with students, but beginning with them helps establish the atmosphere. When my students talk, I talk with them. I have learned that there is a difference between talking with students and talking to them. I learn more about their thinking when I talk with them.

Learning From One Another

It is clear to me that my students have much to offer and that they will learn from one another.

> Barbara Smith Livdahl (1993) writes that "Teachers observe daily the powerful influence peers have on a student's learning, and most believe it is their responsibility to provide classroom conditions that are conducive to learning and personal growth" (p. 193).

I tell my students that they will learn as much or more from one another as they will from me. I emphasize learning from one another by inviting them to share their works in progress and by using examples of student work to model a process or to inspire others. Sometimes I ask permission from a student to use her work to help me teach classes which occur later in the day. At other times I forget to ask permission. It surprises me later in the day when a student whose work I have used comes running into the room to tell me that they have heard I used what they had written as an example. It is then that I know that the students are talking to each other outside of class about what happens in class and that they are proud to be seen as examples or as inspiration for others. Some will pretend dismay at having their friends in other classes hear what they have written, but it is evident from the way they stand proudly and from their smiles that this is but a momentary embarrassment. Others will hand me something they have written saying quietly, "You can use this if you want to, it's okay with me if other people hear it." Sometimes I ask students if they will come to the beginning of another class period and share what they have written.

I ask Jim to do this one day after he has shared what he has written with his own classmates. I write a note asking permission from the teacher he has the next period, and it is only moments later that he bursts back into the room waving his paper in his hands. "Where do you want me to sit? Can I sit here on the stool? Okay, I'm ready now!" As the class grows silent, I formally introduce Jim and tell them that he has something to share with them. We are all working on writing stories based upon a study of immigration for the children in nearby elementary schools. Jim clears his throat and begins to read:

> It was a cold winter day in New York city, just off the coast and Tommy could feel the crisp wind rushing against his cold face and on his nearly frozen ears. He was walking home on December 11, 1941. Just like he had every day. But today seemed different to him. He couldn't quite put his finger on it, but something was different that day. Tommy could feel soft snow crushing to water under his feet. As he walked, he couldn't help but think about what they had been studying in school, Immigration. They

would have a test on it the very next week. He tried to recite to himself the major periods of immigration, the dates that is. Something stopped Tommy right in his tracks as he walked through the alley. It was a boy, a little taller than Tommy, but he still had the face of a young boy. The boy kept calling out to Tommy, saying, "Excuse me can you show me how to get to 59th street?" The boy was carrying a loaf of bread. He was wearing dirty overalls. The dirt on his face and clothes seemed to cover the boy. Tommy answered to him that 59th street was no longer here. He noticed that the boy had a powdery, almost ghostly look about him. This frightened Tommy so he kept his distance from the boy. The boy sat down as a tear dropped down his cheek and splashed on the snow. Tommy asked the boy what the matter was and the boy answered sadly, "I'll never find a good job here. Everything is too hard." "Can you read, boy?" inquired Tommy. "No," said the boy. "Well then, I will you teach you," said Tommy, and they sat down together on a crate. In the freezing snow as Tommy taught the boy to read, the boy taught Tommy more than he could imagine about immigration. Periodically, Tommy would wonder how the boy knew so much about immigration, but he always kept it to himself. Before he knew it, it was almost time for the test. He was sure he would pass as he had met with the boy in the alley every day for one hour all week. The two boys had bonded and had become friends. On the day before the test the two of them realized silently to themselves that they would have to go their separate ways and that they probably would never meet in the cold, wet alley to study again. . . .

Jim concludes this reading of the first part of his story to rousing applause from his peers. The questions fly as they ask him "Where did you get the idea?" "How did you write that?" and "What's going to happen next?" Jim answers that he got the idea from a book called *Ghost Cadet* (Alphin, 1992) he had found in the school library. He tells them that he had stayed at his desk writing that day because I was sitting beside him writing and he didn't think he could "goof around" under those circumstances. Jim then draws their attention to the point in the story where he has written that the boy looked ghostly. "See here, that's some foreshadowing, I'm giving you a clue about what's going to happen." He explains that the boy looked ghostly because he was a ghost from the past and that Tommy would discover how to help him even though they existed in different time periods. As the exchange continues, I am reminded of the words of John Dewey (1944) who wrote that "The process of living together educates. It enlarges and enlightens experience; it stimulates and enriches imagination; it creates responsibility for accuracy and vividness of statement and thought" (p. 6). Jim and his peers are "living together" and are "enlightened and enriched" as they talk about what he has written. Jim has shared what he has written and is then called upon to be both accurate and vivid as he responds to their questions.

It is also interesting to note that Jim has written about two boys who are learning from one another. Tommy gives the boy knowledge of reading and the boy tells Tommy about the past, sharing with him the knowledge gained through his experiences. Students frequently refer to working together or learning from one another. Bet refers to the problem solving which occurs when we work together, stating, "Like in our group, you have three or four other people to talk to and if someone might have the answer, and you might have the answer to someone else's problem."

Sue refers to permission from me, the teacher, as she discusses the working arrangements within the classroom:

> You let us write the notes on the note board to our friends, you let us write the questions, you let us read our books with friends. You give us those group activities to do with our friends.... in other classes I've had, you had to do everything all by yourself.

Providing opportunities for our students to work in the classroom both individually and in collaboration with others and finding time for them to share their processes as they read and respond to literature expands the meaning-making process. School is no longer a place where students listen to the teacher and then go home to read and respond in isolation. The classroom becomes a place where we construct knowledge and understanding as we learn from one another.

Honoring the Products of Learning

We exhibit a respect for our students when we honor the products of their learning. This is another way of saying that we display their work within the community of the classroom and perhaps outside of that community in the hallways of the school, in the administration building, or at professional conferences. I have a wad of what we call ticky-tack (a material which is used to fasten papers to cinder block walls) the size of a football. Our walls and the walls in the area around our classroom are filled with an ever-changing display of student work. At first I hung up only a few examples of what we had done. Then I was bombarded with plaintive questioning by students who wanted to know, "Where is mine?" and "When are you going to hang up my work?" When I saw the attention given to the work hanging on the wall, I realized that we could learn from each and every member of the community. I now hang up the work of every student unless I get a request not to hang a particular work. I can almost predict what will happen as each new display goes into place. In the first few minutes of class the students will search for their own work. They may then stand near their work and point it out to others. After that, students begin to look for the work of their closest friends, sometimes dragging them in by the hand between classes to help them find it. The work will be discussed and often the students will choose several they think are the best examples of that particular response. It should be said that the best examples are not the work of the same group of people chosen over and over again. We are different people with varying talents and ideas and each of us will have an opportunity to be the best at something during the course of the year.

Commitment to the Literacy Community

A final aspect of the continued creation of a literacy community is that of caring. Caring may be a reflection of the respect we have for one another. Sometimes it is the little things we do almost unconsciously that our students remember the most. This excerpt from my journal reveals my thinking about one of those moments:

September 1

There is a boy, Antoine, who sits in the back of the room. He hasn't said a word out loud since the beginning of school several weeks ago. He seems to want to melt into the background, but maybe he is just getting his bearings. One day I asked him a question in class (I wish I could remember what it was, but I didn't realize the importance at the time—it was just a question about something we were reading) I responded to Antoine the way I usually do, probably noting something interesting about his response. That night, before I left, a note on the board caught my eye. "Dear Mrs. Van Horn, I really like your class. Antoine." The next day Antoine brought me a chocolate chip cookie he had made in homemaking. I could see a couple of kids teasing him a little about it as he went to his locker. The experience made me stop and think. Talking about a literacy club is one thing, but we must remember to extend personal invitations. For some students, merely asking them to respond aloud is an invitation. I don't think Antoine was going to join in on his own for some time, but responding to a question from the teacher was okay. And then, when the teacher responded back to him, class was fun. The community grows as we invite participation. If this is true, then it might seem obvious that part of my job is to look closely at who is talking and who is not and to find a way to invite the silent students to join. Attention to details is important—when someone does share a thought or something he or she has written it should be an event.

At other times, we may exhibit care through our understanding of the needs of others.

As I write this I am thinking of Carolina. Carolina is new to our school this year. She has transferred here from a nearby middle school where she says she was "bad" and that she was "mean to all of my teachers, not like this year." When we read, talk, and write about literature Carolina does not volunteer to read aloud. She most often chooses to sit beside me. On this particular day, she is sitting beside me as we read. She is reading *I Have Lived a Thousand Years: Growing Up in the Holocaust* (Bitton-Jackson, 1997). Carolina is fascinated by this period in history. She borrows books from the classroom library and takes them home with her so she can read as much as she can about that time. In addition to this book, Carolina has read *The Big Lie: A True Story* (Leitner, 1992), *The Final Journey* (Pausewang, 1996), and *The Devil's Arithmetic* (Yolen, 1988), as well as informational material on the subject.

As we are reading, Carolina whispers to me, telling me what she is thinking as she reads about Livia and her mother, who are starving in the concentration camp at Auschwitz and who have just learned that their father and husband is dead. "I feel bad for the little girl 'cause she don't have a daddy anymore to like take care of her. She only has her mom. They think they're alone. Just the two of them in this place without their other family." As Carolina continues, she begins to reflect on what she is reading about the strained relationship between Livia and her mother, comparing it to her own relationship with her mother. She tells me, "I felt real scared when I read this. And see, like me and my mom, like we didn't have that much of a good relationship. But if that would have happened to me (if I would have been in a concentration camp with my mother), we would just get closer. . . . " As I talk to Carolina about her reading, it is clear to me that she is reflecting on events described in the novel. She is considering both the history of the text and her own history. Her final remark shows me that she is also wondering how her life might be different if she were confronted with the situation in which Livia finds herself.

Later, during another conversation with Carolina, I ask her to talk to me about her experiences in our class. I ask what she thought about when she first came to this class and saw that we were going to be reading out loud and talking about books with one another. She smiles and tells me, "I was really worried. 'Cause I didn't want to do anything out loud. . . . Now I just want to *stay* in here." I say to her, "You might have hated it in here and, yet, you're always telling me you want to come in here now. What happened that let you know it was going to be okay?" Carolina says, "Well, just knowing you. The way you acted I knew that you weren't going to make us do anything we didn't want to do." "What do you mean?" I ask her. She explains, "Like if they tell you to read something, like in some other classes they tell you to read and if you don't want to read out loud, they still tell you to do it. . . . It just gives me a bad feeling." When I ask her what she will remember most about the class, Carolina tells me, "My memories of being with you and talking about books and all that. . . . I got a better thought of what other people in the class feel like and think. We really got to know each other because we like to read books and we like to discuss and share our thoughts."

Listening to Carolina, I wonder what might have happened if I had insisted that she read aloud. If I had made her feel powerless by forcing her to agree to read based upon my authority as the teacher, would Carolina have felt free to do what she has done this year? Would she have asked me to borrow books to read on her own at home or shared her thoughts about what she is reading? Would she have shared her personal interest and talent in art as she did when she helped other students illustrate stories they were writing? And would she, who began the year sitting alone in the corner, have come to sit beside me and then to join the others? Would she have said that what she would remember most was getting to know each other as we read, talked about books, and shared our thoughts? Or would Carolina have remained in the corner, sitting alone, feeling powerless? I had accepted and recognized Carolina's reluctance to read aloud as being right in terms of it being a right way to feel or a right way to believe. I understand that Carolina and others may be reluctant to read aloud for a number of reasons. When our reasons, our actions, or our concerns are accepted by others as legitimate, then we may begin to feel cared for and to extend care to others.

L. Beck (1995) writes of organizational structure, defining the three activities associated with caring as follows: "(1) receiving the other's perspective, (2) responding appropriately to the awareness that comes from this reception, and (3) remaining committed to others and to the relationship" (p. 12). According to Beck, caring evolves from being a "conditional act dependent on merit or whim, and moves toward being an unconditional act marked by acceptance, nurturance, and grace" (p. 20) through the growing commitment that people have for one another.

In our classroom, as we listen and respond to one another we move away from the noncommittal safety of silence. We begin to talk and to think about how our thinking is the same or different from the thinking of others. We begin to consider ourselves as people who belong to a group and as people who care about the group itself. In the words of one of my students, Jenny, "I have learned to respect my classmates and accept them for who they are. This is something you learn from someone who cares."

People often ask me how I motivate my students or what I do about students who are reluctant to participate in the literacy activities of our classroom. Each of these aspects is reflected in the ways in which we develop and sustain our literacy community. I have found that when students come to a place where the teacher is excited about what is occurring, where it is expected that everyone will participate in the learning experience, where it is openly acknowledged that each of us has something to contribute and that we will all learn from one another, where the products of our learning are celebrated and in evidence, and where we are constantly striving to show one another that we care, they will find a way to join and participate. I must also realize and remember that each of us comes to this room with different past experiences and expectations and, as such, it may take longer for some of my students to find a way to join our community. My goal is to help them find that way.

Expanding Our View of the Literacy Community

The meaning and power of a literacy community is reinforced as connections are made to outside communities. This process requires us to alternate between perspectives, to move between looking at our own community and looking at outside communities. The process might be compared to that of a photographer who looks through the lens of a camera, alternating her view of the far and the near as she focuses and refocuses on distant and nearby objects. Our own community lies within the walls of this classroom; and, yet, we are empowered as we interact with other communities and compare our experiences and the meanings we have constructed. As we focus and refocus, the students compare their own experience with that described in a fictional text. At other times the students contrast their experiences with those of their older brothers and

The Literacy Community

sisters who have been a part of this classroom in prior years. Further connections are made as the activities of our community are related to those described in texts or to the community made up of the authors of texts. As students correspond with authors and as they share their responses to literature with other communities within the school or the neighborhood, the students begin to feel that their literacy community is a part of a larger network of communities and that the people in those other communities care about what they think.

A New View of the Community

My students and I further define and begin to expand the idea of community as we read a chapter entitled 'Ethan Explains the B and B Inn' from E. L. Konigsburg's (1996) book *The View From Saturday,* a moving story about the bonds people form when they begin to work together and to share their lives. This chapter ends with what I consider to be a description of a literacy community—a place where we have permission to explore and to extend our thinking, a place where we do and say that which we have never done before or develop and embellish that which we have begun to do:

> Something in Sillington House gave me permission to do things I had never done before. Never even thought of doing. Something there triggered the unfolding of those parts that had been incubating. Things that had lain inside me curled up like the turtle hatchlings newly emerged from their eggs, taking time in the dark of their nest to unfurl themselves. I told jokes I had never told before. I asked questions I had never asked before. When it was my turn to tell what day I would like to live over, after Nadia had finished, after Noah and Julian had too, I told mine. The Souls listened and were not embarrassed to hear and I was not embarrassed to say, "I would like to live over the day of our first tea party. And look," I added, "every Saturday since, I get to do just that." (p. 93)

In response to the reading and discussion of this chapter as well as connected readings, we begin to look outside of the immediate context of the classroom and in to the community of the school and the surrounding neighborhood. We decide to take pictures of people and places in our city and create our own book we call, *The View From Our City.* We are inspired by *Journey* (MacLachlan, 1991), a book about a boy named Journey who sees the importance of his life and his relationships through photographs. To show how other people have worked from photographs I share excerpts from *Something Permanent,* a book of poetry written by Cynthia Rylant (1994). Rylant's poems are paired with photographs taken by Walker

Evans during the Depression era. As she writes, she responds to the photographs, telling us the story behind the images.

To write in response to photographs of our own surroundings we would need photographs. Thinking about the possible problems associated with asking each student to bring a photograph to work from, I decide to take the pictures myself. I am concerned that it could be weeks before each of us would take a picture, have it processed, and bring it to school. Some of the students might not have access to a camera. With that in mind, one Sunday, I ask my husband to drive me around town while I hang out the side window of the car or get out to take pictures of places which might be meaningful to the students. He is a willing participant and we have quite an afternoon photographing scenes from the local park, restaurants, playgrounds, schools, auto repair shops, motorcycle riders, and even a car accident. When I bring the photographs to school I number them so we can place the poem behind the photograph it references. I then spread them out on the floor and invite each student to pick the photograph they want to work from.

Writing in response to photographs of our school, some of the students reflect back to their first day here. Shelby writes, exposing her fear of being the "new kid" in school and reminding us of the times when we wished we could be invisible:

>Today is the first day at a new school,
>in a new town,
>and a new grade.
>As I walk in the school
>and wait for the bell,
>I see the place swarming.
>I lay my head down and hope I will disappear.
>And then,
>all of a sudden
>someone comes and taps my shoulder.
>A girl about my age
>introduces herself to me.
>I can't believe it,
>I have made a new friend.

If we take a deeper look at a portion of Shelby's written response to the photograph of the school, we can see that what she has written represents her feelings about school and/or attachments within the classroom community:

>As I walk in the school . . . I see the place swarming (and)
>I lay down my head and hope I will disappear.

With these words she reveals a sense of helplessness in dealing with being in a place where she knows no one and where she is not known. For some students, even for those who are not "in a new town" as Shelby is, school can be a place where they feel unknown or anonymous amidst a swarm of people. Here, in this school, surrounded by a swarm of people, Shelby expresses her feelings that she is not the kind of person who can go up to other people and begin a conversation. Her fear or reluctance leads her to wish that she could disappear.

Later, during an interview, Shelby talks to me about her first year here. She talks about her relationships with Jess and Sarita, both of whom are in this class with Shelby. She starts by describing her friendship with Jess, saying:

> And here (in our classroom) we just started talking and she's like the only person I can really talk to. At lunch, we sit with other people, but I wouldn't tell them what I tell her.

I ask her "Does that make school different when you have a best friend here?" In answer, Shelby refers back to the subject of her poem, her first day of school, and her meeting with Sarita:

> Yeah, cause I remember when I sat here (refers to the place she sits in our classroom) I knew Sarita because we were both new and nobody had our papers. They (the school officials) didn't know we were coming even though we had signed up, so we were in the cafeteria and she was with her mom and we started talking. So I knew her and that's why I wanted to sit by her (in this classroom).

Shelby had asked to sit beside Sarita, someone who was also new to the school, and someone who quite possibly shared her feelings of confusion and doubt on the first day of school. From this place of safety, Shelby began to enter into the activities and conversations of our community. Both she and Jess were empowered through their friendship. Shelby does not speak of it here, but as I think about the two of them I am reminded of the many times that Shelby or Jess took on leadership roles in our classroom—of the times that they shared their reading, writing, and their thinking with the rest of the group. In each of these moments they began by looking at one another as if to say, "I can do this because of you," or "I can share this thought with others because first, I have shared it with you."

Shelby's poem is an example of the way that students, through their writing, often give us the keys we need to help them find their place in the literacy community. If we read carefully what our students have written we may see what worries, provokes, or confuses them. We may also see strengths we can help them to recognize and build upon. When I read what my students have written, I try to read both the words and the feelings behind the words. When I see something in the words that I wonder about, I ask my students to talk with me. I hope to show them through my actions that their thoughts and ideas matter, that writing is more than form and talking is more than answering the teacher's questions.

Are We Doing it Right?

As we continue to establish our community we almost instinctively reach out to former communities; it seems as if we want to see if we are "doing it right." Our portfolios are one means of making connections between literacy communities. Students presently in the class read and share the portfolios of their older brothers and sisters who have been in the class in previous years. One day, Deb brought in her older sister's portfolio for a read-aloud related to our current study. After reading a poem written by her sister Deb told us that Shelley, now in high school, had stated the previous night, "I don't know what's happened to me. I never write like that anymore. I'm not as good as I was then." As we talked about Shelley's remark we came to the conclusion that her writing in high school might be more tightly structured. For this reason, she might feel as if she is exercising less personal creativity than she had in middle school.

John is in my class this year. I taught his sister, Amy, last year. In the first few days of school, as we discussed the characters in *The View From Saturday* by E. L. Konigsburg (1996), John commented, "Last night I was reading Amy's portfolio from last year. She had written a definition of an outsider in there before the class read *The Outsiders*. I think Amy's definition reminds me of these people (referring to the characters from Epiphany Middle School). They are outsiders in their school." John's comments reveal that the discoveries we make when we read through the portfolios can generate new thinking on a topic.

One morning John's sister visits our classroom at John's request to help him locate something from *Chicken Soup for the Teenage Soul* (Canfield, Hansen, and Kirberger, 1997) that he wants to share as "Reader of the Day." She stays to watch John read. While we listen, she whispers to me, "John asks to read my portfolio every night. I don't know why he has to look at it every night." I tell her it might be that he is reading, experiencing, and thinking about the things he is doing this year and that he wants to see what she had thought of them when she was in 7th grade.

The Community of Literary Texts

I find picture books to be highly engaging to the students and to myself. I display a collection of picture books related to the theme of our current unit of study on a table at the front of the room. I have used them for a variety of purposes, including the introduction of ideas, genres, language patterns, and aspects of fictional and informational texts as well as models for our own writing. As the students and I read the texts and look at the pictures, I have found that they also serve as models of the activities in which we are engaged. In other words, we make connections between our activities in this classroom and those of the characters in the picture books. In this way we make connections between our community and the community described in literary texts. For example, in the first few days we will be talking about what it means to read and why people read. To help introduce this idea I have *Aunt Chip and the Great Triple Creek Dam Affair* (Polacco, 1996), a book about a town which has abandoned reading and uses books only to prop up sagging doors and plug an old dam. Also on the table is *The Library* (Stewart, 1995), a book in verse about Elizabeth Brown, a character who is a renown bibliophile. In the opening days, I will be presenting the students with spiral notebooks we will call Reader/Writer logs. In these logs we will record our thoughts and ideas about literature and language. To help me talk about the kinds of things we might write, draw, or collect in our logs I have *Carl Makes a Scrapbook* (Day, 1994), a wordless book about a dog who creates a scrapbook about his life with his human family, and *Amelia's Notebook* (Moss, 1995), a book which looks like the actual notebook of Amelia and chronicles her journey to a new town and her efforts to make new friends. In the first week we'll be thinking about our past experiences and what we bring with us to this community. We'll be reading a poem called "Remember" by Joy Harjo found in the book, *Celebrate America in Poetry and Art* (Panzer, 1994). To provide an example of a memoir and to help us get started thinking about our own lives, I have the picture book *Walking the Log: Memories of a Southern Childhood* (Nickens, 1994). Making connections between our activities and those described in texts seems to further authenticate our literacy experiences and our literacy community.

The Community of Authors

Behind the picture books are framed letters from authors such as Gary Paulsen and Caroline Cooney. There is a story connected with each of these letters, and I like to tell a story or two to illustrate some of the potential for a literacy community which reaches beyond the walls of this classroom. For instance, I may tell the story of how one of my most embarrassing moments became a wonderful experience for the class as I show them the framed letter from author Walt Morey's daughter. One year, during a study of survival and adventure books, I chose Walt Morey's *Death Walk* (1991) as a read-aloud to accompany our independent readings. Each chapter ends with a hook and left the students demanding that I continue reading. We enjoyed it so much that we wanted to write to the author and tell him about our experience with his book. On the inside flap of the book there was a photograph of Mr. Morey as well as the address of the publisher, Blue Heron. With this information at hand, each of us wrote a letter which we mailed to the author in care of the publisher. Several weeks later we received a letter from Mr. Morey's daughter telling us that Mr. Morey had passed away. She wrote to us that her father "had been worried that, at past 80-years-old, he might not be able to 'grab' his audience as he had in his earlier books." She wrote to us that our letters "would have reassured him that he hadn't lost his touch." She also told us that her mother had requested that Blue Heron send us a set of his books. Several weeks later we received a box of books inscribed "To the six 7th Grade Classes at Westbrook Intermediate. Mrs. Walt Morey wanted you to have a set of the Walt Morey Adventure Books." The pride and excitement of the students was overwhelming. I gave each of them a copy of the notes from Walt Morey's daughter and the publisher. We read the books and then held a dedication ceremony in which we presented the books to the school library with much ceremony and picture taking. Each book contained a dedication plate written by one of the students. As a result, even though I had neglected to check to see if the author was living in my enthusiastic response to my students' desire to write to an author, we had learned that our reading and what we had to say about what we were reading was of importance to those outside of the immediate community.

Sharing the Thoughts of Our Community

When we display our work in the hallways of the school or the administration building, we are reaching out to other literacy communities. The results are sometimes surprising. Teachers from other classrooms may take their students on a tour of the hallways to see what is being done. Other teachers read the work and attach Post-it notes to the authors. One morning before school, as I was hanging life-sized paper characters from the novel *The Outsiders* (Hinton, 1989) on the walls in the central hallway, I was confronted by our new school janitor, a young man of about 25. He stopped sweeping the floor and walked from character to character, whispering almost to himself, "There's Ponyboy, and Bob, and that's Cherry, isn't it?" He went on to tell me excitedly, "I remember these guys. . . . *The Outsiders* was one of the best books I ever read. . . . I'll never forget it. . . . I still have my own copy!" I told him that many of my students felt the same way. We talked about the connections that readers make to their own lives as they read the book and of how continued readership fosters connections between students and their older brothers and sisters or even between students and their parents who have also read the book.

One evening during a social event I was introduced to a woman from a local business. As she shook my hand she told me that she had recently visited our district's administration building, and while waiting she had read some of the "amazing" children's books our students had created. I was thrilled to hear her reaction. It is my belief that people are interested in what happens in schools. Displaying our work provides an opportunity for them to learn about what we are doing. In cases such as this, the interest of the community and the elementary schools with which we shared our books prompted funding for this project in the years to come.

Our school librarian is an enthusiastic partner in curriculum planning. She is also a participant in the process of honoring student work. We often bind our writing, creating class books which she then enters into the catalogue of the school library. These books are checked out by students as well as teachers. In this way we can see where we have been, where we are going, and share our thoughts with others.

During our year together, members of the school board, the community, and a local university come to visit and to read the thoughts of the students about reading and writing which have been hung on the walls. As they meet and talk with these members of the larger literacy community, the students begin to feel that they are a part of a larger network. After an encounter with university students studying reading and language arts, one student remarks, "People really care what we think don't they?" Another concludes, "We're getting famous in here!"

EVALUATION/ASSESSMENT

At the beginning of the year as I talk to my students about what to expect, I explain that each of them will play an important role in the learning experiences within our classroom. I tell them pointedly that "this won't work without you." I have devised what I call a "Meeting Objectives" checklist which helps me track the progress and participation of my students (see appendix B). I keep the checklist for each class group on a clipboard that I can carry around the room with me. Blank spaces at the bottom of the pages or blank pages inserted behind each checklist serve as a place for me to record specific statements by the students and to note the progress and needs of each class group. Each week I print out a new checklist, marking the date and the activities in which we will be engaged across the top of the form. For example, the columns in appendix B are labeled "SSR" for sustained silent reading, "R/W L" for Reader-Writer log, "ROD" for Reader of the Day, "DIS" for discussion, "PRES" for presentation, "LIB" for library, and "RP" for response project. In any week a student could be expected to read silently, write in his or her Reader/Writer log, bring something to read aloud to the class as Reader of the Day, participate in a discussion of text, make an oral presentation, check out a book at the school library, and work on a response project to literature. I use the Meeting Objectives form as an observation checklist, and each student receives one weekly grade for taking part in the learning experiences of that week. I have also found it extremely helpful as a tool when I am conferencing with individual students and/or their parents and when I am planning for future learning experiences in the classroom.

SUMMARY

As students reflect on the possibilities entailed in a literacy community, we begin to get a sense of how they envision the construction of the power of the group, and how this power enables them to begin to formulate meaning. It is possible to conceive of this construction in terms of a continuous, recursive, upward spiral which turns back upon itself and gains in intensity. Within the spiral are the emotional-psychological and physical elements of the community which contribute to meaning making and power. The following table reflects the elements which make up this spiral.

Elements of the emotional-psychological realm	Elements of the physical context
Listen to one another.	Environment rich with the thoughts and responses of members of the community.
Engage in risk-taking by sharing ideas.	Print constructed by and related to the experiences of the members of the community.
Recognize, acknowledge, and support diversity.	Comfort derived through access to materials.
Recognize, acknowledge, and support commonality.	Comfort derived through access to members of the group.
Trust one another without fear of betrayal.	
Foster a sense of family through trust.	
Foster a sense of freedom as we come to believe that diverse meanings exist and will be acknowledged and accepted as valid. give ourselves permission to express our ideas and to see what and how we are thinking. learn from the teacher and from one another.	
Understand that our community is acknowledged by outside communities.	
View our community as a participatory environment.	

A classroom community is grounded in the words, actions, and interactions of the people within its walls. Community develops as we come to know one another. Coming to know one another involves listening to what others have to say. For these students, the elements of power and meaning related to the group or the community stem from an awareness and acknowledgment of the ideas of others which occurs as they come to know one another, as they listen to one another, and as they engage in risk taking by sharing their ideas with their peers.

The physical context of the classroom may be conducive to the development of a community. Notions about what a literacy community should contain are familiar to us as teachers. We know that environments should be print rich; that a variety of texts and writing supplies should be available to students; and that there should be comfortable places for students to read, write, and interact with one another. A sense of belonging and comfort as reflected in the physical context is critical. Belonging is reflected in the physical context when the print rich environment is rich with the thoughts and responses of the members of the community. Comfort, as described by the members of this community derives from their access to materials as well as their access to the people within the group through their choice of seating. This implies that the physical aspects of community may be fostered when the context reflects the thoughts, ideas, and works in progress of the students themselves and when student input is used to formulate seating arrangements.

Awareness and acknowledgment are the result of an ongoing process of community building through shared experiences, perceptions, and language. We must acknowledge and respect the diversity among us as we seek to identify what we have in common. As we continue in our efforts to create and to sustain our community, students refer to the need to look beyond the surface and to accept and to support the differences among us. Ideas about the power of acceptance and support in a literacy community are linked by the students to feelings of trust within the group. The concept of trust emerges as we acknowledge and talk about our differences as well as our similarities. We began with discussion of our definitions of reading, the students' written reflections about the makings of a good reader or writer, and why people read or write. Discussion is continued through the response of students who voluntarily share their thinking with the group. Students enter this realm cautiously, well aware of the risks involved. Those who share serve as examples for others in the group. As students share what they are thinking and writing, the response to this sharing is also motivating to others. Students in this classroom have expressed a willingness to undertake this risk based upon their feelings of trust, which they describe as the absence of fear of betrayal. Through the ongoing interactions among the students and among the students and myself, this trust develops further; and the community is then transformed and renamed by the students as a place which feels "like a family."

From this feeling of family emerges a sense of freedom which these students attribute to their belief that they will not be viewed as "children" or novices and that their statements and opinions about meaning will be considered on an equal basis with those of the "experts." The feelings of freedom expressed by the students emerge from their reflections about the overall process of building and sustaining the community. Students refer to a sense of freedom when they describe particular events such as being invited to learn along with the teacher and with one another and in sharing their responses with others. As these students come to view the community as a participatory environment in which their ideas as well as their confusions are viewed as relevant contributions, they may begin to experience the empowerment which is central to the transformation of the learning experience of oneself and others. This empowerment may be compounded through the acknowledgment of their own community of learners by those from communities outside the immediate classroom environment. Further reflection by the students reveal that freedom stems from a belief that diverse meanings exist and that those diverse interpretations will be acknowledged and accepted as valid. Finally, the students attribute freedom to the feeling that they have permission to express themselves, to say what they feel, to "go free" and to "see" what they are thinking and how they are thinking.

Chapter 2 will begin to examine the roles enacted by myself and students as we transact with text and interact with one another. As the members of this community begin to explore concepts of self and others as readers, writers, and thinkers, they reflect upon the experiences of the group and begin to individualize the power and meaning of the group. Central questions for the students are "How does this compare with my prior experiences?" and "What does this mean to me?" and "How will I make this knowledge a part of me?" This chapter contains several subsections which describe the simple to the more complex ways in which the students come to know themselves and to further understand one another as they examine their identities through reading and writing.

2

Defining Ourselves— Revealing the Literacies Inside Us

The Power of the Individual

Before I can ever gain true friendship, I have to like myself. Because if I like myself, I will know that I do not need a facade, or friends who cannot accept the real me, and I will show the world who I really am, take it or leave it. And only when I do this will I meet people who like me, because they will befriend the person, not the mask. . . . This is the thing teenagers are exposed to day after day, the struggle to feel accepted and approved of, and the struggle to make friends that become our friends only if we sacrifice ourselves and who we are just for their acceptance. One of the greatest battles I will ever encounter is that where I am struggling to stay me and to never sacrifice myself for the acceptance I might desire from others. Surviving in modern times, and in the so-called 'safe' suburbs, might not mean hiding in an attic from Nazi soldiers, but having the strength to be able to simply stay yourself.

Anthony

Anthony's "battle" is a reflection of the struggle to balance the value of individuality within the community of the group. Anthony has recognized and come to know and to value his individuality. He acknowledges the individuality and the power of his thoughts within that of the group.

Anthony writes that he "will show the world who I really am, take it or leave it," and yet he reflects a belief that his own desire for acceptance puts his individuality in jeopardy. It is possible that Anthony has experienced moments in which he subdued or relinquished his own thoughts or feelings in order to be accepted by another and that he is fearful that it could happen again.

School Literacy Experiences

Anthony's words reflect the inner turmoil of adolescents who are struggling to identify themselves and to identify with others. One of the most difficult aspects of this struggle may be to truly come to know who we are and what we believe.

> As stated by Jesse Goodman (1989) in an essay on education for critical democracy, "An individual's ability to focus on his/her desires, fears, hopes, dreams, and creativity in order to existentially 'know oneself' is important for any society that wishes to promote freedom and human dignity" (p. 93).

As we reflect upon these processes through which we attempt to know what we think and who we are, we find, as Wooldridge (1996) has written, that "We have to start with ourselves before we reach beyond ourselves" (p. 51). For some students, school is not a place where they have been asked to reflect upon their own literacy in terms of who they are and what they believe. During an interview about his history as a reader, Antonio describes his past reading experiences in school as follows:

> We read like little paragraphs and we did summaries on them. Then we read books and did book reports on them.... we read books with lots of chapters and then we do like tests on them.

When asked to describe a memorable reading experience, Antonio could think of nothing. When asked if he read on his own, he said that he reads comic books "sometimes, when I'm bored." When asked what he would change about his reading experiences in school Antonio replied, "I want to be able to read faster. Read things over to understand better ... practice with those words per minute programs." It appears that Antonio thinks of reading as something we have to do quickly in order to answer questions, write reports, or complete exams. He does not read at home or anywhere else for pleasure. His school experiences have not required him to go further with his reading than to respond to queries and demands made by others.

Defining Ourselves—Revealing the Literacies Inside Us 39

Alfredo's reflection on his history as a reader reveals his "need" to read is initially motivated by his desire to be perceived as operating in a manner sanctioned by the school. Alfredo describes himself as taking on the outward appearance of a reader or seeming to comply with school-sanctioned behavior for readers. It is during one of these reading "performances" that Alfredo realizes reading could be meaningful if it is preceded by a desire to "know." In other words, reading is not something we pretend to do in order to comply with the school culture, it is something we might do for ourselves. He describes this to me, saying,

> *In the fourth grade, like we used to have to read all the time. . . . and we'd get a book from the shelf. It would be like on Friday or something. And I never read. I just like looked at the book and talked to my friends and everything . . . And then one time she (the teacher) like passed by me and I started acting like I was reading. I was really reading this time, and the book was kind of cool. And I was like in the middle. And then I read on and thought, I want to go to the beginning, 'cause I want to know what they're talking about.*

When asked to talk about what he is now reading, Alfredo says,

> *I kind of like autobiographies on people. . . . I always see tiny things I can relate to. Leonardo da Vinci. He was like really cool to read on. Umm, that's 'cause everybody thinks of him just as an artist, but he was like a scientist, a philosopher, he was like all kinds of things. And I always like, I like philosophers. I just think that's cool that somebody would think about the world and I always think about the world, like why are we here and those questions and stuff.*

Once Alfredo began reading for his own purposes and to learn what he wanted to learn, he became self-determined. His search for information and his reading of autobiographies are a way for him to find people he can relate to as he confirms his own identity. Alfredo shows us that we may begin by pretending to read, but that reading begins to have meaning and to be empowering when we have an inner purpose for reading and when reading enables us to know or to understand more about our own identity.

During one-on-one interviews with my students, frequent comments are made about the opportunity or the denial of opportunity to reflect on their own thinking within school literacy experiences. Ranita talks about previous experiences, saying, "I didn't really like reading. 'Cause they used to always make us read and read and read and read and read, and so it would get pretty boring." When I ask her what she did after she read Ranita tells me, "Like we would write about it. We would summarize the story. I mean that's not really kind of what we would *like* to do." Nettie talks about why it is important to be asked what we think:

> Well, you (Van Horn) put your thoughts into the story and you told us what you thought of it. In most classes you just, you know, read this, read that, and they don't really ask you to talk about it afterwards. You know, they don't want to see what you think. I really, really like when me and my mom really get into a story and we talk about it, we don't just go over the surface of it, and just, you know.

Nettie's statements suggest that power is equalized when students are asked to think about or to talk about what they think. She notes my modeling of the process, saying, "you put your thoughts into the story and you told us what you thought of it." Nettie's words show us that school can be viewed as a place where students might only be told what to do and not as a place where they are asked to reflect upon or to share what they think. Her final comment in which she describes her reading experiences with her mother at home, saying, "we don't just go over the surface of it" reveals Nettie's belief that literacy experiences in school "just go over the surface" unless students are asked to express their thoughts about reading and/or to make connections between their own experiences and texts.

Making Connections With Text

The relevance of the connections we make between the texts and ourselves is revealed in further statements made by the students during one-on-one interviews. As I reflect on the statements of these students, I am confronted with the possibility that our reading and thinking about texts enables us to define and think about ourselves. As students make connections between their lives and the lives of those who exist in the text, they may feel empowered in three ways: first, because their understanding or meaning making is enhanced; second, because they have made a connection between their own life and their literacy; and finally, because in the making of that connection, they may have learned or acknowledged something about their identity.

Anita talks about the connection she makes between her own experience of being "picked on" as a child and that of Johnny, a character in *The Outsiders* (Hinton, 1989), saying:

> I'll read a book and I'll say yeah, that was kind of like me. It was like if I put myself in his (Johnny's) shoes. Why wouldn't he defend himself, why wouldn't he do that? I was just saying that he would be kind of like a coward and that he would let anybody beat him up. Because, I used to be picked on because I used to have a big gap in my teeth. And so, they would pick on me and I'd go so what. I'm proud of me. And so, I'd rather be myself (and not fight back) than be ashamed of what I am. So I just let them pick on me.... sometimes it really hurt.

Anita finds her reasons for Johnny's behavior in her own history and in her identity. Perhaps Johnny, too, is proud of what he is. Perhaps he too fails to see the value in fighting or "picking on" others.

Others describe a process in which readers "try on" situations from the text in order to find what they might do or think or feel. Sandy explains,

> Like in a book, when you're reading it, you're like, "why did this happen to him?" It's so scary. And you're thinking of it happening to you too. And you're just like, like in a book if someone's dying, you imagine yourself in their place, thinking "what did I do to deserve this?"

Jess talks about sharing her read aloud from *A Child Called It* (Pelzer, 1995) and how it prompted her to think and to talk about her own life. She describes how her life helped her to understand the life of David, portrayed in the book:

> When I was younger until about six I had a pretty good life and then you know, it dramatically changed. So, by that I know how hard it is for some people, and I understand how people are going through life and you, know ... a lot has happened in my life, so that helps me a lot.

For many students the opportunity to think about their own experiences and perceptions, about who they are and what they believe, may come about through overt invitations to participate in literacy experiences in which they must confront themselves. As my students and I transact with literature and interact with others in the literacy community, we are constantly reflecting back to ourselves asking "How does this compare with my prior experiences?" "What does this mean to me?" and "How will I make this knowledge a part of me?" As we listen to ourselves, we come to know ourselves in new ways. Our efforts to know ourselves and one another and to make connections between our lives and literacy experiences, like those of organizing, sustaining, and expanding a literacy community, are ongoing, evolving processes.

> Maxine Greene (1995) writes, "A reflective grasp of our life stories and of our ongoing quests, that reaches beyond where we have been, depends on our ability to remember things past. It is against the backdrop of those remembered things and the funded meanings to which they gave rise, that we grasp and understand what is now going on around us" (p. 20).

Constructing Life Maps

We begin the process of coming to know ourselves or defining ourselves as we remember and reflect upon our life stories—the events which have helped to create us.

> Maxine Greene (1992) refers to this in the context of Freire's concept of learning new things, stating that the different stories of our lives help us to "make sense, to make meaning, to find a direction" (p. 257). Ultimately, in Greene's words, this enables us to "reach out for the proficiencies, capacities, and the craft required to be fully participant in this society and to do so without losing the consciousness of who they (we) are" (p. 257).

We begin to remember the stories of our lives and to symbolize these events or stories as we construct what I call Life Maps. Through this process the students will take a mental journey, returning to moments in their lives which, in the words of William Zinsser (1987), "take us back to a corner of his or her life that was unusually vivid or intense—childhood, for instance—or that was framed by unique events" (p. 21).

I introduce the experience to the students by making a connection to our earlier process of defining reading, suggesting to them that we are somewhat defined by the events in our past. In answer to groans of "I can't even remember what I did yesterday!" I suggest that the art of remembering is something that we have to practice. I show the students my own life map, a sheet of paper containing a series of small pictures connected by lines. I have made a transparency of my map, and while I talk the students are passing around the original for a closer look. Explaining that each picture symbolizes an important moment in my life, I suggest that we might choose a symbol and then tell the connected story. Sam asks about the drawing of the aquarium; and I begin to talk, telling my story. This represents my 4th-grade teacher, Mrs. Edwards. I will never forget her because watching her made me want to become a teacher. We had a classroom aquarium, and I think it was much more than something interesting to look at. We learned about life from that aquarium. Inside the aquarium there were problems. The angel fish was most aggressive. Every day we noticed that the other fish stayed far away from the angel fish. Some of them were missing parts of their fins as if something had chewed on them. One morning we came to school and found that the skink (a lizard like creature) had somehow gotten out of the aquarium. He was lying dead and dried up on the shelf above our geography books. It appeared that he had lost his life in an effort to escape the dreaded angel fish. Something would have to be done. Mrs. Edwards suggested that we have a drawing and that one lucky student could "adopt" the angel fish and take it home. To this day, I remember that it was Thomas McGehee who would win the angel fish. I end my story, saying that I will always remember Mrs. Edwards because, as I watched her and took note of all the things she did for us, I began to think about the ways that teachers create a place where students can learn.

Jeff laughs out loud and remarks that the skink had committed "skinkicide." I tell him I'll have to add that to my story. We spend a few minutes working on the maps. We will return to them in the days to come after the students have had time to remember. Day by day the maps grow more elaborate. Jimmy painstakingly draws tiny feet connecting the events of his life, saying, "See, this is my walk through life and those are my feet, getting bigger as I go along." When the maps are completed, we have a visual representation of where we have been. Not all of the stories are as lighthearted as the one I shared with my students. An excerpt from my journal reveals my growing awareness of what my students carry inside them as they enter the classroom.

September 5

Today as we looked at our Life Maps I suggested that we choose a picture and write about it in our Reader/Writer logs. Chris wrote about the birth of his niece and the death of his nephew which happened in the same year. I cried when I read his words about how he would give anything if he could have been at home to save his nephew from drowning. Brandon wrote of being in the car when he and his father were in an accident and watching his father die. I am stunned by the amount of tragedy some of these children have experienced and the strength that they possess. I truly admire them with all my heart.

When we complete our maps, all but a few of the students want to hang them on the walls of our classroom. Before class begins and during transitions, I watch them studying the maps and listen to them talking to one another, describing the events behind the symbols. Liz decides to create another map, drawing the covers of books she has read, trying to remember just when she read each one of the books. She says that "these books stayed with me and became a part of me." Justin looks at his map hanging on the wall and concludes, "This is my life here. . . . I hadn't really thought about it before." He laughs, saying, "I was just busy living it!"

We will stop and think about our lives many times in the days to come. As we think we will make discoveries about ourselves, discoveries which may help us make connections to the characters we read about as well as to the people with whom we are reading. I may also use the Life Maps as a way for the students to engage in storytelling. Students in pairs or small groups can ask to hear the story behind a particular drawing in much the same way I have told them about the aquarium in Mrs. Edward's classroom. These storytelling sessions may lay the groundwork for the writing of personal narratives, poems, or plays.

Reader of the Day

Judith Langer (1995) states that literature "sets the scene for us to explore both ourselves and others, to define and redefine who we are, who we might become, and how the world might be" (p. 5). As such, reading enacted in school may become a highly individual process existing within a social context. To view readers and the act of reading from this lens is to say that readers bring their individual imaginations to bear within the social context of the classroom. If the culture of the classroom is such that readers are both enabled and compelled to participate, then it may be possible for the reader and the society of listeners to impact one another through their interpretation of the reading event.

> According to Frank Smith (1988), teachers have a responsibility to ensure that children are admitted to the classroom club and that "meaningful and useful reading and writing activities where participation is possible without evaluation and collaboration is always available" (pp. 11–12).

On the first day of school, I ask my 7th-grade reading students to complete a survey about reading. One of the questions invites the students to reflect on their history as readers. Jake's comments in a follow-up interview are representative of the response to this question.

Jake: When I was in 5th grade all we did was, um, she played a tape and we listened and followed along in our book.

Van Horn: And when you finished reading, what did you do?

Jake: We put the book back up.

In response to a query about talk, Amy replies "We couldn't express what we thought about a story, we couldn't talk about it. . . . we just read it and we took a test on it." It is clear that these students think of reading as something to be done and put away or to be done in preparation for a test. Our biweekly visits to the school library reveal that a number of my students experience difficulty when confronted with choice. It is not uncommon to see them spend the library period aimlessly searching the computerized card catalog or wandering up and down the stacks, running their fingers across the spines of the books. In an effort to help students who seem to be confounded by the task of choosing a book, I begin asking "What is the last thing you have read and enjoyed?" In response to this question and others that follow, many of the students can not come up with a title, author, or topic. Student surveys and interviews about reading show me that many of them chose books at random based upon the cover or size of the book. Still others reply that they can not remember a book they have read aside from those assigned in school. Within the curriculum of this classroom the students will be presented with choices of texts within genres; however, as I consider their initial responses to reading, I begin to look for other opportunities to actively involve them in the process of choosing and talking about texts.

My search leads me to think about my own experiences in sharing and talking about texts. For the last several years I have spent the first month of the summer in the National Writing Project Summer Institute at a local university, reading, writing, and talking about reading and writing with my fellow teachers. At the beginning of each day one of us would read aloud to the others, and then we would talk about what we had read. For the most part, we shared children's literature. Our talk centered around how we might use literature to evoke a mood, to exemplify a particular type of writing, or to foster a response. Our sharing led us to discover new authors, new books, and new ways of thinking about texts. With this in mind, I begin to envision a Reader of the Day activity, similar to this experience and to that of Author's Chair. As described by Harste, Short, and Burke (1988), children who sit in the Author's Chair usually share their own written texts although they may read a favorite book. Teachers use the Author's Chair to share readings from a variety of genres. The readings may also be used as models for writing or invitations to children to "try this in their own pieces" (p. 126).

Reader of the Day will be different from Author's Chair in that the choosing, sharing, and discussing of texts will be generated solely by the students. I want to extend an invitation to my students to share their personal reading within the social context of the classroom. It is my belief that an opportunity to choose a reading and lead the group in a discussion will empower the students by giving them a means of expressing themselves as individual readers and thinkers.

Meredith Cherland (1994) defines this process as a reflection of critical pedagogy which calls for teachers and students to demonstrate that "voice" (p. 18) as it refers to the ideas of individuals is an important and valued part of participation in school.

As I describe the way that Reader of the Day occurs in my classroom during the first few months, I will use a framework of activity settings as defined by Gallimore and Goldenberg (1993) and what I have learned through one-on-one interviews with the students. Through this we can examine the influence or extent to which Reader of the Day enables the students to define and explore themselves and others through their choices and conversations.

Introducing Reader of the Day

At the beginning of each class period I share my idea with the students, telling them that "Reader of the Day is a way for you to talk about what you're reading outside this classroom, outside of school." I continue, saying "It is my hope that as you share what you are reading others will hear what you read and what you have to say. They might get ideas about books they could read, or they might find that there are others who like to read the same kind of books they are reading." Within moments the questions erupt: "Does it have to be a whole book?" "What about poems . . . can I read a poem to the class?" What about magazines—that's what I read at home?" and the inevitable "Is this for a grade?" As we talk, we decide that our readings will consist of short pieces of poetry, excerpts from fiction or nonfiction, and/or articles from newspapers or magazines. Reader of the Day sharing will occur at the beginning of the 90-minute period and, as such, will take the place of short focus activities or warm-ups which occur in other academic classes. Participation will be voluntary and students will not be evaluated or receive a grade for their participation. Given this, I expect that the students who volunteer to share will be those who have read something they enjoyed, have read something they want to share, and/or are comfortable with the idea of reading aloud to the class.

I hang a laminated calendar on the door and, in the next few days, students begin to sign up and share. We formalize the way we will go about the process. On the days that we have a volunteer reader, class begins with the introduction of the student and what will be shared. The reader then sits on a stool at the front of the classroom, and I take his or her place sitting among the other students. During the read aloud and the discussion, I try to jot down some notes about what is occurring. When the reading and discussion are concluded, the reader adds his or her name and a description of what has been shared to our Reader of the Day list which is posted at the back of the room.

As I read over the notes in my journal after the first week of the Reader of the Day activity, it becomes apparent to me that there might be more occurring within the process than the sharing of personal reading for the purpose of providing a forum for open discussion of diverse types of literature. Through Reader of the Day we might accomplish more than a reference point from which to choose literature for our own reading. My journal entries of that week reveal the beginning impressions of what might come. I note details of Betsey's "teacher-like" method of sharing, writing, "She previewed the section of the novel she was going to read as she described what had occurred earlier in the story. . . . " and "She stopped during the reading to define a word for us." I observe the reaction of students to Tim's reading of a poem, writing, "Everyone in the class wanted to keep the copy of the poem Tim had made for them. . . . several of them said they wanted to take it home with them and show it to their parents."

According to Gallimore and Goldenberg (1993), the Reader of the Day process would be defined as an activity setting. Activity settings as envisioned by Gallimore and Goldenberg, consist of interactive factors which they categorize as the *participants* or actors engaged in an activity, the salient *cultural values* associated with the activity, the *operations and task demands* of the activity, *scripts for conduct* employed by the participants, and the *purposes* or motives of all those engaged. After several months of Reader of the Day, I can see categories emerging in terms of who is reading (participant), what is valued (cultural value), what is required of the readers (operations and task demands), how the readings and discussion occur (scripts for conduct), and why particular readers may have chosen particular texts (purpose). With these factors in mind I can take a deeper look at the process.

Who is Reading?

As I look at the growing list of readers and titles posted at the back of the room, I note that readers in my six class periods have shared 45 times during the first few months of Reader of the Day. Using the terminology of Gallimore and Goldenberg (1993), these readers are the *participants* or those who are engaging in the activity. Who are these readers and what differentiates them from those who are not volunteering to share? Within these 45 sharing events, 28 of the readers are female and 17 of the readers are male. I might conclude that Reader of the Day is more appealing to the girls in my classes than it is to the boys. And yet, as I look further at the names on the list, I can see that the individual personalities of the students are also a factor.

Due to the fact that this is a voluntary, ungraded program, those who read aloud are often academically self-motivated. These students seem to view Reader of the Day as an invitation to become further involved in the literacy club. Because the readings become venues for expressions of feelings and interests, the students who share are confident in their own beliefs and are willing to publicize those feelings, seemingly without fear of censure by their peers. These are not always students who would be viewed as the socially elite; more often, they are students who appeared to derive power from their own literacy. Some of them acknowledge this feeling, as does Emelda when she introduces herself at the beginning of the semester with the statement, "All my life people have called me 'Miss Perfection.' I wanted to be the best reader and writer, and now I am. Just like Mary Poppins, practically perfect in every way."

As I look further at the list, I can characterize those who are reading in terms of their ability/interest in reading. First, those who read aloud are usually, though not always, those who believe themselves to be proficient oral readers. Second, those who read aloud are more apt to be those who are willing to have it be known that they take an interest in reading outside of school. Publicly, my students tend to deny reading as an activity of choice, stating that they prefer to engage in sporting events, movie viewing, shopping, or spending time with friends. Privately, in conversations among cohorts, they admit to reading to relax at the end of the day, to fill time when they are grounded, or when there is nothing else to do, to find out about things they want to know, and to experience things vicariously (my word) that they have not experienced for themselves.

Finally, I consider the social context of each of these six class groups. Social context refers to the unique characteristics of each group of students and their interactions among themselves and as a group with myself—the outward manifestation or personality of the six individual literacy clubs. Differences among the groups might be expressed in terms of the group's acceptance of those who extend themselves academically. The greatest number of readers are in the third- and sixth-period classes. Both classes consist of a large proportion of students who are interested in the activities of school and in academic success. Both groups are supportive in nature, showing outward approval of those who excel through applause, positive statements such as "Way to go Jordie!" and emulation.

One quarter of the students in the seventh period are participating in the readings. Participation in this class appears to pivot around the influence of several students who are both vocal and powerful in their impact. They have been labeled in the past as discipline problems and have now

Defining Ourselves—Revealing the Literacies Inside Us 49

decided to become full and enthusiastic participants in the literacy club and all that it entails. J. B. illustrates the sense of empowerment that may be derived through participation in sanctioned activities. He is a frequent participant as Reader of the Day. On this particular day, as J. B. is sharing, the assistant principal stops by the classroom for a visit. J. B. concludes his reading and announces triumphantly, "See Mr. R., I'm gonna be good this year. . . . you can take my mom's number off the speed dial on your phone!"

One third of the students in the fourth period participate as Reader of the Day. This is an atypical class in that there are only 13 students, with the usual number of students being around 25. It has been difficult to establish a solid social context with this group. This may be attributed to the frequent influx and outflow of students due to transfers within the district and student absence. The students who regularly attend have made a valiant attempt to establish a literacy club.

Three of the 21 students in second period and one of the 27 students in eighth period participate as Reader of the Day. In both classes there are students who might have shared had they been a part of another class or social context. As Sergei confides, "There are some people in here who think that they're pretty cool. . . . I'm not in that group. I don't want them to you know, laugh at me." Cindy tells me privately, "I might share one day, but right now I just don't know some of the kids in here. I don't feel comfortable reading in front of the people I don't know yet." Both classes contain students who are academically motivated and who have expressed an interest in reading outside of school. The difference in participation may be attributable to the social context in that these students do not yet feel comfortable within the group, so they are unwilling to share feelings and beliefs or to let it be known to what extent they may value reading.

Class Period	Total Number of Students	Number of Students Who Participate As Reader of the Day
2	21	3
3	17	12
4	13	5
6	30	17
7	28	7
8	27	1

What is Valued?

Reader of the Day is viewed by the students as an opportunity to have direct input into the curriculum. Cade compares this to his previous experiences in school, saying, "Got more choices. And more open to what we want to read, our comments and thoughts and opinions and observations—very important!" For a few moments on the days in which there are sharing events, students have the opportunity to lead the class using material of their own choosing.

During Reader of the Day, some students share what they like, making introductory statements such as "This is one of *my* favorites." For the most part, readers choose texts which they believe will be of interest to their peers. Jess describes her thinking as she chose to read excerpts from *A Child Called It* (Pelzer, 1995), the autobiographical account of an abused child:

> There was some words in there that were kind of inappropriate and then I wasn't sure the whole class could take it because it's like really emotional. But, I decided to go ahead and bring it and read the first day, and then if people liked it, I would read some more.

In some cases students describe the process as one in which they read several stories and think about which one "people would like the most." Still others note the readings which are well received and choose material of a similar nature to share with the class. An example of this may be found in the sharing of excerpts from *Chicken Soup for the Teenage Soul* (Canfield, Hansen, & Kirberger, 1997). This book is a collection of short personal narratives and poems, most of which contain an obvious message. *Chicken Soup for the Teenage Soul* directs itself to what the authors presume are the interests and concerns of teenagers. It is written to follow the format of a previously published *Chicken Soup for the Soul* which addresses the issues of the older generation. The readings from *Chicken Soup for the Teenage Soul* usually consist of the sharing of more than one narrative. Those who listen beg for more. Those who do not "get" the obvious message are tutored by their peers who loudly, and sometimes derisively, explain the point of the story. Those who read hold the book authoritatively. The books are often rifled with Post-it notes. Readings are accompanied by comments from the reader such as, "you'll love this one," "this is one of my favorites," or "would you rather hear the one about . . . ?"

One of the most favored stories, "The Bible," (Canfield, Hansen, & Kirberger, 1997) tells of a young man who has been promised money to purchase a car upon his graduation from high school. On the night of graduation, the young man receives a Bible. He throws down the Bible and leaves the house, never to return until after his father's death. While going through his father's personal artifacts, the young man finds the Bible, opens it, and out drops a check for the purchase of a car, written the day of his graduation from high school. Students who had not previously been involved in literature discussions refer to this story weeks later during the reading of *Canyons* (Paulsen, 1990). A comparison is made between the relationship of the central characters and their parents.

Reading of these stories from *Chicken Soup for the Teenage Soul* also provides students with an opportunity to discuss their reading strategies. After reading several stories aloud, Emelda comments that the ending of a particular narrative has not surprised her, even though that is clearly the intent of the authors. Emelda surmises that the reading of these short stories is like the reading of a mystery. "They always give you a clue!" she exclaims. Emelda proceeds to take us through a reading of "Always Return Your Phone Calls" (Canfield, Hansen, & Kirberger, 1997), a story of a young girl who was prevented from taking her own life because of a phone call from an absent friend. As she takes us through the story she directs our attention to particular phrases which foreshadow the events to come, concluding that "You just *knew* Charlotte was going to try to commit suicide and you *knew* that Angela's friendship would save her—the clues were there!"

Reader of the Day is also valued by the students as a means by which they can collectively construct knowledge.

> Robert Everhart (1983) calls this regenerative knowledge, or knowledge which comes from the experiences of those present and their interaction with one another. Regenerative knowledge differs from the reified or predetermined knowledge which is often the basis of literary studies.

Tim's reading of a poem entitled "A Pizza A Party and A Moonlight Ride" by an anonymous author, is an example of knowledge proposed by a student within the context of the classroom and collectively constructed through discussion. The poem tells the story of a young girl who goes out with a boy who drinks too much and makes a pass at her. The poem ends as the boy and the girl are involved in an automobile accident and both of them die. Tim has typed the poem himself and made copies for the class. As he reads aloud there are audible murmurs of approval from the group. When Tim completes the reading several students gasp aloud with surprise at the ending. The talk which follows is centered on the power of the writing and the message of the poem. In reference to the power of the writing, students comment that "Whoever wrote this really knew how to write!" "The ending shocked me!" "The way he described everything . . . I could see it happening!" Students' comments reflect their understanding of the message of the poem as they say, "I would never have gotten in the car with that guy." "My parents aren't going to let me date until I'm an old woman." "Things turned out so bad for them." and "Sure doesn't make drinking look cool." The power of the poem and the presentation is evidenced by the number of students who ask for copies to keep or to share with friends. Tim's reading is of cultural value within this class group and perhaps to others outside of the class, as it is then shared with parents, siblings, and friends. The learning which takes place during Tim's reading has much in common with formal literacy experiences within the curricular framework. Students discuss the title and author of the poem, make predictions, analyze the writing, draw conclusions, and connect the reading to their own prior knowledge and experience. Yet the lesson is different because it is peer driven.

> Penelope Eckert (1989) states that "although an individual may be strongly influenced or even transformed by one teacher at some point in life, the average adolescent probably learns more from peers than from any other category of people" (p. 184).

> Frank Smith (1988) states that "Children do more than use fellow members of their clubs as resources for providing the knowledge and understanding they need. They learn from what the others themselves do: the learning is *vicarious*. . . . *children actually learn from what other people do—provided they are the kind of people the children see themselves as being*" (p. 8).

Finally, the students who value Reader of the Day view it as an activity which they can call their own and one in which they can take active control over the accumulation of knowledge. As students listen to literature and conversations about literature, they begin to exhibit signs of ownership. If I neglect to include Reader of the Day, I am reminded by the students. Several groups want to extend the activity by having more than one reader during a class period. At times we have as many as three readings and conversations occurring in one class period. Students stop me in the hallway to talk about their reading. Angie, a reluctant reader who has been introduced to the Goosebumps series through Reader of the Day stops by one morning to say, "I just read 10 chapters of a Goosebump book last night. At the end of every chapter something happens that makes you just have to keep reading to find out what comes next!"

> This sense of control is expressed by James Coleman (1961) as that of a passive versus an active role. Coleman states that "adolescents are not content with a passive role. They exhibit this discontent by their involvement in positive activities, activities which they can call their *own*" (p. 315).

What is Required of the Readers?

As I consider what is required of the readers who participate in Reader of the Day, I reflect back to the terms used by Gallimore and Goldenberg (1993), *operations and task demands*. As I see it, the *operations and task demands* of Reader of the Day are reflected in the ways that the students prepare to share and share a reading. A close look at readings by Betsey and Emelda illustrates what I mean by this.

Betsey is the first Reader of the Day in the sixth-period class; and as such, she is in a position to set the standard of operations for this group. Betsey comes to class with a copy of a book from the American Girl series entitled *Meet Addy: An American Girl* (Porter, 1993). Betsey sits on the stool in front of the class, and I take my place at her desk. She previews the section she is going to read by telling us that Addy's father and brother have just been sold to another plantation and that Addy is distracted by this as she attempts to perform the task of pulling the worms off of the tobacco leaves. The excerpt Betsey reads reveals that Addy is missing many of the worms due to her distraction. The overseer makes Addy eat the worms she has missed. Betsey pauses during the reading to define the word "overseer" for us as "like the big boss." Betsey has prepared for the event much as a teacher would prepare to share a piece of literature with her students. She previews what she is going to share and sets the stage for the reading by giving us the background knowledge we will need about characters and events as well as the definition of a word with which we might not be familiar.

Another method of preparation is exemplified in the reading shared by Emelda. Emelda chose excerpts from *A Real Diary: Go Ask Alice* (Anonymous, 1971) written by an anonymous teen who describes her descent into drug addiction. Emelda has come prepared with Post-it notes which are placed on pages of the book and numbered in the order that she wishes to read the excerpts. Emelda begins by reading a note from the editors which explains that the book is based on "an actual diary of a 15-year-old drug user." The rest of the note is a statement which conveys the editor's hope that the book will "offer insights into the increasingly complicated world in which we live." The second statement read by Emelda is an entry in which Alice writes about how her world had begun to change overnight:

> I was thinking that the grass had never smelled grassier, the sky had never seemed so high. Now it's all smashed down upon my head and I wish I could just melt into the blaaaaa-ness of the universe and cease to exist. (p. 7)

The third excerpt read by Emelda reflects Alice's initial curiosity and fear about drug use:

> I'm sure if I hint around she'll see that I get to try pot just once,

> then I'll immediately go home and forget the whole drug set-up, but it's nice to be informed and know what things are really like. . . . I can't take a chance on anyone reading you, especially not now! (p. 37)

The fourth excerpt deals with Alice's dependence and growing disillusionment with drugs:

> Anyone who says pot and acid are not addicting is a stupid, raving idiot, unenlightened fool! I've been on them since July 10, and when I've been off I've been scared to death to even think of anything that even looks or seems like dope. All the time pretending to myself that I could take it or leave it! (p. i)

The fifth excerpt deals with Alice's attempts to start a new life without drugs:

> I think I'm scared witless inside about going back to school but in my head I know it's going to be all right because I have Joel and my new super straight friends and they'll help me. . . . Diaries are great when you're young. . . . I think when a person gets older she should be able to discuss her problems and thoughts with other people, instead of just with another part of herself as you have been to me. (pp. 187–188)

The final excerpt read by Emelda is the epilogue which states that Alice has been found dead of a drug overdose. No one could determine if the overdose had been accidental or premeditated. With the reading of six excerpts from a diary, Emelda has summarized the events which led to the demise of Alice. Her preparation consists of carefully choosing the excerpts that will most powerfully depict the essence of the diary.

Conduct for Readers and Listeners

As my students and I engage in Reader of the Day we develop expectations of how readers and listeners will act, what Gallimore and Goldenberg (1993) would define as *scripts for conduct*.

Erving Goffman (1973) writes that "when the individual presents himself before others, his performance will tend to incorporate and exemplify the officially accredited values of the society" (p. 35). Goffman surmises that "when an individual does move into a new position in society and obtains a new part to perform, he is not likely to be told how to conduct himself" (p. 72).

The behavior of the readers, in most cases, is modeled after what has been determined as typical classroom procedure. Readers understand that they are to sit at the front of the room in an elevated position, introduce the text, and read loudly enough so that all can hear. When a reader fails to adhere to these unspoken rules, the listeners make their dissatisfaction known. In other words, listeners prompt reader scripts through verbal questioning and instruction such as: "What's the title?" "Who wrote that?" "We can't hear you." "Read louder." "I can't see." "She reads for too long."

I had expected that the readers would initiate the discussion following the reading. For many, this proves to be a daunting task. Some simply shut the book and dismiss the practice with a comment such as, "Well, that's all . . . " Others leave the stool and hurriedly return to their desks. I realize that it will require time, practice, and encouragement from the listeners for these readers to assume the "part" of discussion leader. Nettie's comments provide an example of student thinking about talk. As Nettie would say at the end of the year, " . . . in the other classes I wasn't really outspoken about what I felt. Other kids and you have inspired me to say what I'm thinking, not just close it up."

Other students are more able to talk about what they have brought to share. As Anne perches on the stool, clutching a note in her hand, she tells us how she had not been expected to live when she was born. Anne proceeds to read aloud from a note written by her mother and given to her on the occasion of her first Christmas. As she reads the note in which her mother describes her love for Anne, she stops to tell us "This is a sentimental note that I'll keep forever. Even though I didn't understand it when my mother first gave it to me, I understand it more as I get older." Anne is able to open up the discussion as she talks about her growing understanding of her mother's love for her. Some who listen to Anne are then able to reflect upon their own experiences and respond with stories of their own.

The listeners, too, have *scripts for conduct* modeled after typical classroom procedure. The *scripts for conduct* of the listeners call for their silent attention and outward expression of interest as well as their participation in the ensuing discussion of the reading. The listeners convey their interest to the reader as they refrain from movement which might distract the reader and as they withhold comments and conversation during the reading. There are, of course, instances in which listeners are released from the script of silence—those instances in which the text is exceptionally provocative, as with the readings of "A Pizza A Party and A Moonlight Ride" and several of the excerpts from *Chicken Soup for the Teenage Soul* (Canfield, Hansen, & Kirberger, 1997). In these cases the conduct of the listeners diverts from the script due to their need to show interest, approval, and enthusiasm for the reading. Readings may be interrupted by the listeners' questions or whispered comments about the text.

Though I had initially decided my own *script of conduct* would require that I sit in a student desk within the listening group and that I should not in any way influence the response or the reading, I soon determine that I should intervene. As the readers conclude their reading and prepare to leave the stool amidst applause from the listeners, I see that discussion is not going to be a natural outgrowth of the reading. To prompt discussion, I decide to ask questions and/or demonstrate a possible response to the reading. For example, Jess shares the poem "Somebody Should Have Taught Him," from *Chicken Soup for the Teenage Soul* (Canfield, Hansen, & Kirberger, 1997). She tearfully concludes this reading about a child who has made the decision not to drink and is later killed by a drunk driver. The listeners clap solemnly and wait. I ask, "Does anyone have anything they want to say?" Bet responds with the phrase, "Don't drink and drive." Again there is silence. I decide to model a possible response with a story about a boy I had known in high school. My telling of the story seems to give Jess time to think about what she wants to say. Through her tears she relates the story of her uncle:

> My uncle, he had problems. He was drinking one night and he was coming back from a club and he either fell asleep at the wheel or something and he crashed into a tree and he flipped over three or four times and he fell into a field. They didn't find him until three or four days later. I have his ring and it's bent and stuff, but I keep it in my drawer at my house.

I ask Jess if this poem might be meaningful to her because of the experience. She tells us that she cried the first time she read the poem. We then wonder if the author of the poem wrote from experience or imagination. As we finish wondering, Burton and Bet join the conversation to tell related stories of their own.

Choice of Texts

The fifth and final interactive factor of this activity setting is that of the *purposes* or motives of those engaged in the activity. As might be expected, this factor of the activity setting reveals the most information about the readers themselves.

Erving Goffman (1973) reflects upon the words of Robert Ezra Park, author of *Race and Culture*, who tells us that the first meaning of the word "person" is mask. As such, "this mask is our truer self, the self we would like to be" (p. 19).

Readers reveal their identities or the identities they want to assume by the putting on and taking off of masks which are revealed through the literature they share with the group as Reader of the Day. Readers are constructing an identity through their readings in order to gain approval from their peers. Through read alouds readers have sought acceptance from their peers, confirmed, resisted, or reinforced personality type or role, and revealed their interests or fears.

> As stated by P. Eckert (1989), "Whereas family acceptance is based on ascriptive (kin) status, the peer group awards acceptance on the basis of the individual's personal qualities" (p. 73).

Seeking Acceptance

The readings of Chris may provide a more clear picture of the emergence of identity reflected through a collection of readings. Chris is a student who has recently immigrated from the Philippines. She had previously attended a private girls' school. Chris considers herself to be a highly literate individual as evidenced by her first reading of a poem she has written herself. The poem is one which Chris has apparently shared at an earlier time with another group of students. It has been commented upon favorably by other teachers and by the students themselves. Thus, Chris appears to believe that the reading of this work will remind us of her interest in reading and writing and, therefore, speed her entry into this new literacy community. The second time Chris reads for the group, she chooses a piece from *Chicken Soup for the Teenage Soul* (Canfield, Hansen, & Kirberger, 1997). Excerpts from this book have already been read by another student and "approved" by the group. Chris reads a poem called "Paintbrush" by Bettie B. Youngs. The poem speaks of the need to cover up our true selves until we believe that others will accept us as we are. The ultimate goal, as expressed in the poem, is for us to accept ourselves. Until that point, we must rely on the paintbrush in order to cover up what we do not like about ourselves or what we believe others would not like about us. With this second reading, Chris reveals her self-doubts about the process of making new friends. It is as if she is asking permission to be herself in this new place. Following her reading, we talk about how people sometimes try to be something they are not in order to win the acceptance of the group. When asked to reflect on her readings, Chris says "It's important to me that people know how I am as a person. I'd rather have a few close friends who really care about me than be one of the popular people." She adds, "Sometimes, I'm quiet because I don't know what people will think of me." Our discussion following Chris' reading of "Paintbrush" allows us to see that there have been times when each of us has experienced self-doubt and a desire for acceptance.

P. Eckert (1989) states that many adolescents remember "a need not simply to get to know people, but to confirm their emerging sense of identity through the recognition of others and a sense of place in the social structure" (p. 86).

Confirming Personality Type or Role

L. Rosenblatt (1995) proposes that the reading of literature gives us a sense that there are others who feel as we do. She states that "The very fact that the reader's situation is not unique, that it at least parallels what others evidently understand and have lived through, gives him some perspective" (p. 191).

Other readers appeared to use Reader of the Day as a way of expressing a world view. They believe they are perceived as a certain personality type and use the readings to confirm this belief to themselves and others. Margaret is perceived by the group as a "nice girl" with strong religious beliefs. She shares excerpts from Chris Van Allsburg's (1985) *Polar Express*. Margaret gives a brief summary of the story up to the point where the boy unwraps the last present under the tree. She reads aloud from the moment when the boy reads the note from Santa Claus and his parents comment that the bell, a gift from Santa, is broken. The narrator of the story goes on to state that not everyone can hear the bell. Only those who "believe" can hear the bell. Margaret then leads the group in a discussion of how important it is to have beliefs and that our beliefs may determine who we are and what we become.

Resisting Personality Type or Role

The platform of reader is also used to resist roles as perceived by the group. Randy resists the social pressure to conform through his readings. Randy is known by his peers as someone who resorts to hitting and kicking when frustrated. This behavior goes against that sanctioned by the school and often results in office referrals. Several of the students have shown their frustration with Randy through their requests that they not be seated near him. Randy chooses particularly violent scenes from *Lord of the Flies* (Golding, 1954) to read aloud to the group. His readings about the treatment of the child nicknamed "Piggy" seem to reflect his own feelings about the appropriateness of harming those who are considered to be inferior. It is possible that Randy predicts reading about the treatment of this character and the general acceptance of this behavior by the other characters in the novel might sway the thinking of his own peer group.

Unfortunately for Randy, this is not the case. Although the group does seem to enjoy the reading, they continue to oppose violence as a means of controlling others. When asked about his reading and the response of the group Randy reacts by saying, "I don't care what they think of me." He dismisses the others in the class with the comment, "They're all nerds anyway."

Reinforcing Personality Type or Role

Guy appears to use the platform to reinforce the roles established within his class group. The class group in which Guy is a member demonstrates a belief in strictly segregated stereotypical roles for males and females. It is verbalized within this group that "guys don't show their feelings and stick to the facts." The attitude of this group reflects observations made by M. R. Cherland (1994) about the residents of Oak Town, that "men read for utilitarian purposes" (p. 84). Guy is an active participant in other class functions. He wants to share during Reader of the Day but bemoans the fact that he cannot find anything to share. Finally, one day while at the library, Guy finds something which will, in his opinion, be socially acceptable to share—an excerpt from a piece of nonfiction about snakes. Guy reads the excerpt with a great deal of expression and drama, as one would read a piece of fiction. He then leads the boys in the class in a discussion of snakes they have encountered. This is met with silence and comments of "oooh" and "yuck" from the girls. It seems that Guy has indeed reinforced his belief that males are a different breed who read "different stuff."

Revealing Interests or Fears

Finally, as represented by the readings of Emelda and Tim, some readers shared pieces which exemplify their interests or fears. Emelda's sharing of excerpts from the diary of a girl whose interest and fascination with drugs leads to her death reflects her own awareness of the issue of drugs and a connection with what she is learning in school. This piece was shared shortly after a drug awareness program presentation in the students' science class. Emelda is not a likely candidate for experimentation with drugs. It is more likely that she has read the piece because she has heard of it from older friends. The reading of the piece reveals to Emelda a world which is different from the world in which she lives. She is drawn to the horror of the situation; thus, the sharing represents both her interests and her fears. The same could be said for the reading by Tim of the poem, "A Pizza A Party and A Moonlight Ride." Tim's mother found the poem and shared it with him. As reported by Tim and his mother, the poem had sparked a family discussion on the dangers of drinking. In reading it to his peers, Tim shares the warning with those he cares about. Death is something to fear, and this is a way that a young person could die.

Collaborative Curriculum

Reader of the Day, because it is based upon readings chosen by the students, offers a change from the standard fare of texts chosen by teachers or curriculum coordinators. As such, it presents an opportunity for us to view curriculum as something created by students or the learners themselves. The students accept the opportunity and transform it through their inclusion of personal writings as relevant readings and through discussions which occur during and after the reading.

> Ira Shor (1992) speaks of dialogue as a means of "putting limits" on the authority of the teacher. Students are called upon to "codevelop a joint learning process" (p. 90). As Shor explains, the teacher may then use student interests and concerns as a part of new curriculum which is developed collaboratively.

> Etta Hollins (1996), who writes of culture in schools, might see Reader of the Day as an opportunity for students to direct their own learning. Hollins describes "empowerment" as one of four essential elements of meaningful learning in secondary schools (p. 112).

As stated earlier, the students who choose to read aloud are those who have read something they enjoy and who are comfortable with the idea of sharing through a read-aloud. Shelby explains further,

> I like reading and I think it's cool to read out loud and stuff, and like when I'm done reading and everybody starts clapping . . . it's just like, it makes people feel good. So, I share because I read a lot. . . . and then there's stuff that I want to tell people.

Shelby's statement reveals that she reads because she has something to share, because it makes her (and others) feel good when the reading is appreciated, and finally, because she views the read aloud as a way to share her thoughts with others.

Some students are uncomfortable with the idea of reading aloud. Others may be reluctant to read aloud because they feel they are unable to choose something which will be well received by their peers. Ranita is reluctant to share until she sees that excerpts from *Chicken Soup for the Teenage Soul* (Canfield, Hansen, & Kirberger, 1997) are enjoyed by her class group. She then decides that she will share, saying excitedly, "Maybe I'll sign up. Maybe I can find something from that book that I can read."

Increased Awareness

> Louise Rosenblatt (1978) writes of the importance of comparing thoughts on literature:
>> Learning what others have made of a text can greatly increase such insight into one's own relationship with it. . . . Through such interchange he can discover how people bringing different temperaments, different literary and life experiences, to the text have engaged in very different transactions with it. (p. 146)

The process of the sharing of literature and ideas found within Reader of the Day may instill an added dimension of awareness to the participants—an awareness of both self and others, as well as an awareness of how our interpretation of text is colored by our own experiences and the context of the reading.

> Judith Langer (1995) writes that the reading of literature may help us to note that "ways of reading are complicated and implicated by personal and group histories" (p. 144).

All too often, our students come to the reading of a text with an expectant air of waiting to be told what it means and what they are to think about it. An increased awareness of text is evident in both students who share aloud and in those who listen. Jess' reading of excerpts from *A Child Called It* (Pelzer, 1995) prompted several students to purchase their own copies of the book. Jess tells me how it made her feel, saying, "After I read it they were coming up to me saying, 'Can I read the book?' I was like honored because they really liked it."

Students who do not read aloud share in the process as they listen to the readings, comment on the text, and as they use what they have heard to help them make choices about what they will read on their own. Carolina is uncomfortable with reading aloud, yet she comments on the book Jess has shared with the class, saying, "That was good . . . that was a sad book. I liked it." She tells me that she bought the book and read the rest of it to herself. Carolina and others frequently choose to read books which have been shared during Reader of the Day.

> According to Paulo Freire (1985), "Education at any level will be more rewarding if it stimulates the development of this radical, human need for expression" (p. 21).

It is my assumption that Reader of the Day, based as it is upon student choice, reflects students' needs in terms of social and emotional issues. In many cases, the choices made by students were an expression of their needs; for example, Chris' need to express her discomfort at being in an unfamiliar situation and her need to be accepted by her peers, Randy's need to gain acceptance for his method of dealing with frustration, and the needs of Emelda and Tim to grapple with the issues of adolescent use of drugs and alcohol. Bet's words reveal what may happen when students share their concerns through reading and listening to one another. She talks about Jess sharing a poem she had written about her despair over her situation at home:

> When Jess read the poem she wrote, it made me think about my life. It just made me have this hope ... made me feel hope for her. Made me feel like I knew exactly what she was talking about.

Reader of the Day is a venue for the members of a class group to come to know one another and to share their concerns. Jake describes how hearing what others read helps him come to know them, saying, "You get to know all the people because they share all this different stuff. Sometimes they bring personal stuff and read that, so you just get to know people a little better when they do that."

Participating in Reader of the Day is empowering to students. As Jake stated at the end of the year, "When all these other people are listening to what you're saying and you can get your point across, when you're up in front and they're looking at you, you just feel like really *powerful*."

Merging of Personal and Academic Literacy

As has been said by many others, the reading of literature provides a means by which we can gauge our own experience against that of others. Literature is a means of grappling with issues which we may face in our own lives now or at some time in the future. Reader of the Day is a means of bringing a hidden literacy, that of personal reading, to the forefront of the classroom and, in so doing, making private practice public in an effort to merge two distinct forms of literacy.

As Ranita talks to me about her reaction to readings from *Chicken Soup for the Teenage Soul* (Canfield, Hansen, & Kirberger, 1997), she says:

> *It was pretty good. My aunt bought that book for me and we were reading it, and I read the one about the starfish. A guy takes one starfish and puts it in the water and the other guy asks, "Why are you doing that? It's not going to help, you know. You can't get all the starfish." So the first guy is like, "Well, one fish makes a difference and I'm saving one of them." ...I liked that one.*

Ranita's words prompt me to think further about Reader of the Day. Every student did not experience the activity in the same way. Each of us played a part in the process—some read while others listened, talked, thought about a personal issue, or took something away to read on our own. Each of us made a difference. Perhaps, if we and our students were able to merge our personal and academic selves and to cease to categorize individuals as those who succeed in the achievement club and those who fail, our learning would have a deeper meaning and school would no longer be something we simply "do" but something we live.

Jamie Myers (1992) states, "If personal and academic literacy clubs were the dominant social contexts in school activities, students might not feel a division between their own knowledge of the world and academic knowledge of the world. They also might not feel a division between those who succeed in the achievement club and those who fail" (p. 321).

Defining Ourselves Through Objects of Personal Significance

At this point, we have come to see ourselves as reflected through the events in our lives as well as through the literature that we value. Through a study connected to our reading of mysteries, we will learn that we are also defined by the objects we hold dear. While reading and talking about mysteries, my students and I became fascinated with the diversity and the potential meaning of objects as clues. For example, students who are reading *Wanted* (Cooney, 1997) wonder about the significance of the information contained on the computer disk that Alice has retrieved from the files of her murdered father. How does the information saved on the disk explain what may have happened? How does it connect Alice and her father? Why do others want the disk? We talk about how the clues are significant factors in the mystery—factors which may help us to reach conclusions about the characters and events portrayed in the story. It occurs to me that the clues may be seen as objects which describe and define the characters as well as the plot.

As I listen to my students talking and as I read what they are writing to one another about the clues in their Reader/Writer logs, I begin to think about ways for us to consider the objects in our lives. I had just finished reading *Poemcrazy: Freeing Your Life With Words* in which poet/teacher Susan Wooldridge (1996) describes her own exploration with words and objects. Wooldridge begins with collecting the words themselves, stating that "The great thing about collecting words is they're free; you can borrow them, trade them in or toss them out. Words are lightweight, unbreakable, portable, and they're everywhere" (p. 9). Wooldridge goes on to describe a process of creating a collection of words by cutting words from magazines and gluing them to tickets. These word tickets are then placed on a variety of objects. For example, the words *abandon* and *boundary* are placed on an old globe. The word *anger* is placed on a burned out green candle. As Wooldridge concludes, "Suddenly it seemed the objects could speak. Their labels changed the way we saw them" (p. 15).

Reflecting upon what I had read, I surmise that creating a word collection and labeling objects with words could be a way of engaging my students in a study of words through a new experience, as well as offering an opportunity for them to utilize labeling as a foundation for the formation of new concepts. If these concepts were developed using objects of personal significance to the students, they might further reflect on their identity and life experiences and increase the depth of their knowledge of themselves and one another. This process involves participants in choosing an object of personal significance and in labeling the object in a manner which reflects that significance. As the personal meaning of the object comes to light through this redefining process, students create index cards that indicate the thought behind the words they have chosen and the meaning or significance of the object. These new meanings and considerations of self are shared within the classroom and then displayed in what we call the Museum of Objects and Ideas.

Collecting Tickets and Objects

I begin by asking each of my 150 students to spend a few minutes clipping words and gluing them to tickets. I am soon bombarded with questions: "Is this a good word?" "What kind of words do you want?" "What does this word mean?" "Do verbs count?" I answer that any word, as long as it is of interest to them, will be an excellent addition to our collection. As the word tickets are completed, we drop them into a glass fishbowl on the counter. I let the word collection rest in the bowl while I make my plans. Though I had not anticipated it, this too creates some excitement and curiosity. "When are we going to do something with those word tickets?" "What are we going to do with these?" Finally, the day arrives. As the students prepare to leave class, I say, "The next time we meet we are going to play a game with our word tickets. Please bring an object of personal significance to school with you so you can play the game." To illustrate what I mean, I show them a geode cut in half and lined with amethyst crystals. As I hold the geode in my hand, I explain that this object is of personal significance to me. I relate a bit of my story, telling them that long ago my mother cut a geode in half and presented part of it to me and part of it to my younger sister. On the night that she gave us the stones she said to us both, "Just like these two fragments of stone, when united you are whole." There is silence in the room; and I watch my students thinking about what I have said, perhaps reflecting upon objects in their lives which are personally significant. Our reveries are interrupted by the bell signifying the end of class. Now, I must wait to see what will happen next.

The moment I enter the building the next day, I sense that something wonderful has happened. On the way to my mailbox, I am swamped by an entourage of excited students. Tracey waves a green army hat in front of me. "Look what I brought for my object! It belonged to my real dad!" Bart asks if he can bring his object to our classroom and put it in the cabinet where it will be safe. He clutches a box which contains his baby shoes, telling me "Yesterday, my mom and I went up into the attic to look for some shoes for my little brother and I found these. My first pair of Nikes! Can these be my object?" As I proceed through the crowd, Martin approaches and gently unfolds a rumpled bag, bringing forth a baby scrapbook. He speaks softly, saying, "My mom made this for me when I was a baby. She says I had better take good care of it." These are but a few of many examples. Veronica and Suliya brought their first books. Laura, an avid member of the school band, brought her drum sticks.

I agree with Martin that we will take care of his scrapbook, thinking that we will need to take care of all of these items. It is clear to me that the students have come to school bringing objects of great personal significance. These are not *things* grabbed in haste on the way out the door, but objects chosen with a great deal of care and sensitivity.

Creating the Museum of Objects and Ideas

My plan is to have each student draw 5 tickets at random from the bowl. They will then look up the definition of each word in a dictionary and write both the word and its meaning in their Reader/Writer logs. Next, they will choose a word or two to fasten to their object. The word or words applied to the object should make us think about the object in a new and different way. We will then create an index card on which we will write the name of the object and the words and definitions applied to the object as well as an explanation of our reasoning in choosing this particular word for the object. A second index card will explain the personal significance of the object. Finally, the objects and index cards will be displayed in a "Museum of Objects and Ideas."

Before we begin, I model the process, choosing an object from the shelf—a stuffed pink pig given to me that year by Kristine. I ask the students to define the word, "some" ("being of an unspecified but appreciable quantity, amount, extent or degree") and "pig" ("a young swine weighing less than one hundred and thirty pounds"). I fasten these words on the stuffed pig and then ask the students to tell me what thoughts come to mind when they see the words on the pig. After a second or two comes the shouted response, *Charlotte's Web*! We talked about how our answer reflects a common childhood experience, the reading of E. B. White's (1952) *Charlotte's Web*. We realize that these words on the pig might have little meaning for those who have not had the same prior experience. I create a statement of the personal significance of the object, writing about my love of the book and about how much the gift of the stuffed pig from Kristine means to me as a teacher.

We are ready to begin. The room is charged with excitement during the drawing of the word tickets and then grows silent as the students search through dictionaries for meanings. Later, while helping a student who can not locate a word in the dictionary, I glance to the front of the room where there seems to be some commotion. "What are you doing?" I ask as I move forward to see several students vying for an opportunity to get their hands in the word bowl while others flip through words tossed out onto the table. "Getting more words," Tim replies, clutching a handful. "I can't find the ones I need," remarks Anthony as he carefully considers and rejects ticket after ticket, turning over the ones he has read. "You want to look up more words?" I ask doubtfully. I had expected them to settle for the words they drew, given the fact that they had to look up each word and write down a definition. "Well, I need the *right* word," Veronica replies, looking at me as if this should have been obvious.

As the students complete the index cards and fasten the word tickets to their objects, they place them at the front of the room. I suggest that we file past our "exhibit" and look at the objects as if we were in a museum. Suliya has fastened to her book the words "helped," which she defines as "aided," and "education," which she defines as "knowledge or skill obtained." She explains her reasoning for choosing these words to place on the book, writing on her index card, "Refers to my later education and schooling. This book motivated me to reach a goal in kindergarten which I did, and it now motivates me to continue reading and writing." Suliya describes the personal significance of her first book, writing, "Listening to my family members read me this book, and finally reading it myself, I found out how wonderful reading is. This was my first book. I will always keep it and treasure it." Tony fastens the word "ambitious" to a gold pen, writing that the word means "full of or motivated by ambition." Tony writes, "I chose this because my grandpa gave me this pen. He gave it to me because I made better grades than my cousins. So I desired to win and I did, and got the pen." Tony describes the personal significance of the gold pen, writing, "This pen is important to me because my grandpa gave it to me. My grandpa is old, and this is one of the few items he has given me. I take good care of it because I don't want to lose it. I love my grandpa, so I really like the pen."

Reaction to the Museum of Objects and Ideas

We display our objects and ideas for all to see in a glass case in the school commons, a gathering place for the students before school and at lunch time. In order for all the students to show their objects and ideas, the exhibit is changed every few days. As I attempt to change the display there are times when I can barely make my way through the crowd of students viewing the objects. Before and after school, parents come in to see the exhibit. It becomes a place for reflecting on old memories; evoking laughter and tender thoughts. "That's my guitar!" shouts David proudly. "My mom gave it to me so I would have something to keep me busy and out of her hair." "I remember making that quilt for Catherine. She was my daughter's best friend. I had no idea she still had it," whispers one mother with a pleased smile. "Can you believe my feet were that small?" Bart remarks. "You're still a shrimp, Bart!" Amber laughs, as she rumples his hair playfully.

Extending the Exploration

As I think about the reactions of the students to labeling and noting the significance of these personal objects, it occurs to me that we could extend our exploration even further. It might be possible to further navigate the world of reading and writing, returning to the pages or the pen with a new understanding of the familiar through our journey. I had come across an essay written by Lewis Nordan (1997) called "The Dimestore Teapot." Nordan wrote about a teapot he kept on his writing table in the attic. The essay was based upon an object and the memories it evoked. As I read the piece, I was reminded again of a statement by William Zinsser (1987), editor of *Inventing the Truth: The Art and Craft of a Memoir*:

> The writer of a memoir takes us back to a corner of his or her life that was unusually vivid or intense—childhood for instance—or that was framed by unique events. . . . a memoir is a window into a life. (p. 21)

The further study of an object from childhood might provide another point of embarkation for a journey into the past. Could a tangible object provoke intense memories, and enable us to write through the windows of our lives?

Being a reading teacher who espouses writing as one of the primary means of responding to reading, I was intrigued by the potential to connect our reading of Lewis Nordan's essay to the creation of our own essays based upon the memories surrounding objects of personal significance. Could we enter the world of "The Dimestore Teapot" (Nordan, 1997) and emerge with an understanding which we could apply to our own writing?

> Regie Routman (1994) writes that literature often provides the best models of language.

> Bernice Cullinan (1993) illuminates the connection between reading and writing and the importance of writing as a response to reading with this statement:
>> Reading teachers know that we need to engage students in writing if we want to teach them to read. We know that teaching students reading without including writing is like teaching them to swim with one hand tied behind them. (p. 2)

> Donald Murray (1996) believes that the essay "is usually the best way for a beginner to enter the writer's world" (p. 57). Murray feels that the writing of a personal essay allows him to "discover who I am. . . . celebrates my difference, authenticates who I am, justifies my existence" (p. 55). He continues, making the point that writing a personal essay encourages him to "make use of my experiences. . . . explore the lives I have lived and am living, even those I may live in the future" (p. 55).

In the description and examination of the process which follows, I will provide an example of the students' earlier insights through personal essays, and then continue with the process as it emerges through our study of objects of personal significance. As we continue, in the words of D. M. Murray (1996), to celebrate our difference, authenticate who we are, and justify our existence, the students examine and analyze text in search of a model. They talk to one another about the objects in attempts to find their stories, their voices, and the voices of their objects. As the students write, they discover that their voices are strengthened by these objects which "talk to me inside (and) tell stories of many things."

Prior Experiences With the Personal Essay

Earlier in the year we had written personal essays based upon an experience in our lives. After reading an excerpt from *The View From Saturday* (Konigsburg, 1996) in which the character, Ethan asks his friends "If you could live one day in your life all over again, what day would it be? And why?" (p. 91) I had suggested to my students that they write about a day that they would like to live all over again. My suggestion was greeted with looks of consternation and frustration as several students murmured, "I can't think of anything," and "What should I write about?" The following excerpts are representative of these personal essays:

Suliya wrote,

> If I could relive any day in my life it would be the day my parents took me to a Rockets game. It all started in November when my sisters and me were really bored so we sat down in front of the T.V. Our dad was already sitting there watching a game. We had never really cared for basketball but as he explained the game to us, we became more and more interested. From then on we all started watching the games.

Rob wrote,

> If I could relive one day in my life it would be the first day in Colorado I saw it snow. I remember throwing it at people and trying to make snow angels. In recess we had a rule-no throwing snow, but people did it anyway. In the winter we could go sledding we never did but that's one reason I would want to relive the two years I lived in Colorado.

The students had, as suggested, written about an experience in their own lives. For the most part, the essays consisted of brief, unelaborated snapshots. As we shared the essays aloud I hoped that questions from their peers asking for details and clarification would prompt further writing; however, few students were interested in revising or adding to the essays. It appeared that there was little personal involvement or ownership in the process despite the potential of the invitation to write of personal experiences.

It is evident to me that if we truly want to celebrate our difference, authenticate who we are, and justify our existence, we must go further. I decide that we will return to the personal essay. With this new encounter the students will have tangible points of reference in a piece of writing and in an object of personal significance. Concrete objects might help them to further visualize and bring their memories to life.

Reading in Search of a Model

In order to move to the next step on our journey, I introduce my students to Lewis Nordan's (1997) "The Dimestore Teapot." As we conclude our first oral reading of the essay, I suggest that we might try writing our own essays modeled after Nordan's and based upon our objects. With this suggestion, I hope to demonstrate two aspects of writing to my students; first, that writers sometimes model an original piece of writing on a work of literature and, second, that writers might use their own experiences as the basis for writing.

> Donald Graves (1994) emphasizes the importance of helping our students to find topics for their writing:
>> Unless we show them how to select topics from the ordinary events of their own lives and expand them into fiction, an essay, or a personal narrative, they can only draw on the experiences of others, which they do not necessarily understand. (p. 58)

> Mary Mercer Krogness (1995) reminds us of the difficulties many students have as they attempt to find, expand, and refine a topic:
>> Finding the story poses huge challenges for both students and teacher. Many seventh and eighth graders think they have nothing to say, and even if they believe they've found something worth saying, they fear they don't know how to say it. (p. 163)

It is my belief that the object of personal significance will stimulate memories and provide us with something to say, while Nordan's (1997) essay will help us see how to say it. We read the essay a second time in order to determine how the author created a mood and a story based upon an object. Our rereading is driven by the question, "How did the author do this?"

> Ralph Fletcher (1993a) writes of the roots and wings which may be found through reading literature, quoting novelist Robert Cohen who says that he reads everything twice, "Once to enjoy it, and a second time to steal everything from the author." Cohen goes on to explain the value of analyzing a work of literature from a writer's point of view with the statement that "In the long run, such wondering nourishes the young writer far more than the ability to recapitulate what the book is about" (p. 12).

Rereading to Analyze the Essay

During the rereading, we note that Nordan (1997) begins the piece by describing where the object is located, "The teapot is scrunched over in a corner of the table alongside some computer diskettes, a box of Kleenex, a filthy coffee mug, a ginger-ale can, and some beanbags I used to try to juggle until I lost one" (p. 92). After locating the object in the room, Nordan writes about who sees the teapot, "No one sees it anyway. I am the only person who ever enters this room. . . . I see the teapot only when I write. Mornings I am glad to find it there, as I sit in my chair to begin" (p. 92). He follows this with an elaborate, two paragraph, description of the teapot. Once Nordan completes his description of the teapot, he writes the history of the object, beginning with the words, "A half century ago when my step-father purchased it in Miss Bee's ten-cent store in Itta Bena, Mississippi, its cost was a few cents, only that." Later in the history, Nordan writes, "When the teapot first passed into my hands I imagined new rituals of romance, warm scones, finger sandwiches, special china." He then writes of what the teapot cannot do and what it can do, "This teapot is not for sharing, at last I understand. No friendships have ever been made or cemented in its warmth." and "This is a vessel designed for solitude. One person alone may use it well, no more . . . It is quiet, quiet, almost invisible, and yet not a listener or a witness. . . . You don't share this teapot with a friend. It is the friend" (p. 93). Nordan concludes his essay with a statement about what his stepfather might have thought as he purchased the teapot, "He might have seen it shiver beneath her feather duster, might have chosen it from the others. 'This one would be just right,' he might have said. . . . Maybe he knew his stepson would be a writer and have need of memory, a friend who does not forget" (p. 93).

As we proceed through the analysis, we compare Nordan (1997) as a writer to a photographer who is constantly changing the focus or angle of a shot. It occurs to us that Nordan has utilized a varied perspective in order to help us to consider the object from all angles or to see the unfamiliar in the familiar. We will follow the suggestion of author Robert Cohen (Fletcher, 1993a, p.12), and "steal" these perspectives as we look at our own objects, using Nordan's essay as a guide for our writing. Our essays will begin by showing the reader the object at a middle distance, showing the reader where the object is located. We will then step back from the object and write about those who see the object. We might imagine ourselves as we first perceive the object and describe it carefully, in minute detail. We can then pull back a bit and reflect on the history of the object and how it had arrived at its present state of significance. As we move in closer again, we will write of the object in relation to ourselves, clarifying what it can or can not do for us. Finally, we will return to the perspective of others as we try to imagine the thoughts and intentions of the person who placed the object in our lives. During our analysis, I keep a record of our "outline" on the overhead projector. With this in hand to guide us, we are ready to begin to navigate a writing based upon our own experiences.

First Steps: Talking and Listening

Before we put pen to paper we spend some time talking and listening in order to help us find the story.

Lucy Calkins (1994) writes of the importance of talking and listening:

> When children receive this kind of listening attention, when their stories and information and ideas and lives are heard and celebrated and channeled onto the page in this way, they respond.... they race off to get more paper; they toil over a list of all the chapters they plan to write; they buy themselves new notebooks, and, gathering around us, say, "Listen to what I've got" and "Will you hear my story?" (p. 17)

As students vie for a chance to talk about their objects, one of them remarks, "This reminds me of Show and Tell, like we used to do in elementary school." I am somewhat surprised by the candid reflections and personal details which emerge as even the most quiet students are now willing to share with their peers. As I watch, I listen to the voices of the students as they relate the stories connected to their objects. I wonder if a return to childhood objects and childhood experiences such as Show and Tell allows us to mentally return to childhood, shedding the reticence to reveal ourselves that we sometimes adopt as we grow older.

Tom begins, holding up a stuffed coyote dressed in camouflage gear. "This is Wylie. When I was little I used to take him everywhere with me." He turns and faces the class, pointing to a stain inside Wylie's mouth. "See this stain here? That's from when I used to try to feed him. I always gave him Cheetos and Kool-Aid." There is much laughter following this revelation, and the reminisces begin to flow in earnest. Carter, the ultimate jock, tells us that he keeps his stuffed basketball on his bed and dreams of the day he will be a professional ball player. Martin carefully turns the pages of his scrapbook and holds it up to show us his baby footprints. He compares his size ten feet to the tiny feet represented on the page. As he looks further at the book he muses, "My mother must really love me.... she's got everything I ever did in here."

> Ralph Fletcher (1993a) might view this talk about our objects as more than an attempt to find our stories. Fletcher writes about the loss of voice experienced by students in upper grade classrooms. He might see our talk as a way for the students to regain their voices in order to write with voice. Fletcher notes the "intimacy not just between the writer and subject but also between the writer and audience" demonstrated by young writers (p. 74), and wonders if an adolescent tendency to be self-critical in terms of writing, as well as "tougher demands from the outside world" contribute to the loss of voice experienced by older children (p. 73).

We conclude that in writing about these objects of personal significance, our charge is to listen to the voice inside of us as well as to the voices of the object in order that we may reveal the history as well as the significance of the object. One by one, as the stories are told, our memories unfold, and we begin to find what we will write about. As the voices of ourselves and those of our objects are engaged, talk dies down and pens are lifted. I sit down to write and to observe what happens.

Writing Our Own Essays About Objects

> M. Bakhtin (Holquist, 1996) reflects upon the voice associated with the objects themselves, stating that the "object has its own history," which consists of "the internal contradictions (or aspects) inside the object itself" as well as "the multitude of routes, roads, and paths that have been laid down in the object by social consciousness." The writer's charge is then to create "artistically calculated nuances on all the fundamental voices" of the object (pp. 278–279).

Stuart chews on his pencil tip, grabs another piece of paper, and writes on. His stuffed bear, nearly identical in size, watches over the process from the seat next to him. Florina opens her music box and listens to a few notes, then closes it with a smile and continues writing. Deb writes with one hand clutching her rubber duck which occasionally emits a squeak and startles us all. The minutes tick by and Martin exclaims, "This is amazing. I can't believe all the things I'm remembering." Stuart interrupts, proudly waving several pages over his head, "I'm flowing here. I've written three pages already and I'm just on the description of my bear." When the bell rings, students groan, and I overhear someone say, "I don't want to go. I just want to stay here and keep writing." As others agree I rejoice in their enthusiasm, saying, "I wish you could too, but this will give us something to look forward to."

On the next day, class begins without me. I enter the room from hall duty to find students reading aloud to friends, sharing what they have written. Others are turning on the overhead projector to look at our outline or silently rereading what they had written during our previous meeting. As the room grows still and the students return to their writing, I move from desk to desk, silently reading over their shoulders. Rob has begun writing about "My Greatest Poem," describing where it is located:

> Deep down in my notebook for school, I find a poem that I wrote the day my friend wanted me to give a letter to the girl he liked; something normal that a boy would think about a pretty girl.

Janice writes, describing those who see her cheerleading uniform:

> The uniform hides in the darkness of my closet most of the time, and is hardly seen. My mother may see it every once in a while, when she hangs up my clothes. My friends may see it when we go through my clothes. Yet I see it almost every day as I skim through my clothes every morning. I seem to grab the same thing, my uniform. It is wedged between all of my clothes and yet, I still seem to find it. Or maybe it finds me.

Tony describes the gold pen he received from his grandfather in minute detail:

> The gold pen shines in the light of the sun with great brightness. On the side of the pen lies my grandfather's name. Engraved on the side, it says, Rafael M. Aristo. The ink that comes out of the pen is the color of the water on the beaches in Mexico.

Deb reflects on the history of a yellow rubber duck and how it arrived at its present state of significance as she describes the night she received the duck, a present from her favorite swim coach, and flower crowns made by the older girls:

> I still remember the banquet so clearly. It was on a warm, breezy night, in a large park. Lynn took my sister and all of the girls in her age group, which weren't very many, and talked to them on a grassy hill. She then taught them how to make flower crowns out of the wild flowers growing in the park. I wanted to be older because I wanted to know what they talked about. It made me feel

like a nuisance since I was excluded from their group. To this day, I don't know how to make a flower crown, but if Lynn had taught me as she taught that group, I know I would remember deep down in my heart forever.

Floriana writes of a music box once owned by her Aunt Vin and its relation to herself as she describes what the music box can do for her:

The notes fill any room with warmth and happiness. The music is soothing and comforting. The soft music flows out and into your brain, turning it into a soft and lovely mush that makes your eyelids droop and feel heavy with a long awaited and uninterrupted, deep, sweet sleep.

Stuart imagines the thoughts and intentions of his parents as they purchased Edward the Bear. He then moves further away from himself as he includes the thoughts of others involved with the bear:

"Wow, that is a neat bear. I think Stuart might like it," my parents might have said as they bought him. "It's time for harvest," a cotton picker might have said when he was first being picked. "Oh good, my shift is almost over," a worker in the toy factory might have said. "Good, a new load. I hope I can sell them by Christmas," a Macy's owner might have said. "Hello. How are you? What is your name?" a fellow stuffed animal might have said. "Were you the favorite bear of Stuart, my great great grandfather?" a child might say as he is rummaging through the attic. He might wonder what I was like.

Suliya writes of her first book:

It stands forgotten like an old warrior among the others. It is a book, squashed and half unseen on my bookshelf. With it are concealed my first joys of reading. Whenever the old, browning tape of the spine catches my eye, I remember. The tape was put on many years ago. The book was deeply loved, meaning it is almost in shreds. The cover is scratched and the corners bent. Almost every page is worn down with the hand of time and scribbling from earlier times. One page is torn right in half. Instead of taping it, it is glued, overlapping the pages and making it almost impossible to read. The cover is a deep turquoise blue that sometimes seems to shine with the radiant glow of an aquamarine gem. Every inch is covered with millions of little scratches. The large jumbled letters of the title, Are You My Mother?, are just slightly crooked and bold. Every inch of white paper and illustrations are turning brown with age, but to me they seem to be glowing with experience. The book was bought in an ordinary bookstore, I'm not sure which one of us it was originally purchased for, probably my oldest sister before I was born. She outgrew it and handed it down to my next sister, but she and this next oldest sister didn't want it. Thus, it came into my hands. I gave it all the love possible. Now it reeks of memories. It became my favorite book in time. I carried it with me everywhere and forced everyone to read it to me all the time. They soon grew wary of it and taught me how to read, or at least tried. I bragged that I could read, but I had some faults. For instance, I turned the page at the wrong time and couldn't read individual words. They figured it out in a short time and they never let me forget it. Soon after, I really did learn to read and it was the first book I ever really read. It has great significance to me and it does many things that only I know. It comforts me and makes me think. It encourages me and makes me feel happy. It tells stories of many things and talks to me inside. It has earned a special place in my heart where my most precious items go.

Further Exploration

As the year unfolds and our journey as readers and writers continues, we will often refer back to this experience. During an interview about her history as a reader, Suliya again talks about her first book. "I really liked it a lot . . . but I didn't know how to read . . . they tried to teach me but I didn't learn. . . . and so I just memorized it and told them I knew how to read." Through her writing, Suliya has explored her thoughts about this childhood book and the special place it has in her heart. As she continues to reflect upon what she has written and to think about her history as a reader, Suliya concludes that through writing and talking about this book—her object of personal significance—she can now see the book as the beginning point in her own literacy.

Others return to their objects, making them the subject of further writings. Deb writes of the yellow rubber duck as a memento passed down from generation to generation, in a story based upon a study of immigration. She writes a poem about the flower crowns made by the older girls on the night that her swim instructor gave her the duck. As she continues to explore her thoughts and to write, we decide that her portfolio will reflect this study of the yellow rubber duck and all the associations surrounding the object.

Thinking About the Experience

The development which took place in the writing and the thinking of the students can be seen as we compare the quality of these pieces with their earlier personal essays, written after reading the excerpt *The View From Saturday* (Konigsburg, 1996). There is also a marked difference in the students' reaction to what they have written. Many exclaim that this is the best writing they had ever done. When I asked them to explain why they think this is so, their answers echo the thoughts of Donald Murray (1996) on the importance of making use of our personal experiences in our writing. The students share their thoughts on the importance of talking and listening as a means of finding our stories and regaining our voices. Their statements reflect the idea that talk helps us return to the moment. When we return to the moment and tell our stories aloud, some of that spontaneity and feeling can then be transferred to our writing. The students also reflect upon the role of the literature, both as a source of inspiration and as a model. Suliya says, "When we first read 'The Dimestore Teapot,' I thought there's no way I could ever write anything like that. But, after we read it over and over and looked at how he did it, I felt more like I could do it and . . . well, I like what I wrote!" With a view that reading can help to make us better writers, the students come to a conclusion similar to that of Robert Cohen (Fletcher, 1993a) who might describe reading and thinking about reading as the wondering that nourishes writing.

Later that year when we read a statement by Eudora Welty (MacLachlan, 1991) which said, "It is our inward journey that leads us through time—forward or back, seldom in a straight line, most often spiraling," (p. iv) we talk about what this might mean. Kent compares these words to our experience in writing about objects of personal significance, saying "An inward journey is a journey to find out about yourself. . . . and that's what we've done. . . . *that's* just what we've done."

Defining Ourselves Through Poetry

As the year progresses, I reflect back to our process of rethinking the significance of objects as we attached word tickets to them giving them new meaning. A shiny gold pen becomes *ambitious*. A pair of wooden drumsticks is a *sacrifice*. As I consider the ways in which our view of these objects has been transformed as we rename them, I wonder what would happen if we renamed ourselves.

According to Susan Wooldridge (1996), "writing about ourselves doesn't mean we're self-involved. We have to start with ourselves before we reach beyond ourselves" (p. 51). Wooldridge suggests that we consider ourselves in a new light: "What sound am I? What animal? What song? What number? What car? What piece of furniture? What food? What musical instrument? What place? What element in nature? What kind of tree? What is something I am afraid of? What is the world hiding behind my eyes?" (p. 54). I decide to use her suggestions as a model for our own thinking and writing.

The process begins with an invitation to the students to think about and construct a representation of another, myself. As I model the process, encouraging my students to think of me as a sound, an animal, a song, or a number, I find that I am viewed or defined in different ways by different groups of students. Examination of the students' writing about themselves reveals that this reconceptualization of self may enable them to express the complexity of their identities, as well as their hopes and fears about themselves.

Introducing the Idea

As the students enter the room on the first day of the experience, each of them finds a list of these questions on a sheet of paper placed on their desk (What sound am I? What animal? What song? What number? What car? What piece of furniture? What food? What musical instrument? What place? What element in nature? What kind of tree? What is something I am afraid of? What is the world hiding behind my eyes?) (see appendix F). "What's this?" "What are we going to do with this, Mrs. Van Horn?" I answer by darkening the room and turning on the overhead projector, saying, "I thought we would think about ourselves in a new way." They are quiet, sitting in the semidarkness. "This looks hard," murmurs Kim. "It may be . . . " I answer. "What if we start out writing one together? Could you help me write one about myself?" Before I can pick up my overhead pen the suggestions are flying. "Let's try starting at the top," I suggest. "If I were a sound, what sound would I be?" Josh says, "We know you like classical music. What about a symphony, could you be a symphony?" "Great idea, I'll write that down, Josh." Bit by bit the poem emerges. As I read our poem aloud, there are audible sighs and whispers of amazement, "Wow, we're pretty good!"

I am

A symphony in the night,

a dove calling to the morning on

Moon River.

Defining Ourselves—Revealing the Literacies Inside Us 79

> Fast and lean—
> A Spider Veloce.
> I am a love seat with arms to hold you.
> I am silky chocolate.
> I am a French horn;
> golden and lilting
> in Paris.
> I am a flower, a rose,
> a magnolia.
> I am afraid of the dark and being alone.
> The world hiding behind my eyes is
> a fairy tale
> I hope never to leave.

The students in my third period class write:

> I am a shriek of excitement.
> A new born baby bird.
> Wooow! I feel good.
> I'm a Little Richard song
> to a googolplex.
> I am a Pinto on one wheel sitting real low;
> sparking down the street.
> A lamp to see by.
> I'm a chocolate covered cherry
> with powdered sugar and chopped
> nuts on the side.
> A melodious eagle,
> a big, red piano in Paris.
> I'm the ocean,
> Intimidating.
> A hurricane, spinning.
> A mimosa, spilling pink skirted
> ballerinas on point.
> Afraid to be without a book,
> the world behind my eyes is sometimes sad.

As I do this with my students throughout the next two days, it occurs to me that I am different things to different groups of people. The first group sees me as someone who is living out a fairy tale and who is peaceful and protective of them, "a love seat with arms to hold you." The second group has a different vision. To them, I am a "shriek of excitement," spinning and dancing, one who can sometimes be intimidating. As I reflect upon what they have written I realize that as a teacher I adapt my own persona to meet what I perceive to be the needs of individual students. As I watch my students in the classroom, listen to what they have to say, and read what they have written, I attempt to position-take with them, putting myself in their place as much as possible in an effort to see what is happening from their perspective, to look at our world through their eyes. In doing this, I hope to learn more about my students as I help them learn more about themselves.

Students Writing About Themselves

When we meet again, it is time for the students to start thinking about themselves. We begin by talking to one another and sharing our ideas. I work alongside them, trying to write something about myself that has not already been said. The quiet in the room is almost deafening. I look around. Everyone is writing or thinking. Satisfied, I return to my own poem. A few minutes later Vance comes to sit beside me asking, "Can you take a look at what I've written?" Ordinarily I might have Vance read to me, but the room is quiet and I hate to disturb the others, so I read what he has written to myself:

> I am Vance,
> the deathly silence of the night.
> The king of the seas, a shark.
> The song, "We're Not Gonna Make It."
> The number one because you only get one chance in life.
> A 1963 T-top Stingray Corvette, fast and black.
> An ebony carving of any proportion and shape.
> The spice pepper,
> a little can change a lot.
> The trumpet, loud, soothing, and different.
> The Bermuda Triangle, mysterious and deadly.
> The element of death which everyone fears.
> A big, oak tree, spooky at night.
> Afraid of getting hit in the braces.
> The world is a phantom hiding from my sight.

As I finish reading, I am dying to talk to him but I remember to first ask, "What do you think of it Vance?" He looks at the floor to hide his smile and then looks back up at me and whispers, "I think it's pretty good." I wait for a moment to see if he has anything else he wants to say, and then I begin. "Vance, this is really powerful. Just listen to the words you've used. . . . 'deathly silence of the night,' 'shark,' 'fast and black,' 'mysterious and deadly,' 'a phantom'. These words are so . . . dramatic. I can 'see' what you're writing about." "But," I add hesitantly, "Vance, there's a line here that doesn't seem to fit with the rest of what you've written. See here where you have 'Afraid of getting hit in the braces': Everything else you've written is so . . . and yet here, braces?" "Do you see how that's creating a different mood?" Vance looks up at me in exasperation, "But Mrs. Van Horn, you asked what I'm afraid of . . . my braces really do hurt, you know. And I *am* afraid of getting hit in the braces. . . . I was just being honest." Given that explanation, what can I say? I concede, saying, "Well, perhaps you're right. It is the way you see yourself. It is the way you are, in a way. Part of you is very dramatic and grown up and the other part is wearing braces and afraid of getting hit in the mouth." Vance leaves, satisfied that the conference has gone well and satisfied with the way he has defined himself.

Later in the day, during my conference period, I read what Ken has written:

> I am Ken Delaney
> I am the wind full of fresh air.
> A sly fox striding through the woods.
> I am the calm music of rain dropping on the ground.
> A number twenty-seven to remember what date I was born on.
> A limo that always starts out quiet.
> I am a bed that never wants to get up in the morning.
> An ice cream bar, always cool on hot days.
> A clarinet playing a solo during a concert.
> I am a library, calm and quiet.
> I am gold, very valuable.
> A pine tree that grows real tall.
> A boy frightened of ever losing his parents.
> A student ready to achieve his goal.

As I read my heart starts to pound. This from Ken! Ken who sits quietly in class, never saying much. Whose parents worry that he has given up on school. It is as if he is talking to me as he writes, revealing his innermost thoughts and fears—his concept of himself. It seems that he is acknowledging his quiet manner and yet telling me that he has confidence as he is a "sly fox striding through the woods." He recognizes his own worth as he compares himself to "gold, very valuable." He admits the importance of his parents in his life and his fear of losing them. Finally, he tells me that he is ready to "achieve his goal," ready to go about the business of being a student. I have got to tell him what this means to me. Picking up the phone, I dial the number of the math class where Ken will be and explain to his teacher that I will only take a moment of his time. She tells me that Ken will be happy to talk to me as he has just gotten a detention for not having his homework. She is right. The next day, Ken's mother calls to tell me how much my call meant to Ken. She tells me that he is "having a hard time keeping up with the work." I tell her that Ken's poem and his words to me show that he has not lost his confidence. The writing of this poem seemed to mark a turning point for Ken. It is almost as if he is publicly announcing his intention to succeed. From this day on he will become an active member of our community, reading, writing, and talking with us sharing his thoughts.

For others, the poem would be a means of reaching out, a revelation of inner despair. Cindy, who I would later learn from the school counselor had recently experienced the death of a sibling, wrote the following:

> I am a noise that makes the ears bleed,
> the human that kills the brain.
> I'm swallowed six times.
> I'm the Camaro that speeds.
> I'm the chair that breaks every time you sit down,
> the spoiled piece of meat that
> makes you sick.
> I am a flute that squeals on every note.
> I'm the burning lava of a volcano.
> I'm the dark, deep hole that you can't bury.
> I'm the large oak tree that you can't cut down.
> I am the big monster who hides under your bed
> and in your closet.
> The dark, vicious, empty beast that I see
> when I look in the mirror,
> and the beast that I see is
> what I'm afraid of.

After I read the poem and talked to the counselor, I spoke privately with Cindy. She told me that she felt empty inside and that she wondered why she was alive and her sister was dead. She said that she felt as if she and her parents would never be a family again, that they would always be grieving the death of her sister. By this time I knew that Cindy and her parents were involved in professional counseling. I knew that I did not have the answers to her questions. I could encourage Cindy to continue to write about her feelings. As the year progressed Cindy appeared to derive self-esteem from her ability to write about the "dark side" of life, as she put it. It was Cindy who would provide us with insight, leading class discussions about characters who had experienced hardships in their own lives. She became the "expert" on adversity. At the end of the year, Cindy wrote a collection of poetry in response to her reading of *Nightjohn* (Paulsen, 1993) and related informational texts. She would continue to write, sending me poems during the summer. The next year Cindy would return to the classroom to ask me to help her prepare some of her poems to submit for publication. During one of our visits she helped me to understand what had happened, saying, "You and Mrs. B. accepted me for what I am. You let me write about what I was thinking. It wasn't always good. . . . the thoughts, or the writing. Sometimes it was pretty depressing. But I'm getting better. . . . getting better."

Overt invitations to the students to consider themselves as aspects of the physical world within a literacy experience may be empowering. As students redefine themselves they may come to see the complexity of their own identities. This understanding of self may enable them to recognize and/or relate to the complexities in the lives of the characters who live within the texts they read. For others, a consideration of self through this literacy experience may provide an opportunity to express their hopes or personal goals. This expression of a hope or a personal goal makes an inner thought tangible. It is possible that putting statements about self on paper and having these statements recognized and acknowledged by others is representative of "trying on" an identity, finding that it is accepted by the social group, and then taking steps to incorporate those aspects of identity into self. Other students may express fears about their identity and their world as they write about themselves as aspects of the physical world. Acknowledgment of this fear may be empowering. For Cindy, the acknowledgment provides her with insight into the lives of characters and into her own life as she continues to respond to text and to her own experiences.

Evaluation/Assessment

My students and I have developed a variety of ways to evaluate and assess our literacy activities. At times we will engage in a discussion to determine the specific requirements after I have introduced the project. For example, after we talked about my Life Map, we decided that their maps would include a minimum of 10 symbols. Each map would begin with the birth of its creator. When several students suggested that they would like to include their future plans at the end of the map, we expanded our initial expectations so the maps would include 12 symbols. When we work together in this way with our students, they have ownership of the process and the evaluation/assessment. The students begin with a clear understanding of what they will do, and in most cases they meet or exceed our initial expectations.

At other times, when the activity is more complex, I have found it helpful to provide each student with a planning sheet. I began to do this when I noticed that no matter how closely they seemed to be listening during direct instruction or demonstration, we could not move in to and engage in the process without a barrage of questions. No matter how clear I thought I had been, I found myself repeating the same statements and suggestions I had made at the beginning. With the planning sheet in hand, students can read and review what we have discussed as they work. Planning sheets are also helpful to parents who are interested in what we are doing in the classroom. I consider the planning sheets to be points of reference. As we work through a project, my students and I may revise our initial plans; and these revisions can be noted on the sheets. For example, when I introduced the idea of the Museum of Objects and Ideas, my expectations were that students would bring an object to school and would label that object with a one word ticket that made us think about the object in a new way. When the students brought objects of personal significance and when many of them wanted to put more than one word ticket on their object, we revised our planning sheet to include the possible use of more than one ticket and a statement about the personal significance of the object (see appendix C for the final planning sheet for the Museum of Objects and Ideas).

Students are empowered and can often be more successful when we involve them in the development of evaluation/assessment documents. This can be done through the use of rubrics (see appendix D for the rubric for the Museum of Objects and Ideas and appendix E for the rubric for the essay about the Object of Personal Significance). Working together to create a listing of the critical aspects of a project and assigning point values to these aspects helps students break down the process and analyze the qualities of each part. Repeated experiences in codeveloping rubrics enables the students to plan, execute, and evaluate their own work. As they engage in discussion with one another and with me they ask themselves, "What am I trying to accomplish?" "What is the best way to do this?" "What will I do first, next, and next?" and "How will I know I have succeeded in each part of the process?"

We develop the rubric for an activity early in the process. For example, we constructed the rubric for the essay about the Object of Personal Significance (appendix E) after analyzing the essay by Lewis Nordan (1997) and developing the outline for our own essays. In this manner, the rubric serves as a guidepost/checklist for the students. Again, we may make changes as we work through the experience and note these changes on our rubrics. When the projects are completed, I ask my students to review their work with the rubric in hand, evaluating what they have accomplished. They might pencil in the points they expect to earn. The rubrics are then clipped to the projects and the package is handed in for my review and comments. Through the use of rubrics my students take an active part in the evaluation/assessment of their work. They are rarely surprised by my own evaluation/assessment.

SUMMARY

Now we must return to the opening of this chapter and the thoughts of Anthony, who writes:

> Before I can ever gain true friendship I have to like myself. Because if I like myself, I will know that I do not need a facade or friends who cannot accept the real me, and I will show the world who I really am, take it or leave it.

As students come to know more about themselves and as their individuality and knowledge are recognized as an integral part of the literacy experience, it may be suggested that both meaning and power are enhanced. Within this classroom, overt invitations are extended and specific experiences are enacted in order to stimulate thinking about self. These experiences take place within the frame of the curricular activities. As we engage in the creation of life maps; share excerpts from our personal readings; identify and write about objects of personal significance; consider ourselves as elements of the physical world; as we reveal our fears and desires through reading, writing, and talking, we define ourselves. Through this process we may find an acceptance or acknowledgement of ourselves and our meanings which is empowering.

When students are asked to reflect upon their histories as readers, their recollections indicate that they feel that reading is a performance or that response to reading is to "do tests" or to "summarize the story." Through analysis of student statements, it appears that students may feel that their voices are not heard or that their thoughts are unrecognized in school literacy experiences. Power may be equalized when students are asked to think about or to talk about what they think. As students are encouraged to express what they think about themselves within the frame of literacy experiences this stimulates the possibility that they will make connections between text and self—a process which empowers them in a number of ways. First, students are empowered because their understanding or meaning making is enhanced; second, they are empowered through the connections they have made between their own lives and literacy; and finally, because in the making of these connections, they may learn or acknowledge something about their own identities.

When students in this classroom are invited to symbolize the stories of their lives through the construction of life maps, they may, as suggested by Maxine Greene (1992), "become fully participant in this society. . . . without losing consciousness of who they are" (p. 257). This experience takes place early in the academic year and, as such, provides an introduction to reflection about ourselves through our literacy—an invitation to "make sense, make meaning, (and) to find direction" (p. 257) for ourselves and our literacy experiences. For these students, the invitation may indicate that here in this classroom they will be asked to think about and to talk about their past experiences.

Further invitations are extended as students are provided with an opportunity to bring their personal literacy into the classroom through the Reader of the Day experience. During this activity, as participants engage in the process of choosing, reading, talking, and listening related to text which is of personal significance or of meaning to those who read aloud, readers bring their individual imaginations and voices to bear within the social context of the classroom. Analysis of Reader of the Day through the components of an activity setting reveals that students who volunteer to read aloud are more frequently those who exhibit one or more of the following characteristics:

- Comfortable being the focus of attention
- Confident in their beliefs
- Derive power from personal literacy
- Believe themselves to be a proficient oral reader
- Willing to have their interest in reading outside of school known to others

There are indications that the social context of the group may also impact the level of participation in this voluntary activity. The level of participation is greater in class groups in which a number of students exhibit one or more of the following characteristics:

- Acceptance of those who extend themselves academically
- Desire for teacher approval
- A feeling of comfort within the class group

Statements of the students indicate that the sharing of personal literacy through Reader of the Day is valued in terms of the following:

- Choice of material is student generated
- Knowledge is collectively created (i.e., students learn from one another)
- Active control and ownership of the knowledge
- Opportunity to know and to relate to others

As students choose, read, talk, and listen within the Reader of the Day experience they engage in operations and tasks which call on them to choose and preview texts, provide background information, and to enact and describe strategies in which readers define words in context, note incidents of foreshadowing, or summarize text. Scripts for conduct are devised and enacted by both readers and listeners. These scripts, for the most part, are reflective of and modeled after typical classroom procedures related to presentation, in that readers speak loudly enough for all to hear and listeners attend to the reading.

I have suggested that Reader of the Day is an activity through which readers engage in the construction or consideration of identity. This is exemplified through the students' choice of literature as well as their related performance during the read-aloud. Within this classroom, students have made use of the sharing of personal reading to:

- Share feelings
- "Tell" others about themselves
- Confirm a perception of personality type attributed to self by self or others
- Resist a perception of personality type attributed to self by self or others
- Resist conformance to standards of acceptable behavior determined within the social group
- Reinforce gender roles
- Reveal interests or fears

Further reflection of self occurs as students are asked to redefine and write about objects of personal significance. For the most part, the students in this classroom chose to write about an object which was significant to them in early childhood. As we redefine and write about these objects from childhood, it appears that the students regain the voice of childhood, gain new insight about the past, connect their past and present experiences to those reflected in a text, and arrive at realizations about what they know and what is important to them. As we continue in the process of coming to know ourselves, the students consider themselves as elements in the physical world. As they choose and write about physical objects that they believe represent themselves, the words of the students reveal the complexities of their identities, and their hopes as well as their fears.

These experiences, which take place within the frame of our curriculum, are founded upon overt invitations and experiences designed to foster thinking about ourselves. As students think, talk, and write about themselves, they may come to deeper realization of the meaning making and power of the individual within the group and to define an individuated identity within the social context of this literacy community. As reflected in the ideas expressed by Anthony, we acknowledge our feelings about ourselves, voicing to the world an aspect of who we truly are. Maxine Greene (1995) has written that "once the distinctiveness of the many voices in a classroom is attended to, the importance of identifying shared beliefs will be heightened" (p. 42). Now that we have begun to define ourselves, revealing the uniqueness of our many voices, we are ready to expand or to extend that which we can create together.

Chapter 3 will examine the students' generation of questions, comments, and observations during whole class readings of a single text, independent reading supported within a small group, and/or private readings outside the classroom. Central issues of concern are the influence of the process on public and private transactions with text, on student empowerment and interaction, and on the meaning-making process. Within the examination of these issues will be further inquiry into the roles of myself and the students, as we transact with text and interact with one another, as well as a discussion of the perceptions of the students regarding the power relations within our transactions and interactions.

3

Transacting With Text

Questioning the Text

I like writing the questions. 'Cause if you don't understand the book you can write about something you don't understand instead of something you might already understand that the teacher is making sure you got. I think it's better to have something you don't understand, that you write up on your own. If I could change anything, that's one of the things I would change in schools. In reading, instead of having to do all those worksheets, not just because I didn't like all the worksheets, but mainly because you already understood that stuff, 'cause those were the main questions, like, "oh duh!" I mean, well they were like, "Why did Sarah run away?" Because she got in trouble or something, you know what I mean

Tammy

As I consider the possible meanings of Tammy's statements about writing the questions, it occurs to me that she may be making a claim similar to that of Nettie in the previous chapter, that school literacy experiences may be such that we only "go over the surface" of the text. For Tammy and others like her, school can be a place where we "just go over the surface," a place where teachers are "making sure you got" what you have been told. Tammy evaluates her experience of writing the questions, stating that "I think it's better . . . that you write it up on your own." She views writing the questions as a form of ownership, a way of expressing what *she* wants to know about the text. Tammy has a need to address the issues she doesn't understand, to participate in her own learning. Her desire to write the questions indicates that she acknowledges a sense of responsibility for her learning. Tammy's later remarks indicate that this participation in the learning experience is something she would like to change about school. She predicts that this change would move her away from rethinking that which she has "already understood," thinking about the obvious or the "oh duh" questions, to thinking about that which she does not understand or to the creation of new understandings. As my students speak of their literacy experiences, they show me that they have come to view active participation in their own learning as a form of empowerment.

> Paulo Freire (Shor & Freire, 1987) states,
> We should not submit to the text or be submissive in front of the text. The thing is to fight with the text, even loving it, no? To engage in a conflict with the text. In the last analysis it is a very, very, very demanding operation. (p. 11)

> L. S. Vygotsky (Dixon-Krauss, 1996) stated that "passivity of the student is the greatest sin since it relies on the false principle that the teacher is everything and the pupil is nothing" (p. 18).

Louise Rosenblatt (1978) argues that readers take an active stance as they read, drawing on past experiences and returning to earlier parts in the text to clarify new ideas. She describes a reader who is "not only paying attention to what the words pointed to in the external world, their referents . . . (but) also paying attention to the images, feelings, attitudes, associations, and ideas that the words and their referents evoked in him" (p. 10). Rosenblatt states that readers create "poems" as they come together with the text, engaging in "an active, self-ordering and self-corrective process" (p. 11). She uses the term transaction to denote a process that places the reader and the text in a reciprocal relationship wherein the reader "interprets the text (the reader acts on the text)" or "the text produces a response in the reader (the text acts on the reader)" (p. 16). Not all of my students are aware that reading is an event in which they must pierce the surface of the words and look deeper, thinking and wondering about what they find.

In seeking to help students transact with text, I began by verbalizing my own thoughts as I read aloud. I was relentless in my efforts to pose questions to my students which would engage them in higher order thinking. We *would* analyze, infer, interpret and evaluate! I knew I had made some progress when Leonard was caught drawing a blueprint in math class. The blueprint was his way of determining the guilt of a character we had read about. But what about Tom who replied to my query, "What do you think?" with a bemused expression on his face, saying, "I *said* I'm finished reading that chapter, what do you mean?"

As I demonstrate the process, posing possible questions to the students, my actions are reflective of an ongoing tradition of teacher efforts to engage students in meaning making or in transaction with text through the use of questions posed by themselves or others (authors of commercial reading materials) outside of the context (Guszak, 1967; Shake and Allington, 1985). My questions to the students represent my own wonderings or my own attempts to demonstrate ways of thinking about text and, as such, may not be representative of the students' thinking or wondering about the text. It is possible that my failure to invite students to add their voices or wonderings to my own may distort the growing sense of the equalization of power in our classroom.

W. S. Carlsen (1991) states that "teacher questions . . . may reflect and reinforce authority relationships in the classroom" (p. 159).

The generation of questions is both critical to meaning making and to the empowerment of students in that through the process they are engaged in meta-cognition or reflection on their own thinking. Through the process of question generation during reading, students may construct meaning and/or "assume responsibility for determining what needs to be understood and for directing their own learning processes" (Metsala, Commeyras, & Sumner, 1996, p. 262).

Rosenshine, Meister, and Chapman (1996) call this a "self-regulatory cognitive strategy" (p. 181). They define cognitive strategies as "procedures that guide students as they attempt to complete less-structured tasks such as reading comprehension and writing" (p. 181), a concept which they state "helps us focus on identifying or developing procedures that students can use to independently assist them in their learning" (pp. 181–182).

Much of the research conducted on the subject of student generation of questions concerns itself with the ways and means by which students would be taught strategies or frames which would enable them to generate their own questions (Alvermann, 1981; Collins, Brown, & Newman,

1990; Palincsar & Brown, 1984; Paris, Cross, & Lipson, 1984; Raphael & Pearson, 1985). My inquiry is concerned with the students' questions as well as their comments and observations about text. Central to the inquiry is my examination of the questions, comments, and observations which emerge through a process in which students are provided with a means of communicating their ideas publicly during the reading of text. Demonstration and feedback, rather than the direct teaching of strategies, is utilized during the reading and following the reading. Given this, the students, as well as myself, become models of the process of transacting with text. Using the frame of a complex adaptive system to examine the process has enabled me to see that my students are doing what proficient readers do. They are defining unfamiliar words, organizing basic information about the plot, and clarifying confusions about characters or events. The students are comparing knowledge and views with one another and/or with their prior knowledge. They are responding to one another on paper; reflecting on prior questions, comments, and observations; and returning to the text for further information. Finally, the students are making discoveries, forming predictions and inferences, and drawing conclusions about the text.

In the next few sections of this chapter, I will provide a view of my recognition of the need to engage the students further; our initial efforts to publicly generate questions, comments, and observations; and my analysis of the process across a series of readings and across the reading of a single text.

Student Involvement

Despite my efforts to demonstrate my own transactions with text, it soon becomes clear to me that I must go further in my efforts to involve the students in thinking about the text. Perhaps they are too comfortable. After all, they must only wait for me to express my thoughts or pose my questions. I begin to realize that my own thoughts and questions are not enough to provoke them to engage with the text when Deb looks at me one day and asks, "Mrs. Van Horn, when are you going to give us the chapter questions?" "Chapter questions?" I ask, seeking clarification of her meaning. "Well, last year, our teacher gave us tons of chapter questions on worksheets. . . . we had to write down the answers to the questions after we finished reading each chapter." "Well, yes," I stall for time, thinking about how I will answer Deb. "That's one way of thinking about literature," I began. "I was thinking that we might want to build on that experience a bit. . . . consider developing our own ideas about what we are reading." Greeted with puzzled, expectant looks, I continue talking. "When you are reading you are also thinking. . . . thinking about what's happening in the story, about the characters in the story. You might be remembering similar events in your own life or maybe you don't agree with what the character has done, and you're thinking about what you would do. Sometimes you are noticing things about the words the author uses. . . . in other words, lots of things are happening inside your head while you read, right?" Bet says, "Sometimes I'm just trying to figure out the words I don't know." Cal states matter-of-factly, "I don't even read the stuff. . . . I just skim through and look for the answers to the questions." Tran laughs and says, "Sometimes I'm just trying to get it done. . . . to finish reading." I agree with them, adding, "We do all those things. Reading can be so much more, reading is like another life. . . . a life inside our minds." Anthony exclaims, "I know what Tran means, I compare myself to a sponge when I'm reading; sometimes the water (words) just seem to run over me. Other times I'm soaking it in and I'm really thinking about what I read and what it means to me . . ."

As Anthony talks I continue to think. Some of the students seem to understand the concept of transacting with text, others clearly do not. What is their stake in the process? How can I create a level of discomfort at which true learning occurs within a safe framework?

> L. S. Vygotsky (Cole, John-Stether, Scribner, & Souberman, 1978) describes this level of discomfort as the zone of proximal development or: ". . . the distance between the (child's) actual development level as determined by independent problem solving and the level of potential development as determined through problem solving under adult guidance or in collaboration with more capable peers." (p. 86)

Can we learn from one another if we make our transactions with text public? What will happen if students are invited to develop their own questions, comments, and observations? Can the teacher be a participant, generating and writing thoughts along with the students? Rather than to directly teach a specific question-generating strategy or strategies, I want to examine the influence of this invitation to my students to construct their own questions, comments, or observations about the text. My initial interest is in engaging my students in the public writing of their questions, comments, and observations and, then, in examining the possible patterns which emerge as the students are made aware of the questions, comments, and observations of others while the reading occurs. I begin the process of finding the answers by asking the students for questions.

Reading Together

We start with a whole class reading of the same text, *Journey*, (MacLachlan, 1991). Each student has a copy of the novel. I start by reading a passage aloud. When I pause for a few seconds, one of the students will "jump in" and continue the reading. When this student pauses, another will begin to read. This experience is differentiated from round robin reading in that no student is required to read aloud, and the order of reading is random. Students who are not reading aloud are asked to read along silently in their copy of the novel. This way of reading is new to my students. At first there are problems. Casey tries to entertain us by reading a few words and then stopping in the middle of a sentence. Tom cuts in and begins reading when Pete stops to catch his breath. This and comments such as "He's hogging it. . . . I want to read." "When's it gonna be my turn?" and "Read louder, I can't hear you," prompt us to create some "rules" for the reading. Each person who reads will read at least one paragraph and no more than a page at a time. We will not start reading until the person who is reading pauses for at least three seconds. When these rules are in place our thoughts can turn to the literature itself and away from the process of reading it aloud. Before long, there is no sound in the room other than that of the words flowing as one reader gives way to another.

Thinking Together

Now that we are reading together, it is time for us to start thinking together. I tape a large sheet of bulletin board paper to the front blackboard, writing the name of the novel, the class period, and page number at the top. On a stool beside the paper I place a cup full of markers. "What's that for?" asks Casey. I tell him and the rest of the students that this is a place where we can write down what we are thinking about while we are reading. I suggest that we may have questions we want to ask. We may have comments we want to make about the literature itself or about how we are connecting what we read to our own life. Or we may notice something in the text, a development in the plot or something about a character that we want to remember. Calling these our questions, comments, and observations, I model the process of making a comment. After reading aloud from the text the words, "before spring crashed onto our hillside with explosions of mountain laurel, before summer came with the soft slap of the screen door, breathless nights, and mildew on the books" (MacLachlan, 1991, preface), I write, "I like the way the author uses words to create vivid descriptions such as the soft slap of the screen door." Brandon asks, "Do we have to put stuff like that?" I reply, "Certainly not, you may be noticing something like this when you read, or you may have a question in your head, or maybe you will want to comment about what you are reading and what it means to you personally. There are many things you may write; write what you are thinking." A few minutes later, as the class reads the description of the character, Cat, cutting up carrots in the kitchen which includes the word "thwack" three times, Brandon steps up to the paper purposefully and writes, "I like that the author made sound effects." He looks to me as if for approval and mouths the words, "Is that a good thing to put?"

As he writes about the author's use of onomatopoeia, Brandon is modeling his comments after my previous comment about MacLachlan's use of descriptive words. In the early stages of generating questions, comments, and observations, it appears that the students will mimic the behaviors of the teacher until they can come up with something on their own. Later, as I write "What do you think the expression 'the camera knows' means?" Brandon writes, "Look, the camera knows—it sounds like the camera knows Grandmother is sad." Grandmother had been showing the character, Journey, pictures of his mother looking dissatisfied with life. She had asked him to compare his mother's face with the faces of the other family members in the pictures. Brandon seems to be relating to the text through this questioning which is happening at the moment he is reading. This exemplifies a transaction, even though at this early stage it is prompted by teacher modeling.

Looking at the Process

My initial efforts to study the students' questions, comments, and observations centered on an examination of possible patterns. In order to determine if over time descriptive patterns of system-wide behaviors could be identified, I examined the written questions, comments, and observations of a single class group of students as they read four common texts (see appendices G, H, I, and J) during the course of one academic year. I found that a complex set of transactions emerges as students who are reading a common text, write questions, comments, and observations for discussion on paper posted where all participants may see the process unfolding. In a sense, the group experienced multiple transactions as students noted individual ideas and reacted to the ideas of others during the reading. My analysis of these written questions, comments, and observations reveals a complex system of interdependent textual transactions which may provoke readers to interact with text at a richer level than that achieved independently.

Complex adaptive systems cycle through stages which may be categorized as regularities, differentiation, coupling or information flow, and self-organization (Patterson & Hirtle, 1996). For the purpose of describing the written questions, comments, and observations, regularities may be characterized as events where students are sorting through input for regularities or patterns to guide schema development. Regularities exemplify comprehension at the literal level. Examples of regularities found in the writings of the students as they read a common text are instances in which students are seeking to define words with which they are unfamiliar, attempting to organize basic information about the plot, or clarifying confusions about characters or events within the novel. Comprehension develops further through differentiation and coupling or information flow as students refine their understanding. Differentiation occurs when students are comparing knowledge and views with one another and/or comparing the current textual experience with their own prior knowledge. Coupling or information flow is exemplified by students going back to the text to augment the information flow, responding to the observations and questions of peers, or reflecting on prior questions and comments. Self-organization or learning/accommodation may be seen in events where students are making a discovery, prediction, inference, or drawing a conclusion about the text. Self-organization or learning/accommodation represents comprehension at the inferential level. I consider the following questions as I examine the written reflections of the students:

- Is self-organization (comprehension at the inferential level) preceded by a particular pattern of behavior?
- If there is a pattern of behavior, does the pattern remain consistent across the reading of the four novels?
- Do certain novels inspire a greater number of self-organizing events?
- As the group works together over time, is there an increase in the frequency of self-organization (inferential comprehension)?

The students read the following four novels in the order presented:

- *Double Trouble Squared* by Kathryn Lasky
- *Canyons* by Gary Paulsen
- *The Outsiders* by S. E. Hinton
- *The Giver* by Lois Lowry

The students were asked to walk to the front of the room and write thoughts about the novel during the reading event. Prior to and during each of the experiences, I periodically demonstrated my own thinking about text.

In order to analyze the thinking of the students, each set of questions, comments, and observations was coded according to the aforementioned categories, those being regularity (literal comprehension), differentiation and coupling or information flow (refined understanding), and self-organization (inferential comprehension). For example, within the questions, comments, and observations written by this group of students as they read the novel *The Outsiders* (Hinton, 1989), the following series of responses was written:

Written Response	Category	My Reflections
Is Johnny the only one still in the hospital?	Regularity	Organizing information about the plot/character
If Johnny lives, will he still be a Greaser even though he can't walk or fight if he gets in trouble?	Self-Organization	Inferring

cont.

Transacting With Text 97

Does it feel weird to Johnny that he had a feeling one day he wanted to kill himself and his wish almost came true?	Coupling or Information Flow	Reflecting on prior questions and comments, going back to the text
If Dally and Tim Shepard are friends, why do they beat each other up?	Differentiation	Comparing to prior knowledge and experience
Because of this stuff happening, they all got a lot closer friendship.	Self-Organization	Drawing a conclusion
These poor boys have had such a hard time. All this stuff. The death of Dally, the death of Johnny. I haven't had such a loss in my entire life! I guess I'm lucky, very lucky.	Differentiation	Connecting to prior knowledge and experience
Is their gang slowly disappearing?	Coupling or Information Flow	Going back to the text, responding to the observations and questions of peers
Are the Socs and Greasers going to become friends?	Self-Organization	Predicting
Why do they have to separate the Socs from the Greasers? They're just looking at clothing, style, cars, and money. Why can't they get along by means of personality or what's on the inside?	Self-Organization	Inferring, drawing conclusions

In reference to my first two questions about the written reflections of students, self-organization or inferential comprehension is preceded by varying patterns of thinking which do not appear to be consistent across the readings of the four novels. In general, reflection proceeds in a manner such that students search for regularities, differentiate through comparison of views or comparison to prior knowledge, and return to the text or reflect on the prior questions and comments of peers (coupling or information flow) to reach self-organization. The pattern may go through several cycles of regularities, differentiations, and coupling before self-organizing. Once self-organization has been reached, the group may stay at this level, move back to coupling and return quickly to self-organization, or begin anew as students again search for regularities.

Self-organization during the reading of the first novel, *Double Trouble Squared* (Lasky, 1991), was preceded by more regularities (12) than differentiation (5) or coupling/information flow (8). During the reading of the second novel, *Canyons* (Paulsen, 1990), self-organization was again preceded more frequently by regularities (19), followed closely by coupling/information flow (16), with few instances of differentiation (4). Self-organization during the reading of *The Outsiders* (Hinton, 1989), was most often preceded by differentiation (7) with regularities and coupling/information flow preceding self-organization three times each. During the reading of *The Giver* (Lowry, 1993), self-organization was most often preceded by coupling/information flow (17), followed by regularities (13) and differentiation (6).

Stages Leading to Self-Organization

Novel	Regularity	Differentiation	Coupling or Information Flow
Double Trouble Squared	12	5	8
Canyons	19	4	16
The Outsiders	3	7	3
The Giver	13	6	17

During the reading of the first two novels, *Double Trouble Squared* (Lasky, 1991) and *Canyons* (Paulsen, 1990), it appears that the students were engaged in more schema development through literal thinking as they sought to define words, organize basic information about the plot, and clarify confusions about characters or events within the novel. When the students were reading *The Outsiders* (Hinton, 1989), differentiation (comparing their views with the views of others in the group, or with their own prior knowledge and experience) most often preceded self-organization. This may be due to the fact that the novel contained characters and events with which the students could most easily relate. The preponderance of coupling/information flow before self-organization during the reading of *The Giver* (Lowry, 1993), a dystopia, might be attributed to the need to return to the text and to the comments of peers in order to understand a different world view. It appears that students are more apt to search for regularities when they first experience the process of generating questions, comments, and observations. The questions asked are similar to those which might be asked by a teacher seeking to establish the general knowledge necessary to operate with a given text. For example, students reading *Double Trouble Squared* (Lasky, 1991), asked the following questions: "What is a beefeater?" "Why did Sir Arthur Conan Doyle want to kill Sherlock Holmes?" and "Why did the man say that the

Transacting With Text 99

Tower of London was filled with ghosts?" Each of these questions contributed to the establishment of a framework of understanding from which to build meaning. Later, perhaps as the students grew more confident in themselves and in the process, they responded to text in ways which most help them to achieve self-organization (inferential comprehension) or meaning making. From this we might conclude that the pattern of events which precipitate within a complex adaptive system organized around students' questions, comments, and observations about text may vary depending upon the text itself and the students' adaptations in order to derive meaning from the reading.

My third question asked if certain novels inspire a greater number of self-organizing events. A count of the self-organizing events within each set of the group's questions, comments, and observations about the text reveals the following:

- *Double Trouble Squared*   15%
- *Canyons*   22%
- *The Outsiders*   27%
- *The Giver*   30%

These percentages may be used to reflect upon our final question: As the group works together over time, is there an increase in the frequency of self-organization or inferential comprehension? From this analysis, it appears that this may be a possibility. However, this is not surprising, as it would be expected that a growing sense of trust among the members of the group, as well as an increased knowledge of the ways of thinking about text and deriving meaning from text would lead to an increase in self-organizing events within a complex adaptive system.

Taking a Closer Look

To return to the metaphor of the photographer and the camera used in the previous chapter, I now want to move from a position behind a camera, focused on the process as a system in which events are categorized and counted across a series of readings, for a closer look at the process, as it occurs within the reading of a single text by a single class group. As I examine and explain the process as it occurs within the reading of *The Outsiders* (Hinton, 1989) by the students in a single class group, I will try to reenact the students' process of reading. In order to do this, I will provide a brief summary of the text; list the questions, comments, and observations as they appear on the sheets; and then examine the possible meanings of what the students have written.

The Outsiders (Hinton, 1989) is a young adult novel depicting the friendship and conflict among two social groups, the Greasers and the Socs. The reading takes place during the second 6-week period of the school year. During the course of our reading, the students in the focus group wrote the questions, comments, and observations in the order in which they appear in the tables which follow. The first dozen notations reflect the kind of thinking that occurs as we enter the text. The writings are generated in response to the first chapter and several pages of the second in which readers are provided with introductions to the setting and central characters of the novel through the narrative of Ponyboy, the protagonist.

Question, Comment, or Observation	My Reflections
Why was Dally waiting? SM	
Dally, Johnny, and me (whoever that is) love mischief. MM	Monica's response after reading about Dally, "He had been arrested, he got drunk, he rode in rodeos, lied, cheated, stole, rolled drunks, jumped small kids . . ." (1989, p. 13). She draws the conclusion that the boys enjoy causing harm or damage.
Are all the fights gang related? MC	Maria uses the term "gang" even though the text states that the Greasers and Socs are "small bunches of friends who stick together" (1989, p. 13). She reflects on her own knowledge of the term, using the words "gang related," a frequent phrase in the evening news.
Why does Dally like to steal so much? SE	Sue questions the actions and motives of the character.
Why did Dally need those two packages of cigarettes? SM	
Why does Dally seem to go around trying to break laws? AD	
Is the Dingo the main place that they always go to? GS	
They must like a lot of girls. MM	
Why did he want to embarrass the girls? AB	
What was the number that was the most on record? SM	
Why would they go into places and make them get things (steal things) because we all work for things and get money and we buy our own things. MM	Monica relates to the previous questions, comments, and observations. She reveals her doubts about the reasoning behind the characters' actions and compares herself and her peers to Dally and Two-Bit in a somewhat judgmental response.
Why do they like the girls, for what? SM	
Why is Ponyboy so embarrassed about Sodapop dropping out? Why doesn't he just let him do what he wants? MC	This comment reflects Maria's confidence in herself and her acceptance of others. Later during discussion Maria will conclude that this might be an example of why the Greasers are looked down upon and/or held to a lower place in society.

Transacting With Text 101

The following notations reflect our thinking as we read about a meeting between the Greasers and the Socs at the neighborhood drive-in movie. Cherry, a Soc, and her friend Marcia have left the company of their dates, Randy and Bob, who have been drinking. Johnny, Ponyboy, and Dally engage the girls in conversation as they sit together on the bleachers at the back of the drive-in. Dally tries to flirt with Cherry and she throws a soda in his face, telling him to leave her alone. Dally leaves and Johnny and Ponyboy agree to "protect" the girls. As they continue talking, Two-Bit, a fellow Greaser, approaches from behind, pretending to be an angry Soc. Johnny is frightened.

Question, Comment, or Observation	My Reflections
Is Johnny a shy kind of person? RN	Ranita, rather shy herself, wonders if Johnny's fear is a sign of his own shyness.
Does Cherry have any other friends? SM	
Why does Cherry do so many mean things to him? GS	Gina questions Cherry's actions.
If I would of knocked someone's tooth out they would of sued me, and plus my mom would ground me for life! (Plus, I wouldn't of) MM	Gina's question reminds Monica of an earlier portion in the text where we read that Dally knocked out someone's tooth and went unpunished.
Dally has a bad attitude just like someone else I know. JP	Jess lets it be known that she thinks someone in our group has a bad attitude. We are always in the process of communicating with one another even though it might be presumed that we are strictly "communicating" with the text.
I think it was very nice of Johnny to help Cherry. AB	
Was Johnny jealous of Dally? SM	
Does Cherry kind of like Dally? MC	Maria returns to Gina's question about why Cherry is mean to Dally. She makes a connection based upon her observations of her peers in social interactions in which people who like one another are sometimes combative and then infers that Cherry may like Dally.
I wonder why Two-Bit tried to scare Johnny and Ponyboy? JP	Jess questions the intentions of Two-Bit.
My mom makes a lot of imitations like Two-Bit and if you tell her to act like something or someone, she will. MM	Monica notes Two-Bit's characteristics and compares them to those of her mother.
How could sometimes Cherry tell if Two-Bit was drunk or not? SM	
Is Two-Bit really drunk? AB	
Why do they sit out at the drive-in and watch people get drunk? SH	Sue builds upon the two previous transactions and questions the actions of the characters.
Cherry's just like my sister, sarcastic, but she's also dramatic!!! MM	

As we continue to read, we learn that Johnny has been badly beaten by a group of the Socs. This event, coupled with the abuse he receives at the hands of his parents, provokes him to carry a knife or a "blade." Ponyboy says Johnny will "kill the next person who jumps him" (1989, p. 33). Johnny, Ponyboy, and Two-Bit attempt to walk Marcia and Cherry home after the movie, but they are stalked by the Socs. As Randy and Bob pull up beside them in their blue Mustang a confrontation is narrowly avoided. Before leaving with Randy and Bob, Cherry tells Ponyboy not to be hurt if she doesn't talk to him at school. They both know that the Socs and the Greasers live in different worlds. In this section of notations we move between considerations of three central ideas as we write about Johnny's vulnerability, Cherry's relationships, and our growing sense of what it means to be a Greaser.

Question, Comment, or Observation	My Reflections
Why do they carry a blade around? SM	
I think all the girls like Soda, even Cherry. MM	
Johnny's situation at home reminds me of the child in the book Jess is reading to us. LV	I note the intertextuality between this situation and that portrayed in a book Jess is sharing as Reader of the Day.
If I was Cherry I wouldn't hang out with the Socs, I would hang out with the Greasers. MM	Monica puts herself in Cherry's place. Later explains that the Socs were "meaner" than the Greasers. She relates to characters she perceives as being nice.
Was Johnny getting beaten a memory, or did that happen presently? RN	Ranita wonders if this is a flashback.
It sounds like Ponyboy is kind of scared of girls—he likes the "nice" girls. LV	
If I was Johnny I would run away or do something to his parents. JP	Jess reacts to my comment, making a connection between the book she is reading to the class, their response to that book, and to this text. Jess puts herself in the place of the character, Johnny.
Why did they beat up Johnny? AB	Anita returns to the core of the idea, that Johnny is beaten by others, as she seeks a reason or explanation for his mistreatment.
Why isn't Cherry like the others? NT	Nettie wonders how Cherry can be different from the other Socs who taunt the Greasers. How is it that Cherry can relate to the Greasers?
I wonder why the Greasers chose to be like that? JP	
It seems like everybody in the neighborhood is outsiders and they always get in fights and their parents beat them. MM	

cont.

Transacting With Text

If I was Cherry I wouldn't go with the boys. I would call my parents because you never know what the boys are going to do because she doesn't really know them that well. MC	Maria considers her own experiences as she makes connections between the life of a character and her own life. She wants to warn Cherry in much the same way her parents have warned her.
Soda crying—I can't picture it. JP	
It's good Ponyboy is Sodapop's brother because by now Ponyboy would be hurt. And it's good that Johnny is the gang's pet because he would be hurt by now too. MM	
Ponyboy needs to think before he speaks. JP	
I have been chased by three cars before and once three guys were in a truck and the truck pulled to the curb and me and my cousin started walking and one of them started talking and pulled the handle and me and my cousin started running. MM	
Why does Cherry like Dallas after she said she hates him? MC	Maria reconsiders her earlier assumptions about the relationship.
Cherry wants to go out with Dallas for protection. TR	Ted reacts to Maria's question and suggests a motive for the character's actions.
I thought Cherry liked Soda. Why did she say she could fall in love with Dallas? SD	
I think Cherry really wants to hang out with the Greasers, but she just won't say it. MM	Monica begins to find evidence that the character, Cherry, may feel as she herself does about being friends with the Greasers.
I think Cherry really likes Ponyboy and just won't tell him!! JP	
Why do people hate the Greasers? AB	
Are they outsiders because they always get in fights and their parents beat them or do these things happen to them because they are outsiders? MM	Monica thinks about the previous question and makes a connection between the title of the novel and the status of the Greasers.
What is so bad about the Greasers? Why do they call them the Greasers? HC	
I think that Greaser is a cool name!! BL	There is some disagreement about the positive and negative connotations of the name, the Greasers. In discussions that follow we compare these groups to groups at our school (Greasers = Bangers; Socs = Preps)

As we read further Ponyboy and Johnny escape the anger of their families and seek refuge in the neighborhood park. The Socs arrive, insults are exchanged, and a fight ensues. Johnny watches as Bob repeatedly plunges Ponyboy under the water in the park fountain. Fearing for Ponyboy's life, Johnny stabs Bob and kills him. The other Socs run from the park, and Johnny and Ponyboy are left to confront the deed.

Question, Comment, or Observation	My Reflections
I think that Ponyboy should have gone home in the first place, but plus Darry should never have hit him. MM	
Why did Johnny kill Bob? AB	Anita suggests a consideration of who is to blame for what has happened. She begins, asking for reasons.
I don't mean to say this, but I think Johnny did right in a way because the Socs hurt everyone else! MM	Monica responds to Anita's question. She gives the impression that she believes Johnny has killed Bob in retribution because he is a Soc and the Socs have hurt others including himself.
I think it was all the Socs' fault that Bob died. SA	Sarita reads what Monica has written and agrees with her.
I wonder how Johnny feels now? AD	Amy tries to imagine the feelings of the character.
I wonder why the other four Socs didn't kill Johnny or Ponyboy. MM	This question will be discussed further as we consider whether the Socs running away represents fear or a lack of loyalty to their friend, Bob.
Why did Ponyboy get scared about the electric chair? He didn't do anything. SM	Sandy moves beyond the thinking expressed by Ponyboy in this passage of the text. Her notations remind us that he has done nothing.
Don't you think that Johnny is going to die? The other three Socs know what had happened. GS	Gina predicts that the Socs could later return, seeking retribution for Bob's death. Her question and comment lead Jess and Maria to join the exchange.
I really think Johnny is going to die. But not like that! JP	
I think that Johnny is going to die also. MC	

As we continue reading, Ponyboy and Johnny seek help from Dally who gives them a gun, money, and instructions to hop a train to Windrixville where they can hide in an old, abandoned church on Jay Mountain. Ponyboy and Johnny bide their time in the church, worrying about what has happened and what will happen. They try to disguise themselves by cutting off the long, slicked back locks which characterize them as Greasers. As we encounter this new setting and situation, our notations again reflect a need to clarify what is occurring.

Transacting With Text

Question, Comment, or Observation	My Reflections
Ponyboy is real wrapped up in Cherry because he is still thinking about her even in a crisis. BJ	
Why can't he like Cherry? AB	
It was very nice of Dally to help Johnny. AB	
How long do you think they are both going to stay at the church, or even if they will go? GS	
I hope Johnny was wearing more than a sweater. SM	During an interview when Sandy looks at this she says "I was thinking that boys say they're strong, some boys think they're tough, and Johnny is really fascinating because he's not like other boys. . . . he tells them that he's cold and he wishes he had more than a sweater on."
He was wearing jeans, sorry. SM	
I'd be scared if I had a gun laying by my head while I was asleep. SE	Sue puts herself in the character's place, thinking about how she would feel.
I feel sorry for Johnny in a way because he had to be dragged through running away, but plus he got away from his parents! MM	Monica infers that life will be better for Johnny because he has gotten away from his parents.
How do Darry and Sodapop feel about Ponyboy being gone? AD	
If I was him I would go to reformatory because I wouldn't want Johnny to go to the electric chair! MC	Maria considers what she believes to be the options of the character.
I would be scared if Johnny wasn't there because they're in a place they have never been. MM	Monica notes the growing closeness in the relationship between Johnny and Ponyboy. For this moment she is thinking of herself as Ponyboy.
Who is Buck? CW	
I think Johnny and Ponyboy are pretty good together. BL	Bet makes a judgment about the relationship.
When Ponyboy gets up he likes to worry a lot. MM	
Did they eat anything else than chocolate? SM	
I can't believe Ponyboy let Johnny cut his hair. AB	
Where are going to get money to buy food for the rest of the time/how will they make a living? GS	
Ponyboy keeps sleeping on Johnny because first he slept on his leg and then on his shoulder. MM	
Who's the fuzz? SM	

cont.

I think it's the police. MM	Monica replies to Sandy's need to know the meaning of the word "fuzz."
My mom is a Pepsi addict too. MM	
What are they going to do and where are they going to go after a while? RN	Ranita expresses her knowledge that the situation cannot remain as it is and sets herself up to make predictions about what will happen next.
Why did they tell the police? SM	
I think it's good Cherry's helping. Maybe she likes the Greasers but won't confess. MM	
Why does he want to turn himself in. NT	Nettie tries to understand the relationship between Johnny's current statement that he wants to turn himself in and his previous action of running away from the problem.
Wouldn't they catch him if he turns himself in? GS	Gina has not yet made the connection. She will need to acknowledge the change in Johnny's thinking and attempt to understand his reasoning.

As we read further, Dally, Ponyboy, and Johnny leave the church to eat at a nearby restaurant. When they return they find that the abandoned church is now in flames and several children who have been picnicking in the area are trapped inside. Ponyboy and Johnny make their way inside the church, saving the children. In the process Johnny is badly injured. The first several notations exemplify the public transactions or written "conversations" which occur as we respond to the reading.

Question, Comment, or Observation	My Reflections
Ponyboy and Johnny are really brave for saving the little brats from the fire. BJ	Burton draws a conclusion.
Why did the kid bite him? JB	
He was young and scared. BJ	Burton helps Jarod understand why one of the children has bitten the hand of the boy who tried to save him.
On the way to the hospital it seems as if Ponyboy is surprised that he's not in trouble. LV	
Sodapop is a nice brother. MM	
That would be awful if Ponyboy and Sodapop had to go to a boy's home after Ponyboy saved people's lives. LV	
I can't wait until the rumble! BL	
Don't the cops want to get these two people for manslaughter? GS	

cont.

Transacting With Text

What will happen to the gang if Johnny dies? LV	I reveal my prediction that Johnny will die from the injuries he has received. My wondering is an attempt to stimulate thinking about the relationships within the group and Johnny's role in the group.
I think that it wouldn't be the same. GS	Gina responds to my question.
I hope Johnny doesn't die. AB	Anita hopes that I am wrong in my prediction.
If I was in the hospital I would be more worried about my health than a book. MC	Maria finds Johnny's request for *Gone With the Wind* unrealistic.

Finally, we read of Johnny's death. The night Johnny dies begins with a rumble between the Socs and the Greasers. Following the rumble, Dally and Ponyboy go to the hospital to tell Johnny of the victory of the Greasers over the Socs. Johnny dies while they are with him. Ponyboy is suffering from a concussion due to a blow on his head during the fight. He refuses to acknowledge Johnny's death, pretending to himself that it hasn't happened. Dally, angry and hurt, robs a nearby market and then waves the unloaded gun he is carrying at the police. He is shot down in the street in front of his friends. Our notations begin with an acknowledgement of our own sorrow, sorrow over the death of Johnny and the effect it has had on Ponyboy.

Question, Comment, or Observation	My Reflections
Why does Ponyboy think that Johnny isn't dead? NT	
I feel so sorry for Ponyboy because he has to deal with Johnny's death. AB	
I feel bad because Johnny was Ponyboy's friend. AD	
I would have gave Ponyboy a towel for his head. MC	
I hope Ponyboy's head is okay. AB	
Dally was stupid for raising that gun, but it's too late, he's gone. JP	This comment prompts us to think about the reasons for Dally's actions.
Why did he do this right when Johnny died instead of praying for Johnny? RN	Ranita reflects her difficulty in associating the actions of Dally with the actions that she would take.
Dally did that because of depression. GS	Gina responds to Ranita.
Why did Dally pull out the gun and bluff like that. Did he want to die? AB	Anita builds on Gina's thought.
Dally wanted to die because he missed Johnny. JB	Jake pieces together the clues provided in the text; statements about Dally not having a family, Dally protecting Johnny, and Johnny's hero worship of Dally as he answers Anita.

cont.

I don't blame Dally, I would have done the same thing. CH	
I think Dally wanted to be with Johnny, so he raised the gun so the police would kill him. JP	After reading what others have written, Jess no longer thinks of Dally as "stupid."
I think Ponyboy needs to take it easy. AB	
Dally was a good friend to Johnny and Ponyboy. BL	Bet sums up the change in thinking about Dally.

Remembering my desire to have the students relinquish passivity and engage with the text, I create a list of my impressions of what has occurred. As we write questions, comments, and observations in a public place, we model our thoughts during a read-aloud of *The Outsiders* (Hinton, 1989). Members of the group ask factual questions which are answered by others. At times, when we ask "what is an outsider" or "what is a Greaser" we consider an abstract, contextual meaning of terms. Members of the group draw conclusions, question events in the text, and define words in terms of our own experiences. We make inferences and predict possible actions and outcomes based upon our perceptions of the events which occur, or the actions and statements of the characters. We seek clarification of the motives of characters. When we do this, we consider the meaning behind the thoughts and actions of the characters or the possible reasons for their thoughts and actions. When we think about why Ponyboy is ashamed and embarrassed that his brother Sodapop has dropped out of school, we think about the meaning of his shame and the possible reasons for his thinking. We conclude that dropping out of school may represent the Greasers' rejection of society and their willingness to accept the labels and even the hatred inflicted upon them by others. As we consider labels we begin to associate the characters' statements or actions with personality types, saying that Ponyboy is "nice," the Socs are "mean," or Johnny sometimes acts "like a girl."

There are instances in which the members of the group appear to judge the actions of characters. Our judgments may be based upon a consideration of what our own response to the situation would be. As we compare ourselves to the characters, there are moments in which we seem to look for ourselves in the characters. At other times we may try on the persona of a character, wondering how it feels to be this person. In order to clarify our responses, we may locate and seek to explain the connections or disconnections between the experiences of the characters and our own experiences.

We build support for our thoughts as we associate the ideas of others. The statement "I think Ponyboy and Johnny are pretty good together" is a conclusion found within supporting statements about the loyalty and need for closeness between Johnny and Ponyboy, as well as examples of the trust they place in one another. Support for our ideas is sometimes found as we return to the text. Jake tries to help us see that Dally pulled the gun on the police because he wanted to die. He returns to the text and finds the reasons for Dally's hopelessness and his inability to face the loss of Johnny.

Finally, we ask, in light of what we know, do the characters' actions and/or statements make sense? We do this when we wrestle with what we perceive as the changing loyalty of Cherry. We do this again when we think about Johnny lying near death, burned and broken in the hospital, and asking for a book. Sometimes we are forced to acknowledge that the characters' actions or statements may not make sense, just as our own actions or statements may not always make sense. It is then that we must return to our thinking in search of the reasons the character might provide for his actions.

The Students' Perspectives

I now want to move in closer with the camera in order to capture the perspectives of the students as they reflect upon the writing of questions, comments, and observations about text. I want to understand how they view the process. My desire for a closer look may have been prompted by the fact that we are now placing our initials after what we have written. While this makes it simpler for us to refer to specific individuals in later discussion of our notes, it also makes it possible to see which of us are participating in the process. Some of the students still appear to need permission to write what they are thinking. They stop beside me on their way to the board, urgently whispering "Can I ask . . . ," or "Can I put this . . .". Others are reluctant to participate. It occurs to me that inviting participation, demonstrating, and reinforcing the responses which are made may not be enough.

During the course of conducting one-on-one interviews with the students in this class group, I ask the students to pretend that I am a new person in the class and to explain the process to me. As they talk to me about the process of writing what they are thinking as we read, the students reveal their initial feelings about writing, describe their impressions of the purpose for placing their initials after what they have written, reflect upon the process and what it means to them, and offer evaluative comments.

Their Initial Feelings

Sandy's thoughts may help to explain why some students might feel apprehensive or nervous about going up to the front of the room to write:

> Some people sit in their seat like, "I'm nervous to go up there." At first I was nervous, but I'm the first person that wrote anything. I think that once I got up there

> everybody started feeling different and starting coming up here. I felt weird at first, I was just like, "Oh my gosh, I'm nervous to go up there." Well, sometimes people think they have something on the back of their pants or something and they're nervous to go up there 'cause they don't want it showing or anything. And I was just like, "Well, I really don't have anything on the back of my pants, so....why don't I just go up there?" And I went up there and I just started writing.

Sandy's words remind me of the deep concerns with personal appearance that I so often see in my students. Christie gets her special socks wet during gym class and wants to call her father at work to ask him to bring her another pair, rather than go through the rest of the day wearing her old gym socks. Joel spends every moment between classes in the bathroom, wetting down his hair and slicking it back into perfection. Tom crushes Sam in a Thursday class, saying "Hey, you wore that shirt on Tuesday." As teachers, we can not provide our students with the "right" clothes or hairstyles, but we can acknowledge that their fears of being different from others may prevent some of them from participating fully in the learning experience. Ted talks about how he feels different from the other students:

> I used to go to another class for reading, you know, this is my first time not to be in resource reading....Kids are messing with me because I get lower grades, I'm failing Science this six weeks. But, you know, I just stick with it, I don't really care.

He too, has been afraid to write what he is thinking because of a girl in the class whose personality seems to overwhelm him. During the interview, Ted talks to me about the situation and how he has overcome his problem:

> I didn't write because someone, like, you know Maria...I mean some person wouldn't want me to do it. I mean, I thought she might not give me the marker or something. Well, then I had something to write and it was at the end of class and she had already left. So, I just went up there real quick and wrote that.

Ted's remarks help me to think about other ways I can help the students become involved in the process. I suggest that the students leave their desks and sit in a group, closer to the front of the room and to the sheets on which we are writing. They quickly respond, some sitting on the floor and others moving to the desks at the front of the room. In this way we have narrowed the distance between one another and between ourselves and the sheets on which we are writing. A feeling of camaraderie begins to emerge. I also suggest that students who are still somewhat reluctant may write down what they are thinking in their Reader/Writer logs. This dilutes the interaction somewhat, but provides a way of beginning for those who are not yet ready to share their thoughts publicly.

Nettie talks about her own concerns that what she writes might not make sense to the others:

> I have so many questions I want to ask, but I just can't get them out into words. 'Cause the way I think of it, you know, it seems like everybody else would understand it, but when I write it down, it just doesn't make any sense, but it makes sense to me.

She explains why she thinks some people might be reluctant to write down what they are thinking:

> Some people might be a little more advanced and you're still on the same subject, but you're just so far up there that it seems like it has nothing to do with what we're reading or something like that. And you know, kids just probably look at you weird or something like, "why are you asking that question?"

For Nettie, it appears that there are two issues at stake. First, she is concerned about her thoughts making sense to others. What she is thinking about what she reads makes sense to her, but she is not yet confident in her ability to articulate these thoughts. This fear may be connected to her second statement in which it appears that she is concerned about how her questions will be received by the other members of the group. It appears that she may believe that others will judge her as a person and perhaps label her as "weird" based upon what she writes.

Sandy expresses an awareness of the reactions of her peers to what she has written:

> Some of them will kind of say like, "Why did you put that stupid question down?" They don't do that here, they just look at the question and sometimes that's their same question. 'Cause Monica wrote a few questions down that I wanted to ask. It was like, it's hard to say. But some person is thinking something and you're thinking the same thing.

This idea, expressed by Sandy, that "some person is thinking something and you're thinking the same thing" may provide the students with a sense of confidence about what they are thinking which will contribute to their empowerment. Students who have been reinforced by seeing thoughts similar to their own written and accepted may venture to write down their own questions, comments, and observations.

Gina refers to several of the central ideas of community (comfort, acknowledgment, and acceptance) and to the equalization of power as being elements which enable students to write their thoughts publicly:

> It's comfortable for everybody else. Then they go up there and they write without someone to stop them or anything. They can just go up there and write it and they're comfortable the way they are.... you give a lot of respect in this class. You're just like equal to us.

Remarks about how important it is to be able to write what you are thinking without fear of being laughed at by others, as well as Gina's statement about the respect and equality in the classroom, remind us that a literacy community must be a place where people feel safe and where they feel that their opinions are respected.

Ownership of Ideas

As I continue to talk with students, I learn that the act of placing our initials beside what we have written has significance to them. Monica's response indicates that she views the initials as a way of owning an idea. She tells me, "Everybody signs it so people will know who had the idea and what's going on in their life and in their head." When I ask Monica why it matters who is thinking what, she replies, "So that we know who's thinking that and who really knows what's going on in the story. Just so we can all communicate better."

For Bet, who says, "We put our initials afterwards so everyone knows how we're feeling at the time," initializing what we have written is a way of letting others know how we feel. It appears that while engaging in this process of writing transactions with text, the students may also be reflecting upon themselves and/or one another as readers and writers or as people whose individual personalities are reflected in what they think and write about text.

As the interviews continue, each of the students tells me that the knowledge that people are reading what they have written, and thus reading their ideas, their level of understanding, and their "personality" as well as what may be going on in their lives, does not prevent them from writing. Amy's comments are representative of those made by other students in the group. As she continues talking about reading the thoughts of others and sharing her own thoughts, she tells me, "I feel more comfortable actually. So people know what I'm like. I just don't think that I know about other people, but they don't know about me." While this may be true for these students, it occurs to me that there may be other students who realize what they reveal about themselves when they publicize their thoughts and who could be reluctant to participate fully because of this. For this reason, I must continue to provide opportunities for students to write their thoughts privately; and I must not make it a requirement for students to place their initials beside what they have written.

The Process and What it Means to Students

As I continue to talk to the students I gain insight about their perceptions of the process and what it means to them. Jake talks to me about the question, comment, observation sheets:

> These are our things—when we're reading a book. Whenever we want to we can just get up and write an idea about the book or a question. And then somebody else that has the answer to that question can come up and write that answer. So you can find that out and you can find out stuff like this, "I think Johnny and Pony are pretty good together." 'Cause that's just a comment. 'Cause some people might not think that, but you know, you can just say that.... And sometimes there's other words, like somebody is just saying something that could really help someone who's lost and they don't know what's going on. Sometimes when you just look at these, it can help you out.

As I think further about what Jake has said about writing questions, comments, and observations in a place where all of us can view them during the process of our reading, several things occur to me. Jake reveals a sense of ownership of the process when he begins by saying, "these are our things." His words indicate that he views the sheets and the process of constructing the sheets as one which belongs to the students rather than as one which is imposed on them from outside and/or controlled by others. As Jake continues, he describes what may be construed as the students' perception of the rules for this process. He tells me, "whenever we want to we can just get up and write an idea about the book or a question." Jake's statement is consistent with statements made by the other students who see this as an event in which they are free to engage and one in which they may write whatever they are thinking.

Finally, Jake explains his ideas about how writing our questions, comments, and observations about text where they can be seen by other readers may help students clear up confusion or come to new understandings. Jake's statements suggest an awareness that the questions, comments, and observations represent socially constructed knowledge. This knowledge may be empowering on several levels: First, because it emerges from the students themselves; second, because it may emerge as students become aware of the thoughts and ideas of their peers; and finally, because the students understand how the process may help them when they "don't know what's going on."

As Shelby talks to me, she describes how writing down questions, comments, or observations during a reading allows her to save the idea and frees her to focus her attention as she continues to read:

> And when you just get a thought, you know like sometimes you feel like reading and reading, or talking, and you just forget. If you write it there, then it doesn't go away. Then you can talk about it.

For Shelby and others, writing down our thoughts as we read is a way of making them permanent. When we write our thoughts, we can continue reading. We can later return to these thoughts and talk about them. As we make our thoughts public in this way, students who are transacting with the text—those who are paying attention to both the external world referred to by the words and to the feelings, attitudes, associations, and ideas evoked in themselves by the text—are indeed serving as models for their fellow readers.

Evaluation of the Process

During the one-on-one interviews with the students, I have them look back at the sheets filled with their questions, comments, and observations about *The Outsiders* (Hinton, 1989). As the students read what they have written, they return to the experience, reflecting on what has occurred in terms of meaning making and in terms of their own sense of empowerment.

As Jake reflects on the experience, he talks about the importance of beginning with literature that may be of relevance or interest to our students—literature that stimulates thinking:

> Like, if you're not interested in something, you're not going to be thinking all this good and bad stuff. You're just not going to be even paying attention. But if it's something you like, you're going to be paying attention and you're going to be going up there and writing stuff or just sitting over there and thinking of stuff in your head.

I tell Jake it sounds as if he is saying that "one of the number one things for a 7th-grade reading class would be to get stuff people are interested in reading." He replies vehemently:

> Yeah. You gotta read cool books and stuff. 'Cause if you're reading like a boring book and kids aren't interested, they're not going to do anything. You're not going to have anything to do because they don't want to do anything.... honest opinion. Yeah. You gotta get cool books. You can tell that to my teacher for next year. Say 'Get Jake some cool books. He don't want none of these stupid little books.'

As she looks at the questions, comments, and observations she has written, Sandy explains what happens *inside* her as she writes in response to the reading:

> I put "why" because I'm wanting to know why it is happening. Or if I put "what," like what is happening. What's going on in his mind or something like that.... and why, why is it happening.

Sandy's words reveal that the students have internalized questioning strategies using words like who, what, when, where, why, and how to help them think about their reading.

As the students talk to me further, they continue to evaluate the process, telling me what it means to them to write their thoughts about what we are reading. Jarod and Gina talk about the difference between attending to their own thoughts and answering a teacher's questions. Jarod says,

> When you write them on the sheets, it's like everybody gets to see them—it's not like a test or anything. Afterwards you get to talk about it. But if it's on a test you have to write it down and you can't talk to nobody about it.... it's just you and the test. The questions on the test are just questions that the teachers made up. And these are the questions that we thought of, that we wrote down. That we would like to talk about.

Jarod's initial comments reflect a sense that the process of writing questions, comments, and observations is meaningful in that it is an action which provides a source for talk unlike that of taking a test. For Jarod, school can be a place where students may not be encouraged to express their questions or to talk. Jarod needs to express his ideas through talk. He suggests that students engaged in testing situations may conceive of the situation as representative of oppositional relationships with tests and/or teachers. I do not believe that Jarod is suggesting that he should be allowed to talk while he is in a testing situation. It is more likely that he is making a comparison between his feelings in situations based in talk and situations based in test taking.

Jarod's final comments, "And these are the questions that *we* thought of, that *we* wrote down. That *we* would like to talk about . . . ," reinforce the idea that in writing their questions, comments, and observations these students are socially constructing meaning and are experiencing a sense of ownership in the process. He emphasizes the word "we" each time he uses it in these last two statements. This, in conjunction with his earlier statement that questions on tests are "just questions that the teachers made up," reveals that he feels powerful when he is asked to contribute his own ideas to the classroom.

As Gina compares the experience of writing questions, comments, and observations to one of writing answers to questions on a worksheet, she adds her voice to those of Jarod, Tammy, and other students in this classroom as they reflect on their literacy experiences. She says,

> Well, the questions on the worksheets, those are what the teacher knows and sometimes they are questions that we don't know about the book and we want to know. Sometimes they're the questions that are obvious, that are on the worksheet, and we just write those down. It's like the teacher doesn't care, but. . . . the things we write on the sheets in this class, it's like I don't know how to put it, we get involved. In reading, I feel like I'm more involved.

Gina is restating the view that teacher generated questions are representative of what a teacher knows and has decided that students should know. Teacher generated questions may also be based upon the "obvious," or as previously suggested by Tammy, "something you might already understand that the teacher is making sure you got." One of Gina's most dramatic statements begins with the words, "It's like the teacher doesn't care." This remark, coupled with her continuing statements about her own involvement in the process of writing questions, comments, and observations about text, suggests that Gina may feel that teacher generated questions are both arbitrary and nonresponsive to the needs of individual students.

For Monica, the value of the process is centered in the picture it gives her of what other people are thinking:

> I think it's cool, because if I don't catch on I can get people's ideas. And plus, I don't know what people are thinking about when they're reading because I can't see

> *through their mind. And so, it's better that way, so I can look at their questions and think about what they're thinking.*

As I reflect upon what Monica has said, I am struck by her words, "I don't know what people are thinking about when they're reading because I can't see through their mind." As she talks about what she values, Monica helps me to see that students are empowered through this process in which we make our thoughts during reading visual or explicit. As we engage in multiple, visible, concrete transactions with text, my students and I are, to paraphrase Monica, seeing through the minds of others.

Jess and others envision the process as one which stimulates further thinking and prompts them to return to the text to clarify their thinking. Jess describes how reading what Jarod has written on the sheet and then comparing her own thoughts to his, prompts a return to the text. As Jess rereads, she searches for further meaning so that she might understand how Jarod has arrived at his interpretation. In Jess' words, writing questions, comments, and observations about text helps her to understand:

> *Because I can see what other people ask and what they think of the book. And then, I, uh, I forgot which book it was, but Jarod wrote something about a part in the book, and then I thought differently. Then I went back and read that part he was talking about and I could see how he thought that. Like I could understand how he thought that. It helps me understand the books better and I haven't done that in any of my other classes or for any of the other books I had read. It really helps me understand books and makes me want to read more and more.*

As students are invited to talk about the process of writing questions, comments, and observations, they engage in an examination of their initial feelings and their impressions of the purpose for initializing what they have written. From these students we hear that personal appearance; perceptions about academic success; and concerns about how their questions, comments, and observations will be viewed by others may inhibit their entry into the experience. These students conclude that comfort, acknowledgment, acceptance, and the equalization of power are aspects of the classroom that may enable them to write their thoughts publicly.

As they describe the purpose for initializing their questions, comments, and observations, the comments made by these students indicate that initializing is representative of their feelings of ownership of both the process and of the idea which is represented on the sheet. Further reflection by these students indicates that they view initialized questions, comments, and observations as reflections of self or, as Monica states, of "what's going on in their life and in their head." For these students, reading the questions, comments, and observations of others and thinking about what this reveals about our personality, our life, and our feelings is a further way in which we come to know one another.

As the students continue to examine the process, they clarify what it means to them and offer evaluative comments. Further statements are made about the ownership they feel for the process. It appears that the students envision writing their questions, comments, and observations as an extension of their freedom—in this case, the freedom to write when they want and what they want. The reflections of these students about the process reveals that they envision this as a means of socially constructing knowledge. This is indicated in three ways: first, as students state their awareness that the ideas which emerge and are represented on the sheets are a product of the thinking of themselves and their peers; second, as students refer to the understanding which stems from their readings of the thoughts and ideas of their peers; and finally, as the students refer to their understanding of the ways to work within the process to construct meaning.

As these students evaluate the process, their comments are indicative of the particular aspects which they may value. These students view the writing of questions, comments, and observations as a way of making their thoughts tangible and permanent and as a way of holding a thought while they continue reading. The process may engage them in active consideration of text as they read with a view to what they will write—thinking about what they know, what they don't know, how they feel, and how they will contribute to the ongoing transaction. As these students read the questions, comments, and observations of their peers, they relate that they learn from what others have written or, as stated by Monica, that they "see through the minds of others." This suggests that the students are modeling the process of transacting with text for one another.

Finally, as these students evaluate the process, there are frequent references to ideas of community, empowerment, and involvement which stem from their participation in the generation of questions, comments, and observations—a process in which they and not the teacher generate the ideas.

Moving to Silent, Independent Reading

How can we retain that feeling of connecting with others as we move from reading as a large group to silent, independent reading? What happens when students are allowed to choose their own books within the framework of a particular genre? Will these students transfer aspects of writing questions, comments, and observations publicly to their private transactions with text? In this section, we will examine these issues through a study of genre conducted in the classroom. During our study of myster-

Transacting With Text 119

ies, the students will be presented with a number of books from which they will choose. The students will be reading independently and interacting within small groups formed on the basis of their book selections. As the students begin to transition from whole class reading and response to reading independently and interacting within a small group, we must adjust our ways of working. Through their questions, comments, observations, notes to one another, and double entry journals, we will retain the central aspects of the question, comment, observation process. One-on-one interviews with students will allow us to see their perspectives about the process of student-to-student writing of questions, comments, and observations in Reader/Writer logs and provide us with a view of how this process may be transferred to the personal reading of these students.

Introducing the Books and the Process

I begin by covering the chalk rail and the floor beneath it with multiple copies of mysteries I have collected over the years. Under each set of books I hang a sheet of paper with title of the book and the class period written at the top. Standing back to survey the scene, I mentally check off the titles, preparing for the book talks I will give today:

- *Something Upstairs* (Avi, 1990)
- *Wolfrider* (Avi, 1993)
- *And Then There Were None* (Christie, 1991)
- *Driver's Ed* (Cooney, 1994)
- *Wanted* (Cooney, 1997)
- *Wilderness Peril* (Dygard, 1991)
- *The House of Dies Drear* (Hamilton, 1984)
- *Deadly Deception* (Haynes, 1994)
- *A Candidate for Murder* (Nixon, 1991)
- *The Kidnapping of Christina Lattimore* (Nixon, 1992)
- *The Other Side of Dark* (Nixon, 1992)
- *The Stalker* (Nixon, 1992)
- *Whispers from the Dead* (Nixon, 1991)
- *Sweet Friday Island* (Taylor, 1994)
- *A Ghost in the House* (Wright, 1991)

Moments later, the first students of the day enter the room and I am swept away from my position at the chalk rail. My wonderings about how they will react end as I hear the words, "What are these?" "Wow!" "Do we get to pick what we want to read?" "Can I take this book now?" "Hey, I'm going to read that one!" "Can we read more than one?" and "How many can we read?" I literally have to herd them to their desks in order to be heard. "Yes, you get to pick the book you want to read!" and "Yes, you can read more than one!" I begin. "But first, wouldn't you like to hear a little about each one?" As I watch them lean forward in their desks to listen, I search for just the right words to say about each of the books. We are reading on many different levels within this classroom. I include a short remark about the length of the book or the complexity of the plot in order to help the students choose a book they will be able to read independently. Finally, I talk about how our reading will be organized. Each of us will sign up for the book we want to read. Those who are reading the same book will choose a place in the room where they can sit together—a meeting place. We will read to ourselves because, as I ask, "Can you imagine what it would sound like in here if we were reading all these books aloud at the same time?" They laugh. We will bring our Reader/Writer logs to the meeting place. Each time we read, we will exchange logs and write a note about our reading to another member of our group. I will take turns, reading and writing with a different group each class period.

"Can we go and pick now, Mrs. Van Horn?" asks Matt impatiently. It is evident from their faces that my time to talk has come to end. "Sure, let's go!" I reply. There is a surge of motion as students climb over desks and one another in order to reach the books they want and to sign up on the lists. When the frenzy dies down, I choose a book and sit down, indicating that it is now time to read. Before long, the groups have settled into their meeting places with their mysteries and Reader/Writer logs in hand. The reading begins.

Difficulties and Transformations

In the days to come there are difficulties to confront. Paco insists that he cannot read alone. I sit with him in the doorway where we won't disturb the others. We whisper as we read aloud to one another, passing the book back and forth. Paco reads slowly, but fluently. As we whisper to one another about Taylor's *Sweet Friday Island* (1994), Paco's face is animated. He laughs at the list of camping gear Peg Toland and her father are taking with them to an island located between Baja California and the western coast of Mexico. He tells me that he too, always brings plenty of toilet paper when he goes camping with his dad. Later, Paco authoritatively corrects my mispronunciation of Camino Diablo, "the old Devil's Highway" (Taylor, 1994, p. 10). After several days, Paco decides that he is ready to join his group. He does not say anything to me about his decision, but I wonder if it might be that Paco simply needed more time with the interactive process of the read-aloud before he was ready to read on his own. Sitting in the floor in the back corner now, surrounded by others who are also reading *Sweet Friday Island*, Paco continues reading, slowly, but on his own.

Katy, Melissa, and Jules are reading *And Then There Were None* (Christie, 1991). As I join their group Katy whispers apologetically, "This book is kind of confusing. . . . we haven't read very far." I ask them if they want to try another book, but they want to stay with this one. They are intrigued by the poem about the ten little Indian boys I had read aloud during the book talk, and they want to find out what happens to this group of people who have been invited to Indian Island for a holiday. In the beginning of the mystery, Christie writes several chapters of introduction to multiple characters. Katy, Melissa, and Jules are having difficulty keeping track of the names and background information for each character. For several days we write back and forth to one another, sharing our questions, comments, and observations. For the most part, they write questions and I write answers until they establish an understanding of the characters and the plot which allows them to continue on their own. It appears that these students were able to use the process to formulate specific questions about their understanding. Their success as they continued on their own, corresponding with one another indicates that the initial difficulties they experienced may have been attributed to their lack of background information (these characters are all adults) and/or their need to test how the process of writing questions, comments, and observations would transfer from whole class to small group by writing first to me.

Ani's log reflects how the process looks as individual entries in the Reader/Writer log are influenced by the whole class experience of publicly noting our thinking in terms of questions, comments, and observations about text. As she reads *The Other Side of Dark* by Joan Lowery Nixon (1992), Ani records her thoughts in columnar fashion, dividing the pages of her Reader/Writer log in half and noting what she wants to know (her questions), and what she knows (her observations and/or comments):

Things I Know	**Things I Want to Know**
Stacy's mom was murdered.	Who killed Stacy's mom?
Stacy's 17 and she thinks she's 13.	Who is that dude in Stacy's backyard?
Donna's pregnant and married.	Who is Jeff Clinton?
Stacy's going to a party.	Who was that guy on the phone?
B.J. and Jan are her best friends.	Why does that guy keep calling Stacy?
B.J. and Jan are giving her a makeover for the party.	Has Stacy met Jeff before?
	Is Jeff the killer?
	Did Jarrod make those freaky calls?
Stacy accused Jarrod of killing his mom.	Is Jarrod the killer?
	Is Jarod insane?
	Why did Detective Markowitz say the attorney dude was one "devil's advocate"?
The justice system sucks.	I need to know if this is a REAL story.

cont.

Stacy has suffered a major loss, her mother, her respect, and four years of her life.	
	Why did Jarrod whisper "my friend" to Stacy?
Jarrod is a liar, because he has the same eye color as the killer.	Was Jarrod really in San Antonio when Stacy's mother was killed?
I know Jarrod may try to kill Stacy, he has tried before.	What did Jarrod have against Stacy's family?
I know Jarrod has brought havoc upon Stacy's family, and caused Stacy to lose her respect in the city she lives in.	
Jarrod may have been a killer before.	Why did he constantly call Stacy's home and hang up?
Stacy's mother. Mrs. Cooper is her new neighbor and has kept a watchful eye. Jarrod is being a little pain.	Or is it just a prank?
Detective Markowitz is helping a great deal.	
Jeff is helping Stacy in a way that makes me think that he had nothing to do with her mother's death.	How does Jeff know Jarrod so well?
Jarrod supplies Tony with narcotics.	Who is Tony?
Mrs. Lathan is the person Stacy talks to about what she can remember about her accident and her mother's death.	How does Tony know Stacy?
	Why did Tony invite Stacy to his party?
	Does Jan know Jarrod well?
	Is there an accomplice to Stacy's mother's death?
	Was Jeff or Tony the accomplice if there was an accomplice?
What is up with the media and a murder in their town? They invade people's privacy which is just plain wrong.	Is Jarrod a stalker?
	Has he been watching Stacy from the start?
The justice system really really sucks sometimes.	Well if he does get out of jail will Jarrod kill again and switch guns?
Jan is letting Stacy come over for dinner.	
I can see Stacy really wants to kill Jarrod, but she won't because she knows she'll be just like him.	Why is Tony being so secretive about Jarrod? Is he afraid he'll get busted?
	What kind of narcotics is he being supplied with?
	Why is Jeff with Jarrod so often?
	Is Tony lying about being friends with Jarrod?

cont.

	Why does Jarrod have yellow eyes?
	Has Jarrod gone under a fake name before?
	Is Jarrod having a seizure?
	Is it drug related?
	Is Jeff lying to Stacy?
Jarrod has escaped from the jail in a mad dash, shooting someone in the leg.	Why does the media have such a fascination about death? Is it a fetish?
	Why does Jarrod want to get out so bad?
Jarrod may find Stacy and finish the job he didn't four years ago.	
	Why won't Jarrod stop with this killing?
	He's killed one, wounded another, won't he stop?
	Is Jarrod really going to get Stacy in the tree house?
	Is the tree house stable enough to hold Stacy?

When I read these thoughts, I feel as if I am inside of Ani's mind—wondering, needing to know if this is "real," indignant, angry, suspicious, fearful. I am living in the book with her.

I had planned for the students to talk in small groups, sharing their questions, comments, and observations, and using them as a basis for discussion in much the same way as we do in our whole class experiences. During a debriefing after the first day of sharing, Marla points to a potential problem saying, "Mrs. Van Horn, this could be tricky. We're not all reading at the same place in the book. These are mysteries. What if I read what someone else writes and it gives the whole thing away?" Together, we decide to include page numbers with our entries, and to turn down pages in our Reader/Writer logs which deal with parts of the novel others have not read. We will begin our discussions with a group decision about how much of the book we will cover.

Writing Notes to One Another

In order to extend the experience, I suggest that we might write notes to one another based upon our questions, comments, and observations. Together we brainstorm a list of possible opening topics. As the students and I begin to write to one another, we write about why we chose our book, how we feel about the characters, and how we compare ourselves with the characters.

Jan is reading *Wolfrider* (Avi, 1993). Surprisingly, no one else in the class has picked this book to read. I tell Jan not to worry, that I will be in his group. At first, he is nervous about writing to me. "No one wants to be in my group 'cause I can't spell," he announces to me. "They wouldn't be able to read my notes to them." "I will read your notes," I assure him. This is Jan's first experience outside of a resource reading class, and I want to ease the transition and encourage him to participate fully. I suggest, "Let's start by writing about why we chose this book."

Jan writes to me:

> Dear Mrs. Van Horn,
>
> The rizin I chos this book is it sonde relly exizon.
>
> The opioning pirgaf was relly exizon.
>
> The arthion chose a relly cool way to opon the first pigraf.
>
> After the page 6 got me cofe about how Andy, Paul & Zeke is, do you know?
>
> a good book
> Jan

Later, I ask Jan if we can write about how we feel about the characters. Are they believable? He answers:

> Dear Mrs. Van Horn,
>
> I thank Andy is believrelbe.
>
> Andy is like a nombr purson. He is out going.
> Then he can be the shiy tipe.
>
> I do no someone like Andy that purson is me.
>
> To be trouful I would go and try to save her from getting murde.
>
> good book
> Jan

Jan will later build upon his comparison of himself to the character Andy, writing:

> Dear Mrs. Van Horn,
>
> The way I camper my salf to Andy is how he is oupsate abot no one bleves hem and some times that is how I fell bescas my mom sometimes dos not bleves me. And that makes me mad just the same way Andy fells. Then people asck him questions, then thay asck me questions. So I gest you can no we are alike each outher.
>
> from Jan

As we continue reading, Pete and John exchange notes about why they chose the book *Wanted* (Cooney, 1997) and how they feel about the central character Alice:

> Dear John,
>
> I think that it was kind of stupid the way Alice handled things. I think that the reason why I chose this book was because of the title. It sounded exciting. Like I was saying, I think that it was stupid of Alice to hide under the car when the killer was in the house with her. If I was her I would have gotten into the car and busted through the garage door with it. I thought it was also rather weird the way the killer acted. Oh! I almost forgot. The book is about to get a lot more interesting from the point where you are. While you are reading the next part make sure you keep in mind that she still has the floppy discs. Oh! I also thought it was stupid the way she went back into the house after someone had just broken in, and to top that took a shower!
>
> Sincerely,
> Pete

John responds with some additional thoughts about Alice, comparing her to his own sister Tina:

> Dear Pete,
>
> Alice is very believable, don't you think? I could just imagine her as a '90's mall kid. She is a typical blond to me. She puts fashion before other priorities. The only other person I know who would do that is my oldest sister, Tina. I do not know if I would do all the things Alice did. I would not go back in the house to take a shower. I probably would have faced the intruder person-to-person. I know my house better than anyone. The intruder would be playing on my turf. I'd have the advantage. I would not have done something that stupid. I would put my family above fashion if I was Alice. Who cares what I look like? When my father tells me to do something I know he means business. I would not have wasted one moment.
>
> Your pal,
> John

Shawn, writing to Matt, also reflects on the vanity of Alice and compares the actions she takes with what he sees himself doing in the same situation:

> Dear Matt,
>
> I think Alice is too much concerned with how she looks. Like when she was painting her fingernails and wondering what purse to wear. She had to take a shower after she was under that car in her own house. I think that she worries about herself too much. Like when her dad said to drive the car. Heck, I would have sprung up from where I was sitting and driven the discs to my dad. I think I also would have copied the phone number directly from Caller I.D. My sister acts the same way. She thinks everything has to be perfect. Her hair, clothes, etc. I wouldn't have done the same thing because think about it, if she hadn't had to pick out her purse and change clothes, she wouldn't be where she is now. I still can't believe that she took a shower after those people came in her house.
>
> Your pal,
> Shawn

Our notes reflect continued thinking about the text. Jan sees himself in the character, Andy. He, like Andy, is sometimes outgoing and sometimes shy. Both of them get angry when people ask them questions and then disbelieve the answers. Pete disagrees with the actions of Alice. Rather than hide under the car as Alice does, Pete writes that he would "have gotten into the car and busted the garage door down with it." Pete is further along in the book than John, the student with whom he is exchanging notes. He does not want to give away the plot, but he offers a helpful hint to John, writing, "While you are reading the next part, keep in mind that she still has the floppy discs." John and Shawn both consider their own knowledge of girls as they read about Alice, comparing her to their sisters. Shawn thinks that Alice "worries about herself too much," and draws the conclusion that if "she hadn't had to pick out her purse and change clothes, she wouldn't be where she is now" (in deep trouble).

Reading and Thinking on Our Own

I want to know how this process of recording our thoughts and writing notes to one another with the framework of a small group works for my students. Monica talks about her thinking as she read *The Final Jour-*

ney (Pausewang, 1996) during a study of historical fiction and survival, saying:

> It lets me know. 'Cause I don't catch on to some things. Like in The Final Journey I didn't catch on and then I read some of Gina's questions in her Reader/Writer log and I caught on. Like I didn't really get the part about the grandma and then I read her questions and that's what got me. 'Cause she put answers off to the side too.

Looking into Gina's journal provides Monica with a similar experience to that which she had as we wrote our thoughts on sheets of paper where the whole group could see them. As we move from whole group to small group reading and thinking, it appears that we take our process of transacting with text along with us.

Later in the year, during interviews with the students, I learn that they have continued thinking and writing about text as they read on their own outside of the classroom. Carolina tells me,

> Well, when I took it (the book she is reading) home I was reading it and I really started imagining things in my mind. And I could see how it really happened. And every time I would get to a good part, I would just stop and just wonder what would happen, and just wonder what would happen to me if that happened to me.

Monica's words reveal that she has transferred the processes she uses in her school reading to the reading she does at home:

> I'm reading a book at home now. 'Cause I'm getting more into reading. Last night I read about eighty pages and I wrote down questions and answered them to myself.

Sandy tells me what happens when she moves away from simply reading the words and starts to think about what she is reading. For Sandy, thinking about the book is a way of "getting into" the book itself:

> When you're like in the book you're reading...at first it's boring, but then once you get to the exciting parts and you're wondering "what's happening, what's happening?" You're asking...you're like getting into the book. It's coming up, like 3D (three dimensional) and you're really in it! It's like a magnet. It like (she slaps her hands together) sucks you in!

Reading *can* be like a magnet that "sucks you in." As I think about this analogy, I am reminded of Anthony's comparison of himself as a reader to a sponge that could soak up the water (make meaning) or just let the water run over it. When I think of all of us reading and thinking together in this room, I know that no one can explain what happens better than Anthony does in his note to me about reading class:

> This year is special because this is the year I moved to Texas, and met you and all my other friends. My thoughts took on a new dimension now that I had people to share them with. I will remember until the day I die, the warm, happy memories of when we all got together right next to that big window inside your classroom to read. Carmen, Katie, Michelle, Jessica, and Ashley would all pile up next to the window and lay down basking in the afternoon sun as we delved deep into literature. Other people would be scattered about and we'd be like a little island, where we lived in a world of fantasy: the world of Brennan Cole, Macbeth, Journey, Ponyboy Curtis, Jonas, and others... and there we found happiness, love and learning... we have learned so much from each other.

Evaluation/Assessment

As I study our question, comment, and observation sheets, I can evaluate both the progress and the needs of individual students and class groups. I may transcribe the lists and write my reflections as I have done in this chapter. Or, I may mark directly on the sheets themselves, coding the statements by level of comprehension. The students and I refer to these sheets as we discuss aspects of comprehension and the processes of successful readers. This is empowering to them because they can see the physical evidence that they are exhibiting and/or developing these processes.

A review of the question, comment, and observation sheets also helps me to make instructional decisions. As I examine the sheets, I can determine the need for additional background knowledge, vocabulary study, related readings, and/or demonstrations of particular comprehension skills. I may also use what the students have written to help me design response activities which relate to their particular interests or concerns about the text and, thereby, further acknowledge the relevance of their thoughts.

SUMMARY

As we examine the processes of these students as they generate questions, comments, and observations about text, we can see that meaning making and empowerment are enhanced as transactions with text become foregrounded and public and interactions among the student are, stimulated. Through the initial responses of these students to the concept and the process of generating their own questions, comments, and observations about text, it is revealed that questions generated by the teacher and/or those created by the authors of published materials are viewed in two very different ways by the students. For some students, questions from others represent an expected, accepted, and perhaps, less risky means of responding to reading.

More frequently, students relate perceptions that teacher questions may be representative of issues which should already be understood by the students and, as such, teacher questions may be utilized as a means of checking that understanding. For some of these students, a focus on questions generated by the teacher or by others outside the context indicates to them a lack of care or perhaps a lack of interest or respect for the questions they might have asked. For these students, a focus on questions generated by the teacher and/or others outside the context could be degenerative to the empowerment and meaning which is developing through the creation and sustenance of the literacy community and to the ongoing process of coming to know ourselves through our literacies.

Examination of the patterns in the questions, comments, and observations of a single group of students across the readings of four novels reveals a complex system of interdependent textual transactions in which the written reflections of the students cycle through stages which represent the various levels of comprehension. The questions, comments, and observations written by the students as they read the first two novels (*Double Trouble Squared* and *Canyons*) contain a greater number of regularities or searches for word meaning and information related to the plot or to the characters, as they establish a frame of information from which to construct meaning. In the reading of the second two novels (*The Outsiders* and *The Giver*), the sequence diversifies; and the students' growing sense of trust in the process and in one another, as well as the focus on the ways of thinking about text inherent to the process, contribute to responses which more frequently lead to self-organization or meaning-making events.

An examination of the process as it occurs within the reading of a single text (*The Outsiders*, Hinton, 1989) by the students in a single class group reinforces the view attained through the previous analysis. As we further examine the responses of the students in the focus group, we may envision this process as one in which the students alternate in and through considerations of text, self, and others as they formulate and respond to questions, comments, and observations. A further look at the critical or representative transactions during the reading reveals that the students

- Relate word meanings to personal knowledge and experience
- Question or comment upon the motives and actions of characters in ways that refer to actions they themselves would take, what they consider acceptable, or what they value
- Respond in ways which are reflective of their identity or the way they believe their identity is perceived by others
- Interpret the actions of characters through their own observation of social interactions among their peers
- Make connections to texts shared by their peers in read-alouds
- Put themselves in the place of characters, reasoning and/or feeling from the point of view of a character
- Express personal concern for a character or characters

In each of these critical transactions students respond through connections to personal experiences, feelings, identities, and/or values. This personalization enables them to generalize, draw conclusions, make predictions, and to consider central issues or themes. During the reading of *The Outsiders* (Hinton, 1989), these students are in frequent if not constant communication with others in the group as they answer questions posed by the members of the group and as they make comparisons between the characters and the members of the group. Through personalization and communication these students come to consider issues of the abuse and labeling of individuals by others as well as the psychological reasoning and motivation behind Johnny's murder of Bob and what appears to them to be Dally's suicide over the loss of Johnny. Meaning is constructed by these students as they personalize their transactions with text. Those who have internalized this reflection and connection to self are empowered. Therefore, it may be said that to deny students the opportunity to personalize knowledge is to restrict both power and meaning.

Examination of the statements of these students as they talk about writing their questions, comments, and observations reveals that this process is one in which they are engaged in continual reflections about self, others, and the community or group as they transact with text and interact with others.

Consideration of Self	Consideration of Others	Consideration of the Group
I need to overcome concerns about physical appearance.	Others may prevent me from writing.	We have been asked to contribute our thoughts.
I need to discover what I think.	What I write (think) may not make sense to others.	

cont.

	Others may see what I write and think of me as someone who is behind or does not understand.	
I need to narrow the distance between myself and the sheets.	I need to narrow the distance between myself and others.	
I need to write in my R/W log before I can make my thoughts public.		We are free to write when we want to write.
When I initialize what I write I "own" the idea.	When others initialize what they write they "own" the idea.	These are "our" things; what we write belongs to us as a group.
My individual personality or identity is reflected in what I write.	The individual personality or identity of others is reflected in what they write.	We are free to write what we want to write.
When I write I reveal what's going on in my head.	When others write they reveal what's going on in their heads.	We learn about one another.
When I write I reveal what's going on in my life.	When others write they reveal what's going on in their lives.	
I write to say what I feel.		We become involved in our own learning through the process.
I write to state an opinion.		
I write to ask a question.		
I write to show what I have observed.		
I read the sheets to find answers to my questions.	What others write may answer my questions.	
	What others have written may help me when I am "lost."	We read the thoughts of others to clear up confusions.
I read the sheets to see alternate views.	What others have written shows me an alternate view.	We read the thoughts of others to get alternate views.
I read the sheets to get ideas.	What others write stimulates my thinking.	We read the thoughts of others to stimulate our thinking.
I write to hold a thought while I continue reading.	Reading what others have written and watching them as we read makes me feel like we are a family.	We learn from one another; "seeing" through the minds of others.
I reread the text and think about what I want to know.		Seeing what others think makes us feel like a family.

cont.

| I reread the text to get further ideas. | | |
| I ask myself who, what, when, where, why, or how before I write. | | We will use (authenticate) what we have written when we talk about it. |

    The comments of these students reveal that as they engage in the process of writing questions, comments, and observations about text and posting their responses publicly, their awareness of their own meaning-making strategies and those of others is enhanced. In addition, the comments of these students reflect a deepening awareness of the relationship between self and literacy—for example, how response to literature may be a reflection of self. The statements of these students about others and about the community or group indicate that issues related to the equalization of power and empowerment underlie the process. While they may have some initial trepidation about engaging in the process and their individual contributions to the process, these students state that they are empowered when they are asked to contribute their questions, comments, and observations. This empowerment is reflected in their statements that they have control of what and when they write, that they are "seeing" or learning from what others write, through their descriptions of the emergence of a feeling of family, and in their comments about the authenticity of the process.

    As we transition from whole class to independent reading supported within a small group and/or private readings outside the classroom, the students enter a period in which they must actively consider the ways that public transactions through written questions, comments, and observations may be applied to small group or individual transactions. Extension of the process through note writing is a way in which small group or whole class talk about texts is simulated.

    Chapter 4 will examine the students' whole class and small group discussion of texts. In this chapter, I will focus on the influence of whole class and/or small group discussion of text on the meaning-making process of the students, the roles of myself and the students as we interact, and the perceptions of the students regarding power relations as reflected in our interactions.

4

THE POWER OF TALK

DEVELOPING IDEAS ABOUT TALK

It's different . . . because, see we talk about it. And you know how we debate on how we think that it should be? I think really, if there's questions about reading . . . I really don't think there is a wrong and a right answer, because other people think of the story differently. . . . so, I don't have anything against reading tests, but I, I don't know . . . I like doing this 'cause you see what other people are trying to say about that question. If somebody says, "Well, I think this is saying," and you're, "Well, no, I think it's saying." Like I said, there is no right or wrong answer. . . . I think if reading was that easy people wouldn't go anywhere; people wouldn't have that big of an imagination.

Nettie

As I write this, I can "hear" Nettie's voice as she speaks to me about our classroom conversations about literature. Each of these statements is made emphatically, punctuated with raised eyebrows and hand gestures. As Nettie talks, her expression of concentration and the emphasis she places on the words suggest to me that she is making a discovery through our dialogue. Nettie has come to value the ambiguity or the possibilities entailed in a reading of text. Nettie views our talk about literature as an ongoing "debate" in which we attempt to convince one another of the validity of our interpretations. As she refers to reading tests, saying, "so I don't have anything against reading tests, but I, I don't know" her hesitation indicates a belief that reading tests are a call for one right answer which, in Nettie's thinking, is not always possible. This, coupled with her remark that "other people think of the story differently," shows us that Nettie believes that we have a right to think about what we are reading and/or that we do not always come to the same conclusion or agree upon a single interpretation. Her statement that "if reading was that easy people wouldn't go anywhere" reveals that Nettie views thinking and talking about literature as acts which are arduous but worthwhile, because these acts may enable her to come to an understanding or to develop an interpretation of what she has read.

Susan Hynds (1990) has written that teachers must "create classrooms where students are creating unique interpretations, not guessing at predetermined answers" (p. 176). Hynds and others suggest that we must provide our students with opportunities to engage in conversations about text—conversations through which they may come to expect and accept a diverse range of impressions or views about literature (Hynds, 1990; Almasi, McKeown, & Beck, 1996). It has been noted that the patterns of interaction reflected in classroom discussion of literature are often controlled by the teacher who may initiate the question, call for a student to respond, and then evaluate the response (Cazden, 1988; Dillon, 1981). Teacher evaluations of student responses may be used to discourage diverse views and to shape or illuminate predetermined answers.

---

bell hooks (1994) suggests that teachers are responsible for fostering an environment in which students listen to one another seriously. She notes that students often make judgments about their own responses and those of their peers based upon the evaluation of the teacher; "if the teacher doesn't seem to indicate that this is something worth noting, few students will" (p. 150). This, according to hooks, "raises a whole range of questions about silencing." Specifically, "At what point does one say what someone else is saying ought not to be pursued in the classroom?" (p. 150).

---

bell hooks (1994) views "coming to voice" as "a complex recognition of the uniqueness of each voice and a willingness to create spaces in the classroom where all voices can be heard because all students are free to speak, knowing their presence will be recognized and valued" (p. 186).

A teacher generated pattern of initiation, response, and evaluation, intended to stimulate talk about literature may actually cause a silencing of student voice and result in teacher controlled simulation of a true discussion. Kletzien and Baloche (1994) define a true discussion as "an exchange of ideas and opinions about topics that may not have easy answers" (p. 541). As such, students engaged in a true discussion will not be searching for predetermined answers. Students engaged in true discussion control the content as well as the nature of the discussion. Content is developed as the students originate the questions and/or topics to be discussed. The nature of a true discussion is reflected in the students' responses, which are primarily student to student rather than student to teacher (Cintorino, 1993).

> Calfee, Dunlap, and Wat (1994) state that when "the teacher controls the discourse and manages the direction of inquiry . . . it is likely that we "create perpetual novices, students who have yet to experience the task of designing and implementing genuine discourse strategies around problems that they have played a role in framing" (p. 553).

> Fielding and Pearson (1994) suggest that we should attempt to change the pattern of discussion in classroom talk about reading "to allow more student input and control" and "to accept personal interpretations and reactions" (p. 66).

> As we move away from teacher directed discussion toward an exploration by multiple voices, we create what James Moffett (1968) describes as a cognitive collaboration:
>> A conversation is verbal collaboration. Each party borrows words and phrases and structures from the other, recombines them, adds to them, and elaborates them. Inseparable from this verbal collaboration is the accompanying cognitive collaboration. A conversation is dialogical—a meeting and fusion of minds even if speakers disagree. (p. 73)

In order to foster true discussion in classrooms, we must transform teacher-student interaction patterns. The transformation of our discussions in this classroom begins with the creation and maintenance of a literacy community that nurtures both the group and the individual, continues as the voices of individuals are coaxed into being, and further evolves as students are then invited to contribute to the formative ideas of discussion through the construction of questions, comments, and observations about text. Yet, even as we move through this cycle, our attempts to enter into transformative discussion of literature may be impeded by a lack of understanding about how to proceed or even a fear that others will not listen to us or acknowledge that we have something to say. As we attempt to enter into true discussion, we experience a complex range of emotions. Nettie's response to discussion exemplifies this complexity. Nettie, who forcefully declares that people think differently and that "there is no right or wrong answer," also shares with me her fear that she may not be allowed to speak:

> You know how everybody is gathered up at the front and people are just talking and you're like waiting for that pause, for you to get in, but they just keep talking and you say, you know... and you're just like sitting there waiting. Nobody sees you, they're just looking straight over you. That's how I felt sometimes.

At this point in the chapter, it may be helpful to note some of the features of our initial conversations attending to aspects that serve to impede or to promote our entrance into true discussion. The following section includes excerpts from a representative conversation about our reading of *Journey* (MacLachlan, 1991), descriptions of the students' decisions about conducting conversations about literature, and excerpts from my journal. The combination of these elements provides a representative view of our initial experience in conversations about literature.

OPENING CONVERSATIONS

We gather on the floor silently. The tape recorder in the center of our circle clicks on and calls to mind images of ancient civilizations assembled around campfires to tell the stories of their culture. Stories which will be retold, altered, and pondered. We are not here today to tell stories. Rather, the members of this 7th grade reading class are here to engage in a dialogue based upon the questions, comments, and observations that have occurred to us as we read a common text.

And so, I find myself seated on the floor, looking at a sea of expectant faces ready to engage in a discussion of *Journey* (MacLachlan, 1991), ready to exchange ideas and opinions about topics which may not have easy answers. Taking a deep breath, I begin:

Van Horn: Wherever you want to begin...

                Pause...

Sue: Can we read our own questions?

The Power of Talk

> Van Horn: It doesn't have to be number one, if you want to just scan through the questions and pick some things you want to talk about.
>
> Go ahead, it's your group.
>
> Pause . . .
>
> Tanya: It's our group. Well . . .
>
> Pause . . .
>
> Janice: Well, how about we start?
>
> Pause . . .

As I wait for the students to begin my mind journeys to a consideration of the potentialities within discussion. My plan is to enter into conversations about literature with my students—conversations that will be based upon the questions, comments, and observations the students have recorded during the whole class reading of a text. I expect that other issues will arise as we talk, but the written responses of the students will provide an entrée into discussion and a reference point during the discussion. It is my intention to be a participant in a collaborative role with my students during the discussions. I hope to provide an opportunity for my students to engage in naturalistic, evolving conversations about literature or, as suggested by Smith (1981), to provide the students with demonstrations of how we might talk about literature within the meaningful context of an actual conversation. In order to do this, I will attempt to background my position as a teacher who leads the class and manages the discussion in favor of a position in which I encourage the students to make decisions, to lead, and to manage the discussion. Included in this process will be opportunities for myself and the students to talk about the content and process of our discussions and, thus, to examine the impact of our talk as well as the decisions we make about talk.

L. S. Vygotsky (in Cole, et al., 1978) emphasizes the role of language and dialogue in mediated cognitive growth, comparing these elements to tools which give rise to new mental structures. According to Vygotsky (in Dixon-Krauss, 1996), higher order thinking occurs when learners consider new ideas as they relate to their own prior knowledge, thus constructing new knowledge. He states that this development or cognitive growth occurs during social interaction as learners verbalize their thoughts, seeking the reaction and response of others. Vygotsky further clarifies the theory and relates it to the discussion of literature, stating that "this strategy enables students to represent language in the form of a tool to be used, in a public manner, to solve the problem of understanding these texts and their inherent themes" (p. 121).

Short, Kaufman, Kaser, Kahn, and Crawford (1999) suggest that "Students also need opportunities to reflect on the content and process of their group discussions" (p. 384).

According to Shor and Freire (1987), "Dialogue seals the act of knowing, which is never individual, even though it has its individual dimension" (p. 3, 4).

The recorder continues to whir on through the silence, ready to capture our voices as we verbalize our thoughts, seek the response of others, and develop our understanding of the text. Reality confronts me as I meet with each group of students and encounter similar hesitation about how to proceed. The floor beneath me grows harder and harder as I try to resist directing the students in the art of conversation. One group devises a complex system in which one student wields a yardstick, authoritatively pointing to the next topic on the question, comment, observation sheet as another caps and recaps a red marker, efficiently checking off the topics which "we're finished doing." In another class, the students decide to raise their hands when they have something to say. The manner in which the hand is raised signals to the student appointed director who should be called upon. One finger signals that the speaker wishes to address the current line of talk. Two fingers indicate that the speaker wishes to change the course of the discussion by introducing a new idea. It occurs to me that the students are replicating what they consider to be critical features of classroom discussion, reenacting former discussions in which a teacher has asked the questions and called upon students to answer the questions. The process feels more like a rapid-fire check for understanding than a conversation. Excerpts from my journal reflect some of the issues we are confronting as we attempt to engage in conversations about literature:

September 3
Second period didn't get off to a very good start today. When we had a discussion about the book, the students seemed unfocused and made off-task remarks. They seemed to want to keep reading even though they didn't have an understanding of what was going on in the story. I felt as if I was losing my patience when I told them I would rather have us read fewer pages and really understand the meaning of what we were reading. Randy said it was a

The Power of Talk

stupid story and that nothing happened. Someone else tentatively agreed with him. I tried to explain that it wouldn't seem as if anything was happening if we didn't understand what we were reading.

September 5

I noticed that the time we spent looking at the cover of the book and making predictions has made a difference in the students' discussions. I saw Kendra and Don looking at the cover of the book and whispering to each other, "That's Grandpa." Later Brian said, "When we read about the photograph taken when the airplane flew over—there's the photo on the cover of the book." Jim referred to a line in the text where the author writes that there was mildew on the books and Jody responded to him, asking "Why is there mildew on the books, cause they haven't read any books?" Interesting connection.

September 7

Some of my students' experiences remind of what I am reading in Spradley's book on participant observation and an experience I had over the weekend. I went to Castroville to participate in the baptism of my new niece, Kristine. Jerry and I are her godparents. The baptism was held in a small Catholic church. Castroville is a small, historical town. Julie, my sister-in-law comes from a large, close knit family. She has a sister and two brothers. Her sister had a baby several months before and one of her brother's wives is now pregnant. Each family has at least two children, if not more. So different from my family. I found myself standing in church watching the others to see what to do during the ceremony. The priest had given us little booklets so we could read along. Later, in the kitchen when everyone was preparing the lunch, I again felt myself watching everyone to see what I should be doing and how I should behave. I can see my students doing this too. They watch me and each other to see what is expected. When they try something new, or join the group, I always to note that in a public or private way. I think it is sometimes scary for them to be "out on their own" the way you are when you talk about books. We watch and we learn from one another.

September 8
Today was a stupendous day. I really need the transcripts of the discussions to talk in detail about what happened, but I will try to recreate the feeling. In sixth period we sat in a tight circle around the recorder. What an experience. I reminded the students that I wanted them to try to respond to one another rather than to me, watching what I said or did during the discussion. They went for it in a big way, even so much as to say things like, "Way to go Jordie!" when one of them made a good point. I like that. When we paused for a moment I had to tell them what I was thinking. I spoke briefly about how when we were reading I really didn't know the details of their thinking about the book, but when they spoke out aloud and enlarged upon their written responses I could see things about the book that I hadn't seen before.

September 10
Randy made fun of Bart's spelling on the question, comment, observation sheet. I said it was the thought that counted here. A few minutes later when we were discussing what we had read, Carl read one of Bart's questions aloud and said that we should discuss it, that it was a good question. I like that Carl did that. He wanted to make sure that Bart wasn't hurt. As he and Randy are friends, I was somewhat surprised by his reaction.

As I reflect on these excerpts from my journal I begin to note the students' emerging concepts about our discussions. As we talk and as we talk about the process of talk, the students come to a realization that our conversations help us to develop understanding and to make meaning of what we are reading. We may even come to appreciate a particular type of literature as we talk about how it is different from other things we have read or our perceptions about what makes it unique. My own demonstration of ways to make predictions and to think further about literature is taken up by the students as they note places or events in the text which are reflected on the cover of the novel. As the students begin to note the details in the text they may use this awareness to introduce new ideas or to support their thinking during our conversations.

We continue to watch one another to see how to "do" conversations about literature. During our discussions I demonstrate aspects of conversation such as looking at the person who is talking and responding to what has been said. When we talk about the process, I may explicitly reference these aspects of talk. The students also refer to the content and process of our discussions during these debriefing sessions. After a long session of unelaborated question and response, Katrina sighs with exasperation, saying, "Our discussion was boring!" When others agree, I ask why they think it was so. Anthony exclaims vehemently, "All we did was read the questions and answer them." David evaluates the questions, comments, and observations on which the discussion was founded, saying, "The stuff we wrote is too easy. We know all that now; there's nothing to talk about." Jennifer suggests, "We need to write about things we would want to talk about, not just the stuff we know." Nan agrees and adds her ideas about how she envisions a discussion, "We need to stop and talk about things, not just say one answer and go on to the next thing. We need to go deeper and say what we really think."

Finally, the moment arrives when, in the words of Cathy, "We *must* discuss!" After a few hesitant remarks about how to begin, we fly into discourse which is punctuated by emphatic agreement, disagreement, exasperated sighs, revelations, and quiet reflection. The following is an excerpt taken from a transcript of a 45-minute discussion of *Journey* (MacLachlan, 1991):

Sue:	Are we going to go around in a circle so we don't interrupt each other?
Van Horn:	This class is very good at taking turns so I don't think you'll have to do that. Just sit for a minute and look at the questions. I think Cathy has got one. You don't have to raise your hand in this kind of thing.
Cathy:	Okay. Could taking pictures, could it be like a bad thing to do? Like, could it get you in trouble or hurt someone? 'Cause, I don't know where it was, but he asked umm. Could taking pictures be a harmful thing?
Van Horn:	What do you think? What do you think? Cathy, why could taking pictures be a harmful thing?
Cathy:	'Cause, I read in the book, I think it was in chapter 11 or

something that Grandfather took a picture of some kind of animal and that it came back and poked him on the arm. And he was talking to someone. I don't know who it was, and he showed that wound to them and then he asked this question, "Could it be harmful to take pictures?"

Jennifer: I think it is. Because, like say somebody like has a secret. Remember how he said the camera knew everything? And say somebody has a secret and it, the picture, kind of tells the secret, and it can be harmful to that person.

Katrina: Like up there (on the question sheets) it says, "I understand how Journey feels about Grandpa taking pictures of private moments." Like it's, like it's frustrating.

Nan: Yeah. And sometimes there's moments that you don't want the camera to know because they look too deep. Like Jennifer said, and that's not what... I think Journey's learning that there are certain times to take pictures for happy families—they aren't, and it's just not the time.

Sue: Like when Journey's upset or something and you know when his mom first left and Cat gave the camera away and his grandfather was taking pictures and he was upset about that because he was upset and he didn't want those moments to be captured. He didn't want to remember those moments. He probably wanted to remember the happy moments in his life.

Jennifer: I mean like people you know, nobody ever takes pictures ... everybody takes group pictures, everybody smiling. Nobody just, here you go, psssh.

Nan: But those are all fake pictures because everybody tries to put on a smile or something. I think the best kind of picture is when you just capture somebody. When they're not looking.

Katrina: I know. It's funner to look at pictures like that. Like last year I brought my camera. Like it was the last day of school and I was taking pictures of people and they didn't know it and I'd go, you know, "Mandy," and take a picture and they'd have some funny look on their face. Yeah.

Anthony: I think there are two classes of pictures. I think there are the pictures where the camera knows. The camera catches you—it can see through what other people can't see, and those are the real pictures that show the real you and those are the pictures that can sometimes make you feel like it's violating your privacy and that might harm you, but

The Power of Talk

and I think that the other pictures . . . and when Mrs. MacDougal said, um, where did I put it? "Sometimes the truth is hidden behind the picture."

I think what she would mean is when you pose. I mean in that picture it said she was smiling but her brother was pinching her like crazy and but she, but you would never have known it because the truth was hidden behind . . . I think those pictures are the ones where you can't really see anything because it's just a fake picture. It's just a picture.

Jennifer: Everyone just puts a face on, you know. You can't really tell what's happening.

Katrina: A "picture face." Cheese!

Anthony: And I hate that when they say pose or you gotta get in a group. I would rather just say, call your name and take a picture.

Katrina: Why do you think Grandfather likes to take pictures? It's because like it said in the book—how like um Grandmother has her cat . . . Grandma has her cat and um Journey keeps it all bottled up inside and Cat has a garden and that's like Grandpa's refuge.

Jennifer: Everybody has their own thing that they do.

Cathy: Why do you think Grandpa takes pictures?

Katrina: It's his refuge.

Jennifer: He's nosy and he wants to know other people's secrets.

David: He wants to replace the pictures Journey's mother tore up.

Sue: That's what I think.
Oooooh.

Jennifer: I like that one.

Katrina: Maybe that's what he's trying to do.

Jennifer: There's lots of hidden things in this book.

In looking at this excerpt from a transcript I can see instances of students relating the text to their own prior knowledge, verbalizing their thoughts, and seeking the reaction and response of others. They are using language as a tool in order to develop an understanding of the text and its inherent theme, concluding that there are different types of pictures and that some pictures might reveal things about ourselves that we do not want others to know. They believe Grandfather may take pictures as a refuge from his emotions or because he is nosy and wants to know other people's secrets. In a more literal interpretation, Grandfather takes pictures because he wants to replace the pictures Journey's mother has destroyed.

Just as there are "lots of hidden things in this book," there are "lots of hidden things" in this dialogue between students. As I examine this portion of the transcript, I begin to note the ways that students respond and interact with one another. Jennifer responds to Cathy's initial question about whether taking pictures could be harmful, first by answering Cathy and then, by referring to a statement in the text. She then elaborates with her own idea about how picture taking could be harmful in a psychological rather than a physical way. Katrina and Nan further extend Jennifer's comment. Katrina refers to a comment written on the question, comment, and observation sheets. Nan prefaces her remarks by agreeing with Nan and referring directly to Jennifer by name, saying, "Like Jennifer said." Sue then returns to events in the text and reviews what we know from our reading. She reinforces or supports Nan's statement, "I think Journey's learning that there are certain times to take pictures for happy families—they aren't, and it's just not the time," by looking for examples from the text. Jennifer, Nan, and Katrina then engage in an exchange that reflects their prior personal experiences and views on picture taking. As they complete the thought, Anthony has time to draw some conclusions about what has been said thus far. He explains what he feels is the difference between a picture which reveals our inner self and one in which we are performing a role. He, Jennifer, and Katrina then comment on his idea of "a fake picture." Katrina moves the conversation along when she introduces another question related to picture taking, "Why do you think Grandfather likes to take pictures?" She offers her own thoughts about why this might be—that taking pictures is "Grandpa's refuge." Jennifer and David offer other suggestions. When David says, "He wants to replace the pictures Journey's mother tore up," Sue agrees as others "oooh" in approval. This is followed by further affirmation from Jennifer and Katrina. Finally, Jennifer acknowledges both the text and the meaning emerging through their conversation of the text as she says, "There's lots of hidden things in this book."

As we engage in further discussions of other novels and related readings, the process of searching for meaning continues. I record and transcribe these discussions, looking at the transcripts in an effort to discern a method of examining both the meaning making and the power structures within student conversations about literature.

BALANCE OF POWER IN CONVERSATIONS

During interviews with the students, I asked them to look at transcripts of our conversations and to recall their feelings and thoughts during the interactions (for a sample, see appendix K). Their comments reflect an awareness of the power that exists during conversations of text. Interviews with the students help to clarify aspects of the culture of the social group and of the classroom that work to create a balance in which individuation (the power of the individual) and solidarity (the power of the group) work together, rather than in opposition.

For example, Burton talks about the importance of revealing ideas and how writing or stating thoughts about literature reflects an inherent need. He says, "I mean like people need to talk out and say what they like, you know, what they're thinking about. Even if people don't think it's good. I mean, it's just good they said it anyway. It doesn't matter what other people think, that's theirs." His words represent both a belief and a value system. According to Burton, we own our ideas—a fact which remains despite the reactions of others to what we say. The indication is that people should be respected no matter what they say. His claim reveals that individuation and solidarity coexist and achieve balance in the culture of this classroom because they are based upon an acceptance of differences, rather than an insistence on conformity.

Maria expands this thought as she reflects on her participation in the conversations, saying, "You let everybody like have their own opinion and stuff. And we don't have to take turns or anything. We all just sit in a circle and we all let out what we want to say. . . . cause this is the only class that we all like speak out and feel free." The statements of Burton and Maria and similar comments by other students reveal a belief that there is power in talk—a power derived from having a place where they can express their thoughts and ideas. I think of this in terms of a power expressed through permission, indicating that we begin to feel powerful when we are permitted or when we permit ourselves to express what we are thinking without censure. Burton explains this further, saying, "I don't like some classes 'cause you have to talk about . . . you just have to say what the answer is. You can't like say what you really think about anything, you know like whatever it is. Everybody can memorize an answer, but it takes like you gotta have at least a little bit of your own thoughts." He elaborates further on the idea of permission saying, "You could say whatever you want really because like everybody thinks so differently and we still try to evaluate whatever they're saying."

The statements of these students and others reveal that individuation and solidarity act in tandem within the culture of this classroom. We may disagree with what others say, but this disagreement will not negate the individual with whom we disagree. In further comments, Burton remarks on his internalization of the reactions of others to what he says during discussions of text, saying, "Maybe some other people will make good gestures about it and you'll feel a lot better about yourself." Over and over again, students refer to the confidence they derive from the supportive gestures, expressions, or remarks of myself and other members of the group. As I reflect on their comments, I can see that they derive the power to continue talking as well as the power to "exceed the limits" they have imposed on themselves when their statements are supported by others. In these exchanges, individuation is expressed and acknowledged by members of the group. These expressions of support and the feelings of solidarity which emerge indicate that the group may be empowered as individuals propose ideas which lead them to think further. I think of this as the power we feel when our thoughts and ideas are reinforced by the supportive actions or words of others—the power of self-exploration through self-expression in a supportive environment.

During my interview with Ted, I ask him about an exchange in which he tries to make a point and is ignored by the rest of the group. I ask, "So what are you thinking about as you keep trying to make this point and people just keep talking? It's a good point." He replies, "Well, yeah, but . . ." I ask him if he knows that it's a good point. In response to this question, Ted replies, "A little . . . " and then tells me that the tape recorder is making him "lose my mind." It is clear that he does not want to discuss his feelings at this point. Later in the interview, we talk about a time in which the group agrees with something he has said. I ask him "How does that make you feel when you say something and everybody agrees with you?" He says, "Well, great mainly, because half the class doesn't like me." He explains that he thinks of the other students in this class as the Socs and himself as a Greaser or an outsider. The revelations of Ted and other members of the group remind me of how important it is to be accepted. The power of acceptance, like other types of power may be used for constructive or destructive purposes. We add to or reinforce the power of others when we accept the thoughts they express. We subtract from or disassemble the power of others when we deny their thoughts.

Further in the process of the interview with Burton, I point to an exchange in which Burton uses the word "sucks" as he argues in support of his vision of Darry as a bad guy. When I ask Burton what he thought about using the word "sucks" in a class discussion, he responds in a manner which may reveal a tacit understanding held by the students, saying, "I mean like, not to be like, you can't water everything down, you know what I mean. You gotta tell it like it is, 'cause if you water things down people might not even get your point." When I ask Burton how he knew he could do that, he explains:

> See, if it's the appropriate time to say something inappropriate they'll (teachers) let you, you know what I mean. 'Cause they know you have to explain something, there's certain ways you have to explain it so other people will get your point. . . . I knew I would be able to say it. 'Cause I knew I had expressed my point. So I couldn't just say (in an effeminate voice) Well, Darry he's a bad guy, people wouldn't have felt it like I said it.

Anita too, talks about expressing her point of view even though it may differ from the views of others:

> *I know it's just a book, but it's kind of like when you read it you get really into it and it becomes real. And then when, when people talk about it I feel sad. I mean, I just want to say, no, don't talk about them (the Greasers) because it's not right. What if this was real? How would you feel if they were talking about you that way?*

She continues, saying, "If I wanted to say that I'd be afraid of how they'd react. Because I mean, they could all say something and then I'd feel hurt." I ask Anita if that has ever happened to her and she answers, "At home . . . so I feel like at school I can really say what I want to say and get my opinion out better." As I talk with Burton, Anita, and others in the group, I begin to see the power they derive as they resist the interpretations put forth by others. They seek opportunities to express their views or they initiate new ways of using language and new ways of thinking in the classroom. I think of this as the power to initiate or to exercise initiative in our conversations with others.

In other exchanges, students make connections to and/or build upon the statements of others. Anita tells me that she feels encouraged when she sees that other people are listening to her and making connections to what she is saying. She says, "Then I hear their thoughts and I, even when I think something's wrong, when they kind of change it around, and I might change my thoughts into another point of view and I'm 'oh yeah' . . . " In a later interview, Bet describes how she connects her comments to Anita's statements, saying, "I listen to what she says and then I respond. She then remarks upon the effect Anita's statements have upon her own thinking:

> *It just made me think about that. I mean it was just like, I don't know. This class is sort of like different because I mean you can tell . . . you can say something, and no one's like afraid to say anything.*

During the course of our conversations, students interact with one another in ways that allow them to rethink their initial interpretations. As they listen to one another, they consider alternate positions or ways of knowing. As students hear what others have to say and formulate a mental or verbal response, they have the opportunity to revise their original thinking. This is the power we have when we are enabled to adapt or adjust our thoughts—the power of revision.

The power of revision may be inhibited or blocked in several ways. We may inhibit revisions in thought when we, as teachers, direct discussion through a fast-paced question and response mode in which we attempt to engage a number of students as we call upon them to provide answers. Burton's comments about the difference between giving an answer and expressing your own thoughts indicate the reason that revision is inhibited in this mode. The implication for students engaged in this form of discussion seems to be that that they will provide an answer and wait passively until the next time they are called. There may be little opportunity for them to revise their thinking and respond further after hearing what others have to say or to express something and think further about it, considering what may be right or wrong about it. When discussions are directed by the students and when time is allowed for reflection, the students begin to think openly about the ways that their thoughts are revised as they interact with one another. Burton talks about the importance of being able to reconsider his initial thoughts:

> *If you never do it, you'll never know if it was going to be a good idea or a bad idea. If it's a bad idea, you could maybe change it and start thinking about other possibilities. . . . 'cause like in my mind I go through all the possibilities and that's kind of hard, 'cause you have to think about everything kind of like early, you know, until you find the best answer that you think, the best answer to you.*

Revisions in thought may also be inhibited or blocked due to a belief that there is a single correct interpretation of the text. Students who have internalized this belief may be searching for *the* correct answer which they believe is already known by the teacher. Through overt statements to the students, I have emphasized my belief that literature may be interpreted differently by different people as we consider the text through the lens of our own personal experiences and as we relate what we are reading to the knowledge that we already possess. The students' statements regarding the "right" of everyone to an opinion indicate that they are developing resistance to the idea that the text or the teacher provides a single correct interpretation.

During an interview with Sandy, I ask about an exchange in which she has made a connection between the text and her own life experiences. Sandy tells me, "When somebody will say something about their life time, you're like, 'Oh, I had something like that happen to me'. And it's just like once you see somebody talking about what happened in their life, you're like, 'Oh, we can talk about that?'" When I ask her why we talk about our personal lives, she answers, "We do that because it's just kind of like a trait. It's part of us." Further in the interview, Sandy tells me that talking about "personal stuff helps us understand more about that book." She tells me about a time that she was reading a book about a girl "becoming a woman" and how as she read she thought that "This girl was going through the same thing I am going to have to go through." She concludes, "And so, when it like starts to happen, I'm like thinking about that book and I don't get scared or whatever." Interviews with Bet and others corroborate Sandy's statements. Bet tells me that talking about a personal experience is "like, well, putting in what happens in real life compared to what's in the story . . . it makes it, it makes people understand better and understand the meaning." Burton examines the need for a feeling of security before making personal connections to the literature in public discussion, saying, "I mean because like in certain other classes, I ain't telling them nothing." The statements of these students and others reveal the importance of being able to talk about the connections we make between the text and our personal experiences. These students realize that making personal connections to literature is a natural process or, as Sandy says, "a trait, a part of us," but that the desire to do so does not necessarily result in action. We must be granted the power to personalize our interpretations as we read and, then, to further personalize as we talk about our experiences with others. As the students grow to value one another and to value the community they are creating, the power to personalize is foregrounded.

Within this group's culture, the balance of solidarity and individuation is possible because of underlying cultural themes: "We are a family who tolerates difference among ourselves." "We are a family, all of us are different, and this difference is understood and mutually appreciated." It is through our discourse and our reflection that the students and I have developed a place where our solidarity and our individuation are expressed, a place where we will succeed because it has become a place where we are free to assert the powers of being within ourselves. In order to address my perception of the needs of my students to formulate concepts about interaction and discussion of texts, I began by involving them in whole class discussions of literature—discussions which were based upon their comments, questions, and observations during the reading of the text. Through these lived experiences the students began to engage in naturalistic, evolving conversations about literature. Our discussions were transformative in that they revealed alternate ways of talking about text and of talking in the classroom. Rather than responding on call to teacher generated questions, these students became involved in the creation of their own frames and formats for conversation. As Jess describes it:

> I mean it's like, it's just kind of like nature. It just goes with the flow. Somebody might say something and it might start a whole conversation. And somebody might say one little word and it starts a whole new conversation. And I

think that's how we work.... we're just a bunch of conversations.

As these students accepted invitations to think and to talk about themselves, their literacy experiences, and their responses to literature, they began to exercise distinct and insightful voices. They spoke of freedom, of power, and of family. They devoted themselves to sustaining and expanding the freedom of individuals within the bonds of family. The voices of these children and of other children like them reveal much to us about the impact and the influence of our pedagogy. They may also open the door to further understanding of the meaning of empowerment and what can happen when social modes of power are equalized. Through the equalization of social modes of power, we may extinguish the silencing of others as we come to understand, respect, and honor the differences among ourselves.

It was my belief that we must develop a common ground or base of understanding about the discussion of literature before we could successfully engage in small group discussion. In the following section of this chapter, I will demonstrate and examine our transference of this experience to small group discussions.

Talking in Small Groups

The following is an excerpt from a small group discussion between several members of the representative class group. The discussion took place during our study of survival across time. This group is reading *I Have Lived a Thousand Years* (Bitton-Jackson, 1997), a memoir written by Livia Bitton-Jackson, a survivor of the Holocaust. Maria is out of the classroom on school business during this discussion. Carolina, Amy, and Bet are also in this group but do not speak during this exchange. Sue and Stacy are the remaining members of this group. We are sitting together at a small table near the front of the room. Each of us has our Reader/Writer log and a copy of the book. While we talk, the other students in the classroom are sitting in small groups, whispering to one another as they review information about the time period of the book they are reading and make plans for a response project.

Van Horn: Now everyone has read to a different place. So the way you've got to start when you meet in your book club is by figuring out which page is the highest number that you have all read to and then stick your finger in there and don't talk past that. So 23, we can talk up to 23?

Sue: Um Hmm. But we don't know what Maria has gotten to so...

Van Horn: So 23 for you guys and that's going to be the maximum. Hopefully, she's made it to there.

The Power of Talk

Sue: Well, she's gone the whole period so she . . .

Van Horn: Right, so she may not have . . . So why don't you go ahead and start.

Sue: What, like talk about what's in our journal things?

Van Horn: Sure. It's all right, it's all right. . . . Stacy you had an interesting comment . . .

Stacy: I'm too far ahead of them.

Sue: Go ahead and say it.

Van Horn: I don't think it will mess up the story.

Stacy: You want me to read that little section?

Van Horn: Um hmm. That's an interesting and exceptional way to begin Stacy, Good idea.

Stacy: It says, "All Jews are to be removed from the town and relocated in the ghetto in another town. . . . In five days every Jewish family must stand ready for deportation to the ghetto. Every Jewish family may take along to the ghetto personal possessions and one room of furniture. Everything else must be left behind exactly as is. Keys must be delivered to police headquarters prior to departure." I didn't know they used "ghetto" way back then.

Van Horn: And you were surprised about that weren't you. Here, I got you a dictionary. Why don't you read what it says in the dictionary.

Stacy: "A usually poor neighborhood in a city where the poor of the same race, religion, and ethnic background live."

That's not really how it is today.

All the races live in . . . .

Sue: Well, not really. In Houston there's ghetto. Like the fifth ward is a ghetto.

Stacy: I live in a ghetto. I live in the Camden Heights and everybody says that a ghetto and it's not really a ghetto, it's just the last three streets where mostly Mexicans and black people live.

Sue: Not just Mexicans and black people live in ghettos. White people live in ghettos too.

Stacy: I know but those last three streets of my neighborhood are like really, really ghetto.

Everybody thinks that Westfield City is so beautiful and everything, but . . .

Sue: Well, in some places it's really pretty, but in other places when you go deep down it's not too pretty.

Pause

Van Horn: Carolina, what were you going to tell them that you discovered about the book?

Sue: Say whatever you want.

Stacy: Well, I have something else to say. On page 17 . . . I want to know why the Hungarian military police came knocking on the doors or windows at 3:30 in the morning.

As we begin to talk in this small group, we must make some organizational decisions. This process is similar to that experienced in the large group discussions; although, here we must delineate the parameters of what can be talked about as we are reading independently rather than as a whole class. Once the group agrees on a stopping point, we can begin. At this point, Sue asks if we are going to talk about "what's in our journal things." She is referring to the questions, comments, and observations the students have written as they read on their own. I agree with Sue, supporting her suggestion.

My next comment is to Stacy. She is new to our class, and I want to encourage her and draw her into the discussion. Earlier in the day, Stacy had shown me a passage in the text describing the deportation of Jewish families to the ghetto. As Stacy reads the passage to the group, she is modeling a moment in which a reader returns to a particular point in the text, rereading in order to think further about what has been read. Her remark, "I didn't know they used 'ghetto' way back then," indicates that she has encountered this word in the text and then made connections to her own experience of the word. She needs to align her understanding of the word with that presented in the text.

At this point, I ask Stacy to refer to the dictionary. I want to provide an opportunity for Stacy to compare her personal understanding of the word, her understanding of the word in context, and the formal definition. After Stacy reads the definition, "A usually poor neighborhood in a city where the poor of the same race, religion, and ethnic background live," she expresses her doubts. When Stacy says, "That's not really how it is today," she indicates that her personal experience does not align with or reflect this definition.

Sue supports and makes a connection to Stacy's statement. She then builds upon it, referencing what she considers to be an example of a ghetto. Stacy then makes a personal connection in which she argues against her impression that other people think her own neighborhood is a ghetto. The conclusion of her statement, "it's just the last three streets where mostly Mexicans and black people live," prompts a response from Sue, who disagrees emphatically. At this point, Sue and Stacy enter into a brief exchange in which they attempt to clarify their reasoning. It is interesting to note that much later, near the end of the discussion when I ask if anyone has anything they want to add, Stacy reintroduces this earlier topic of the ghetto. Again Sue will counter Stacy's comments in a way that suggests that she wants Stacy to stick to the facts even as she is making a personal connection to the literature.

Sue has come to think of herself as someone who can model the conventions of a fruitful conversation. During our interview Sue tells me:

> Sometimes I'm scared to say something 'cause someone will disagree with me, but usually I'll put in my two cents, 'cause you know everyone's gonna have their own opinions about what you say. It's like, well, you can have your own opinion, this is my opinion.

Later in the interview when I ask Sue about the role she plays in our classroom, she responds:

> I talk, but then I listen really well. I take in a lot of information of what people say and then I put my... if it's not important I usually won't say it, but usually I say what I want if it's important—at least I think it is...

Sue's earlier reflection that "white people live in ghettos too" is an example of something she felt was important to say to Stacy, a newcomer to our school and to our community.

The next excerpt is from a discussion between Burton, Jarod, and Jake regarding their reading of *I Am Regina* (Keehn, 1993), a fictionalized account of Regina Leininger's capture and adoption by the Allegheny Indians during the French and Indian War. Burton, Jarod, and Jake are sitting at the table at the front of the room, and I am working with another group.

Jarod:	Let's read some of your questions.
Burton:	Let's read some of Jake's questions.
Jarod:	I don't know why the Indians tried to burn her.
Blake:	The Indians tried to burn her because she was a . . .
Jarod:	Because she wouldn't shut up.
Burton:	Yeah, she tried to get away! She tried to get away, so they had to teach her a lesson. Now read some more of his questions.
Jarod:	Why did the lady help her.
Jake:	No, why did the lady help Sarah. Like, you know, the Indians were like beating them with axes and . . .
Burton:	Oh yeah. Well she was a nice lady, very nice Indian.

Jarod: Why did the Indians want Sarah to be an Indian?

Burton: Well, because that one dude's son had a dream of her being his wife.

Jarod: Oh yeah.

Burton: Read some more questions. . . . read some more questions.

Jarod: Um, let me see . . . Why did the Indians

Jake: Why did the Indians burn down the farm?

Burton: Well, I don't know why the Indians burnt down the farm. I think because they hated the White people so much because the White people were taking over their land they just wanted to burn down their houses that they had put on their land. . . . they just wanted to get rid of them.

Jarod: Yeah, how could you go trade with a white man and you can't even speak their language?

Jake: I know.

Burton: Yeah, back then, they were trying to like take advantage of them. They'd be like "we take your land, is that okay?" And they'd be like, "Yeah." They don't know what they're talking about.

Jarod: How you gonna trade with somebody when you can't even speak their language. I mean that's totally stupid.

Jake: Yeah, I know.

Burton: That's messed up, but they didn't know, they thought they were like good people, you know.

Jarod: Yeah, and I'm gonna go up to the store. I speak Spanish. And this costs $159.00 for a banana. "Okay, here's the money".

Burton: I know . . . I know.

Jarod: Sheesh!

This portion of the conversation begins with Jarod and Burton's decision to read Jake's questions. Jarod reads from Jake's Reader/Writer log, "I don't know why the Indians tried to burn her." They are referring to a threat to burn Regina's sister Sarah. Burton attempts to answer the question. Before he can complete his sentence, he is interrupted by Jarod who attempts to complete the thought. Burton supports and builds upon Jarod's comment in a rapid, perfunctory manner, saying, "Yeah, she tried to get away! She tried to get away, so they had to teach her a lesson." He then demands of Jarod, "Now read some more of his questions."

At this point Burton attempts to find something he wants to talk about. Burton has described himself as an interpreter whose role it is to "interpret everybody's opinion and then evaluate it and tell them my opinion." He also sees himself as someone who keeps others "on track." During my interview with Burton, he describes this as a rule, saying, "You can talk about it a little bit, how it relates, but then you get back on track. You can't just go totally off the subject on to the news and everything."

As the conversation continues, it appears that Burton reverts to a question and response mode while he hurries the group through the next exchange. Jarod starts to read Jake's next question and Jake enters the discussion, clarifying and elaborating as he says, "No, why did the lady help Sarah. Like, you know, the Indians were beating them with axes and . . ." Burton interrupts Jake again in an impatient manner, saying, "Oh yeah. Well she was a nice lady, very nice Indian." When Jarod follows with his own question, an attempt to connect and build upon Jake's earlier question, Burton answers him quickly and repeats his demand for more questions.

Jake again interrupts Jarod's reading of his (Jake's) question, asking, "Why did the Indians burn down the farm?" This opener is accepted by Burton, who then settles into the conversation, providing his interpretation for the others based upon his knowledge of American history. Burton suggests that the Indians "hated the white people so much because the white people were taking over their land." Jarod then connects and builds upon Burton's statement, suggesting that it may have been difficult for the two groups to communicate without a common language. Jake supports Jarod's comment, saying, "I know." Burton then connects to and builds upon Jarod's statement as he creates an imaginary scenario or interaction depicting a possible miscommunication between the two groups.

Jarod appears to want further confirmation of his statement, from Burton in particular. He repeats his earlier remark in a slightly altered form, exclaiming, "How you gonna trade with somebody when you can't even speak their language," adding his assessment of the situation with the statement, "I mean that's totally stupid." Again, Jake supports Jarod, saying, "Yeah I know." Burton agrees and then provides a possible reason or interpretation of the feelings of the Indians. Jarod still appears to want affirmation from Burton. He takes up Burton's earlier mode of response and creates his own imaginary scenario in which he, because he speaks Spanish and not English, is charged and agrees to pay $159.00 for a banana. Through the replication of Burton's use of the imaginary scenario, Jarod finally receives affirmation from Burton who agrees, "I know, I know." At this, Jarod indicates his pleasure with a drawn out "Sheesh!"

Within this excerpt of conversation, the transference of patterns of interaction from the whole group to the small group are exemplified. I have suggested that Burton's enactment of a question and response mode indicates that he is searching for a topic he wants to discuss. This reenactment of a traditional pattern of classroom discussion may also be reflective of a period of adjustment, the same period of adjustment experienced within the early whole group discussions.

These final excerpts are from an exchange between John and Shawn who are reading *Nightjohn* (Paulsen, 1993). This is the story of Nightjohn, a slave who has escaped to freedom and who returns to teach reading to those still in captivity, and Sarny, a 12 year old girl who wants to learn. John and Shawn are sitting at the table at the front of the room with Dan, a visiting teacher from a nearby school district. These students are both vocal and enthusiastic participants in the classroom, and it was my belief that they would enjoy this opportunity to talk to someone from outside our literacy community about their reading.

Dan: Why do you think language and the ability to read is such a big deal in this setting of slavery?

John: Because with knowledge brings dreams and they want to keep . . . the masters and overseers want to keep the slaves and the black's spirit and dreams to minimal as possible and they think that if they have the knowledge to read they're going to want to do more and if they read about other people's dreams, other people's adventures that they're going to want to go out and have their own dreams and have freedom and that would be more trouble for them. I think John was brave to let them actually, to actually come back. He had freedom, he had it in his hand, he clutched it. And he, well to him it meant more to be able to give the blacks the privilege, the right and to the right that they had, that's owed to them the entire time to be able to read and write about these times. And he, he did something brave, he put others before himself. He could have just stayed back there and said, "tough, live it out, do what I did," but he came back.

Shawn: And I think also . . . what if you couldn't speak. What would they do about them? Because the blacks they didn't know how to read, write, they didn't know sign language wasn't probably even made up because you couldn't write. All they could do is hear. . . . they couldn't respond, you know. They couldn't say what they really felt. But if you know how to write and read, you would have more enjoyment because then you could write to people and tell them what you're feeling and what you think about each subject that you're talking about. You could write it down, and talk. You could write and the teacher will talk to you about it and then you could write something back on the paper.

As John and Shawn talk about the ability to read in the setting of *Nightjohn* (Paulsen, 1993), they not only express their interpretation of the meaning of the text but they also reveal their own beliefs about the power of literacy. For John, reading fosters knowledge and freedom which keep the spirit alive and nurtures our dreams. As John talks about Nightjohn's return to the plantation to teach the slaves to read and write, he uses the words "the privilege ... the right that they had, that's owed to them ... to be able to read and write ..." John expresses the belief that all of us have a right to learn to read and write; that this knowledge is "owed" to us.

Shawn elaborates upon John's ideas. His statement, "They couldn't say what they really felt," exemplifies his understanding that reading and writing are means by which we think about our feelings and convey them to others. Near the end of his statement, Shawn makes a connection between writing and talk, saying that "You could write it down and talk." For Shawn, reading, writing, and talking are of value because they are ways in which we communicate with one another. If reading, writing, and talking were denied to us, all we "could do is hear." In this next excerpt, John introduces his idea that the author's use of strong language in the text is effective because it reflects the reaction of the slaves to their treatment at the hands of others.

John: See later in this book. I don't want to spoil anything, but later in this book it has a bit of cursing, but it doesn't, in this case, it doesn't really seem wrong the way they're using it. It almost seems right, or, it almost seems right. It almost seems like it belongs there, you know. Because I mean, look what all they're doing to them. They're beating them and raping them and whipping them and tearing their flesh off, and I mean just cussin' about it. You know how usually if you hear somebody cuss, another person cussing, it seems wrong and you punish them for it.

Shawn then makes a connection and builds upon John's naming of the tortures to which the slaves were subjected through a return to an incident described in the text.

Shawn: I think, you know when that lady was hanging, when they had already whipped her and stuff. I think the thing that was going through her mind was that it was hurting, and then I bet she was sweating. And all that sweat would fall into those wounds. And it would hurt really bad, 'cause I know when I get cut it really hurts a lot. And she didn't have any flesh. 'Cause it was all badly whipped.

As Shawn talks, he predicts what might be going through the mind of the character and makes a personal connection to his own experiences with pain.

Dan: You guys have talked about two ways that the white slave masters controlled them. They tried to stop them from learning language and torturing them physically. Is there any other way that used to try to keep them down that maybe you noticed in the book or that you know from other things you've read or watched?

Dan supports the statements of the students, briefly reviewing the ideas they have proposed. He then suggests that these are ways to keep the slaves "down" and asks them to expand upon this concept. John mentally returns to the text and provides descriptions of a number of ways that the slaves were kept "down." In order to respond in this manner, John must draw upon his understanding of events which are depicted throughout the text he has read thus far. His response indicates that he is able to generalize his thinking about the text and then to apply this generalization to the concept proposed by Dan.

John: Well, they worked them so hard that they wouldn't have the energy to be able to, to be able to run away. They'd feed them in little troughs like they do pigs. They'd feed them cold food. They don't even let them worship God or have any religion for example. It said in here, that Mammy would put her head in a huge pot and that's where she would pray knowing what little she did about God because they would whip her until the flesh tore off if they caught her praying. And that's another way they would keep their spirits down. And the worst way is showing them what they would do to them. They would hang, they would hang the person on the spring wall for hours and hours until everybody had finished their work and then they would sit everybody down, have some person with a bunch of salt and they'd whip the person horribly and just make the people sit there and watch.

Dan: Like making an example of someone?

Dan supports John's remarks in this brief statement which gives a name, "making an example of someone," to John's last description of slaves being forced to watch as their fellow slaves were tortured. Shawn then connects and builds upon this idea of "example" as he creates an imaginary scenario of a failed escape attempt and the resultant death of a slave.

Shawn: Yeah. Yeah. I think that would you know, I think the reason they probably did it, but it's wrong, is 'cause you know if they ran away they would release the dogs and let them tear them up. And then take them back alive and let them die, and make the people watch them die and say this is what's gonna happen if you try to do that. So they won't do it, that'll scare them.

The Power of Talk

Shawn concludes that examples are used to scare the slaves and to stop them from trying to gain their freedom. After listening to Dan and Shawn, John comes to the conclusion that the harsh treatment of the slaves will only "fuel(ing) their anger, their passion to get away." He then invites Dan and Shawn to make a personal connection along with him as he talks about how anger fosters resistance.

John: The way I see it, when they whip the blacks and the slaves, they're not really hurting them. All they're really doing is fueling their anger, their passion to get away. So they were doing something that they thought would help them have the advantage. They thought well if I can beat them so hard and so brutally, so tremendously painful, then they won't run away. Well, that's wrong. All that's gonna do is make them madder. Have you ever had someone, you did something wrong, but you had somebody come up to you, you had somebody, like yell in your face and tell you that you're wrong. It only makes you angrier. Makes you want to do it again, harder. And, and, like, when they ran away, all it did when they were laying there is give them time to, they were either thinking of two things. How to get away faster and cleaner this time, or they want to die. Because for them it was either life or death.

Later in the conversation, Dan invites John and Shawn to make predictions about how the story will end.

Dan: You guys are about halfway to the end of the book. What do you think is going to happen in the end?

Shawn: I think she's gonna try to run away. That's what I think. I think she's gonna realize what the other people are thinking, reading, and hearing about those places where there's freedom and stuff. I think she's gonna try to run away. I think it will be kind of happy and kind of sad. Because I think she would run away and her mother, I think she will stay because that's all she knew is how to do that. You know she knew how to stay away from being whipped. She just minded her own business. And then here's her daughter, you know, it's gonna hurt her that she has to leave her mother just so that she can have freedom. And I think she thinks to herself I think I should have freedom, but if it's okay if my mom wants to stay, but I need to go because I can't take it anymore. Watching these people get like this. And then she would run away and I think she will talk about what kind of job and . . .

John: Here's a metaphor for it. To her it's like being locked inside a room, a chamber all your life, a dark dismal chamber where there is no hope, nothing else. Then all of the sudden, a light comes out, a window, her hope, her opportunity. She's gonna want to grab, she's gonna want to go for it, grab that light and chase it until it's hers, no matter what the cost is. Then she'll have a hopefully better life.

As they talk about the book, Shawn and John reveal their own feelings abut the value of freedom. For these students, a lack of freedom suggests a state which cannot be born, "a dark, dismal chamber where there is no hope." As John talks about what he hopes will be a better life for Sarny, he returns to his original consideration of the meaning of literacy.

John: Life wouldn't really seem like life without reading or writing. It seems more like a necessity. Something owed to you that you should be able to read. Life without reading or writing, the only thing you know is by word. So if somebody forgets, if somebody forgets, if somebody was told the proclamation of the world and they forget a part, they forget something, I mean how is anybody going to know. They don't have it written down on paper. All they have is their mind. So they have to sharpen their minds. And they have to be able to remember everything. Remember everything. They're under tremendous pressure to be able to perform. To be able to get out there in the field and do their work or clean the house and do everything right, 'cause I mean I'd be scared too. If you didn't do the right thing, you'd have somebody hanging over your head with a whip.

As John speaks, he makes a connection between life and literacy. Literacy for John is "something owed to you," "a necessity." John has spoken to me many times about the pressure he feels to perform in school. For John, who is a strong reader and writer, this pressure is for the most part self-imposed. For other students, this may not be the case. There may be times when our students do feel they are under tremendous pressure to perform. There may be times in which they perceive the school experience metaphorically or, to paraphrase John, when they experience school as something hanging over them with a whip. Our conversations about literature provide us with a voice, a way of expressing what we understand and what we feel about what we read. This voice may be exemplified through our solidarity or through our individuation. Together, as we talk, we may find the answers to our wonderings. Curt tells me that talking is different from writing answers on a worksheet:

> *With the worksheets you don't get to work together and hear other people's opinions and stuff, so you think that your opinion is the world and if it's not right, then nothing's right. If other people join in, then it's like they're all one. It's all one. It's all one.... and it's not the end of the world if your opinion isn't right.*

Our conversations may alleviate feelings of aloneness and further bind us as a group who is "all one." Amy describes our participation in conversations about literature or coming to voice as a learning experience. As she talks about the students in her class group, she tells me,

> *There are people in this class who like to talk and there are other people that are more quiet. But then, that's a mix. Everybody will talk, will just, you know, not just one person... they learned, and then they were able to do it themselves.*

Over the summer I receive a poem in the mail from Jolene, a former student. As Jolene writes about her struggle as a young Latina woman, she illustrates what it means to feel that she has found a place where her voice can be heard:

> It is a struggle to fight for one voice to be heard....
>
> You fight and fight until you are heard....
>
> You come, risking your life just to be free.
>
> Finding a place where you are guaranteed you will succeed.

Evaluation/Assessment

I have approached the evaluation of our conversations in a number of ways. When we talk about literature in our classroom, I make audio recordings of the conversations. This allows me to return to the moment and reflect/analyze our processes in the same way that I have described in this chapter.

When students are engaged in small group discussions of books, I move from group to group, listening, facilitating, and taking notes about what I am hearing. These notes help me think about the content and nature of their conversations. At the end of each class period, we come together as a class to share our discussions. Using excerpts from my notes about their conversations, I can provide the students with specific examples of their meaning making. I can help them to see when they are activating prior knowledge, returning to the text to clarify a misunderstanding or to find evidence for a point they are making, making connections to what others have said, referring to other texts, relating the events or emotions portrayed in the text to personal experience, and so forth.

At times, I have had each small group record their conversation and write a brief summary to go along with the tape. (Our school library has a number of tape recorders available for check out.) I then listen to the tape and record my own comments and suggestions at the end of their discussion. At the beginning of their next meeting, the students listen to my comments and then continue their conversation. As you might imagine, in middle school where we may have as many as 150 students engaged in 30 different book discussions, this method can be overwhelming. With this in mind, I generally use this procedure for our first small group discussion or when I have students who need more intense facilitation and feedback. At other times during the year, I may have one or two groups per class period taping while other groups work on response projects.

While the students do not receive a separate grade for engaging in conversations about literature, their participation is reflected on the Meeting Objectives checklist (see appendix B) and through the response activities in which we engage. Talk is a means of response that refines and enriches understanding. This understanding is then applied to and reflected through other response modes. I consider these tapes of whole class and small group conversations about literature to be artifacts of my students' developing literacy. Though I have not yet done so, I would like to see tapes of small group discussions of literature included in the students' portfolios.

Summary

As I reflect upon this examination of my students discussions of literature, I find myself returning again and again to my conversation with Nettie. Her statements that she does not "really think that there is a wrong and a right answer, because people think of the story differently," and "if reading was that easy people wouldn't go anywhere," represent understandings about the critical transformations that may occur when students engage in authentic conversations about their reading. As I have stated, it is my belief that the transformation of our discussions in this classroom is a part of a cycle which begins with the creation and maintenance of a literacy community in which both solidarity (the power of the group) and individuation (the power of the individual) are nurtured; continues as the voices of individuals are coaxed into being; and further evolves as students are then invited to contribute to the formative ideas of discussion through the construction of questions, comments, and observations about texts. As we move within this cycle and attempt to engage in whole class or small group discussions, we are confronted with a need to establish an understanding about how we will proceed and possible fears that we may not be listened to or acknowledged by others.

The Power of Talk

A conversation is an embodiment of a communicative action—an event or situation in which participants draw upon a common-life world and in which they seek agreement or further understanding through rational expressions and references to this common lifeworld. Action may be demonstrated through the consensus that is achieved. In this setting, action may also be represented in exchanges that conclude with a need to seek further information. I might also suggest that action is implied when these students realize that they cannot agree upon an interpretation and know that they must look further for possible reasons or explanations for their differences.

It has been suggested that the traditional, and perhaps more frequently used, mode of classroom discussion forms a pattern in which the teacher initiates a topic and then calls for and evaluates a student response. As I have noted, this pattern of discussion can function to discourage diverse views and/or shape predetermined answers. This pattern may, in effect, contribute to a silencing of student voices through what might be interpreted as a teacher controlled simulation of a true discussion.

Our conversations may be viewed as representative of ideas about the power of the individual and the group which have emerged in this literacy community. Students are individuated when they express unique thoughts or interpretations which may or may not counter the ideas reflected by others in the group or when they make statements that resist the implications set forth in the text. Solidarity is expressed through comments that make connections to the themes developed by the group and reference the ongoing nature of the interpretation. As the students reflect on the transcripts of our conversations about literature, their comments suggest a further typology—that of the power represented in the exchanges within the conversation. I have described this power in terms of permission, self-exploration through self-expression in a supportive environment, acceptance, initiation, revision, and personalization. This typology is summarized as follows:

Type of Power	Description
Permission	We are permitted or we permit ourselves to express what we are thinking without censure.
Self-exploration through self-expression in a supportive environment	Our thoughts and ideas are reinforced by the supportive actions or words of others.
Acceptance	We add to or reinforce the power of others when we accept the thoughts they express. We subtract from or disassemble the power of others when we deny their thoughts.
Initiation	The power to initiate or to exercise initiative in our conversations with others.

cont.

Revision	We are enabled to adapt or adjust our thoughts.
Personalization	We have the power to personalize our interpretations as we read and then to further personalize as we talk about our experiences with others.

As the students and I enter into small group discussions of our readings, we find that we transfer and adapt the need to organize our process. As the students talk in small groups, they add to or further embellish their conversations. For example, Sue admonishes Stacy to ensure that her sharing of personal experiences remains based in fact. Burton and Jarod create imaginary scenarios to help them convey possible meanings to others. And finally, through John, Shawn, and Jolene, we learn that literacy is a power which should never be withheld, a power which is "owed" to us, and a power which is worth fighting for.

Chapter 5 will provide a picture of our exploration of dramatic readings and performance as a means of self-expression, meaning making, and empowerment. Each of us plays a part as we work together to incorporate performance of stories, studies of characters, choral readings of poetry written by ourselves and others, and the production of plays in to our classroom experiences. We discover again that learning and making meaning of our experiences works best when we listen to and build upon the ideas of others.

5

Living the Meanings Through Performance

Developing Ideas About Performance

The part that I played in Macbeth was the "witch number one." I liked playing this part because it allows you to be able to act wicked. At first I thought I couldn't do that part of a witch, like the voices and the mean looking faces and I really just didn't think I had it in me. And I also thought that if I act like a witch people would look at me funny, so I thought I was saving myself the trouble of being laughed at. But then I saw everybody getting into it. I thought, "Hey, they look just as funny as I would acting like a witch," so I thought, "Let's be funny together." I thought I was pretty successful at my voice. I made it crackle like a witch and I kind of put expression into it. I really enjoyed that part because it's not everyday you walk around school saying, "When shall we three meet again, in thunder, lightning, or in rain?" in a witch's voice. I would change the parts of me just standing there. I would not just stand still. I would walk around and say what I have to say as if this were in real life.... What makes a play good is if you can base it with reality, reality is kind of a helping point. You could be rehearsing and then say, "Wait a minute, I would be more dramatic in reality." I would make it to where I could get my point across and that would make the scene better, just by doing a reality check.

Kesha

Reading what Kesha has written about playing one of the three witches in our production of *Macbeth* returns me to this moment in our lives together. As I look closely at several of her statements, I begin to think further about the implications of being invited to participate in dramatic readings or performances for Kesha and for other students. Kesha begins, writing that "At first I thought I couldn't do that part of a witch, like the voices and the mean looking faces and I really just didn't think I had it in me." This statement reflects Kesha's discomfort in being asked to pretend to be another, to act out the words and feelings of someone else. Her words, "I really just didn't think I had it in me," reveal her concern that she may not be able to do what she feels is necessary in order to succeed in this role. Kesha alludes to her feeling that school can be a place where we are sometimes asked to do things we may not have done before or things that we feel we cannot do . Kesha indicates her understanding that she has been asked to take on the personality and actions of a character, the witch, and that this character may or may not be like herself. Her use of the phrase, "At first," shows us that she considers what she will have to do to play the part of the witch and that, through this consideration, she is able to transform her initial reluctance and/or self-doubt into a strategy or plan of action. Kesha's strategy is to "base it with reality (because) reality is kind of a helping point." In order to do this, she states that she will have to "walk around and say what I have to say as if this were in real life," and ". . . be rehearsing and then say, 'Wait a minute, I would be more dramatic in reality'."

Robert Probst (1988) writes of creative drama as a strategy for teaching literature. He acknowledges the importance of a level of comfort among the students as he reflects upon the potential of classroom dramatization in meaning making:

> It may take time for the class to grow comfortable with pantomime, improvisation, and role playing, depending on previous experience and how comfortable the students are with one another, but once used to the techniques, the students may find they provide insights into the literature that are inaccessible through other approaches. (p. 62)

The words of Kesha and other students in this classroom suggest that their perception of their ability to engage in dramatizing or performance is related to their sense of comfort and acceptance within the literacy community. Kesha writes that she had at first thought she would save herself "the trouble of being laughed at" by not acting like a witch. Her fear of being laughed at and her reluctance about playing the role of the witch

Living the Meanings Through Performance 167

are alleviated when she sees "everybody getting into it." Blanchard explains this, writing that "we were all ready and we knew that no one would make fun of us on how we played the part because that's not how our class acts." Lucinda expands upon the idea that we are able to perform when we feel secure within the community, writing, "I was successful because I could place myself in the person I was acting.... I was able to believe and live everything that Lady Macbeth was going through." As Lucinda reflects, we gain a sense of her realization that performance provides a further avenue of meaning making as we place ourselves in the position of others, believing and living what they are "going through." As she concludes her statement about performing in *Macbeth*, Lucinda writes that "Our class has many talented people that didn't know they were talented." Her words exemplify those of many of these students as they applaud their own efforts and those of their peers in this dramatization of the words of William Shakespeare. As you continue reading, you will see that it wasn't always like this in my classroom. You will see that we develop our understandings about performance and meaning making through performance in much the same way that we address other aspects of our literacy and our community—defining and reflecting on the elements of the process and engaging in experiences that move us from the simple to the complex.

Was It Always Like This?

I devoured the words of the authors Purves, Rogers, and Soter (1995) who write of drama as a means of engaging students in Rosenblatt's (1978) "lived through" experience. I mentally cheered as I read J. D. Wilhelm's (1997) conclusions that,

> Drama ... proved to be an effective technique for achieving entry into a textual world. Further, it provided a meaningful mode for moving around in that textual world, making meaning of it and in it, and of observing and reflecting on the world and its meaning. (p. 111)

J. D. Wilhelm (1997) later writes that the "mental model(s)" created through dramatization are "an activity that is almost completely neglected in classroom instruction and curriculum guides in reading, and yet every other kind of response and thought about reading depends on this." (pp. 144–145)

While I agreed with these authors and others that engaging students in dramatic activities could enhance meaning making, I was also beset with doubts about how to proceed and concerns about how my students would react to being asked to perform. To a degree, my concerns were a product of reflections about myself in middle school. As I have said to my students, "In middle school I was so self-conscious that I would hide wadded up papers in my pencil bag or purse rather than get up and walk to the front of the room to throw them in the trash can." My memory of performance in school centers on an experience in which I was required to give an oral report on my reading of Salinger's *Catcher in the Rye*. I was fascinated by the book and had labored night after night on the note cards I would refer to during my presentation. Midway during my performance I was interrupted by the teacher who cleared her throat, rolled her eyes, and said to me, "You need to read with more expression—we're falling asleep out here." Needless to say, I was mortified. Clutching my note cards tightly in sweaty palms, I continued doggedly onward until I could return to the safety of my seat.

Having alluded to the possibilities of meaning making and empowerment through performance, I must now return to the beginning and retrace our journey—a journey which might never have begun in earnest without the urging of my students and their efforts to renegotiate what I had originally conceived as an enlivened exercise in the summarization of *The Van Gogh Café* (Rylant, 1995). I have organized the following sections of this chapter in a way that will provide a view of our developing study of meaning making through performance over the course of several months. As you read, envision each experience as following and building upon the previous experience. You may want to refer to my sample of a course syllabus (appendix A) to help you see how all of these activities fit within the overall curriculum. Keep in mind that these experiences reflect general ways of addressing performance in studies of poetry, fiction, short stories, and plays. Any of them could be adapted to accompany alternate texts and/or genres.

CHORAL READING

At first I didn't know what to think, but I knew this class would be different when on the second day of school you were standing up in front, playing like you were a conductor with your yardstick as we read the poem "Journey" out loud. I'll never forget how we made train sounds at the end and said "It's a journey, it's a journey, it's a journey" over and over.

As I read the words Karina has written in her end of the year reflections, I am reminded of our choral readings, thinking about the ways that we orchestrated these performances of the works of others and of ourselves.

Living the Meanings Through Performance

These readings provided opportunities for us to perform within the safety of a small or large group, to blend our voice with those of others.

I often begin the year with a choral reading of "Journey" by Nikki Giovanni (1993). I think of this poem as an invitation, a preview of what is to come. Giovanni, writing in first person proposes that readers come along with her on a journey in which she will be a fellow traveler. To prepare the students for the reading, I make a transparency of the poem that I can project onto a screen so we can all see it at once. We begin by reading the words silently. After this silent reading, we talk together about the poem. We talk about Ra, who is named in the poem; and one of them says, "The sun god, remember we learned that in the 6th grade!" We talk about what Giovanni might mean with the words "autumn's exuberant quilt," deciding that the different colors of the leaves which have fallen from the trees might look like a quilt. I tell them that I sometimes think of this poem as a conversation we might be having early in the school year. Framing my statements around the phrases and ideas expressed by Giovanni, I tell my students that I will be their fellow passenger on a journey we will take together this year. I tell them that my past experiences have shown me that we will come to rough spots, times when it looks as if the road is washing out or as if we cannot find the answers to our questions. But we won't be afraid, we will continue trying. Together we will go on this journey of discovery and invention.

I then divide the room in half, instructing the students to read the lines of the next stanza in unison when I point to their side of the room. Our first efforts are somewhat ragged. After we have read through the poem several times, I suggest that we make a tape of our first choral reading together. At my suggestion, I can see them pulling themselves up, coming to attention. Their faces grow serious . . . this is a performance! It is at this point that suggestions on how to make it better erupt: "Jim's trying to be funny and read real slow." "Cal, you're reading too loud, no one can even hear the rest of us." "Hey, could we make train sounds at the end like we're really going somewhere?" "I think we should fade off at the end and make our voices real quiet. . . . we can say 'It's a journey,' over and over." When the taping is complete they want to listen to themselves again and again. We huddle around the recorder and they point to one another, alternately laughing at and congratulating themselves on their efforts. My announcement that it is time to break for lunch is greeted with groans and someone says, "Can't we just listen to it one more time?" "We'll do more of this," I promise, inwardly thrilled at their reaction.

THE VAN GOGH CAFÉ

As I noted earlier in the chapter, my efforts to involve the students in meaning making through performance began in earnest when I listened and responded to their enthusiasm and prompting. While I envisioned our response to *The Van Gogh Café* (Rylant, 1995) as a somewhat dry series of presentations of chapter summaries, my students convinced me otherwise. This is the way that it happened.

"What are you doing Mrs. Van Horn?" questions Brandi one morning in early fall as she encounters me in the hallway, feet soaked in dew, arms filled with flowery weeds ripped up from the ditch out beside the school. "Just getting ready for class!" I exclaim, somewhat mysteriously. Ignoring her puzzled looks, I rush into Room 157, closing the door behind me. I have only moments to finish the creation of a "café." I have borrowed a vinyl, red-checked table cloth from my friend Jeanne, combed my cassette collection for a tape of Lena Horne crooning the blues, and all that I have left to do is arrange these "flowers" in a chipped vase and place them on the table at the front of the room. As the bell rings I click on the tape player hidden under the table and stand back to admire the scene; this is *The Van Gogh Café!* (Rylant, 1995).

As the students burst into the room, the usual noise intensifies. Tom and Brady plop themselves down in two of the chairs beside the table, Tom stating authoritatively, "I'll have some fries, please." Kristi, wrinkles her nose and refers to the music playing, asking "What's that sound?" "That's the blues," responds Cal, as Lena sings that she "Ain't Got Nothin' But the Blues," and the last of the group, fully assembled, looks at me expectantly. I reach down under the table to click off the player and pick up my copy of *The Van Gogh Café* (Rylant, 1995).

I had recently discovered this book, a collection of tales about a café that had once been a theater, and could hardly wait to share it with my students. The first chapter sets the scene, and the students grow quiet as I read aloud:

> Magic is in the Van Gogh Café in Flowers, Kansas, and sometimes the magic wakes itself up, and people and animals and things notice it. They notice it and are affected by it and pretty soon word spreads that there is a café—the Van Gogh Café—that is wonderful, like a dream, like a mystery, like a painting, and you ought to go there, they will say, for you will never forget it. You will want to stay if you can. Some have for a while.
> (Rylant, 1995, pp. 2, 3)

As it is early in the year and we are just beginning to form ideas about our literacy community, I want this reading to prompt them to make a connection between the café in the book—a wonderful place where people gather, have memorable experiences, and want to stay for a while—to the possibilities for our own literacy community. As I finish reading this passage I tell them that I hope that our classroom, like the Van Gogh Café, will become a wonderful place they will never forget. There are nods of affirmation and shuffling as the students wait to hear what will come next.

Living the Meanings Through Performance 171

"Each chapter of this book tells a different story about something that happens in the Van Gogh Café," I begin. "I was thinking that we could divide up into groups. Each group could read a chapter together and then come up with a summary to let the rest of us who haven't read the chapter know what it is about." Briefly, we review what we know about summarization. I conclude by assigning chapters to the groups: "The Possum," "Lightning Strikes," Magic Muffins," "The Star," and "The Wayward Gull."

As the groups settle in to read, I move about the room listening to the words: "Suddenly a possum is hanging upside down in the tree outside the café window" (Rylant, 1995, p. 7). "Clara and Marc were both at the café when the lighting struck" (p. 13). "The woman drives away to New York, leaving behind two magic muffins on the counter of the Van Gogh Café" (p. 23). "The silent star seems pleased, quietly thrilled, to talk of his work with someone who understands so well" (p. 35). "So now it is February and there is a seagull living on the Van Gogh Café" (p. 40).

Time flies and before long the groups have finished the first reading of their chapters (each chapter is 8 to 10 pages in length). Discussion ensues: "Have you ever seen a possum? They look kind of like a big rat...." "I have a muffin pan at home and you can make muffins as little as this in it." "Lightning couldn't really make that happen...." "It's a magical place, remember?" As I meet with each group, listening and helping them decide what they will include in their summaries, the interruptions begin. Tammy, an emissary from the group reading "The Star" arrives at my side breathlessly. "Mrs. Van Horn, we were wondering if we could fold up pieces of paper and make them look like menus.... we could write 'The Van Gogh Café' on the outside and put our summary inside the menu. Then, when we're doing it we could pretend to be people in the café looking at the menus." "Sounds great," I reply, "Go for it!" Moments later, after hearing this exchange, another group sends a messenger. Sandy pulls on my sleeve to attract my attention, asking, "Can our group bring some coffee cups and pretend like we live in Flowers and we're in the café drinking coffee and talking about what's happening?" "So, you want to have a conversation together and through that give us your summary of the chapter you read together?" "Yes, can we?" "That's a neat idea, I can't wait to see what you do with it," I answer excitedly. As I sit back and survey the energy level in the room, it occurs to me that the answers to my questions about how to proceed with dramatic activities and how my students would feel about performance are forming through the responses of my students to this reading of *The Van Gogh Café* (Rylant, 1995). Before I have time to analyze what is happening, Matt comes to ask if his group can have the piece of poster board on the top of the cabinet to make a refrigerator. "We're doing 'The Magic Muffins,'" he informs me, "And we're thinking that we'll act it out.... Misty has a miniature muffin pan and she can make some and we can put them in foil and put them in and take them out of the refrigerator when stuff happens, just like they did in the book."

"Wow!" is my response to Matt. With the words "teachable moment" flashing in my mind, I pick up my harmonica and blow a few notes to signal a class conference. "Some of you have been sharing your ideas with me about what you would like to do," I begin. "I think it's important for everyone to hear your ideas, so could we take a few minutes to hear from each group?" As each group shares the excitement grows until the room seems to vibrate with voices. Frantically blowing the harmonica to get their attention, I suggest that we spend more time with this than I had originally planned so we can incorporate their ideas into the activity. Cheers greet this suggestion; and we spend the last few minutes of class planning what they will need in order to create menus, props, and costumes. We decide that we will devote the next session to construction and rehearsal and another to the actual performance of the book. That night, I write in my journal:

> This is truly a discovery process. They are discovering what it is they want to accomplish, how they will show what they know, and that they can negotiate the curriculum with me. I am discovering their creativity, how they will go about learning and doing, and that I don't have to have all of the answers. I'm also discovering that the best laid plans can be made better if we watch and listen to our students as they engage and disengage in the classroom. Through this planning of the dramatization of The Van Gogh Cafe we are doing what Purves, Rogers, and Soter (1995) suggest, giving ourselves "permission to talk to each other in new ways" (p. 115) and thinking about new ways to express ourselves!

On the morning of our first performances, I arrive early. Flicking on the light, I drop my bags on the floor and stand silently, smiling to myself as I take in the transformation of our classroom. A brown paper possum winks at me from the lower branches of a paper oak tree taped to our window. On the chalkboard behind the table is a "neon" sign with the words "The Van Gogh Café" written backwards as they would appear from inside the café. Red and white striped paper candy canes dot the upper edge of the blackboard. A yellow cardboard "refrigerator," door slightly ajar, stands behind the café table. The table itself contains the same chipped vase, now filled with flowers from the gardens of the students, and a neat row of assorted coffee mugs. The ringing morning bell, thundering feet, and slamming of lockers in the hallway outside jolt me from my reverie. Today is a day to celebrate.

As the students burst into the room, I sit down in a chair near the front, watching as they make their final plans for the performance. Cal suggests that we play some of the Lena Horne tape between the performance of each chapter while the next group is getting ready. The others enthusiastically agree. Kristin, holding out a cardboard "apron," moans that Sheila is absent and asks if I will play her part of the waitress in their performance of "The Star." We decide that we will begin with my reading of the first chapter and then proceed through the performance of each chapter as it appears in the book.

Sitting in a chair at the café table, I turn to page one and begin to read aloud the words, "The Van Gogh Café sits on Main Street in Flowers, Kansas, and the building it is in was once a theater, which may be the reason for its magic. . . ." (Rylant, 1995, p. 1). With these words read, I reach under the table and the first notes of "Stormy Weather" sound as the magic within these walls unfolds.

From my chair near the front of the room I can hardly believe what I am seeing. One chapter flows into another, broken only by the sounds of giggles and the notes of "I Can't Give You Anything But Love," "Mad About the Boy," and "As Long As I Live" which emanate from underneath the table. "Lightning Strikes" us all as Brady, playing Marc, reads the poetry he has written, "So still and blue waiting waiting it is a long silver night" (Rylant, 1995, p. 16). "Magic Muffins" multiply as Matt and Misty open and close the refrigerator door, dramatically revealing how the muffins have mended the children of Flowers. Cate, "The Star," takes us back to the days of silent silver screen stars in her cardboard top hat and white paper tuxedo shirt and bow tie. With a debonair mustache penciled in above her top lip, she is both gracious and wistful, bowing her head sadly as she shares a treasured photograph of an old friend. Tom becomes the "Wayward Gull" in white paper wings which reach to the floor as he pretends to settle onto the roof of the café in Kansas.

When the final words are said and the applause dies down, I return to the café table to read the final chapter, "The Writer." With this reading I will invite my students to create their own stories about a magical place somewhere in the world. But that is another story for another chapter. Talking together afterwards, we speak of how creating and watching the performance has made the book come to life and how enacting our interpretations has given us a chance to live inside the pages for a while. Not all of my students have dressed in costume and taken on the role of another. Some have been more comfortable being themselves and "visiting" the café, sitting at the table and talking about their impressions of the chapter. This, to me, represents another way of engaging in drama and performance—a positive step toward a full performance. Our first experience together in dramatizing and performing *The Van Gogh Café* (Rylant, 1995) has shown me that my students are ready and willing to explore drama and performance! As we celebrate, dining on Misty's muffins, we decide that we will look for other ways to include performance in our responses to reading.

CHARACTER INTERROGATION

Imagine that for a few moments we could "forget" ourselves and become someone else, someone who exists only on paper. When we invite our students to engage in improvisation based upon the reading of a text, we ask them to shed their own personalities for a few moments as they extemporaneously create or enact the persona of another. In writing of her own experience with improvisation in the classroom, Mary Mercer Krogness (1995) states that improvisation is a way for her students to "climb into the skin of the character" they are reading about (p. 141). Here, in our own classroom, while reading *The Outsiders* (Hinton, 1989), we have been engaged in a study of character, trying on the "voices" of others through writing. While we do this, we are continuing to develop our own questions, comments, and observations about text. As I think about creating a link between these experiences, I wonder what would happen if we could speak and act as characters? What would happen if we could "meet" the characters and question them about their motives and actions? Through the verbal enactment of character interrogation, my students may become further involved in questioning and reflecting on the motives and actions of the characters.

Along with our reading of the novel, we will read Robin Brancato's (1984) short story, "Fourth of July." Donald Gallo has written a prelude to this short story which previews the text and engages readers in establishing a purpose for reading:

> A former "friend" steals a substantial amount of money from you but never admits to it and never pays for his crime. Would you let bygones by bygones, or would you take advantage of a rare opportunity to get even? (p. 102)

Gallo invites us not only to read "Fourth of July," but to think about what we would do if we were the character Chuck. To imagine that we are a boy in high school and that it is night on the Fourth of July. As we prepare to close up the service station where we have a part time job, Jack pulls up and demands that his gas tank be filled. As Chuck, we remember the past when Jack has tortured us, teased us, and stolen from us. As Chuck, we must decide if we want to just pretend to pump gas into an empty gas can, knowing that Jack will later be stranded on the open road. Or, we might pull the firecracker out of our pocket and toss it into the back seat of Jack's car. Or, maybe we will forget about the money stolen from our bedroom and "let bygones be bygones" (Brancato, 1984, p. 102).

With this in mind, I decide to invite my students to continue in their search for ways to make meaning through performance. The next day, I pull Mark and Jody aside before they enter the room, asking them hurriedly if they will play the part of two characters we are going to read about today. They agree excitedly and we plan our course of action before

Living the Meanings Through Performance 175

we go inside. After the reading, I use our prearranged signal and Mark and Jody retire to the hallway to take on the personas of Chuck and Jack.

Inside the classroom I tell the others, "In a few minutes you will have a chance to talk to Chuck and Jack. They will be here to answer any questions you might have about what has happened." Jason puckers up his forehead, asking "They're not *really* going to come here, are they?" I suggest that they are and that their visit will provide us with an opportunity to interrogate or to question them. "We should get ready . . . each of us should write down four things we want to ask each of them," I add. As we write, Torrie whispers, "This is hard." "I know," I whisper back. I am writing questions myself. It helps me to write along with the students. I can think about what questions they might have, and I can gauge the amount of time we will need to get our questions down.

When we finish, the students begin to share what they have written for the interrogation. "I'm going to ask Chuck why he invited Jack to his house anyway after all the things Jack's done to him," Tammy remarks. Bill, looking over at her, adds, "I think we ought to find out more about Jack's car. . . . how much it cost and did his mother help him pay for it . . ." Torrie adds, "If it's the same amount as he stole from Chuck we might be able to prove that he did it." "No," argues Cal, "He could have just used that stolen money to pay for part of the car." There are other things we want to know. We want to ask Chuck: When was the last time you saw your money? What stopped you from throwing the firecracker in Jack's car? Do you think you've changed since you started going out with Katie? We want to ask Jack: Why are you always doing bad things to Chuck at school? You gave him a soap suds milk shake, forged his name on a nasty note to a girl, and cheated off his test and you call him a friend? Why did you go to Chuck's house that night? Did you know he had just been paid?

As the sharing dies down, the students begin to look anxiously toward the door. I too am improvising, as I pick up the receiver on the telephone and pretend to dial the number of the school secretary, telling her that she can now send our visitors to Room 157. When I hang up I hear a sharp intake of breath and Cathy exclaims, "Let's turn out the lights and shine a light in their eyes like a real interrogation!" Sandy agrees, "Yeah, I don't want them to be able to see who's asking them the questions either. They might come after us later."

There is some relief as "Chuck" and "Jack" enter the room and the students see that we are not *truly* being visited by these characters. Mark and Jody make their way across the semidarkened room to the two chairs we have placed in the "spotlight" of the overhead projector. As they introduce themselves, Cal pulls down the screen behind them and writes on the overhead projector above their heads, labeling Jody as "Chuck" and Mark as "Jack." The interrogation proceeds and accusations fly. Mark, as Jack, alternates between anger and defensiveness as he extends his hands in a plea for understanding. Jody, as Chuck, talks about how his relationship with

Katie has made him see things differently. He slumps in his seat looking repentant, as he tells us that he regrets pretending to fill Jack's gas tank and hopes that "Katie will forgive me when she finds out."

As the interrogations continue, the students in another group plead with me to let them put Jack on trial. I agree, and the students choose their roles. Laura will be the judge, Michael and Sarah will act as the lawyers for Steve and Tim who will play Chuck and Jack. Carrie will be the court reporter and Miguel, whose father is an officer of the court, will maintain order in the courtroom. The others will be the members of the jury. Later that day, Michael stops by for a visit between classes waving a sheet of notebook paper on which he has sketched a blueprint of Chuck's house. Below the elaborate floor plan which includes a tile floor in the kitchen, a washer and dryer, and "things hanging" in the washroom is a cut away view of Chuck's room. None of this is described in the text; Michael has envisioned it in order to help him make a point during tomorrow's trial. Above the drawing, he has made the following notes in reference to the suspicions of some of his classmates that Chuck may have invented the story about Jack stealing the money:

> Chuck couldn't of framed Jack! 1) You can't lay down someone's fingerprints without their fingers. 2) Jack's never been in his room until the money was stolen, so Chuck couldn't of placed his fingerprints. 3) There's only one way up the stairs from the kitchen. 4) Jack would of saw Chuck framing him.

The next day, Miguel comes to class early as I am setting up the judge's table and chairs for the witnesses and the court reporter. His hair is slicked back and gelled into place, his posture erect. "My dad and I talked about how I should do this," he confides to me. Moments later as he instructs the witnesses, Miguel informs them that "When we swear to tell the truth, the whole truth, you can't 'say so help me God' because we're not *really* telling the truth." I watch as Laura raps on the table calling for order in the court and listen as Carrie "types" the account of the trial on a sheet of notebook paper which when tapped upon sounds like the clacking of a typewriter. Michael, who has redrawn his blueprint on the overhead projector, is red faced as he argues excitedly that Chuck could never have framed Jack. Sarah tries valiantly to defend Jack, but her efforts are to no avail. In the end, the jury led by Marcus will come to a unanimous conclusion that Jack is guilty. Marcus, who has previously been a reluctant and distracted participant in the classroom, stands at the front of the room reading from his notes about the "evidence" and the "conclusion." As Marcus reviews the "evidence" he reads "Jack—he threatened Chuck. Proof that he stole the money. Fingerprints were found. He told three different stories. He knew how to get to Chuck's room. He is not telling the truth. He got caught in a lie. Chuck—he got threatened by Jack. His money got stolen. He found Jack's fingerprints. He was good friends with this man." Marcus looks up from his piece of paper and nods authoritatively to his classmates as he continues reading, "Conclusion—Jack stole the money because they had his fingerprints on Chuck's bureau. He knew how to get to the room, he threatened Jack, and we have proof that he stole the money. We the people of the jury find the defendant guilty for one count of robbery and one count of threats and lying under oath."

The drama of the courtroom recedes as we, hearing this verdict, break into spontaneous applause. Confusion abounds and Laura raps the table, shouting, "Order, order!" as the bell signaling the end of the period rings and other students, out in the hallway begin opening the door and asking "What's going on?"

That night, as I think about our experiences with character interrogation and the trial, it occurs to me that there were moments in which it seemed that we were no longer pretending. There were moments in which we had actually "climbed into the skin" (Krogness, 1995, p. 141) of the characters in the text and of those we had created in order to put these characters on trial. At one point during the trial, Steve had become so upset at Tim's testimony as Jack that Tim had stopped talking and asked worriedly, "Steve, you're not really mad at me, are you?"

> Dennis Sumara (1996) writes that: Telling stories, listening to them, and reading them (to oneself or to others) opens a window to other worlds, other persons, and other experiences. Interpreting the way in which our interactions with literary fictions alters our lived experience helps us to more deeply understand what it is like to exist relationally amid texts and among other readers. (p. 85)

New meanings may be constructed as we "enter" and "move about" in the context of the text, making it our own. Improvisation and performance are ways for us to tell stories as we enact and embellish our interactions with text. The students who played the parts of Chuck and Jack, those who conducted the interrogations, and those who participated in the trial have drawn on multiple texts—the short story itself, personal experiences, discussions with others, and their viewing of the proceedings of a lengthy trial on television—in order to tell these stories. The meanings constructed by the students go well beyond that which can be directly attributed to the original text. As I reflect upon this, I think about the ways our character interrogation or improvisation has prompted us to consider alternate meanings and outcomes.

> Robert Probst (1988) who has written of improvisation that:
>> If improvisations vary from the text, so much the better for this demonstrates that the poem is the result of the author's choices, and that other choices could have been made, revealing different values and ideas and resulting in different poems. Just as varying response statements yield discussion by showing alternative readings of a poem, so might varying improvisations reveal the alternatives from which the writer has selected. (p. 63)

Robin Brancato (1984), the author of "Fourth of July," did not elect to have Jack confess his guilt. In fact, Jack asks Chuck "How do you know one of your other friends didn't rip you off?" (p. 110). Chuck was not vindicated through Jack's trial. In fact, Chuck's letter to the judge went unanswered. Instead, Brancato writes that "The judge invited Sager (Jack) to court and slapped his hands, that's all" (p. 104). Through improvisation, interrogation, and the enactment of the trial, these students have revealed their own values and ideas. For them, justice is served only when those who are guilty are made to confess and to suffer punishment for their crimes. As these students construct and enact the poems they have created, it seems that they are indeed "revealing the alternatives from which the writer has selected" (Probst, 1988, p. 63). Through their performances, the students have entered the text world, questioned the characters, argued with the author, and extended the events portrayed in the text in order to form an imaginary epilogue through which they are able to reenvision and reconstruct the text to reflect their own desires. Or, as in Miguel's words, "We lived it!"

The Poetry Café

As we continue to read and talk about the characters in *The Outsiders* (Hinton, 1989), I search for ways to take us further in our understanding of the similarities and differences between Ponyboy, Dally, Bob, Cherry, and others. Ideas begin to take form one night as I flip through a magazine and come across an article about a Poetry Café in a Chicago night club. Images of tables stained with the imprints of wet glasses and rickety wooden chairs merge with those of budding poets reading aloud their latest works to an audience who listens and snaps their fingers appreciatively. I begin to make connections between the poetry café experience, our earlier choral readings of "Journey" (Giovanni, 1993), and thinking and writing about the contrasts between characters from *The Outsiders* (Hinton, 1989). Moments later, I am out of bed and riffling through the book shelf for my copy of *Joyful Noise: Poems for Two Voices* (Fleischman,

1988). My mind is whirling: choral reading, voices—two voices, voices of the characters, similarities and differences, compare and contrast, perform.

Compare and Contrast

The next morning, I begin by asking my students to think and talk about these people we have been reading about. Together we generate extensive lists of similarities and differences related to how the characters look, what they like to do, how they talk, how they interact with others, their hopes and dreams, and how they feel about life in general.

Character	Characteristics
Ponyboy	Has greenish gray eyes and light brown, almost red hair, squared off in the back
	Likes to read and watch movies by himself
	Wants to make the best of life since he has lost his parents
Johnny	Has big, black eyes; a dark, tanned face; and jet black hair combed to the side
Sodapop	Never gets drunk on alcohol, just on plain living
	Wants to make the best of life since he has lost his parents
Darry	Worries too much and is extremely up-tight
	Is rough without meaning to be
Johnny	Is shy, scared, and would kill if he had to
	Walks with a blade in his pocket and is never alone
Dally	Is dangerous, wild, and dirty talking
Two-Bit	Enjoys telling jokes and getting his two bits in
Cherry	Lives in a pampered world and has to make tough decisions
Sandy	Lives in a tough world and has to make tough decisions

Standing back, I survey our list and pose a question, "How could we show what we are learning about the similarities and differences in these characters?" Marcus attempts to stifle a groan, muttering the words, "Venn diagram." "Yes!" I answer excitedly. "We could take what we have here and construct a Venn diagram" or, I counter, "We might try another way."

"Let me show you what I mean," I begin, placing a copy of Fleischman's (1988) poem "Book Lice" (pp. 15–17) on the projector and turning off the lights. We read the poem together all the way through and then, during the second reading, we stop to talk about how the author has structured the poem. Fleischman begins by having each of the two book lice describe the place where he or she was born. This is different for each louse and, as such, the words of the stanzas are different. These stanzas are read individually. In the next stanza, the book lice describe where they now live. This is the same for both of them, so the phrase is repeated and read in unison by both lice.

"Could we use this poem as a model for our own writing about the characters from *The Outsiders*?" I ask. We decide to work in small groups. This will be important later, when I invite the students to pretend that we are in a poetry café and to perform a reading of their poems. "Let's see what you can come up with," I suggest, handing a transparency and marking pen to each group.

As the students write, they discover that they have to restructure Fleischman's format slightly to allow for a greater number of stanzas on a single transparency sheet. Heated discussions about what details to include and who has the best handwriting ensue. "Should we put this in quotation marks like they're talking?" asks Sandy. "Can we say Ponyboy is a pansy if we prove it with details from the book?" Burton wants to know. Maria suggests writing the letter "D" beside stanzas which reflect differences and the letter "S" beside those which reveal similarities to help organize their thinking. When I see that they have finished writing and are starting to share, reading excerpts to one another, I interrupt, describing the article I read about the poetry café in Chicago. "Let's do it," shouts Jake enthusiastically.

Performing Poetry

I give them a few minutes to practice while I get the room ready. Burton, Jake, and Jarod develop some moves to go along with their reading. Sandy, Bet, Ranita, and Gina try singing their poem and then decide they will divide up the parts and read them in pairs. Shelby announces that we "can't say these are poems for two voices because there are more than two of us in each group." My suggestion of "Poems for Two or More Voices" is approved. At last we are ready. I switch off the lights and turn on the overhead projector, our "spotlight."

One by one, the groups come to the front of the room, placing their transparencies on the projector so we can read along with them as they perform. Nettie, Maria, and Ted compare Darry and Two-Bit, writing:

I was voted boy of the year!
When I won I shedded a tear.

                                  I was voted most famous for shoplifting.
                                  I spend my days just drifting.

Living the Meanings Through Performance

We are both tall and muscular. Also very firm.	We are both tall and muscular. Also very firm.
	I love to smoke. Also make a funny joke.
I love the gym, That is why I stay so slim.	
We are both greasers and and very proud of it If you have a problem you will have to deal with it.	We are both greasers and very proud of it. If you have a problem you will have to deal with it.

Another group compares Sodapop and his dream horse, Mickey Mouse, writing:

I never crack a book, even when I am able.	
	A guy owns me and I live in his stable.
When we first saw each other we fell in love with one another.	When we first saw each other We fell in love with one another.
I like Mickey Mouse because I am horse crazy!	
	I love Soda so much that I come when he calls and I chew on his sleeve and collar.
We think we belong to each other because it was meant to be!	We think we belong to each other because it was meant to be!
My parents are dead and I live with my brothers!	
	I don't know who is my mother.
We love each other because we're always together.	We love each other because we're always together.

Later in the day, Liza, Carl, Danny, and Bert speculate about how Dally and Johnny have come to be the way they are, writing:

I rode in the rodeo, And for no reason rolled a drunk to get a ring.	
	I went to the park to find a football one day,

	and Socs came by and didn't want to play.
We gained nothing from this except trips to the emergency room.	We gained nothing from this except trips to the emergency room.
I'm scared of nothing, I have no fears. Johnny what are you scared of? Do you ever shed tears?	
	I was scared at a very young age. Inside of me is building fear and rage.
If you put us together we would be neutral, everything in the world would be balanced out.	If you put us together we would be neutral, everything in the world would be balanced out.

I spend the next few days watching my students as they poke and prod one another into performance. Suggestions for perfecting the readings are accepted or rejected without rancor. Giggles erupt as students take advantage of the dim light and café like atmosphere, twisting and shouting, gesturing and singing along with the words they have written. Each performance is celebrated with rhythmic snaps and taps as we in the audience signal our approval. At the end of the week, creating a little performance of my own, I snap my fingers and whisper to myself:

> Inspired by Fleischman
> we've gone beyond the Venn!
> Compare and contrast
> aren't a thing of the past.
> Model the form,
> We can perform!
> Poetry café
> has shown us the way!

THE RADIO PLAY

From behind the "curtain" (a paper quilt made of index cards tied together), Cal, as Herman, speaks in a solemn tone, saying, "I am sorry for my friend. Now I must go to the castle. I have taken on an awkward mission. I must present myself as an uninvited guest among enemies. I will ruin their spirits with news that will end their hopes of a happy marriage." Mike, as Narrator, breaks in, "Still, Herman was curious to meet Clarissa." Cal, as Herman, whispers to himself, "It will be an adventure" (Glenn, 1994, p. 23).

Living the Meanings Through Performance 183

We listen to the sound of horse hooves clopping on cobblestones as Esmerelda plays a few ominous notes on her cello and then swings into a short rendition of "Here Comes the Bride" while Mike announces a commercial break before Scene 3. A few minutes later, "The Specter Bridegroom" concludes and the applause erupts. Cara jumps from her seat and circles the room, collecting response notes from the "audience" to the performers in a construction paper envelope. "Well, excuse me!" Tod grumbles good naturedly as he jostles Cal in his haste to get behind the curtain and set up for the next radio play, "The Adventure of the Blue Carbuncle" (Glenn, 1994, pp. 4–11).

Today, Room 157 is no longer a classroom in a school. It is now a sound stage where actors are recreating the essence of the radio play, including sound effects and commercial breaks. As I listen to Tod and company deliver a commercial for "Calvin's Carbuncle Cleansing Foam," I think about how we have arrived at this moment, how we had begun this adventure.

Listening to Learn

I had purchased multiple copies of *Mystery in the Spotlight* (Scholastic, 1994) which features adaptations of mystery plays and stories. The book includes "The adventure of the Blue Carbuncle" (adaptation) based on a Sherlock Holmes mystery, "The Open Window" from a short story by SAKI, "The Specter Bridegroom" based on the story by Washington Irving, "The Monkey's Paw" adapted from the story by W. W. Jacobs, and an adaptation of H. G. Wells' "The Invisible Man." As I talked about my plan to have each book group read and produce a "radio" version of one of the plays in this collection, I tried to describe the experience of listening to a radio play. Jack interrupted me excitedly saying that he had a set of tapes of old radio plays at home that he would let me borrow. The next morning he arrived at school early, carrying a box of tapes carefully wrapped and tied in a plastic bag.

We spent some time in class that day listening to these tapes of old radio plays and jotting down lists of things we noticed, the elements we would include in our own productions. The students noticed that radio plays typically had an announcer who introduces the play and the scene breaks and who reads commercials advertising the products of the sponsors of the show. We also noted that music was used to begin the show and to signal scene breaks, commercials, and the conclusion of the show. Finally, we listed the sound effects we had heard: car doors slamming, motors running, rain falling, and paper rustling. We used our notes to create a rubric for our radio plays (see appendix L). Our rubric addresses the aspects we will include in our performance of radio plays: an introduction that, through its mysterious tone, captures the attention of the listeners and activates their expectations; dramatic reading that exemplifies the thoughts and feelings of the characters; sound effects that support the story and enable listeners to visualize the action; a commercial break which advertises a product related to the theme of the play; and finally, a conclusion that utilizes a piece of music, sound effect, or other device to extend the mood of the play. Through the design of the rubric we will ultimately use to evaluate the performances of the radio plays, the students and I have also created an outline of the steps we will work through as we ready ourselves for production.

Practicing and Further Planning

For the next few days I listened to a cacophony of voices as students read and reread the plays, working to get just the right tone and sense of drama into their readings. When I stopped to visit with one group about their plans, Jordy confided in me, saying "You know, I could be a lot more dramatic if I could read without the other kids looking at me." Trish agreed and explained further, "You know, Mrs. Van Horn, some of us are still kind of shy." "And then there are people we really like in here," she continued, raising her eyebrows for emphasis and glancing toward a group of boys in the far corner. "We wouldn't want to look dumb in front of them." "So what do you think we ought to do about it?" I asked. Jordy suggested excitedly, "Why don't we hang one of those paper quilts up in front of the room and we could get behind it and read the play!" With this suggestion the problem was solved and they could return to their reading. A few moments later, I glanced back at the group to see them laughing uproariously as Trish made a face and read in a deep growl.

As the week continued our room became a collection point for keyboards, a cello, a guitar and other instruments, compact disks and compact disk players, and an assortment of strange and varied objects which would be used to create the sound effects for our radio plays. Students began to call one another at night, trying out the sound effects over the telephone. I learned that a bag full of dry breakfast cereal makes a sound like leaves rustling and that a poster board held on one end and wiggled back and forth simulates the sound of thunder building. Whistles blew, keys clinked, doors slammed, coins jingled and clattered, and shoes slid and tapped on table tops as we perfected the sounds for our plays.

Commercial Break

With speaking parts rehearsed and sound effects in place, we turned our attention to the creation of commercials for the "sponsors" of our radio plays. We thought about the elements of familiar radio commercials and developed a planning sheet (see appendix M) which includes a name and description of the product and a slogan for the product. In addition, the students would identify potential buyers and describe why these buyers would need the product—what it would do for them. Finally, the commercial would tell listeners where the product might be purchased and conclude with a restatement of the name of the product and the slogan.

We decided that each group would create one commercial for their play and that the product advertised should, in some way, be related to the theme or subject of the play. For instance, a production of "The Open Window" might be sponsored by a glass company or a company who manufactures window cleaner and a production of "The Specter Bridegroom" might be sponsored by a dating service. With one exception, this thematic relationship between the product and the play proved helpful to the groups as they constructed their commercials. The exception involved a group producing "The Adventure of the Blue Carbuncle." Through their readings the students had surmised that a carbuncle was a precious stone. While brainstorming ideas about a sponsor and a product, Matt suggested that they look up the word "carbuncle" in the dictionary to see if they could create some kind of a play on words or a slogan based on the word itself. Confusion resulted when the consultation of the dictionary revealed that a carbuncle was not only a precious *red* stone but that it could also be "a painful local purulent inflammation of the skin and deeper tissues with multiple openings for the discharge of pus" or "a wicked zit" as concluded by Tod. The group decided to go with the second definition and produced a commercial for "Calvin's Carbuncle Cleansing Foam," a tribute to fashion designer Calvin Klein and a reference to the ever present possibility of a "wicked zit."

Connections

Jeff Wilhelm (1997) writes of drama as "a way of bringing the invisible secrets of engaged readers out into the open, where they could be observed and shared and tried on by other readers" (p. 85). One of the "secrets" of engaged readers is the development of the ability to "see" and to "hear" the words. Our production of radio plays enabled the students to think about, talk about, and perform the voices of characters and the sounds which might accompany their actions. Students who had not "heard" the voices or the sounds as they read now began to listen for these voices and sounds as they read other texts. They began to make the connections between the actions we had taken to make our radio plays come to life and what they could do to make their own private readings come to life. They began to think about and to "hear" the sounds of literature. As we continued in our efforts to weave performance into our experiences of literature, we found that performance could also help to unlock the meanings of words and ideas from long ago.

A Shakespearean Play

Double, double, toil and trouble; fire burn and cauldron bubble! Fillet of a fenny snake in the cauldron boil and bake. Eye of newt and toe of frog, wool of bat and tongue of dog."

The atmosphere in the room is charged with excitement as the students watch three bearded women drop their charms into a bubbling cauldron, calling forth a vision who will speak to Macbeth. As the vision rises slowly from the pot, holding a skull, I catch my breath.

The three women are not "secret, black and midnight hags," they are Jo, Melissa, and Dina. The bubbling cauldron is a plastic pot placed in front of a cardboard screen on which a paper fire rages. These are not Shakespearean actors, they are my 7th-grade students. In the last several weeks as they studied Shakespeare's *Macbeth*, they have become readers, thinkers, thespians, problem solvers, directors, and writers.

Why *Macbeth*?

As the students hurriedly remove the cauldron amid shrieks of "Where's my script!" and "Hey, can you help me tie on my sword?" I take a moment to reflect upon this experience. Scene 10 opens and the narrator speaks solemnly, "Back at his castle, Macbeth becomes more unstable." How did all this begin?

I knew that my students would be reading Shakespearean plays in high school, and I surmised that this would be of greater meaning to them if they came to the readings with some background knowledge and personal experience. I did not predict that my students would become so motivated that they would come early to school to work on sets and rehearse lines or that some of them would spend their evenings at the library researching the time period, viewing other productions of *Macbeth*, or creating costumes. Long before we concluded our study, many students were asking if we could do this again; and I was believing that I did indeed "lead a charmed life." But, I get ahead of myself. Let me begin at the beginning.

Setting the Stage

Our study of William Shakespeare and *Macbeth* began with a reading of Diane Stanley's (1992), *The Bard of Avon*. This is an excellent biography with a foreword describing how historians conduct their investigations and a postscript with interesting information about Shakespeare's use of language and expressions still in use today, such as "the game is up" and "fair play." The students were fascinated by Stanley's illustrations of the Globe Theater and her descriptions of the groundlings who paid only a penny to see the plays and were often quite rowdy. Using an article by Jeff Spencer (1994) which provides an eight-step method of leading students through the process of drawing, we created diagrams of the Globe Theater and learned more about theater in the days of Shakespeare. During a visit to the library, Mike made a copy of a diagram of the theater. He mounted it on tag board and constructed a free-standing model of the theater. Several others would do the same.

During our production, Annie as Macbeth intones, "Stars hide your fires. Let not light see my black and deep desires." She makes us feel Macbeth's inner turmoil as if it is our own. This might not have occurred had we not begun our study of *Macbeth* with an oral reading of a story version of the play (Garfield, 1985). As I read to my students I paced to and from, gesturing and grimacing, wrenching my hands, clutching my heart, and otherwise doing whatever was necessary to illustrate the drama of the words. My reading was interrupted frequently with questions and comments about the language used by Shakespeare's characters. When we came upon the lines later dramatized by Annie, we stopped to decide what was meant by the words, and Tim concluded that, "Macbeth's saying he's excited about what the witches told him and he wants to be king no matter what he has to do to get it. So, like, he should look innocent." Our analysis of these phrases led several students to remark that it would be fun to rewrite *Macbeth* using today's words and phrases. We did not read the actual text of Shakespeare's *Macbeth* in class as this is something the students will encounter in high school; however, some of the students did read it on their own.

Preparing for Production

Our next reading of *Macbeth* was a version of the play from Scholastic's (1994) *Shakespeare in the Spotlight*. This version of the play, the one that we would eventually produce, is 9 pages long and contains 14 scenes. There are parts for two narrators, three witches, Macbeth, Banquo, Duncan, Macduff, Lennox, Ross, Lady Macbeth, Malcolm, a murderer, a vision, a doctor, a handmaiden, and a scout. Banquo's son, Fleance, and the ghost are nonspeaking parts. Scholastic has retained the essence of the play in this abridged version, using many direct quotes from the original. The narrators clarify the action and explain character motivation with lines such as:

> Back at Macbeth's castle, Lady Macbeth gets a letter from her husband, telling her about his meeting with the witches and his new title. Alone, she paces her room. She wants Macbeth to be king - but she believes the only way that will happen is if he kills King Duncan. She doubts he will do it. (p. 34)

Words like *cauldron*, *dire*, *fenny*, and *slay* which may be unfamiliar to students are noted and often defined parenthetically in the script itself. We read the play several times prior to choosing parts and attempting to produce it on film.

During the reading, the students' involvement and understanding increased as they used their own prior knowledge and personal experiences in relating to the characters. When Lady Macbeth encouraged Macbeth to kill King Duncan to assure his own position, one student interrupted, stating, "You know, this is a lot like that song about betrayal where they say, "Will you kill for me?" "Will you steal for me?" She's trying to see how far he will go to satisfy her." When Macbeth opened the door to Duncan's room to reveal the murdered king and his guards, Calvin jumped up from his desk shouting, "Wait! Macbeth messed up. He should have said he killed the guards before they all saw them dead. I would have told them what happened before we got to the room." By now, the students were familiar with the characters and ready to choose parts. I decided to have them sign up for any part they would be interested in playing, including set, prop, and costume design, director, and camera operator. We then drew for parts and made ready to enter "the grim Scottish plain."

During the next few days the students worked in small groups at centers created for each of these aspects of production. Chalk outlines of Macbeth's castle emerged on gloomy black bulletin board paper and swords were fashioned from corrugated cardboard covered in tin foil. Lady Macbeth stood motionless while costume designers draped a bed sheet around her frame and adorned her head with a poster board crown encrusted with "rubies." At another station, directors meticulously copied the words in the scripts onto cue cards for each of the players, admonishing one another to "write big enough so they'll be able to see the words." The players sat in a circle, coaching one another as they reviewed their lines, occasionally standing to practice a movement or gesture.

Filming the Play

The filming itself was an exercise in problem solving and shared decision making. We had learned through our reading of *The Bard of Avon* that sets and scenery were minimal in Shakespearean theater (Stanley, 1992). As such, our set would be a backdrop depicting an exterior view of a castle and Birnam Wood. We decorated a classroom table and chairs to serve in the banquet scene. This same table, covered with a sheet, would represent the bed in which King Duncan slept prior to his being murdered by Macbeth.

Before each scene was filmed we would work out additional details: "Should I try to change my voice when I say, 'When the hurly burly's done'?" "How would a witch sound?" "That's *hover*, not *hoover*!" "I need more blood on me!" "Can we film me getting murdered?" "Can I kind of groan and say, No, not you Macbeth?" "When Macbeth is talking to the bloody dagger we could tie a dagger to some fishing line and make it look like it's really floating." "How would Lady Macbeth look when she's saying, 'Out damned spot. Out I say'? Should I have my eyes open or closed? I'm supposed to be sleep walking, you know." "I'm gonna write for the sword fight on my sword so I don't have to look at the cue cards while I'm fighting." "When Macduff is bringing Macbeth's head to Malcolm, we could hold a sheet under Macbeth's chin so it looks like his head's really cut off!" When this flurry of decision making abated, we turned expectantly to those in charge of direction and filming and waited to hear the words, "Quiet on the set. In five, four, three, two, one—ACTION."

Taking a Bow

The clapping and cheering startles me from my reverie. One by one the students move in front of the camera, stating their name and the part they played in the production, and take their final bows. But it wouldn't end here. Just as Malcolm, crowned at Scone, would plan his kingship, we would reflect upon this experience and make plans for our next adventure. When asked to evaluate our production, Sarah would write:

> Our greatest accomplishment in this production was our teamwork. We were able to work together for a week without fighting with each other. For 23 people to work together, even though they don't always get along is a great accomplishment. We also helped each other to become better actors and actresses by telling others our ideas. No one took the ideas as put downs.

Tom would write, "I think one of the best things was the fun we had. Fun makes us want to do it, which is good because if we want to do it, it will probably be a better play."

The Curtain Closes

As I pull down the paper backdrop and pack away the bent tin foil covered cardboard swords, I think about what this experience has meant to all of us. My students are better prepared to meet the challenges of high school literature and yet, there is so much more. I have a lunch meeting scheduled with Anthony tomorrow. He wants us to go over his first draft of a tale about the three weird sisters and how this all came to be, a prequel to *Macbeth* he calls it. Laura is reading a book of plays, searching for "another good one we could do." Jarod approached me in class to share the first page of his evaluation of the production saying, "I think I'm gonna need a lot of paper. This is my first paragraph!"

What had begun as an effort to enhance our study of meaning making through performance and to establish the background knowledge my students would need for their high school readings of the works of Shakespeare had changed our lives. Our study of *Macbeth* had enabled us to address all aspects of Language Arts: reading the play and associated works; writing an evaluation of the production of the play itself; speaking the lines conceived by Shakespeare; listening to his words as we spoke them; visually representing Shakespeare's words through our sets, props, costumes, and actions; viewing and evaluating our performances; and finally, thinking about the connections we could make to our own experiences with friendship, greed, and ambition. "All hail Macbeth! Hail to thee!"

Evaluation/Assessment

As I noted in the evaluation/assessment section of chapter 2, my students and I often make decisions about what we will do, how we will proceed, and how we will evaluate ourselves as we construct and revise planning sheets and rubrics. As we move to include performance as an aspect of our developing literacy and meaning making, we return to these instruments to help us structure and reflect upon our experiences.

Our first experience with performance, the choral reading of "Journey" (Giovanni, 1993) is one which we evaluate through discussion alone. Our discussions take place both during and after the reading. As I have noted, the students' production of *The Van Gogh Café* (Rylant, 1995) far exceeded my initial expectations. My intention was for us to focus on summarization through the creation of a summary for each chapter of the book. With this in mind, my assessment centers on the summaries presented within each group's performance. As I reflect on this experience I see that I could individualize the evaluation/assessment process by having each group construct a "proposal" in which they describe how they intend to summarize their chapter, being specific as to what will be included in their presentation. With these proposals in hand, I could then respond to the students in writing as I view their performances. I have also had my students develop proposals such as this for other activities (see appendix N). In general, the proposals include statements about the product, the process, and notes from the students to me describing ways that I can help with materials or information.

As an accompaniment to our reading of *The Outsiders* (Hinton, 1989), we engaged in the reading of Robin Brancato's (1994) short story "Fourth of July." Following this reading the students were invited to interrogate two of the characters from the short story, Chuck and Jack. Through this experience in improvisation and interrogation, I wanted to provide an opportunity for my students to become further involved in questioning and reflecting on the motives and actions of characters. With this in mind, I asked each of the students (with the exception of the two who would play the parts of Chuck and Jack) to write down four things they would ask each of the two characters. As I examine what the students have written, I look for evidence of reflection on the motives and actions of the characters. During the improvisation, I make notes about the contributions and responses of the students playing Chuck and Jack, again looking for their developing understanding of the characters.

Features of performance are further woven into our reading of *The Outsiders* (Hinton, 1989) when, using Fleischman's "Book Lice" (1988, pp. 15–17) as a model, the students create poems for two or more voices which compare and contrast the characters in the novel. I think of the students' choral readings of the poems as "presentations." As each group presents their poem to the class, I note this in the "presentation" column of my Meeting Objectives checklist, counting it as one of the literacy activities in which we have engaged in that particular week. Further evaluation/assessment occurs later as I read each poem, examining both the structure of the poem (Is the poem written in a form derivative of Fleischman's poem?) and the elements within the poem (Does the poem describe the similarities and differences between the characters?).

The evaluation/assessment of the performance itself in terms of features such as dramatic voice, gesture, interaction between characters, and so forth, does not really come into play until our production of the mystery/suspense plays as radio shows. It is at this point that I believe my students have enough experience with dramatization and performance that we can begin to look at these aspects. You may have noticed that prior to this we have been evaluating/assessing the writings or concrete products created within the performance experience. As we produce the radio shows and commercials, we utilize what we have learned through our earlier experiences to aid us in the creation of planning sheets and rubrics (see appendices L and M). Later, when we evaluate our performance of *Macbeth*, the students and I work together to create an outline which calls for them to provide their overall impression of the performance and to write about the strengths and areas for improvement of the group, as well as the strengths and areas for improvement in their own efforts.

Summary

As I reflect upon the inclusion of dramatization and performance in our reading class, I realize that this process, too, is a recursive cycle. With each new experience, my students and I must reenvision the process, the product, and the role we will play in the creation of meaning. The words of Kesha and others remind us of the importance of beginning this process from a position of belonging in the literacy community and of ensuring that each of us is allowed to consider how we will participate. Kesha exemplifies the transformations that occur as students move from a belief that "I really just didn't think I had it in me" to thoughts about how to make performance work for them and, finally, to feelings of accomplishment and comments such as "I thought I was pretty successful at my voice" and "I really enjoyed that part."

As we work together to incorporate the performance of choral readings of poetry written by ourselves and others, stories, studies of characters, and radio show and theatrical performances into our classroom experiences, each of us plays a part. We discover again that learning and making meaning of our experiences works best when we listen to and build upon the ideas of others. I may be the one who provides the initial suggestions for a performance, but it is the interplay of ideas and the negotiation of what will be done and how it will be done that gives meaning to our actions. Choral readings are embellished with sound effects and synchronized movements; Sandy and her group transform a summary into a conversation over coffee; Matt and his group write a play to show us what happened in the chapter they have read; while others extend an interrogation of characters with a trial, preparing blueprints and briefs. Over and over again, I find myself noting the impact of this negotiation as my students become deeply involved in what we are doing and move far beyond my original expectations.

As I think further about our experiences with dramatization and performance, I am reminded of a passage from the writings of M. M. Bakhtin (Holquist, 1981):

> The word in language is half someone else's. It becomes "one's own" only when the speaker populates it with his own intention, his own accent, when he appropriates the word, adapting it to his own semantic and expressive intention. (p. 293)

Our performances have enabled us, in a sense, to develop understanding and ownership of the words of others. As these students have read and prepared to perform the words of others, they have had to think beyond the words on the page to the intention of the writer. We begin by thinking and talking about how a writer might have wanted us to view the words and actions of a character. The words become populated with our own intentions and our own accent when we move further, thinking about our own reactions to the character, how his or her actions compare with what we might do in a similar situation, and how we might bring his or her voice to life for others. We further appropriate the words when we physically enact our interpretations of these intentions, not only reading the words but moving through them and living through them until they truly become our own.

Chapter 6 describes our efforts to express the meanings we are constructing from our readings and our lives together through writing. We write before, during, and after reading, trying on and expanding various ways of working. As we write, we continue to find new meanings and continue to learn from one another. We write to understand and to crystallize our interactions with text and with one another.

6

THE POWER OF WRITING

DEVELOPING OUR WRITING POWER

I have only respect and love for the stories that I hear. I love trying to see and feel the way the writers of stories felt. A story is not just a story to me. It is the life that thrives inside each and every one of us . . . Reading and writing are like peering down into someone's soul! You get to see things the way they would. You get to be them for a moment . . . When I need to refill my talent or my inspiration I turn to books to see if they can help kindle my fire, and they do. They make the flames of talent burn high inside me. I write as fast as I can, racing against the end of the flames and the words to come. They appear on the paper for me to read. That is how I write. I write with the fire that burns inside my soul so deep.

Stefano

As I read these words, I can "see" Stefano at his desk. As he begins to write he stares into space, his expression thoughtful. Stefano is a reader who knows that stories are not just stories but a reflection of the life of someone else, a way to "peer down into someone's soul!" When he reads he tries "to see and feel the way the writers of stories felt . . . to be them for a moment." Stefano has personal experience in taking on the point of view of others. He is the youngest in his family, and the only male with four older sisters. Stefano tells me that "I have many different perspectives because of this. . . . when I see something I don't see it one way, but differently, as each of my sisters would. . . . I have a way of knowing how people feel without experiencing it." Before he begins to write, Stefano thinks about the people he has known and the stories he has read. He turns to books to "kindle" his "fire." When Stefano begins to write, his expression changes to one of intense concentration and his pencil flies across the paper, "racing against the end of the flames and the words to come." Later, as he pauses to read what he has written, Stefano, who tells me he is "developing a love for pencil and paper," smiles to himself. As he reads what he has written, he discovers the "flames of talent" inside himself.

Garnet, another avid writer, describes her feelings about writing in school and what motivates her to write:

> First, the way I feel when I write something can be really different. If I am assigned to write something the feeling is just not the same. When I write for fun and pleasure my mind wanders. My mind does not wander as far and deep into the story if I am assigned to write. Something what motivates me to write is turning every day issues into explorations or expeditions. For instance, my mom telling me to clean my room could transform me into a poor maid girl forced to stay in an attic room and clean. I imagine things, just little things, and change them into a story. . . . maybe not one written down, but as one filed in a cabinet in my mind. A thought just filed away for later writing.

Not all of my students see themselves as writers who reflect upon what they have read, get inside the life of a character, and/or create new meanings as they mesh what they have experienced or imagined in life with what they experience or imagine through texts. For some, like Jem who says, "I don't really like writing because I just don't like to write," the physical act of writing itself can be distasteful. Others, like Tenitia, say "I don't like to write because I always have nothing to write about." Some, like Mack, have negative feelings about writing based upon past rejection:

> One time I remember writing a paragraph at home about me. I was so impressed with it. I showed it to my teacher the next day. She told me I needed to improve my language. I was so crushed that I gave up writing by myself

There are many more of my students who have vivid memories of teachers who have inspired them to write. Cara writes about such a teacher:

The Power of Writing

> *In third grade my class was given a writing assignment to write about what we were thankful for. I wrote a poem and when my teacher read it she started to cry. I thought it must have been a terrible poem. She then said it was the most beautiful poem she had ever read. This motivated me into pursuing writing.*

Further on, in this piece, Cara describes what writing has come to mean to her:

> *It seems as if writing is my only escape from reality and all its troubles. As I get older, writing becomes more important to me. The more I see of the world, the more I need to write it down through the eyes of a thirteen year old.*

The words of these students provide a representative picture of the thinking of my students with regard to writing. There are those who are fully engaged in the process of writing and becoming writers, and there are those who "always have nothing to write about" or who have given up on writing. Some write because they are inspired by what they have read; and others are motivated to write by their parents, friends, or teachers. As they write or plan to write, some of my students reflect on the characters they have met in books or their relationships with living people. Others find ideas by imagining themselves as people who live in other places or other times. Still others, like Cara, write because they need to capture and make permanent what they, as 13-year-olds, see and think of the world around them.

As each of my students takes a separate English class, my primary concern as a reading teacher is to provide the students with opportunities to "try on" various ways of responding to their reading. Through written response they will engage in the further development and expression of meaning. Using what I have learned about my students through observations and conversations, I attempt to design experiences that will relate to what we read and to provide an element of choice and of opportunity to make personal connections to the text. The students will write at various points before, during, and after our readings. This enables them to develop further awareness of the ways that readers develop interpretations and construct meaning. Throughout the process, I invite the students to share what they are writing or what they have written with others. Through this sharing we construct knowledge both individually and collectively, in a manner similar to that in which we generate questions, comments, and observations about text, discuss literature, and dramatize texts.

I have organized the sections of this chapter to reflect a variety of our writing experiences, placing them in the order in which they occur during our year together. When thinking of ways to help my students develop their written responses to text, I consider the text itself, noting features of the genre as well as the aspects of writing exemplified by the text. I think about ways to help my students make connections with their own lives and ways that we can build upon our prior writing experiences. With this in mind, you will see that we develop our processes as we cycle through considerations of ourselves to considerations of text and as we move from the simple to the complex within and among the writing experiences.

Responding to Photographs

In an earlier chapter I describe our opening conversations about the novel *Journey* by Patricia MacLachlan (1991). The students talk about Grandfather's statement that "pictures show us what is really there" (p. 19). As they talk, they make comparisons between the photographs described in this novel and what they reveal and photographs of their own lives which may or may not reflect "what is really there." Through poetry we respond to this central idea about what photographs reveal. We begin with the "known," as we write about pictures of our own community.

I want to extend this experience and provide my students with opportunities to delve deeper into the hidden meanings in photographs. I want them to think about inner dialogue, as they consider the question, "If the person in a photograph could talk, what would we hear?" I decide to introduce this experience with a reading that would exemplify inner dialogue and provide my students with a model for their own writing, Judie Angell's (1984) "Turmoil in a Blue and Beige Bedroom." The action in this short story takes place through the thoughts of June as she waits in her room for a telephone call from John, who she hopes will invite her to an upcoming party. The following excerpt typifies the thinking of June and the style of the piece:

> Please let John call.
>
> Please let John call before two o'clock.
>
> If John calls before two o'clock I promise I'll baby-sit Stewie for three Friday nights in a row without arguing.
>
> Now, what will I wear?
>
> I haven't worn my powder blue sweater with the fluffy collar to school yet.
>
> I could wear that with my tan slacks. Or my black slacks. Or my white wool ones? Maybe I'll wear a dress. (p. 72)

The next day as the first class enters the room, I ask them to sit down quickly and write down exactly what they are thinking about. "Oh, noooo," laughs Tim. "I'm not thinking anything yet," George complains. I suggest that they think back to a moment earlier that morning and write/think about that. A few raised eyebrows and giggles later, we are ready to share. Susan reads what she has written:

> I feel grundgy today. Why do I always wait until the last minute to get ready for school? Just a few minutes of extra sleep. Well I got that, but then I had to look through the dirty clothes basket for something to wear and now I'm sitting here wearing two socks that don't even match and a pair of my brother's jeans.

We laugh and talk about similar experiences. Others share and we note the way our thoughts tend to ramble at times, jumping from one subject to another. At this point, our thinking about inner dialogue is activated and we are ready to begin reading "Turmoil in a Blue and Beige Bedroom" (Angell, 1984).

There is much laughter during and following the reading as the students attempt to give voice to June's thoughts and then as they compare their own social dilemmas with hers. While they sit together in a circle on the floor talking, I pull out a stack of photographs of people I have torn from National Geographic magazines, scattering them on the floor in the center of the circle. We look at a picture of a girl floating on her back in an indoor pool, a woman standing on her head, a man wrestling with a sheep, another sitting alone in a gathering of people, a young boy in formal dress beside a cello. "Pictures," I tell them, "of people we do not know." "And yet," I ask them, "can we look at these pictures and see as Journey's Grandfather would say, 'what is really there'?" "Can we 'hear' the voices of these people as we hear our own or as we hear the voice of June as she waits for the call from John?"

I ask the students to spend a few minutes in silence, looking at the photographs and "listening" to the voices they hear. They are then to choose a picture and take it with them to their desks. Without saying a word, we will study our picture and then write down what we think we "hear." I choose a photograph and write with the students. At first, I cannot think of anything. I am distracted, wondering what my students are thinking and writing. They are writing as if "racing against the flames and the words to come." When I begin to hear the whispers of students sharing with one another, I suggest that we might all want to hear what has been written. In order for us to see the photograph as the writer shares, we turn off the lights and "spotlight" the photograph with the light from the overhead projector. Julie reads the thoughts of a woman in a white shirtwaist dress, relaxing, half reclined with her arm thrown over the back of a white wicker chair:

> The house is so peaceful when I'm alone. No rush, no shouts, no kids at each other's throats. Just me. I'm tired, and now's the perfect time for a nap. Warm sunshine, a comfortable chair, and quiet, glorious quiet. It's so quiet in here I can hear the hum of the ceiling fan and the faint buzzing of the lawn mower next door. A nice tall glass of iced lemonade would be perfect right now. I don't want to read, I don't want to walk, I don't want to think. Just soak in relaxation. Just be. I feel warm all over. I wonder if I paid the electric bill. Oh, shut up. Don't you dare start thinking of other things. This time is mine! How often do I just get to sit and be? Never!

Jeff reads the thoughts of a fisherman standing at a wooden counter, gutting a fish. Behind the man, we can see that there are piles of fish waiting to be cleaned:

> What a day. Look at all of these fish. They will sell good in the market. I'm gonna be rich. Today was the best day out in the bay. I'm so proud of myself. Okay, time for filleting 322 fish. This will take forever. I'll never get it done. I sure hope that people will raid the market like the fish raided the bay today. I spent three hours out in my dinky boat, and look what I got. My hands are full of fish guts. I better put on some gloves. Today was cold and usually fish don't come in the bay. They like to be out in the Gulf. I guess I have fisherman's luck. I hope I catch this many tomorrow. I would have more fish than the harbor's fish market. Yeah, what a good idea. I'll sell the fish to the market and then make big bucks. Why waste your time waiting for people to buy it, when you sell your fish to other fisherman? I know. I'm smart. Who can blame me?

Danielle reads the thoughts of a Russian cosmonaut who appears to be on another planet:

> Wow! I can't believe it! I've actually landed on another planet! And before those Americans. Move to the left? Fine. I can't believe they're taking this picture. Oh well. Better make the best of it! Do something? I've just traveled through outer space and you're telling me to do something?!

For the picture? Oh, never mind. Well, I guess I'll do something. Okay, I'm doing something. Take the picture already. Geesh, I'm getting tired of holding this smile. Why am I just standing here? I thought you were just supposed to float around here? These shoes are so ugly! Why do they make us wear these? And this thing is hot! I hope you can't tell I'm sweating. Goodness, I look like an idiot! Hope they don't publish this! They aren't even getting my good side. Forget about the shoes, this whole space suit is ugly. It makes me look fat. Finally, we're done!

A light-hearted mood prevails; and here in the semi-darkness, we laugh and clap as student after student steps into the spotlight. The words they have written allow us to step in to the minds of the characters, the people in these photographs. As the students share, I ask each of them to spend a few minutes talking to us about the writing itself and their thinking as they worked to project the voice of someone unknown to them. As they talk, we discover the commonalities in our approach. Most find the reading of Angell's (1984) "Turmoil in a Blue and Beige Bedroom" to be helpful. As Cal states, "You can see how you should make it look, and how you can just write down thoughts the way they really jump around in your head." For Anthony and others, time spent searching the photograph for details and imagining what the subject might be thinking enables them to "become this person for a few minutes."

Many of the students note connections between the way they perceive the character in the photograph and moments or events in their own lives. For instance, Julie, imagining a woman who wants to enjoy a few moments away from the pressures of the day, imagines how she herself feels when she has a moment to relax after school work, dance, and volleyball. With this in mind, Julie then thinks about the kind of pressures that might be felt by an older woman, referring to what she has heard from her mother and others.

Jeff, who lives near the Gulf and who "goes fishing with my Dad nearly every weekend!" uses these experiences to imagine the thoughts of a professional fisherman. Others, like Danielle, find ways to add humor by introducing the incongruous. It makes us laugh to think that an explorer who has traveled to another planet is thinking only about his personal appearance.

I conclude our discussion by sharing a story with my students about the time I listened to author Walter Dean Myers speak at a conference for educators. Myers shared details about the way he works. He told us that before he begins writing, he and his wife walk through the neighborhoods and streets of the city taking photographs. When Myers chooses the place where he wants to set his story, he and his wife hang the photographs side by side on the wall, creating a pictorial representation of the neighborhood. As Myers views the photographs, he can mentally enter and walk around in the setting. Myers related that he may also use photographs of people from magazines or people he knows to help him develop his characters. These too are hung on the walls to be used as a point of reference when he is writing. My students are fascinated by this connection between what they are doing and what Walter Dean Myers does as *he* writes. "This was fun!" Cal comments as he leaves the room that day. I smile, thinking, "It *was* fun!"

As I think further, breaking down this writing experience looking for the strategies that were helpful to my students, I can see that our writing is strengthened as we use reading strategies. For example, we activate prior knowledge and think about our own experiences when we begin by writing down what we are thinking. At this point I do not use the literary term "inner dialogue." I simply ask my students to "write down what you are thinking." In this way we preview the text we are about to read ("Turmoil in a Blue and Beige Bedroom," Angell, 1984) and set a purpose for reading—to see how writers convey the inner thoughts of a character. Following the reading we talk about personal connections, note the format for writing inner dialogue and, then, set a purpose and a method of reading another type of text—the photographs. At this point, the students are "listening" to the voices they "hear" as they "read" the photographs and then write down what they "hear." Finally, we share what we have written and learn about the method used by Walter Dean Myers. Through this sharing and talk, we continue to build upon our knowledge as we reflect on the writing of others.

Re-envisioning The Van Gogh Café

As promised in the preceding chapter, I now return to our experience with *The Van Gogh Café* (Rylant, 1995). My students had transformed my original vision of the reading from an exercise in summarization into a dramatization of the text complete with conversations, commentary, and costumes. Their enthusiasm prompted me to expand upon this experience still further. As their production of the book came to an end, I moved to the front of the room with book in hand. As they listened, I read to them the final chapter of *The Van Gogh Café*—a chapter I had kept from them until now. This chapter, "The Writer," tells the story of a young man who had once dreamt of becoming a writer. Now he has given up on his dream, and he is delivering telephone directories. He stops in at the café and sits down at a table. "As he sits, the magic in those wall begins its work on him" (p. 52); and he decides that he *will* be a writer, that he does have a book inside him. Rylant tells us that the writer wonders what he might call his book, hinting that he will name it after the Van Gogh Café.

There are several seconds of silence and then a buzz of conversation erupts: "Wow, what an ending!" "Is this *his* book?" "Is this the book *he* wrote? I thought Cynthia Rylant wrote the book!" As we talk, I suggest that Rylant has left us with a hint of mystery. Could the book be seen as a collection of the stories of people who have come to the café? And then I ask, "What do you think about creating our own book about a magical place that used to be something else? You know, the way that the Van Gogh Café was once a theater.... Could we come up with a new place and write stories of our own about the people who come into that place? A place where the impossible becomes possible?" My suggestion is greeted with shouts of approval.

The next time we meet we begin by creating a listing of places—places that were once something and are now something else. I sit at the overhead projector, writing as the students call out ideas. When the onslaught of thoughts wane, we take a few moments and review what we have written. Each class group chooses an original site and a new site on which to base their book. Their choices make it clear to me that they are modeling their titles after the book we have read and making a connection between my name and that of Van Gogh. They decide to write about The Van Horn Steak and Cookie Palace which was once a Magician's Shop owned by Elanini Fatuchini the magician; The Van Horn Community Center, formerly a forest; The Van Horn Classroom which was once a magical toy store; The Van Horn Café which was once a 7th-grade reading classroom; and The Van Horn Library which was once an arcade.

With setting in hand we are ready to begin. I choose an empty seat and sit down to write. Papers rustle and soon there is silence in the room. I put my pencil down and glance around hopefully. Each and every one is writing. Thinking, "*This* is magical," I return to my own writing. Seconds later, a shadow falls across my paper. "Mrs. Van Horn, can you look at this?" whispers Matt. Before I can read the first sentence of the two sentences he has written, we are joined by Mel who shoves her paper onto the desk with a smile, saying, "I'm through! Will you read mine?" Close behind her is Teresa, looking doubtful, shakily gripping a blank piece of paper and biting her lip as she laments, "I don't know how to start." It occurs to me that I need to reevaluate my approach. It is early in the year, and we are searching for ways of working together.

Donald Graves (1994) suggests that:
> Students need to hear the responses of others to their writing, to discover what they do or do not understand. The need to help students know how to read their own work and the work of their classmates provides further teaching and demonstration opportunities. (p. 108)

Thinking that it might help my students to talk about what they are writing, what is working, and what is not working, I ask, "Can we take a few minutes to talk about what we're doing?" "How are you starting your stories?" For the next few minutes students volunteer to share what they have written. Vanita reads what she has written so far, "One night at the Van Horn Steak House a girl named Vanita and all of her friends always went to that steak house every Friday night to go and talk and eat." We talk about how she is using herself as the central character and how she might add details and dialogue to let the reader "see" and "hear" the character. We listen as Cal reads to us:

> One day this lady walked in. Her name is Rachel. Rachel is a newcomer to the city. She doesn't know about the most popular place, Van Horn's Steak and Cookie Palace. She doesn't know that it was once owned by a magician. She walked in because she had a craving for steak and some chocolate chip cookies. She also came in because it was a cold and rainy day. Once inside she was very surprised at what she saw. There was sunshine coming in through the windows.

Together we talk about what Cal has done so far. He has modeled his introduction after those in each chapter of *The Van Gogh Café*. Someone enters the setting, references are made to what the place is and what it was, and something mysterious begins to happen. Once we have this "outline" or model for the introduction in mind, we can return to our writing. For the next several days this is the way we work—writing and sharing, conferencing as a whole class, and learning from one another.

At this point in the year, I am focusing on motivating my students to write, and on building their confidence in themselves as we begin to develop ideas about writing in response to reading. I am also working to help my students recognize and "pick out moments when the writing works well," and "learn how to take advantage of the pleasant surprises that crop up in their writing" (Fletcher, 1993b, p. 15). As we finish our stories, each class group chooses someone to draw a cover for their book. The rest illustrate their stories. I make copies for their portfolios and bind the originals, creating a book for each class group. As each book is completed, we have a read around. Students take turns, sitting on the stool at the front of the room, reading aloud and celebrating what they have written. A look at some of the finished pieces reveals that the students have noted and used the structure of the original text as a model. Others have made personal connections to the text.

For example, Jay, a musician and heavy metal enthusiast, shares his chapter, titled "The Musician":

> *He has been trying to be a good musician for four years. It isn't that he isn't any good. Actually, he is very good. Most record companies don't like Heavy Metal or Alternative. They're more interested in R&B, rap, and country. But he kept true to his music. He kept on trying to get a record deal. But everywhere he went, failure followed him. He kept on trying for about a year. He was just about to give up when someone came up to him and asked, "You play music?" "Yeah," he said. Then she said, "I have an opening at the Van Horn Steak and Cookie Palace. Would you like the job?" "Yeah! I'll take it. When do I start?" "Tonight," she said. So that night at the Van Horn Steak and Cookie Palace the sign read "Opening Tonight. Heavy Metal Star Jamz Hetfeld." Lots of people showed up. Even a few scouts from record companies. That night the musician played for hours. Everyone loved his ripping solos and heavy beats. After the concert a representative from Sub Pop asked him to sign with them. But he said no because he would rather keep his job at the Van Horn Steak and Cookie Palace.*

Jay opens his chapter in the same way as Rylant (1995) has in "The Writer" (pp. 50–53). We are introduced to a character/artist who has a talent which is not recognized by the gatekeepers of the profession. The character is at the point of giving up when he visits a magical place, The Van Gogh Café, or, in this case, The Van Horn Steak and Cookie Palace. Here, in this place, his vision is renewed and he finds the confidence to try once again. Jay continues beyond this as he gives us a picture of what happens next, the musician's first concert here at the Steak House and Cookie Palace. He then shows what might happen as a result. The character is acknowledged for his success but chooses to remain in the setting where he has regained faith in himself.

Jacy's chapter provides another example:

> *One day in the Van Horn Steakhouse and Cookie Palace (formerly a magic shop) a young girl and her family were sitting at the table in the farthest corner from the cash register which is no more than fifteen feet away from the door. The girl was probably five years old. She was holding a small, plastic watch. When it came around to*

closing time, the family left the restaurant. As they left, their waitress noticed the small girl had forgotten her watch on the chair. The family drove away before the waitress could give it to the girl. She cleaned the table and tucked the watch in her pocket. The watch was pink and had a Barbie on it, but all the same, it kept the right time. Every 30 minutes the watch said, "Barbie says it's such and such a time."

The next day all the clocks and watches in Flowers, Kansas, suddenly stopped. The only watch in the city that still had the correct time was the little watch with the Barbie on it. But that was not the only problem. The real problem was that none of the clocks would re-set. The next day there was a riddle on the front door of the Van Horn Steak House and Cookie Palace. It read:

> Eat a fine cookie,
> The best in the land,
> Have some steak
> to go with it.
> Get home and know
> What time it is again.

So, all of a sudden the cafe filled with people, all wanting cookies and steak. The watch started to shake in the waitress' pocket. She took it from her pocket and it started to glow and sparkle. Glitter went all over the floor. That night, not only did the people of Flowers' clocks tell the right time, they noticed that for every cookie they ate they lost one pound.

The next morning, the young girl and her family returned. The girl asked the waitress, "Can I have my little Barbie watch back, please?" "Sure," the waitress said. "You must have dropped it last time you were here." The waitress handed the little girl her watch and the girl

> said, "Thank you," and continued eating. Then, for the next few months, the cafe was quiet, until the next magical thing happened.

Jacy, too, has modeled her response on elements in *The Van Gogh Café*. Jacy's chapter includes elements from several of Rylant's (1995) chapters. For example, in the chapter titled "The Magic Muffins" (pp. 22–29), a glamorous woman visits the café and leaves magic muffins behind. Jacy writes about a little girl who leaves a talking watch behind on a chair in the Steak and Cookie Palace. Rylant's chapter, "Lightning Strikes," (pp. 12–21) contains several poems, some which foretell the future and another that provides clues to the whereabouts of a missing cat. Jacy's riddle/poem tells the people of Flowers, Kansas, how they can restart and reset the town clocks. Jacy concludes her chapter just as Rylant concludes each of her chapters, with a hint of magical things to come.

Ben's chapter, written about the Van Horn Classroom which was once a magical toy store, touches on reality and hints of the possibility of magical things to come in our own classroom. Ben writes about a group of 7th graders who are writing a story, "but the thing is everyone thought the assignment was too hard." While the students are out of the room during a fire drill, a magical red toy truck appears and moves about the room leaving a trail of purple powder tracks which spell out the words "You Can Do It!" The students in Ben's story are encouraged by the purple powder trail of words, and their writing begins to flow. As I listen to Ben read, I think about how my students have shared and encouraged one another in the writing of these stories. Our interactions during this experience reveal the power of large group sessions in which we stop at various intervals during the writing to discuss our processes. As the students read aloud examples of what works and what does not work and as we talk together, searching for ways to confront our difficulties, we begin to see ourselves as a community of writers. I make a promise to myself to continue to search for ways to provide them with experiences which will enable them to see that they too "can do it!"

CANYONS

Making Connections

Canyons (Paulsen, 1990) is the story of two adolescent boys separated by time. Coyote Runs is an Apache boy living in the mid-1800s. His life comes to a violent end during a coming of age raid. Brennan, living in contemporary times and also dealing with the trials and tribulations of impending manhood, finds the skull of Coyote Runs while camping in the canyons around El Paso, Texas. As Brennan becomes more and more obsessed with learning the story of the skull, he feels himself drawn into the life of Coyote Runs. At times, he imagines that he has become Coyote Runs.

Gary Paulsen's words draw us inside the lives of the characters. Before we begin to read the novel, I read aloud an interview of Paulsen printed in a local newspaper. Paulsen describes himself as follows:

> I was from the wrong side of the tracks, I was a poor reader, I skipped school all the time, flunked the ninth grade and had to take it over. No friends, a geek, last one chosen for sports—never chosen, let's be honest here. I was on my way to trouble, real trouble.

Paulsen relates that one night as he took refuge from the cold in a public library, he was "saved" by a librarian who gave him a library card with his name on it. He describes what this meant to him:

> It was such an incredible thing. People didn't give me anything. It seemed like I had to fight for everything. And here's this woman who hands me something with my name on it. It's like, suddenly I had an identity.

As I read on we learn that Paulsen faced continued hardship. He turned to writing and his first book "sold about eight copies," but he persisted. He began writing young adolescent novels. He based his writing on his own life experiences of running the Iditarod and surviving in the wilderness. Finally with the publication of *Dogsong* (1985) and *Hatchet* (1987), Paulsen achieved recognition for his writing.

Reading and talking about this interview of Gary Paulsen helps us to begin thinking about the connections between the writing and the writer. As we talk about the events in Paulsen's life, it occurs to us that small moments can change lives. Paulsen's life was altered when the librarian handed him his own library card.

The frontispiece of our edition of *Canyons* (Paulsen, 1990) contains an excerpt from the novel in which one of the central characters, Brennan, is introduced to his mother's new boyfriend. Later, as Brennan thinks back on this moment, he realizes that this is the moment that his life began to change. He wonders, "How could anything so big come from something so small and simple?" After we read this together, I ask the students to think about what the library card has meant to Paulsen, how meeting Bill Halverson might change Brennan's life, and about moments in their own lives. I ask them to consider the question, "How could something so big come from something so small?" Each of us spends a few moments writing about a critical moment in our lives.

Garen writes about the beginnings of his first friendship with a girl:

> Well, first of all, asking a girl out could start from something small and become something big. One time I

asked a girl out and I thought that she would give me a simple "yes" or "no," but boy, oh boy, was I wrong. When I asked her out, not only did she say "no," she also told everyone that I was ugly and started a rumor about me. After she did this, I think she realized how horrible and embarrassed I felt. I think she regretted what she had done to me. Later she told me that she really felt bad and that she was having problems and didn't mean to take it out on me. I asked her if we could be friends and she said, "Of course." She promised she would never be so mean to me again.

Erin writes about moving into a new place:

It all started about four years ago when my dad said those simple little words,

"Hey, you wanna go for a ride?"

Then I thought, sure why not? That day somehow, some way we landed in the town of _____.

"I'm taking you to a special place," he said. I smiled, but my mind soared. Where could he be taking me? Soon we arrived at a dead end street, and there it was. A lot. Not just any lot, a small green, triangular lot. Triangular, yes triangular! Who would want to build a house here? I looked over at my dad who was obviously in heaven. "Oh, God," I said to myself, "he likes it."

His forehead was twisted to where you could tell he was thinking hard, thinking about the future. I took a step closer to him and he looked at me. "Isn't it great," he said. I nodded untruthfully.

A year later we built our house on that small, plain, triangular lot. I hated it. I did not want to move, nor did I want to spend my summer painting a house. Then school started and I met new people and the school was better, and not as strict. Things just kept on getting better. Now I love it here and I don't ever want to move!

Creating Journals

When we begin to read *Canyons* (Paulsen, 1990), some of my students are confused by the changes in time and point of view as they attempt to develop knowledge about the characters and setting. Paulsen alternates between chapters about the life of Coyote Runs and that of Brennan. Before long, we note that chapters about Coyote Runs are numbered and titled but chapters about Brennan are only numbered. We see that the publishers have printed chapters about Coyote Runs in one type style and chapters about Brennan in another. This, along with our growing sense of the characters themselves, alleviates the confusion. Gary Paulsen's words begin to draw us inside the lives of Coyote Runs and Brennan.

As we continue to read and talk, we wonder "why Brennan doesn't have more friends," "why he likes being alone," "why he resents his mother's relationship with Bill," "does Coyote Runs ever sleep on his boy to man trip," "why he wants the straw colored horse so badly," "what is the 'medicine' Coyote Runs talks about," and "are Coyote Runs and Brennan connected in some way." Debbie confides to me one day that she knows "how Brennan feels about his mom and her boyfriend. I feel that way too sometimes. It's like you want your parents to be happy, but then in some ways you want it to stay just the two of you."

I want to provide the students with a way to think about these issues through writing. Recalling our experience in writing as a person in a photograph, I wonder if we might do something similar, this time writing as a character in a novel. With this in mind, I invite my students to choose to "become" either Coyote Runs or Brennan (see appendix O). As I share my plan with the students, I tell them that each of us will make a journal, either for Coyote Runs or Brennan. Every day after we read, we will spend some time imagining that we are Coyote Runs or Brennan, writing in the journal, expressing what we are thinking and feeling. As I talk, I show them a journal I have made of plain writing paper bound in a cover made from a brown paper grocery sack glued over index paper and tied together with twine. I show them my copy of *The Adventures and Misadventures of Peter Beard in Africa* (Bowmaster, 1993); and we study the photographs of Beard's journal, noting the way he has filled the pages with both words and artifacts. Woven among the record of his thoughts are sketches, newspaper clippings, photographs, leaves, feathers, animal teeth, cartoons, cut up Christmas cards, and coins. We decide that our journals will include artifacts as well as writing.

Each day as we read, the students make notes, recording events, questions, and ideas for their journals. Anne decides to keep a two part journal of both characters, similar in format to the novel itself. Catherine decides to write both as Brennan and as herself. She tells me that she will use two different colors of ink in her journal, "one color will be for Brennan and one color will be for my thoughts about what he is saying." Michael worries how he, as Coyote Runs, will write about his own death at the hands of the bluebellies, "'cause he wouldn't just stop in the middle and write about it." He decides to write in a hurried, messy fashion at the point where Coyote Runs is trying to hide underneath an overhanging rock formation. Then he will make the pen slide across the paper as if the writer dropped the journal in fear and horror when Coyote Runs is captured by the bluebellies. Michael later decides to pretend that he has found the journal of Coyote Runs and to use the remaining pages to write about what has happened to the Apache boy.

We begin to collect artifacts for our journals. Jordie, as Brennan on the camping trip with his mother, Bill, and the kids from the youth group, writes:

> Bill asked if anyone knew a ghost story. Nobody answered so he ended up telling one. It was about the canyons and the Apaches and raids. The kids were into the blood. Then Bill winked at me. It made me feel a little better. He started talking about ghosts and told a few more stories. Then I went to bed. It's beneath a rock. I even took some hot chocolate with me. This trip isn't that bad. I hope Mom and Bill hit it off. Right now the kids are going to bed. I keep hearing cries, must be mountain lions. I've lived so close to this place and never really seen it. Well, I'm tired. Gonna drink my chocolate and go to sleep.

On this page she circles a chocolate milk spill and labels it "hot chocolate." Later, when she writes of finding the skull and shaking the sand and rocks from inside it, she glues a tiny rock to the page. Slowly the pages of our journals fill with words and artifacts. Photographs of rocky canyons, sand, ink splattered to look like blood, sketches of skulls, notes, and measurements, pictures of dreams.

Some days we end the class by reading aloud from the journals. Renee reads as Brennan, her words reflecting his emotions as he learns the details of Coyote Runs' death:

> His name was Coyote Runs. He was my age. He had a hard life. He was shot in the canyons. He must have felt fear. What fear he must have had. I feel for you Coyote Runs. I do. I really do!!. You weren't killed, you were executed. I don't understand. Coyote Runs, you seem as if a friend. A part of me has died with you. I want to know more. I MUST. Lead me, Coyote Runs. Take me to where you want to be.

Anthony reads to us, first explaining that he has imagined himself to have a teacher, named Mrs. Gordan, who has given him (Brennan) the assignment of keeping a journal. Anthony reads his interpretation of Brennan's relationship with Mr. Homesley, the biology teacher:

> Last year, I was nearly flunking all of school. I really didn't care—I didn't study for tests. I didn't put in the effort to do my homework. I didn't pay attention to the teachers, I just sat around letting myself become a nothing in life. I'm not saying I goofed around in school. I didn't socialize enough to do that, I just sat in the back of the class trying to hide from everybody. I was a loser. I had this one biology teacher—Mr. Homesley. He is the kind of teacher you are, and believe me, your group is rare. You're the teachers that care about the kids, the teachers that throw the old-fashioned, boring methods out the window and try exciting things. You're the teachers that love teaching, and don't believe in workbooks and copying out of the book junk, but real stuff; fun stuff. But, I was so busy ruining my life that I didn't see this. Then, one day after school, Mr. Homesley stopped me outside and gave me a lecture on beetles. Then we looked for one. Soon we worked out an agreement; if I brought a different variety of beetle to biology class every day, he would teach me about that variety and give me a passing grade. I kept up my end of the bargain, and Mr. Homesley certainly did. I just didn't pass biology by the skin of my teeth, but got a B! Then, I totally changed.... I wasn't a loser anymore! I was making B's, and had found a best friend. All because of beetles.

The incident between Brennan and Mr. Homesley does occur in the novel. Anthony develops further meaning as he interprets what this might have meant to Brennan. He makes connections to his own thoughts and feelings about what makes a good teacher. He infers why students like Brennan may lose interest or motivation in school. Throughout the process, as the students "become" the characters Coyote Runs and Brennan, they find further meaning as they expand upon and reflect through and beyond the events in the text, merging their own feelings with those of the characters who live on these pages.

Finding Poetry in the Prose

As we continue to read, we respond to the power of the words themselves using Paulsen's phrases to construct "found poems." I think of found poems as a way to honor the words of a writer while reformulating text—turning prose into poetry. I will illustrate what I mean in the same way I introduce the idea to my students.

First, imagine that there is poetry everywhere around you—in all the words that you see—on billboards, street signs, in restaurant menus, and in the pages of telephone books. You can "find" a poem anywhere. You might find it in the pages of a book. For example, pick up the book on your desk, close your eyes, and flip through the pages. Now, stop and call out a page number. Is there a poem on that page? Perhaps so.

I have chosen a page at random from *Canyons* (Paulsen, 1990) and made a transparency of the page so I can project it onto a screen where we can all see it at once. I instruct the class to "Read it to yourself and think about words, phrases, and/or images that stand out for you. We are going to use these words, phrases, and images to create a found poem." As the students volunteer to share, I underline the words we want to work with. For example, on page 90, we chose to work with the following:

> There was no reason to think it. He would not have a much bigger skull when he was a grown man, so why could it not be a man's skull? Or a woman's or girl's skull?
>
> Yet <u>he could not shake the feeling</u> and that night, the first night back, he put the skull back in the closet, went to bed but could not sleep though he was tired from the camping trip and not sleeping well the night before.
>
> At last his <u>eyes</u> had <u>closed</u> and he felt that he was still awake but somehow he dreamed, <u>slipping in and out of the dream.</u>
>
> The dream that night made no sense. He sat cross-legged on a high ridge overlooking the desert and the canyons below, apparently near where they had camped, and watched <u>an eagle flying</u>. It moved in huge circles, taking the light wind, <u>climbing and falling</u>, and he just sat and watched it fly and didn't think or say anything, didn't do anything.
>
> He could sometimes see the eagle very closely, see the feathers, the clear <u>golden eye</u>, then it would swing away and go higher and higher and finally become <u>a small speck against the blue sky and then</u>, in the end, <u>nothing</u>, and he just sat all the time on the ridge watching.

Now that we have chosen the words, we can manipulate them, repeating words or phrases, moving them into a new order, adding in words of our own. Together we create this "found poem":

>Eyes closed.
>Slipping in and out of the dream.
>In and out.
>Slipping.
>I can not shake the feeling.
>Slipping,
>Dreaming
>of an eagle flying.
>Climbing and falling,
>higher and higher.
>Eyes closed.
>Golden eyes.
>In and out of a dream.
>A small speck
>against the blue sky,
>And then,
>falling,
>falling,
>Nothing.
>Eyes close.

Now we are ready to try it on our own. I tell my students to choose a page at random and read through it. They may not want to work with the first page they come to. Amidst the sounds of rifling pages, I hear whispered comments, "I don't see one here!" "This isn't the one I want!" and finally, "Here, here it is!" There is growing excitement in the room as the students begin to see the "poems" on the pages of *Canyons* (Paulsen, 1990). Whispered consultations take place as they talk about repeating words and phrases, rearranging thoughts, and injecting their own ideas into the poem. As they write, some of the students decide to work from more than one page of the text. Others finish their first found poem and want to write another and another. We decide to include a citation of the title of the novel, author, and page number(s) on which the poem was found. Rob writes, comparing the beauty of the canyons to that of a pretty girl:

>Trying to see the beauty,
>watching,
>Watching her brushstrokes.
>Seemed like birds were singing.
>Pretty as a picture,
>So sweet.
>When she passed by
>it seemed like it took
>hours.

The Power of Writing

>Watching the beauty.
>(Poem found in *Canyons* by Gary Paulsen, p. 39.)

Tammy, too, writes of beauty, using a different perspective:

>Beauty.
>Tiny pool of green water.
>Small cotton woods.
>Who?
>Who was the Artist?
>God.
>God was the Artist.
>Trails
>that drop.
>Almost sweet
>Coolness.
>Hard to see beauty.
>Birds singing.
>Silence.
>(Poem found in *Canyons* by Gary Paulsen, pp. 39, 40.)

Danielle writes of Coyote Runs' thoughts and his efforts to be brave as he rides through the night on his first raid, his rite of passage into manhood:

>Lost.
>Many men were lost.
>They made their way in front of all others.
>Yet they still were lost.
>It was truly dark.
>But again,
>Some see better in the dark.
>They continued their hard journey.
>On their own.
>Without anybody.
>With nothing to see.
>With only silence.
>Lost.
>People believe if you pick the trails you walk on carefully.
>You will not lose your way.
>They hoped.
>They hoped they would see
>The many steep drops they might encounter.
>Lost.
>But they are not lost.
>They have each other.
>Now it is possible to see better things.
>(Poem found in *Canyons* by Gary Paulsen, pp. 30, 31.)

Writing to the Author

George suggests that we make a book and send a copy to Gary Paulsen. His idea is greeted with much enthusiasm. For the next few days we spend a part of each class period getting the book ready. The students work together, proofing and editing for one another. When our book is completed, we write letters to Paulsen and mail the package to him in care of his publisher. A few weeks later, I check my box during the lunch break and find a priority mail envelope inside with Gary Paulsen's return address sticker in the upper left hand corner. My hands shake as I open the envelope and read his letter addressed to my students. I make a copy for each student. Later, in the classroom my students pass the envelope and the letter around the room, holding it with reverence as if it were Paulsen himself. Carefully, we file the copies of his letter in our portfolios. Several students ask for extra copies to take home to frame and/or to "hang on my mirror to inspire me!"

We certainly can not *expect* authors to write to us as Paulsen has; but when something such as this occurs, it is a memorable event for us all. We had begun our experience with *Canyons* by reading and thinking about the author, the character Brennan, and ourselves. As the students wrote about the big things that emerged from small moments in their lives, and as we continued to read and respond to the text, the students created imaginary journals of the characters. These journals helped them to further develop their ability to empathize with characters and to write the thoughts of a character. The journals reflected the sequence of events in the novel and provided a place for the students to make predictions and develop inferences and generalizations about these events as they made personal connections to the characters. The process is similar to that of keeping a diary. We begin by writing down the events of the day and then we reflect on those events. It is during our reflection that we think and write about the meaning of the events and the interactions which have comprised the moments of the day. With the writing of the "found poems" and the letters to Gary Paulsen, we returned to our initial consideration of the text and reflections about the big things in life that emerge through small moments. Corresponding with Gary Paulsen reminded us once again of the connections between the writer and the text and of how writers draw from their lives and experiences in the act of creation. Gary Paulsen's expression of appreciation for the writing of my students contributed to their growing confidence and consideration of themselves as writers. As George would remark, "I know Mrs. Van Horn thought I could write, but if Gary Paulsen thinks I can write—I *must* be a writer!"

THE OUTSIDERS

Outsiders and Friends

Ellin Oliver Keene and Susan Zimmerman (1997) write of the importance of activating prior knowledge or schema before reading. As they point out, it is critical that we begin the process using the background knowledge of our students and that we teach this strategy of thinking about the "known" explicitly using a variety of texts. Students can activate their thinking and make connections to what they know through writing before reading. Before we begin to read *The Outsiders* (Hinton, 1989) I ask my students to spend 10 minutes writing a definition of the word "outsider." In these 10 minutes most of them write a page or a page and a half. It is clear to me that they are making personal connections to the word itself. As I read their thoughts, I find myself mentally clipping an idea at a time from the pages:

> *If everyone is a jock and you're not, you are an outsider. That's not a bad thing, it just means you don't have the same interest as they may have. You'll always fit in somewhere.*
>
> *Someone who doesn't know what's going on. Like if you and your friends know something and someone doesn't know, then they would be considered an outsider.*
>
> *An outsider is a person who isn't in the "cool" group. They're ignored by everybody.*
>
> *They like to be alone, or are just left alone.*
>
> *People can just all of a sudden become an outsider because of one decision. They can be really popular one minute, and the next minute they're an outsider.*
>
> *I know people who might be known as an "outsider." I've felt like an outsider before.*
>
> *An outsider is a person that might be different to other people, or who might see themselves as different.*
>
> *If I feel like an outsider I feel real alone. . . . it's like being in a big room that's empty and nobody comes to check to see if you are okay.*
>
> *Some people are like butterflies—they just flutter from group to group. But outsiders don't even hop from group to*

> group. They keep to themselves.
> Most people just ignore and mock outsiders.
> An outsider looks different, acts different, talks different.
> An outsider could be someone who is not wanted or accepted into a group or type of social group. Like in "Titanic," Rose's fiance was rude to Jack just because Jack was poor. Maybe Jack could be considered an outsider.
> Outsiders don't care what others think about them. . . . they pretend they are fearless.
> A kid that is not allowed in a gang . . . the gang might call him an outsider because he is outside of the gang.
> If you are an outsider you may have certain qualities–or disabilities that others dislike, or envy about you, therefore not wanting to hang out with you or do things with you because of your differences.

As the students volunteer to share their definitions aloud, we develop a frame of reference we will return to as we read the novel. We predict that the outsiders in the novel will be people who don't fit in, aren't wanted or accepted, who may be alone, who keep to themselves, who see themselves as different, and who pretend to be fearless. Stefano is in the class which meets just before lunch—ordinarily a rambunctious, hungry group, anxious to get to the school cafeteria. Stefano shares his definition of an outsider, and as we listen we grow quiet and forget our hunger:

> An outsider is not a nerd or a freak. They are not necessarily alone, just kind of cast out. They are people who are not recognized as "in" or "cool." They dare to be independent. They will not be one with the others. Because of that independence, they are cast out. People do not want to have other friends that are different. So, for that reason, outsiders have been cast outside the circle. They are not in the circle of people. They are the people we make fun of everyday. They are the people we consider weirdos. They are the people that sit alone at lunch or meetings. They do not choose their names. They are outsiders because of us. Our failure to recognize these people made them who they are . . . they are the outsiders.

When Stefano finishes reading there is silence for a minute or two. We are thinking of what he has read and, perhaps, recalling moments in which we have been outsiders or times that we have made others feel like outsiders. Finally, the silence is broken by Shawn, who remarks, "Wow, Stefano!" Then we can talk.

The words pour out as students speculate about why this happens and talk about times when they have felt alone. Even thought it is time for us to go to lunch, no one seems to want to leave the room. Stefano sums up our discussion and sends us to lunch with a mission, saying, "Let's all do this . . . when we're at lunch today, let's look for people who are sitting alone and invite them to come and sit with us." The rest of the class accepts Stefano's challenge enthusiastically; and, for this day at least, there are a few less "outsiders" in the Westbrook cafeteria.

In the days to come, as we read and talk about *The Outsiders* (Hinton, 1989) our thoughts turn to friendship and the meaning of the word "friend." We read about Darry who, after the death of his parents, relinquishes his athletic scholarship and his dreams of college to work as a roofer and take care of his two younger brothers, Sodapop and Ponyboy. We laugh with Two-Bit whose sense of humor provides relief to the Greasers as he helps them laugh at themselves and other things. We are saddened as we discover the reasons why Johnny, small and jumpy, is the special "pet" of the gang. We decide that *The Outsiders* (Hinton, 1989) is definitely a book about friends. Our discussion prompts us to think further about the meaning of this word. Kris says the word reminds her of the word "tragedy" because, "They are both deep words that really don't have a single meaning." We wonder if we *could* write a definition for the word friend. Kris laughs, saying, "That would take a whole book!" Her statement sparks an idea. What a challenge. Each of us will write a definition. We can bind all of the definitions together and make a book defining the word "friend." And that is what we do.

Our book becomes a talisman of sorts for the students. Many of them have concluded their definition with the first and last name of someone who is a friend. Some have decided to submit a definition in the form of a poem. We decide that what we have written is important for people to read and that, since it is going to be made into a book, it should be typed. With this goal in mind, we hasten to the technology lab to process our thoughts. The students sit close together as they type. Those who are less skilled at the keyboard are helped by others. There are whispered consultations about the size and style of the print. When everyone has finished, I suggest that we autograph the book. The students in each class group sign together on a single page preceding their poems. I arrange the poems alphabetically by class period and bind the book for them. We call it "Reflections on Friendship."

<u>Seasons of Friendship</u>
by Sandy
Lonely. Like winter. Cold-hearted. Empty.
Harsh words. A blizzard. Stinging. Pounding.
But friends! Glorious spring! Starting anew.
Good times, new times, blooming like blossoms.
Friendship. Ripening like fruit in the summer.
Growing in love. Hard times. Fall.
Good times and memories falling like leaves.
Changing like colors.
Losing friends. Winter.
New friends. Spring.
Keeps going. Keeps growing. Friends.

<u>Friends Are Like . . .</u>
by Kate
A friend is like a chair
That holds you up.
Or the wings of a bird
That help it fly.
A friend is like the lightning
In a storm at Night
That gives you light
To help you see.

Lance writes:

> A friend is pretty much someone who you can always count on. It's someone you can say, "Yeah, buddy," to. They will never do something to get you angry or hurt you. They help you, you help them. It's really a no-lose situation. You hang out with them, go places with them, do a lot of things with them. If you are a sports maniac like me, you play sports with them. If they are down in the dumps, you are the one to get them out. If they have had a bad day at the plate in baseball, you cheer them up. They do the same thing for you. Friends are super important. Without them where would the world be? In total chaos if you ask me.

His friend Pete writes:

> Friendship is something with many definitions. For some it is good and fun. Others dislike it because they think it is another way to get stabbed in the back. I believe that

> *friendship is a bond between many people. It is a relationship between two or more people. One person is just a strand of fabric blowing in the wind. When that person meets and befriends someone, they are intertwined. The more people that intertwine, the heavier the strands become, and the wind can no longer blow you over.*
>
> *The wind is peer pressure, and those who dislike you, or strangers on the street who try to get you to do something you don't want to do.*
>
> *When you get many friends you have something that is like a protective circle that helps you when you are in trouble.*

We keep this book on the table inside the door, opening it to read before and after or between classes, reminding ourselves of the meaning of friendship. Through this experience of writing to define "outsider" and "friendship," the students have clarified and refined their understanding of these words which reflect the central concepts or theme of the novel we will read. This enables us to enter into a reading of the text with a view of the theme and a set of expectations about what we know and what we want to learn. As we read, we will continue to refine and develop our understanding of the concepts "outsider" and "friendship."

Considering the Setting

Ponyboy (*The Outsiders*, Hinton, 1989) walks the streets alone, wishing he had some company. As he walks, he thinks about the clashes between the "Socials, the jet set, the West-side rich kids," and the Greasers, "all us boys in the East Side" (p. 6). He describes his neighborhood as "tight-knit" (p. 7). There are differences between the Greasers from the East Side, "just buddies who stuck together," and those led by Tim Shepard who are "organized" "young hoods who would grow up to be old hoods" (p. 121). As we continue to read, we talk about the friendship between the members of each group and how this friendship is defined by neighborhood as well as social class. We make comparisons between the text and our own lives, talking about our neighborhoods and the people and places that are important to us.

Seeking a way to further develop these ideas about the setting as it relates to the theme of the novel, I decide to introduce my students to another author who has written about neighborhoods, Gary Soto. Soto's (1992) *Neighborhood Odes* is a collection of odes to the wonders of his world. Before reading, we look up the word "ode" and find that an ode is a "lyric poem usually marked by exaltation of feeling and style, varying in length of line and complexity of stanza forms" (Mish, et al. 1998, p. 805). Searching further, for the meaning we find that to exalt is to "glorify" or "raise high" (p. 403).

As I have only 10 copies of *Neighborhood Odes* (Soto, 1992), I decide the students will read in small groups. Each group will start from a different place in the book; the beginning, the middle, or the end. Later in the class period, each group will have an opportunity to share their favorite ode with the rest of the class and talk about why they have chosen this particular piece.

The noise in the room intensifies as the students take turns choosing and reading poems to one another. Soto has written 22 odes. Among these are odes to los raspados (snow cones), los chicharrones (fried pork rinds), Pablo's tennis shoes, fireworks, weight lifting, and weddings. Though written in English, many of the odes contain Spanish words and phrases. My students who speak Spanish become the experts, helping others with pronunciation and meaning.

Later, we gather in a large group on the floor to share. Some groups read chorally, others choose a single person to read. As the students talk about the reasons they have chosen particular odes, we return again and again to the imagery in Soto's phrases. As we continue to talk, we decide that Soto has indeed written to "glorify" or "raise high" all the little things in his life and in his neighborhood.

Deciding to write our own odes to *this* neighborhood and to the little things in our lives, we write odes to anklets, skateboards, turtles, baseball, mothers, books, trees, goldfish, hamsters, fathers, friends, sisters and brothers, and to imagination. As they write, many of the students attempt to imitate Soto's way of describing everyday things in unique ways. In his ode to "my turtle," Jem writes, "walking in the drainage ditch, listening to the crusty brown leaves crumble under my soft, worn Nikes. I hear a grinding noise as if two rocks were arm wrestling in the freezing water...." Antoine writes of "laying in Grandpa's lap, listening to slow, slithering stories..." Matt writes an ode to his new jacket, "the son of my old jacket" that "wraps around me like a security blanket." Cal writes an ode to his garden where "Leaves spring from the stem like needles piercing through clothes" and Maria writes an ode to her dog "with caramel eyes who chases his tail because he thinks it is another dog following him." As I read the words they have written, I can see that reading the poetry of Gary Soto and talking about the imagery he utilizes to bring us close to his subject has had a profound effect on the writing of my students.

Some of the students share what they have written with their families. Calvin reads his "Ode to Mother" to his mom as they ride home in the car after school and reports that she "started to cry while I was reading and we had to pull over." Sam who previously "hated my little sister because she took all the attention away from me," has written an ode to her. We decide that she should have this for her baby scrapbook, and

I make a copy for him to give to her. "She might not understand it right now, Sam," I tell him, "But when she gets older she will read it and know that you truly love her." The students decide they want to publicize their thoughts. I make a copy of each ode; and we back the copies with colored construction paper, fastening a paper "roof" to each one so it looks like a house. We hang our odes in rows down the hallways of Westbrook, as if they were crowding the streets of a neighborhood. Between classes, students stop to read, searching for their own ode or that of a friend. One teacher writes Post-it notes of appreciation and places them on the students' "houses." They are thrilled to receive fan mail from a fellow writer.

This interlude spent reading and writing about neighborhoods gives further meaning to our reading of *The Outsiders* (Hinton, 1989). We continue to read and find ourselves comparing the neighborhood we read about, where tough guys eat at The Dingo or Jay's and go to the Nightly Double drive-in movie, to our neighborhood where kids eat at Taco Bell or "Micky Dee's" (MacDonald's) and spend Friday nights at the Dollar Cinema. We find that Pony, Soda, Darry, and Johnny have little things in their neighborhood and in their lives they could glorify with odes, just as Gary Soto has and just as we have.

Our written responses to *The Outsiders* (Hinton, 1989) have engaged us in defining the central concepts and themes of the novel, making personal connections to those concepts and themes, and comparing and contrasting our own lives with those of the characters in the novel. Meaning is constructed as the students engage in an interplay which takes them from writing to reading and then from reading to writing.

The Mystery

During a 6-week period of our time together, we immerse ourselves in mystery. We read mysterious novels. We write notes to ourselves and to one another, trying to decipher and discover the essence of *mystery*. We pour over mysterious plays and then produce our own versions of them as radio shows, complete with commercials and sound effects. As we read and write, talk and perform, we reflect on our developing understanding of the genre; and we begin to compose our own mysteries.

The Elements of Mystery

I have started writing notes to my students and hanging them outside the door—previews to what we will be doing that day that they can read and (hopefully) think about before they come to class. On this particular day I write only a question, "What's in the bag?" and fasten this to the cinder block wall outside the room.

"What *is* in the bags?" asks Pete, somewhat indignantly, as he enters the room. As the rest of the group bounds inside, sharing jokes and jostling to get to their seats, my question "What's in the bag?" is repeated again and again. When all are somewhat settled, I point to a half dozen brown paper lunch bags strewn across the table at the front of the room. Attempting to sound like Rod Steiger introducing an episode of "The Twilight Zone," I intone, "What *is* in the bags? Here before you are six ordinary brown paper lunch bags. Bags that look like they might appear in any one of our homes, in the hallways of our school, on the tables in our cafeteria; and yet these are no ordinary bags. As you can see, the bags are numbered one through six. You might wonder, 'What is the significance of these numbers?' I will provide a clue. In a few moments you will be asked to form groups of four. Each group will be provided with one bag, one numbered bag. For example, your group may choose bag number two or bag number five. . . ." "Yeah, but what's *in* the bags?" interrupts Mack impatiently. "Clearly you are curious about the contents," I reply, attempting to stay in character. "Inside the bag there is a mystery. . . . a mystery yet unwritten. Only you can shape the story, but first you must look inside the bag and puzzle over the pieces."

The students spend the next few minutes forming small groups. As each group assembles, a representative is sent to choose a bag from the table. Whispers and shrieks of laughter erupt as each group empties the contents of their bag. Inside they find an invitation/planning sheet (see appendix P). Taken together, the planning sheets and the contents of each paper bag reflect elements generally contained in a mystery—setting, clues, event (crime), motive, and characters. There are four clues in each bag, words typed and glued to strips of tag paper with the corresponding bag number on each strip. I could have put the actual items inside each bag, but using the words gives me greater freedom to include things that would be difficult to locate, unwieldy, and/or messy. I have included here a list of the clues inside each bag:

Paper Bag Number	Clues
1	rope red satin high heeled shoe ticket to the opera baseball
2	candlestick car keys half-eaten doughnut cello bow
3	string of pearls train ticket crumpled corsage revolver
	receipt for a crystal vase tube of lipstick

cont.

The Power of Writing

4	chewed leather dog leash love letter
5	brief case containing one million dollars Barney sticker book wet towel a pack of Big Red gum
6	apron half-eaten blueberry pie yo-yo clump of monkey fur

In addition to the invitation/planning sheet and clues, each bag contains three photographs of people from our collection of photographs. These people may become a villain, victim, detective, or possibly a supporting character in our mysteries. The photographs will serve as visual aids and beginning points for the creation of our characters.

By the end of the second day, after introducing the idea to all of my students, I can see that my plan as originally envisioned is not working for them. As I visit with group after group, trying to move them from talking to writing, I get a sense of the problem. "Nobody wants to write it the way I do," laments Tony. In another group Sara tells me, "Melissa and I have one idea and Mark and Jordie have another. . . . we just keep arguing about which one to do!" Cal, more emphatic, sits back in his chair with his arms folded, telling me "I *know* what I want to write and I want to do it *my* way!" As I think about what I am hearing it occurs to me that this is actually a "good" problem. My students are telling me that they want to write a mystery of their own, that they do not feel they need the support of others in this endeavor. I decide that the best approach is to leave it up to them. Of my 119 students, 87 choose to work independently, 14 to work in pairs, 6 to work in groups of three, and 12 to work in groups of four.

Mystery in a Paper Bag

Number of Students	Number in the Writing Group
87	1
14	2
6	3
12	4

In the days to come, we decide that the original groups of four can still support one another. Periodically, the groups will meet so the students can share what they are writing and respond to one another.

As the students begin to move from talking to writing we experience a difficulty much like that described by P. G. Wodehouse's character, Bertie Wooster, who wonders, "I don't know if you have had the same experience, but the snag I always come up against when I'm telling a story is this dashed difficult problem of where to begin it," (Ensign, 1993, p. 1). In an effort to help my students to recognize a number of possibilities for beginnings, I spend a few moments reading aloud to them from a book called *Great Beginnings: Opening Lines of Great Novels* (Ensign, 1993).

> We note authors who begin with the voice of a character:
> You don't know about me, without you have read a book by the name of "The Adventures of Tom Sawyer," but that ain't no matter. That book was made by Mr. Mark Twain, and he told the truth, mainly. There was things which he stretched, but mainly he told the truth. (Mark Twain, *Adventures of Huckleberry Finn*, quoted in Ensign, 1993, p. 12)

> We talk about beginning with an action sequence:
> Boys are playing basketball around a telephone pole with a backboard bolted to it. Legs, shouts. The scrape and snap of Keds on loose alley pebbles seems to catapult their voices high into the moist March air blue above the wires. (John Updike, *Rabbit, Run*, quoted in Ensign, 1993, p. 109)

> We notice that other authors begin their pieces with dialogue:
> "You won't be late?" There was anxiety in Marjorie Carling's voice, there was something like entreaty.
>
> "No, I won't be late," said Walter, unhappily and guiltily certain that he would be. Her voice annoyed him. It drawled a little, it was too refined—even in misery. "Not later than midnight." (Aldous Huxley, *Point Counter Point*, quoted in Ensign, 1993, p. 133)

> Still others may begin with a memory or a flashback to an earlier time:

> When he was nearly thirteen, my brother Jem got his arm badly broken at the elbow. When it healed, and Jem's fears of never being able to play football were assuaged, he was seldom self-conscious about his injury. (Harper Lee, *To Kill a Mockingbird*, quoted in Ensign, 1993, p. 145)

These read-alouds and the discussions that follow enable my students to develop ideas about how to begin. As we consider the words of authors who have used the voice of a character, an action sequence, dialogue, or a flashback to lead us into the story, the students begin to see alternate ways of writing their own opening lines. Later, as I circulate through the room meeting with response groups, I hear bits and pieces of mysteries emerging. Their words reassure me that our discussions of various ways to begin have provided these writers with tools they will use. I hear dialogue, "George Heney report to the ticket booth!"; detailed observation, "11:35 a.m. Amanda Fraser was found unconscious in her car, a half-eaten doughnut still clutched in her hand."; description, "The wind whistled, an eerie sound outside the old, run-down apartment building."; memoir, "I remember two years ago I was sitting at home in the state of California when I got a mysterious call at 1:00 in the morning."; a spoof of the timeworn beginning for a mystery, "Dark . . . dark . . . dark. It was dark and stormy . . ."; and even a breezy play with rhyme, "Intermission at the Corfiel Garden Opera House. A glittering crowd circles up and down the golden staircase. This is the first night of the city's most glamorous music theater. However, it is about to turn from magic to tragic."

For the next several days there is an uncommon, uncanny silence in our room as sheet after sheet of lined paper is filled with words, scratch-outs, and more words. Talk in response groups becomes more focused: "Do you see what I'm trying to do here?" "No, I can't put it that way because . . ." "Does that make sense?" Sometimes our discussions end with humor. For example, one group repeats several times in unison, "Get it?" "Got it!" "Get it?" "Got it!", breaking their clasped hands apart as if in a huddle. The students begin to come to class with fresh, typed sheets or crumpled pieces of notepaper. I hear them saying, "This is what I worked on last night," and "I woke up in the middle of the night and it came to me. I just started writing and I couldn't stop." Others who make remarks such as "Remember what you said to me on the phone about how it was too obvious? What about this?" are clearly conferring with one another outside of class.

As I sit up late at night reading their words, it occurs to me why so many of the students have chosen to do this alone. They have been together enough, reading, talking, and performing; and they are ready to think about their own personal meanings for mystery. Excerpts from a few of the mysteries contained in our two-volume work entitled, "The Lost Files of Sherlock Holmes" will illustrate my point. Pam, a musician herself, has worked with the clues in Bag Number 2—the candlestick, car keys, half-eaten doughnut, and the cello bow. She writes:

> As he entered the dressing room backstage he felt a sense of accomplishment. He had played Pastorle in F Major without a pause in the eighty-third measure or a tremor in the ninety-fourth. He was happy.
>
> He grabbed a freshly baked doughnut from the box on his dresser and turned to shut the door. Something heavy knocked him on the head and his limp body fell into a motionless heap on the floor. A wicked laugh bellowed from behind him.

Ed, working with the clues in Bag Number 3—a string of pearls, a train ticket, a crumpled corsage, and a revolver—writes on his own, away from Dave and Mike who wanted to start their mystery with the words, "It all began at an opera when Becky Gurnsey tore off Meg Jones' corsage and crumpled it to pieces." Ed has his own take on the evidence. His story begins on "a cold, rainy night at the mountain lodge on the slopes of Mount Everest." Detective Jones is working the case, and Ed follows this lead with the words:

> "So," Detective Jones said, "we have a real mystery here." He reached down and picked up a crumpled corsage from the victim's side. Where had he seen or heard about this before? The corsage was linked to the murderer. He had no means of checking police records. The storm had worsened and all communications were out, even the police radios did not work. "Talk about being in the dark," he said. "Looks as if we have to really use our brains on this one." As he stood there thinking, a police officer walked up to him with a plastic bag in his hand. "Detective, you might want to look at this," he said as he handed over the bag. It contained a train ticket from New York to Florida dated October 6, 1996. "Today's date," exclaimed Detective Jones. "If only the radios . . ." He was cut short by an officer coming in saying that the radios were working.

Lance, who dreams of becoming a professional baseball player, and who confided to me earlier in the day that he might "also like to write when I get older," has composed and typed a 10-page story which ends in an epilogue. The epilogue states that Lance's central character, Oleo Odeberry Johnson, a detective, has since retired and is now writing "adult novels such as *When the Time Was Right* and *Death Due to the Bad Man*." As he writes, Lance goes deep inside the life of his central character, the 67-year-old detective, Oleo Odeberry Johnson. Reading his opening words, I can "see" Lance working on his mystery, his face taking on the irreverent, gruff, and sassy look that I imagine Oleo would have:

> "What do you want—it's three o'clock in the morning," I said as the phone woke me up. "I'm Oleo Odeberry Johnson with the Colorado Springs Police Department. At age sixty-seven, I've been on the police force for nearly forty years now . . . What I really can't believe is that Sergeant Reeves (my partner) is calling me at this time in the morning. . . ." "Ode, it's a stalking we have on our hands now," said Reeves. At this, I growled and yelled into the phone, "You are saying that your dumb superiors are giving me a stalker case! Who has the 42-1 record and is world renown in the detective business? Me, just me! What is it, have I suddenly gotten too old for the business of being a detective? If so, I'll ditch you and your floundering police department and step down right now, over the phone! Want me to? I'll gladly depart from this job!" I was out of control and I knew it, but I really was that angry. This old geezer is coming back. I was preparing to continue with my onslaught when Reeves stopped me.

For the next few weeks after the publication of "The Lost Files of Sherlock Holmes," classes begin with writers volunteering to read aloud the stories they have written. As the students read, their pride in what they have accomplished is evident, as is their growing sense of the mystery genre itself. Suggestions are made that we "Try to *really* get this published," and, of a more immediate nature, that we "Do some more stuff like this!"

A Detective's Notebook

Our most recent writing response in the study of mystery has been to create detective's notebooks, what I envision as a mystery in an alternate format. I give each student a notebook which looks much like a steno pad. In actuality, the notebooks are made with an 8 1/2 x 11 sheet of index paper cut in half for the front and back covers and twelve sheets of plain copy paper of the same size cut in half for the inside pages. I then spiral bind the notebook using the school binding machine. Tucked inside each notebook is a description of the writing experience and a rubric (see appendices Q and R). The description or planning sheet includes 10 aspects of the detective's notebook:

- Description of yourself as the detective (may include a photo)
- Photographs and descriptions of the appearance and personality of three characters in your mystery
- Photographs or drawings of at least three clues to the mystery
- At least one sketch, map, or photo of the scene of the crime
- One to two page write-up by you, the detective, describing the scene of the crime and detailing your observations
- One to two page statement from each of the three characters in your mystery
- Your description of the crime and your conclusion (Who did it? and Why?)
- Arrest report with fingerprints of the criminal
- Epilogue—What are the characters doing one year after you solve the mystery?

In the next few weeks as we continue to read, talk, and write to one another about the mystery/suspense novels we are reading, we will also spend a part of each class period working together on our detective's notebooks. Before we address each of the 10 items on the planning sheet, we talk together as a whole class group. At this point, I can provide direct instructions to my students on the particulars which pertain to this item through mini-lessons. For example, as we read and talk about the first writing experience—the description of ourselves as the detective—I ask, "Why don't we start by thinking of new names for ourselves." In response to their questioning looks, I elaborate, saying "Well, for example, I could be Vera Van Schnorn of the Van Horn and Van Schnorn Detective Agency." "Oh, I get it now," exclaims Tony. In the next few minutes the students shout out suggestions and before long they have transformed themselves, becoming Detectives Joker Jackson, Mac Macaroni, Kris Knowles It All, Crisco Varisco, and Ruin You Ripple. I write their new names on a sheet of bulletin board paper. We decide to hang this up when we are working on our "cases." As the work progresses, we "live" the experience. The students bring dark sunglasses, trench coats, or neck ties to wear while they are writing. They begin to call one another by their detective names inside and outside of class.

At the end of each class period, we discuss the next phase of the case. As we talk about bringing in photographs of three characters Mack asks, "Can I draw my characters?" This prompts further thinking. Kris decides she will use her three cats as characters. Mora, using school photos, will write about her best friends. On the day they are to bring in clues, it becomes obvious to me that the students have full ownership of the experience. They bring bits of torn cloth, broken necklaces, and cat foot prints. Others stand on a page of the notebook, making imprints of the bottom of their tennis shoes or cut snippets of their own hair to tape to the pages. Jack sits on the floor with his notebook, biting his lower lip as he tries to attach a golf ball and a broken identification bracelet inside his detective's notebook. "I don't think it's going to stay in there Jack," I remark, kneeling beside him. "What if I take some pictures of your clues? You could glue them inside your notebook." Jack looks relieved at my suggestion and, perhaps remembering movies or television show mysteries, asks if we can photograph a ruler with each clue so, "You can tell what size it is." Anita, watches us taking the photographs. When it is time for us to enter the scene of the crime, Anita comes to class with polaroids of her kitchen at home. There is a knife on the floor and what looks like blood spattered over the counter tops. Laughing at my expression of horror, Anita says, "That's not really blood, it's just ketchup. My mom screamed at first when she saw it, but I told her I was just doing my homework!"

As work on the cases progresses, students offer to share pieces of their detective's notebook with the class. Stefano sits stiffly on the stool in front of the classroom as he shares what he, Detective Catch 'Em All Carranzo, is feeling as he enters the scene of the crime.

> *It was a misty night. Friday night to be exact. The house looked like a ghost house. I touched the cold, hard door knob, embracing the cold metal against my soft, fragile human skin. With a twist of the knob I was suddenly flooded and overwhelmed with new senses. Fear, nausea, excitement, and a sick feeling in my throat. Through it all there was one emotion I could not put behind me. The huge lump in my throat. It was telling me something here was very wrong.*
>
> *It was driving me crazy. I was on the edge of tears. They are right. Men try to seem tough, but there is always something that tells a man to stop trying to be tough. I almost let it go. I was furious. How could someone do this to another human being? No matter how many times it happens I always start to value the thin line that separates the dead from the living. Just the sight of the fragile human being lying lifeless, still, cold. The person seems to*

> *be pleading with me. Pleading and begging me not to let this happen again. For a moment I let everything go. Not trying to stop the emotions. Not trying to keep the tears in any longer. Everything in that house seemed to be crying and mourning the death of the man. Through the tears everything seemed blurry. Still I could hear the cries. It was speaking to me. Then, in a split second it all went away. Lifeless, still, and serene.*
>
> *The world was gray. It was as dead as the innocent man. I had to do something.*
>
> *I had to bring myself back into the real world again. At that moment I made up my mind. This man was not going to die in vain!*

Most of his classmates are visibly impressed, but amidst the murmurs of approval there are a few snickers of derision at the emotion Stefano expresses in his writing. Someone mutters in a sing-song voice, "Are you cryyying Stefano?" He looks up, his eyes serious, responding indignantly, "No *I'm* not crying, but I think I might if I were there. I'm trying to write the way I would really feel. How I would feel . . . I would know I have to do something, but at first . . . at first I would feel this way." Stefano's response to the remarks of some of his peers shows us that the students have to come to value what they can learn from one another as they share their writing and that they will continue to do so despite occasional misunderstandings.

The impact of Stefano's reading and his honest portrayal of emotion reverberates over the next several days. Grady who is in this class group, is at first overwhelmed. He wants to write "as good as Stefano." I try to help him by asking him to first verbalize what he might write or "tell me the story." Together we sit and look at the photograph of the scene of the crime he has glued inside his detective's notebook. Suggesting that he look closely at the photograph and imagine he is there, walking inside the picture, I ask him to talk to me and tell me what he sees. He looks at me sheepishly, at first reluctant to begin. As he talks, I jot down what he is saying:

> *It's a windy day on the streets of San Francisco and see this, there's a lot of dirt blowing in the wind. It gets in my eyes and I squint to see these people. See, these are some bad people walking toward me on the other side of the street. It's real quiet. There's a dog sitting in the*

> *middle of the street. As I walk along my trench coat starts flapping in the wind and the dog starts to bark . . .*

I read back to Grady what he has said to me so he can hear the way that he is composing as he speaks his thoughts aloud. As I read, someone sitting nearby whistles and comments, "Wow, Grady wrote *that*!" I hand him my notes and Grady, head down, begins to write in earnest. Several days later Grady, who has never volunteered to read aloud, offers to share his description of the scene of the crime:

> *The wind is heavy, the sky is dark. My throat is very dry and my hair flies wildly in the wind as if it was a flag. The dogs bark loudly as they sense trouble in the air. My heart beats at a regular speed. I feel a gust of wind against my gray sweat shirt. As I approach the gate of the dock I see a kind of oily substance trailing what seems to be a rather large truck. . . . As I approach the warehouse which appears to empty I see a red Dodge Caravan turn the corner. I desperately try not to be seen, but am spotted. As the van approaches I try to act as calmly as I can, but still, I am very nervous. Out of fright, I suddenly give a sigh of relief as the van drives by and shows no sign of curiosity or care. I suddenly realize I shouldn't be here and I leave.*

As he writes, Grady has changed and embellished the words he originally spoke when he talked to me about the photograph. Talking has provided him with a way to collect his ideas and to gain the confidence to begin to write. At times, I have students speak their thoughts into a tape recorder before they begin to write. They can then play back the tape, making notes about what they want to write and how they want to write it as they listen. As we continue to work on our cases, I reflect in my journal about the experience and the implications for my students:

> *We are working on interviewing the suspects for our detective notebooks. Cory asked, "When it says it could be an interview, can you write it like it had in the mystery plays?" This was so exciting to me. He was taking the format of the dialogue from the play he had read and applying it to his own writing. I truly think that in some way students learn from everything we do. They take things away from the experiences, internalize them, and then use*

them later. In the beginning I thought students might want to try to take the easy way out, but what I've found is that more often than not, they will do much more than they have to according to the specifications or rubric. For example, I asked that they introduce and interview three characters. Many of them had five or more characters in their notebooks. Same situation for the clues. Same for the scene of the crime which could have been a photograph or a drawing. Some of them have included photographs marked by the detective and blueprint type drawings as well as a general area map. I thought the twenty-four sheets of paper inside the notebooks would be more than enough, but I had to open up several of them and add paper today. I think what I am discovering is that I come up with the bare bones experience and as they work with it within a learning community and share their thoughts the experience becomes whole. In other words, the learning continues through the process as they interact with the reading/ writing/ doing and come up with their own ideas. . . . If I had the students do the bulk of the work at home I would lose two-thirds of the learning experience and most of the community building.

As we approach the conclusion of our cases, we must make an arrest. Betty, whose father works in law enforcement brings me a copy of the statement of rights, personal history, and finger print forms used in an arrest. I make a transparency of the forms, and we devote our efforts to "handling the closing paperwork." Each blank on the forms is numbered and we proceed to fill in height, weight, social security number, identifying scars, tattoos, and so forth, along with aliases, type of violation, and place of arrest. As we work our way toward completion of the last of 48 blanks, Joker Jackson sighs and remarks, "Wow, this is pretty tough work. I could use a cup of coffee. I'd hate to have to do this all day." Crisco Varisco responds to his complaint matter-of-factly, saying, "Just part of the job, Jackson!"

Unwilling to end the experience, Tony suggests that we should exchange notebooks with a partner and try to solve someone else's case. To do this, we put paper clips around the conclusion, arrest report, and epilogue. The students curl up on the floor, making notes and chewing the ends of their pencils in concentration as they read descriptions of characters, evidence, the crime scene, and interviews or statements from each character. When we meet to compare notes, comments such as "I knew it," "I figured it out when I read the interview of Marissa Morosco!" "Oh, man, who would ever think that?" and "How am I supposed to figure that out?" reveal that some have been more successful than others in making inferences and developing interpretations of the "data."

That afternoon, the students stack their notebooks in a cardboard box, so that I can read them through one more time. Joker Jackson, whose memory of the drudgery of filling out the arrest reports has already faded, remarks, "Last year writing seemed like work, but this year it's fun—it just doesn't seem like work."

Macbeth: A Myriad of Meanings

In the preceding chapter, I described our experiences as we read several versions of Shakespeare's play, *Macbeth* (Garfield, 1985; Scholastic, 1994), and enacted our own performances of the play. As we worked to visualize the words of Shakespeare, imagining both the actions and the meanings behind the actions, we wrote to express our growing understanding.

Finding Poetry in the Play

While reading and rereading the Scholastic (1994) version of *Macbeth* in preparation for filming the play, our dialogue inside and outside of the classroom becomes enlivened by the words of Shakespeare. Kris, who has dribbled spaghetti sauce on her new blouse, points emphatically to the mess and laments, "Out, out damn spot!" During tutorials, Scotty trying desperately to complete his math homework, holds his pencil in the air before him, dramatically exclaiming, "Is this a pencil I see before me, point toward my hand? Let me clutch you. I have you not, and yet I see you still. Are you but a pencil of the mind, a false creation of a fevered brain?" Later, as he finishes his assignment, he drops his pencil on the desk with a flourish, announcing, "I have done the deed!"

In order to capitalize on this interest in the words of the play, I suggest that we create found poems as we had done during our reading of *Canyons* (Paulsen, 1990). The students begin to experiment with the process, making it their own. Barry pulls a series of lines from the play in order to summarize the action:

> Never shall he see tomorrow's sun!
> My thane, look like the innocent flower,
> but be the serpent underneath!
> Stars hide your fires
> Let not light see my black and deep desires!
> I have done the deed. This is a sorry sight.
> Did you hear a noise?
> I thought I heard a voice cry.
> My hands are now of your color,
> but a little water clears us of this deed.

> How easy it is!
> No time for tears now.
> Let us get away from here.
> I'll go to Ireland, you go to England.
> Being separated will keep us both safer.
> Here there are daggers in men's smiles.
> Macbeth! Macbeth!
> Laugh and scorn the power of man,
> for none of woman born shall harm Macbeth.
> Forget your charm
> I was not born, but ripped from my mother's womb!
> They fight and Macbeth is killed.
> Then Macduff enters and places his bloody sword
> with Macbeth's bloody head upon it, before Malcolm.
> Hail king, for you are so!

Jim chooses a single line from the play, repeating it at various intervals in his poem. He deliberately repeats the words "Hail king, for so you are," coupling this phrase with descriptions of Macbeth's treachery and deceit. Jim's writing reveals his awareness of the irony in the play as well as his growing understanding of the contrast between good and evil and the abuse of power exemplified in the play.

> Hail king, for so you are.
> Bloody tyrant, burning carcass.
> King of courage, king of fire.
> Hail king, for so you are.
>
> Hail king, for so you are.
> Bloody hands, trembling fear.
> Shield of honor, blade of steel.
> Hail king, for so you are.
>
> Hail king, for so you are.
> King of good, king of bad.
> Tyrant of passion, tyrant of betrayal.
> Hail king, for so you are.
>
> Hail king, for so you are.
> Knife of guilt, killer of Duncan.
> Wife that is dead, Malcolm that rules.
> Hail king, for so you are.

Tania chooses specific lines from the play, and then writes her questions or the meanings she has constructed for these lines in parentheses below the lines. Her poem reveals the questions, comments, and observations she is making as she reads and as she writes. As she writes, Tania translates the language of the text into her own way of speaking and thinks about the central issues of the play: "Can you really be what you are promised?" and "Do you really have to be bad to win what you deserve?"

> YOU CAN BE WHAT YOU ARE PROMISED.
> (Can you really be what you are promised?)
> YOU ARE NOT WITHOUT AMBITION BUT YOU ARE WITHOUT THE EVIL WHICH SHOULD ACCOMPANY IT.
> (Do you really have to be bad to win what you deserve?)
> NEVER SHALL THE KING SEE TOMORROW'S SUN.
> (In other words, tomorrow)
> MY THANE, LOOK LIKE THE INNOCENT FLOWER, BUT BE THE SERPENT UNDER IT.
> (Look like an innocent person, but really know what's going on.)
> WHAT? ARE YOU AFRAID TO WIN WHAT YOU DESIRE?
> (Are you afraid to get what you want?)
> WHEN YOU DARED TO COMMIT THE MURDER, THEN YOU WERE A MAN.
> (When you said you would do the murder, then you knew what was best.)
> FAIL? SCREW YOUR COURAGE TO THE STICKING PLACE AND WE'LL NOT FAIL.
> (We will do what we must do.)

Others choose to write their reflections about particular characters:

> Evil Witches
> They don't look like
> inhabitants of the earth.
> They look into time,
> and greet you with great predictions,
> but to gain these fortunes
> you must play most foully.
> These acts are too cruel anywhere.
> The acts to gain this power
> are not worth the reward.
> They are the evil witches
> with beards like men.

> Tragic Crime
> Macbeth . . . who was he really?
> He was a greedy man at heart,
> too famous for killing his royal and best friend.
> Sorrow at ease, and blood upon his hands.
> Smudge of grief across his face
> told us of his guilt.
> Too confused in a dark world that keeps him

> trapped by all his desires.
> Alone in what he wants, is all of his needs,
> and his only crime was
> of his greed.

Reading what my students have written helps me to see that they are building upon our previous writing experiences in response to literature. As they explore the possibilities of form and function in their poems, their writing reveals the development of their understanding of the play. These students recognize the significant events in the play. They are forming questions about the text and hypothesizing about possible meanings. As they focus upon individual characters in the play, the students convey their reactions to the characters. These reactions often include personal judgments about the actions or morals of the characters.

Conclusions About *Macbeth*

After we have completed the filming of our production of Macbeth, I invite my students to respond in writing to the whole experience—to write to solidify and capture their thoughts and conclusions about the play. Later, in high school, when they encounter the original version of Macbeth, they may reread what they have written in 7th grade to help them activate their prior knowledge and reenter the world of the text. With this in mind, I am fairly directive about the structure of the piece. I sit at the overhead projector with each class group as we develop an overview or outline of the piece. Together we talk about each facet of the piece as the students ask questions and offer suggestions. Here, I will provide examples taken from a number of completed essays in order to illustrate each aspect.

We begin with a discussion of the message or theme of the play. I ask the students to think about what Shakespeare may be telling us, considering the questions "What is the message he conveys with this play?" "What have we learned?" "What will we remember?" Their responses include references to power and greed, retribution, and peer pressure. For example, Burton expresses his thoughts on power:

> The message I think William Shakespeare is trying to get across to the reader is that once you do something bad and get power you keep on wanting more power, and then you turn into a totally different person. This is what happened to Macbeth because power corrupted him and changed him from an honorable warrior to a disgraceful murderer.

Martin writes that "you should not let your greed get the best of you. You should just let things come naturally, don't rush things; take life one step at a time." Bet explains her thoughts on the theme of retribution:

I think that William Shakespeare was trying to tell us that whatever you do comes back to you, whether good or bad. I think that is a good thing because if you do something mean to someone else it will come back to you. So if someone makes fun of you for no reason, leave it alone because they will get what is coming to them, maybe not now, but later in life.

Dan and Calvin are among those who view *Macbeth* as a statement about peer pressure. Dan writes that "His message reached out to me. . . . do what's right in your heart; don't be pressured by others." Calvin writes:

You should never do anything unfair or wrong to alter the course of your future because you are who you are and you cannot change that with a lie. Everybody has something good about themselves; sometimes it just takes time to find it. A shorter version of all I have just said is that you should not try to be somebody you are not.

We continue the essay with a brief summary of the events of the play. As they write their summaries, the students may refer to their copies of the script and/or reflect back on the experience of performing and producing the play. While some students elaborate more than others in this section, Calvin's summary is a representative example:

The story starts out with Banquo and Macbeth coming back from a victorious battle. They meet three witches sitting around a cauldron making magic brews. The witches give prophesies that Macbeth will become Thane of Cawdor, and later he will become king. A messenger comes from the king to tell Macbeth that he has been chosen to be Thane of Cawdor. Macbeth thinks that if one of the things already told by the witches has come true, then the other will too. Macbeth later decides that he can't wait long enough for the king to die and he makes plans for his wife, Lady Macbeth, and himself to kill King Duncan and steal the crown from his son Malcolm. One night, Macbeth has King Duncan over as a guest and when he goes to sleep Macbeth thinks that this is the time to kill him. His conscience tells him not to, but his brain says to get it done. Lady Macbeth drugs the guards, and Macbeth takes

> *their daggers and kills Duncan with them. He then wipes his blood on the faces of the guards and kills them too so they can't tell their side of the story. The next day Macduff comes and sees Duncan dead and suspects Macbeth of the whole thing. Macbeth's friend, Banquo suspects him too. So Macbeth hires two murderers to kill Banquo and his son. That night Macbeth holds a feast and sees Banquo's ghost. Later in the story Lady Macbeth goes insane with the guilt of all the murders and kills herself. Macbeth then goes to the three witches to ask what will happen next and the three spirits tell him that Macduff has plans to kill him, that any man born from a woman cannot hurt him, and that he cannot be hurt until Great Birnam Wood comes up to Dunsinane. Macduff and his army come up to Dunsinane with branches in front of them to disguise themselves and Macduff kills Macbeth. Macduff was torn out of his mother's womb, or as we know it, she had a C-section, and so the fact that no one born of woman can hurt Macbeth did not apply to Macduff. Later, Malcolm, Duncan's son is given the crown and made king.*

During our reading and performance of the play, we had engaged in discussions of the various sorts of conflict presented in literature—person versus person, person versus nature, and person versus himself or herself. We categorized these conflicts as being internal (a struggle which takes place within the minds of the characters) or external (a struggle between individuals or between individuals and the forces of nature). These definitions were written down on our word wall and in the students' Reader/Writer logs so they could refer to them throughout the study of *Macbeth*. Now, having addressed the theme of the play and having reviewed the events of the play through their summaries, we were ready to continue with our essays. In this next section, the students would write to identify and discuss the conflicts within the play. At this point, I ask the students to begin by identifying or defining the type of conflict and then to provide an example or examples of this type of conflict from the play. A paragraph from Dan's essay exemplifies the results:

> *Internal conflict means a struggle which takes place within the minds of characters. Macbeth's internal conflict was that he was arguing with himself whether or not to kill the king so he could be king. But his wife made him make that*

> decision to kill the king. Which leads me to external conflict. External conflict means a struggle between individuals or between individuals and the forces of nature. Macbeth's external conflicts were with his wife, Banquo and his sons, and the weird sisters. His external conflict with his wife was a tough struggle. She persuaded him to do a lot of things that he did not want to do and did not want her to do. Like killing the king so he could take the throne, smearing the guard's faces with blood, and doing all the other evil deeds. He also had a struggle with Banquo and his sons. He didn't want Banquo's sons to be king, so he killed Banquo and his sons. Another struggle he had was with the weird sisters. He didn't know whether or not he could believe them, but later he found out what they said was true.

Finally, we talk of justice. We look up the word in our class dictionary and find that justice refers to the quality of being just or fair. This definition is elusive. I ask the students, "Can we elaborate?" "How do *we* define justice?" "What is fair?" "Have we experienced times in our own lives when we felt justice was served or not served?" "Are the events in *Macbeth* just or fair?" Not everyone will agree on the definition of justice, nor will all agree on whether or not justice is served in *Macbeth*. That is what I expect; what I hope for is that each student will come to an understanding that makes sense to him or her and that each one will find a way to express and explain that understanding. I will close this chapter as I began it, with the words of Stefano. This is his written response to the question of justice:

> To me, justice can not be served until the person can admit or understand what he or she did is wrong. You can punish a man for a hundred years and call it justice, but it will do nothing. Until they understand, and admit to doing wrong the person will not learn or feel anything. When someone learns their mistakes their conscience will punish their soul for eternity. Once a person sees they are wrong then, and only then can you punish them and call it justice. If you punish a man who sees nothing wrong with his actions it will only fuel their anger and make them do it again and again. The person will have learned nothing. They will know nothing more than they did before. You can not teach a man to learn from his mistake if he sees none.

> *If a man learns his mistakes he will punish himself more severely than any prison, camp, or man could ever have thought possible.*
>
> *In Macbeth, justice in the end was truly served as Macbeth's conscience slowly, but surely started to eat him from the inside. As we see, he punished himself by imagining that he saw the people he once knew, but had killed. Macbeth realized that he was wrong in his actions but it was too much, and too hard for him to stop. He had to ride it out until the total complete end of him or his actions. When Macbeth was killed it undid a small percent of his evil, but that was only the beginning. In my opinion justice was served. Macbeth realized his mistakes and began to go insane. For the sinner to experience the sin he committed is the best punishment I can think of. Better than any punishment we have today. He felt what he put many people through. He was killed like King Duncan; someone killed him and then took his place before he knew it.*

This experience in writing what may be viewed as a rather complex essay in response to a complex work of literature is possible for several reasons. We are building upon our previous experiences in writing; and we are writing in response to an extensive study of the text in which we have established prior knowledge through reading, speaking, listening, performing, and visually representing the text. As noted at the beginning of this section, I preview the outline for the entire essay for my students before we begin to write. The writing of the essay takes place over several class periods. As we prepare to write each new section of the essay, the students and I begin with a consideration of what it is that we will do and what we know that will help us to do this. Again, I find that breaking down the process and building in time for us to reflect and share as we write helps my students to develop their writing and to develop the meanings they are constructing as they write.

Evaluation/Assessment

As I have described in previous chapters, evaluation and assessment are integral parts of our process as we engage in the various aspects of literacy. In most cases it has been our practice to collaborate and achieve consensus about our writing responses/products prior to and during the actual writing experience. At other times, I introduce the writing experience with a planning sheet and rubric that illustrate the expectations for the writing. This is a strategy I began to use after I learned too late, too many times, that my students did not have a clear idea of what was expected of them, how to approach various ways of writing responses to literature, and/or how to evaluate what they had written. As students participate in discussions and learn to use and/or collaboratively construct outlines, planning sheets, and rubrics, they begin to take an active role in the planning, execution, and evaluation of their writing.

At this point, it would be helpful to review some of the writing experiences I have described in this chapter and clarify how they might be evaluated/assessed. Here, I will keep my description of the experience to a minimum, concentrating instead on the issue at hand. With this in mind, you may want to reread any section that describes a writing experience you want to adapt or include in your curriculum and then return to the following table as you consider how you might evaluate/assess the writing.

Description	Evaluation/Assessment
Viewing a photograph and writing inner dialogue	This is a "discovery" experience. As such the students and I do not construct a rubric before or during the writing. As I read their completed responses, I look for: • attention to the details in the photograph; • dialogue which reflected possible or plausible thoughts of the person in the photograph; • dialogue written in the format we identify in the short story we read.
Writing a short story or "chapter" for a class book modeled on *The Van Gogh Café*.	Discuss/plan with the students. Develop a rubric with the students using student examples as the writing proceeds. Rubric includes: the elements of a story, specific references to the setting and what it was before it became a magical place, and foreshadowing of the stories "chapters" to follow.
Composing a quick-write considering the question "How could something so big come from something so small?"	Students respond in Reader/Writer logs. Evaluation/assessment of this writing experience is part of the overall evaluation/assessment of the Reader/Writer log.
Constructing and writing a journal for a character in the novel *Canyons*	Hand made journal which contains 20 entries and 10 artifacts (see appendix O).
Writing a "found poem" based upon the novel *Canyons*	Develop rubric with the students. Rubric includes: lines excerpted from a page or pages of the novel, written in the format of a poem, citation of page numbers and title of the novel, optional repetition of lines and/or inclusion of original lines and phrases.

cont.

Writing a definition of an "outsider"	Students respond in Reader/Writer logs. Evaluation/assessment of this writing experience is part of the overall evaluation/assessment of the Reader/Writer log.
Writing a definition of "friendship"	This is a "discovery" experience. As such, the students and I decide that their responses may take the form of either a poem or a short essay on the topic.
Writing an "ode" to our neighborhood	Rubric developed with the students during the writing process. Rubric includes: a title structured as "Ode to . . .", subject is something in the neighborhood that is meaningful to/appreciated by the student, a single page written in the form of a poem, the use of imagery which helps the reader to see, hear, touch, smell, or taste.
Writing a mystery based upon the contents of a paper bag.	Planning sheet is provided to the students along with the contents of the bag (see appendix P). Rubric addresses each of the aspects of the planning sheet.
Writing a mystery in alternate format—the detective's notebook	Planning sheet and rubric are provided to the students along with the blank detective's notebooks (see appendices Q and R).
Writing a "found poem" based upon the play, *Macbeth*	Develop rubric with the students. Rubric includes lines excerpted from a page or pages of the play, written in the format of a poem, title, optional repetition of lines and/or inclusion of original lines and phrases.
Writing an essay about *Macbeth*	Outline is developed and previewed with the students prior to and during the writing experience. Rubric addresses each aspect of the outline; i.e., theme or message of the play is noted and discussed, events are summarized, conflict is identified and example(s) is(are) provided, justice is defined, and the student draws conclusions about whether or not justice is served in *Macbeth*.

SUMMARY

We write for many reasons. When asked why people write, my students have responded that people write to "let their emotions out," "so they can tell a special thing that they know or thought of," "to give messages to other people," "to show the world who they are inside," "to play with their ideas," or to "let anger out, to bring happiness in, to tell a story, to remember, or to forget." When asked what writers need, their answers

The Power of Writing

vary from concise lists such as "a writer needs an imagination, pencil, and a piece of paper," to poetic visions such as "to be a good writer a piece of the writer has to go on the paper."

In seeking to write to express the meanings we are constructing from our readings and our lives together, we try on and expand upon various ways of working. We listen to the "voices" in photographs, model our writing after works by others, and compare ourselves to characters and writers as we consider critical moments in our lives and as we attempt to see and write through the eyes of the characters. We find poems in the words of others and define concepts such as outsider, friend, and justice. We put together pieces of puzzling mysteries. We write to understand and to remember our interactions with texts and with one another.

In each of these instances our writing is tied to our readings. We write before, during, and after reading. As we write, we continue the cycle of discovering what we think, finding ways to express our thoughts and learning from one another as we share our struggles and our triumphs. We publish our words in classroom books or hang them on the hallway walls where they can speak to us again and remind us of who we are and what we are thinking. Our writing is not always polished. At times it seems that we are "racing against the flames and the words to come." And yet, each time we put pencil to paper we are growing, finding ourselves, and finding the meanings we make of our reading and our living. Perhaps Michael expresses it most clearly when he writes, "I like to write about normal every day things because when I write about them they don't seem like normal things anymore; they become special to me and I learn more from them."

In chapter 7 our meaning making is further extended as we wrestle with the tangible representation of our thoughts. This chapter includes descriptions and reflections on our process of creating visual representations of the meanings derived from our experiences with texts.

7

The Power of Visual Representation

Reading, Writing, and Works of Art

All my life I wanted to know what it was like to write a book or draw in a book. I remember one time we went to the library to check out a book. I was thinking how fun it would be to find an empty page in the back of the book and draw one of the pictures that I saw on the front cover. When we brought the book back to the library, they flipped through the book and saw that I had drawn in the back of it and my mom had to pay for it. . . . My process is simple. All you need to do is read a lot of books. Then, take notes on how the story tells itself when you read it and how it makes you feel. . . . You know when people say a picture is worth a thousand words? That's what I think.

Jarod

Jarod opens this piece with his earliest memory of reading and drawing—a time when he drew on a blank page in a picture book checked out from the public library. Jarod then describes the relationship he has discovered between reading, writing, and drawing. For him, the process is a "simple" one, a sequence in which one act leads naturally to another. Jarod begins by reading. Reading leads to writing as he "takes notes on how the story tells itself" and how it makes him feel. His written reflections about what he has read and how it makes him feel lead him to draw. For Jarod, drawing is a way to compress "a thousand words" into a single image, an image that reveals elements of the text and the poem (Rosenblatt, 1978) he has created through the reading. Cal too, expresses a sense of these connections:

> I have a little thing called the "Art Cycle" which is reading inspires me to write and writing inspires me to draw and drawing inspires me to read in order to get more ideas to write and then draw again.

Other students may draw to gather ideas or to help them clarify what they want to write. Stacy writes that "Drawing helps me get a better picture of what I am writing. Drawing helps to explain my stories better because people see what I am visualizing while I am writing." For Stacy, drawing functions both as a tool for elaboration and as a key to a reader's understanding of what she has written.

Jarod says that "not a day goes by that I don't pick up a pencil and draw something." Anita writes that "When I draw and illustrate I feel like I'm creating life." For Jarod, Anita, and others like them, drawing may be a way to chronicle or signify personal meaning. The thoughts of these students exemplify the ways that many of my students have come to view drawing. Their prior experiences have led them to conclude that reading, writing, and drawing are interconnected acts of creativity and meaning making. For others, drawing is something "I stink at" or "I hate to do."

Ruth Hubbard (1989) writes that "we need to expand our narrow definition of literacy to include visual dimensions" (p. 150). During our time together I want to provide opportunities for my students to create visual representations which will enhance their literary experiences. The reading and language arts standards for our state include viewing and representing. As described in these standards, this includes "procedures for producing visual images, messages, and meanings to communicate with others," and teaching students "how to select, organize, and produce visuals to complement and extend meaning" (http://www.tea.state.tx.us/teks/). With this in mind, my students and I will work together to explore ways to produce visual representations which communicate, complement, and extend the meaning of our literary experiences. As you read the following sections of this chapter, think about how you might translate or adapt these experiences to fit with the texts you and your students are reading.

Beginning by Remembering

One of my favorite books is *Celebrate America in Poetry and Art* (Panzer, 1994), a collection of poetry paired with paintings, drawings, photographs, and other works of art from the National Museum of American Art. Early in the year my students and I read the first poem of many we will share from this collection, "Remember" by Joy Harjo (Panzer, 1994, p. 33). Harjo writes of our connections to one another and to the earth. Paired with this poem is a photograph of a fan quilt made by the residents of Bourbon County, Kentucky. Each square of the quilt contains a fan made from strips of colored fabric appliquéd on a black background. In the upper right hand corner of each square there is what we presume to be a symbol of the creator of the square. For example, we find embroidered appliqués of a person, a horse, a book, a star, a heart, and three rings linked together. One square, different from all the others, contains only a painted picture of a red barn with a spray of flowers above.

Inspired by the poem and the photograph, we decide to write poems about something we remember and to create our own quilt. Our quilt will be made of strips of colored paper cut with scissors which create zig-zag or scalloped edges on the paper. We plan to write our poems on these strips and then glue our fans to black construction paper.

Author Toni Morrison (1987) has written that "memory weighs heavily in what I write, in how I begin and in what I find to be significant" (p. 111). She describes her process of writing, revealing that she begins with an image or "the 'picture' and the feelings that accompany the picture" (p. 112) which then "tells me what the 'memory' is about" (p. 114). For Morrison, the mental image or picture is the stimulus which allows her to enter and then to write about the memory. I share this with the students, asking them to close their eyes and search for images which evoke memories. Then, without saying a word, we pick up our pens and begin to write.

Corly remembers the agony and the ecstasy of a track meet:

> The sun grilling on my back as I'm bent over the let the
> substance come out of my mouth.
> As I hear my stomach organs clam up.
> I sit back into the little shade that I had sitting next to the
> stand.
> My coach comes to me and asks me if I'm okay.
> I think to myself, "Back up lady!"
> I could throw up any minute now.
> As I picked up my water to quench my thirst,
> I felt my stomach unclamp just a little.
> I get up, looking deformed and demented.
> I get up and start walking across the track to warm up.
> I feel the sweat slide down my face and my skin gets browner.
> I hear the man say 4 x 400 meter relay!
> We run over onto the track and get into our lanes.
> My lead off man, April, gets the good start.
> I start to feel the call of nature as I feel a cold, yet satisfying

breeze come by my shoulders.
Little did I know, it was my friend April in first place, handing
it off to Brittany, and then to Katie.
She took off at a fast pace and got us back into the lead.
The man now says "Westbrook, stand on the track."
I'm feeling sick and have to go to the bathroom.
I get the handout and it was like someone hit all the fear out of me.
I could feel my body just tearing through the wind,
coming around that last home stretch and landing it in.
I could hear my mother screaming at me, "Faster, baby!"
It echoes through my ears.
I come in first and win District Champs!

Corly's memories are centered around her feelings that day. When she closes her eyes and "sees" herself at the track meet, she can then feel again the way she felt on that day. These feelings are then transferred to the page as she writes about being sick to her stomach, hot, thirsty, and so forth, in ways that enable us to feel what she is feeling. While Corly takes us to a track meet, Nettie remembers learning to be a best friend forever:

Remember when we would go to the park on hot summer days.
Remember when we would tell stories of what we had done in the past.
Remember the day we said we would be best friends forever.
I didn't really know what it meant until that day.
Until I saw the boxes and a sale sign in the front.
I remember that day you told me the news.
I was afraid of what would come next.
That day you left as you waved good-bye out of the back
window of the car.
And I went home slowly, wondering if it was true.
I sat on my bed.
I knew what friendship meant.
Remember.

Nettie calls forth a succession of images which depict the critical moments in a friendship. She sees herself and her friend playing in the park, telling stories, sealing friendship, and saying good-bye. Finally, she sees herself alone, trying to remember what it was like to be and to have a friend. Maria, too, remembers a special relationship. She writes about her grandfather:

Grandpa, I remember you.
Remember when I was born.
You were there to hold me and welcome me.

> You were there to care for me and love me.
> Remember you would play with me.
> Then I grew older and moved.
> Remember it was hard to let go.
> Remember we would go visit you and you were so nice to me.
> You would give me things that were special to you and now they are special to me.
> Remember I would sit on your lap and we would laugh together and hug each other.
> We grew so close, but then on February 25, 1998 it all ended when you died of sickness.
> It was so hard to let go of my grandpa, my heart, my everything.
> In March we were supposed to be going to your surprise birthday party,
> but now we stay home thinking of you.
> I just want you to know that I have always loved you and will always miss you.

When she closes her eyes to evoke a memory, Maria sees a succession of images or moments in her life with her grandfather. Using these images, Maria writes to remind him of the things they have done together and to tell him once again that she loves him. As we look at what these students have written, we can see that each of them has focused on a different aspect of the memory. Even so, it is clear that the process of closing our eyes and attempting to visualize and reenter the moment has enabled the students to enter the writing process and to write in ways that evoke the images or feelings associated with a particular time.

The next time we meet, we begin constructing the visual frame for our writing. Colored paper is selected and the cutting begins. Pairs of scissors are passed from one hand to another. Splotches of glue are wiped away with tissue. Questions arise: "How many strips do I need?" "Do I write one sentence on each strip?" "Should I use lighter colors? You can't see the words on the dark ones!" Dilemmas occur: "Hey, my fan is too big for the background!" "Mine's all wiggly!" "I can't cut a straight strip."

While working we talk about adding something in the upper right corner, a symbol to represent the author of each poem. Nettie cuts out a yellow sun. Maria brings in a photograph of herself sitting in her grandfather's lap. Others cut out basketballs, snow flakes, hearts, rocket ships, flowers, stars, and tennis shoes.

One by one, as the students finish their quilt pieces, I ask them to fasten them to the wall. Martin comes in during tutorials and creates a single quilt piece with a red barn, just like the piece in the quilt made by the residents of Bourbon County. Little by little, our quilt grows and grows until someone asks worriedly, "How's this gonna fit on the wall?" As it turns out this is a well-founded concern. Part of our quilt must wrap around onto the front blackboard, but that does not detract from the effect. Comments of "Wow!" "Awesome!" and "This is so cool!" let us know that our work is well received.

This experience reflects an effort to respond to literature in a similar manner to that described by Jarod and Cal; we read, wrote, and then, instead of drawing, we constructed a visual representation modeled after the one we had seen in the book. In this way, we began our experiences with visual representation by analyzing and creating an image based upon an existing image.

Constructing a Collage

The idea for a collage of a scene from the novel *Journey* (MacLachlan, 1991) first came to me as I watched my students pass spiral notebooks to one another before and after class. The covers of the notebooks were carefully decorated with collages of pictures cut from magazines, cartoons, stickers, and school photos of their friends. Inside were notes and poems written in a myriad of colors, from one friend to another.

Asking my students to construct a collage would be a way of building upon something that many of them were already doing outside of class, a way of bringing what Margaret Finders (1997) describes as "hidden" or personal literacies to the classroom. I also considered the way that the construction of a collage of photographs would return us to the ideas depicted in the novel about the meaning and importance of photographs.

We began the project with each student choosing an event or moment from the novel. I suggested that they reread this portion of the novel several times, making notes about the main idea and creating lists of the pictures they might need to convey this idea, before beginning their search. We tried thinking of each event as a scene from a film. As the students completed their notes and lists, they moved to sit on the floor in front of the shelves containing our collection of National Geographic and travel magazines.

I watched, listened, and helped in the search for pictures. As stacks of magazines left the shelves and were strewn across the floor, the sound of paper being ripped and snipped intensified. As we worked we returned to the events in the novel, searching for places, things, and people with the look we had envisioned while reading. "Here's Journey's hand!" "He doesn't look like Grandpa!" "Is this a peony?" "I'm tearing up some pictures to show when Bloom finds the box of photos Journey's mother tore up and put under the bed!" "Can anybody find me a picture of an old car?" "This looks just like Cat, don't you think?" At other times conversation centered on the magazines themselves. "Look at this shipwreck!" "Remember when we read about the Titanic last year?" "Hey, there's pictures of girls with no shirts on in here!" "Where is Madagascar?" "Can I have this map?"

Once the students had collected the pictures they needed to create their collages, we began the process of trimming and arranging the pictures on 8½ x 11 sheets of paper. As we worked, we discovered that it helped to glue down a large, general background picture of a landscape or sky first and then arrange the smaller pictures on top. We also discovered that it was better to plan the arrangement of the pictures before gluing them down. This provided an opportunity to think about how a viewer would "move" through or "read" the collage.

When the collages were completed, we created an exhibition and the students took turns talking about their work. Discussion included references to their reasons for choosing a particular scene, their decisions about what to include and which items to foreground, problems they had encountered, and celebration of elements that worked well.

While reflecting on the process, I came across these words written by Andrea Barrett (1998) in a novel about a naturalist recording all that he encounters on a voyage to the Arctic:

> Why is it so difficult simply to capture what was there? That old problem of trying to show things both sequentially and simultaneously. If I drew that scene I'd show everything happening all at once, everyone present and every place visible. (p. 26)

In choosing a scene from *Journey* (MacLachlan, 1991) and then creating a collage of photographs, we had found a way to "show things both sequentially and simultaneously" (Barrett, 1998, p. 26). Our collages captured an event or moment of the novel in much the same way that a single photograph captures a moment on film. We could "read" them as a whole, seeing and understanding everything at once. Or, we could read them in pieces, one photograph at a time, as we might read a single word or sentence. Placed together, side-by-side, the collages formed a visual representation of the main events, ideas, and theme of the novel *Journey*.

Creating a Wallet

One day while I was cleaning out my wallet, I came across an old card advertising golf lessons. I remembered my friend, a social studies teacher at Westbrook, and I had planned to take lessons together one summer. Moments later, after sifting through and finding a library card and numerous discount cards for local book stores, an idea occurred to me. Our wallets are visual representations of who we are.

At the time we were deep in a reading of *The Outsiders* (Hinton, 1989), and I wondered what my students would make of this idea. The next day at school, I made a transparency of the contents of my wallet. Before showing it to my students, I asked them to tell me what they had inside their wallets. After a few seconds of shocked silence, they began taking wallets out of pockets and purses and examining the contents. Volunteers noted: "I've got a house key." "My lunch money." "A note from Maria." "A picture of my dog." "Not much, I just started carrying one!" I then asked, "Can we learn something about a person by looking at the contents of their wallet?" Continuing, I told them I was going to show them the contents of a wallet and ask them to tell me all that they could about the owner of the wallet. I had included cards from a middle school association, a reading association, a parent-teacher association, a driver's license, a faculty discount card from a copy center, a grocery store discount card, a library card, a discount card for a book store, and a membership card for an international honor society in education.

Surprisingly, it took a few moments for the students to notice my name on the cards. Before noticing this, they observed that this person "probably likes to read," "makes a lot of copies," "might be a teacher," "a middle school teacher," "buys food at _____," and then, the inevitable, "Ooooh, Mrs. Van Horn—it's you! You're *old*!" Thanking them for their observations and for noticing the date of birth on my driver's license and integrating math into the experience, I suggested that we continue.

Together, we talked about how we would go about the process of creating a wallet which might belong to one of the characters in *The Outsiders* (Hinton, 1989). I would provide each student with a sheet of black or brown construction paper for making the wallet, black book tape to hold the edges together, and a sheet of index paper printed with blank cards. Each wallet would contain ten items that would tell something about the owner of the wallet (see appendix S). The students would choose a character and then, as we continued to read, make notes about items they might include in a wallet for this character. For example, when we read that the gang goes to the Nightly Double Drive-In Movie Theater, someone creating a wallet for one of these characters might include a movie ticket or discount coupon for popcorn at the Nightly Double.

We spent a part of each day together working on the wallets. Their enthusiasm far exceeded my expectations. Wallets were embellished with cut out slots for cards, flip out photo holders, and chains. Students brought in old combs, photographs, and pages copied from the book that Ponyboy and Johnny read together while hiding in the abandoned church. They included notes from one character to another, folded and torn, and old hall passes with the name of our school marked over and the name of Ponyboy's high school, Will Rogers High, inserted at the top. Those making wallets for some of the Greasers wanted to include copies of detention slips and typed notes from the principal of the high school.

One day, while remarking on how realistic the wallets appeared, another idea came to me. "What if we pretend that we are somewhere in the town where they all live and we find the wallet? You could write a letter to the character explaining that you have found the wallet and telling them what you have learned about them from looking at the contents." Together, we draft a plan (see appendix T). Each letter will open with a statement about where the wallet was found. This should be a place the character might have been. The writer of the letter should then describe the contents of the wallet and discuss what he or she infers from each item. We later decide to add references to personal connections between the writer and the owner of the wallet. For example, if we are writing about a movie ticket stub in the wallet, we might tell the owner of the wallet about our favorite movie or describe an experience we had while at the movies. The letter should close with a statement in which we make plans to return the wallet to the owner. This is Amy's letter to Ponyboy:

> Dear Ponyboy,
>
> Hi! My name is Amy. You wouldn't believe what I found. I was coming home from school when I found a twenty dollar bill. I looked around and saw a whole wallet. Inside the cards said it was yours, Ponyboy Curtis. I like your name. I found the wallet outside the remains of an old building up in Windrixville. I live on a farm up there. My dad said my grandfather talked to some boys your age one day. They asked for the way to the church. I have been investigating and I bet you are him.
>
> You have some neat stuff in your wallet. I see you have a library card. But seems to me you just like to read. I doubt you were one of those top of the line students. Maybe you were. You went to Will Rogers High School. You know what's strange? The assistant principal at our school is Mr. Rogers. You went to the drive-in movies. Or, did you sneak in? I have some friends that do that kind of thing. But if you did sneak in, you wouldn't have to twice. You got two free entries. What happened to Johnny? How did he die? That's one thing I wish I knew. But, guess what? I went to the Eastside Cemetery. In there was Johnny's grave. Somewhere near there was one of Dallas Winston. Was he your friend? Now I have to tell you a great secret. I was walking around one night, when I heard a noise coming from the ruins of the old church. I saw a ghost, a small one in one corner. It looked like he

was picking up air and throwing it out the window. Then, yells and shrieks like someone was dying. And ambulance sounds. Is that how he died, Ponyboy?

I saw the gas station card, but you're too young to drive. Were you getting food or just hangin' out? Well, you keep up with the important stuff. Your social security card. You must be pretty responsible. Which one is you in the picture? Is that your brother? Your mom looks pretty nice. With your grades and everything, you probably went to college. Your mom must of been proud of you. Did you smoke Ponyboy? You shouldn't of done that you know. It's bad for you.

Well, you used your hall pass enough. I never use mine. You probably just wanted to get out of class. Did you have glasses or is that just an eye exam discount sent in the mail? Did you have green eyes or is that just the picture?

I see you got a bunch of money. I kind of used some for some candy on the way home from school. I get kind of hungry, you know. Like I said, you got a pretty nice wallet. Well, see you around, Pony.

The person that found your wallet,
Amy Carrero

P.S. Write back soon.

These wallets became treasured objects—tangible representations of the feelings the students had developed for the characters and the connections they had made between their lives and the lives of the people portrayed in the novel. We would seal them inside plastic bags before they placed them in their portfolios. Before this, I took the wallets home with me to study them carefully. As I held each wallet in my hands and read the accompanying letter, I could see the connections the students had made. Each item in the wallet served as a visual record of facts gleaned from the text, inferences made from collected details of the thoughts and lives of the characters. I could almost believe that it had actually happened—that we *had* found the wallets of Sodapop, Ponyboy, and Darry, Two-Bit, Bob, Marcia, and Cherry.

Creating Paper Characters

In the first chapter, I mentioned the janitor's reaction to the life-sized paper characters from *The Outsiders* (Hinton, 1989) we had made and hung in the hallway. The first time I did this with my students, we simply made and hung the characters—looking at our paper creations as a means of depicting how we had visualized the people in the book.

In later years, we would build upon this experience. Students created elaborate sets in an alcove including the fountain where Bob is murdered and a view of the back end of the Socs' blue Mustang which appeared to be driving away through the double doors at the end of the hallway. Teachers began to bring their classes down to see the "exhibit." We decided to add information about each character beside the paper cut outs.

Using *The Important Book* (Brown, 1949) as a model, the students wrote poems summarizing the important things about the character they had represented on paper. At the end of each poem, they included a quotation from the novel which they felt revealed the essence of the character. Mandy and Chris worked together to create a paper version of Cherry. As we look at their vision of Cherry, we can also read what they feel is most important about her:

> The important thing about Cherry Valance
> is that she watches the sunset.
> She has fire red hair that perfectly reflects her soul.
> She was in love with Bob,
> but deeply attracted to Dally.
> Cherry was a cheerleader,
> head of the team.
> But she isn't stuck up
> as though it would seem.
> She was a spy for the Greasers,
> and at some point cried.
> Because she regretted
> how her boyfriend, Bob, died.
> She had problems just like Greasers do.
> She had a hard time with her problem,
> just like me and you.
> But the important thing about Cherry Valance
> is that she watches the sunset.

"All Socs aren't like that. You have to believe me, Ponyboy. Not all of us are like that." (Hinton, 1989, p. 33)

I have included the planning sheet for this project in the Appendices (see appendix U). Hanging these poems on the wall beside the characters enriched the experience of both creating and viewing the display. With the poems in place, it was as if my students were "talking to" as well as showing other students the meaning they had made. This particular experience is one which also works well as students read informational text or biographies about real people. They can then construct paper images and write about the most important characteristics, actions, or contributions of these people.

VISUAL REPRESENTATIONS OF A THEME

In the last section of this chapter, I want to describe some of the ways the students have constructed visual representations of a thematic study. These representations have been constructed both before and during a unit of study. In many cases they have remained behind throughout the year to remind us of where we have been, what we have done, and what we have learned together.

Creating Ransom Note Mystery Poems

One year, I introduced the idea of the found poem during our study of mystery. As the students were searching through their mystery novels, putting together lines and phrases, Alvin had an idea. He had recently seen a film in which someone had created a ransom note using letters cut from a newspaper or magazine. "What if," Alvin began, "What if we cut out words and letters and made our found poems look like ransom notes?" "Sounds like a great idea," I replied. "Let's do it!"

Within moments, the floor was littered with words and letters. While I searched through the cabinet for construction paper backing, I listened and smiled at the exchange behind me. "I'm looking for a 'Q'. There's a reward in it for anybody who gives me a 'Q'." "That's easy, I need a 'Z'," "Look out! You're stepping on my words," "No, no! Don't sneeze. You're going to blow it all away!" While in the cabinet, I found not only construction paper but also some plastic bags we could use to alleviate the problem of missing words and letters while the students worked on the project.

When the ransom note poems are completed, we hang them in the hallway with an invitation to others to "Decipher these gems if you will." Each poem comprises a single sheet of words. Viewers must come close to read the words of the poem Lance has found in *Sweet Friday Island* (Taylor, 1994):

> Three rocks exploding,
> slamming into beach.
> Tiny white specks on the sea.
> A boat to help us.

The Power of Visual Representation 257

<blockquote>
Morse code from World War II.

Lost sight.

Lost in despair

in Paradise.
</blockquote>

Nearby is another poem about the same novel, written by Kendall:

<blockquote>
Steeply crooning

over us.

Standing by the spring.

Hey, Hey, Hey

Echoed,

And felt tremendous.

Then silence,

With a Cortez breeze generously,

peacefully shaggy.

Lean to me, my friend.

Comprende.
</blockquote>

The wall resonates with words and letters. It is both a visual representation of meaning making and a work of art as arresting and unnerving as the mysteries from which it arose.

Spelling Out *The Giver*

One year, while reading *The Giver* by Lois Lowry (1993), the students and I decided to construct a visual representation of our questions, comments, and observations. This novel depicts a world where thought is carefully controlled and individual freedom does not exist—a world where all but the Giver and the Receiver of Memory are ignorant of the past.

While reading, the students recorded their questions, comments, and observations about the novel on small slips of paper. "Why didn't anybody know what 'animals' meant?" "It seems like kids are never bad or disobey here. Rules are strict, but kids are kids. Why are they so perfect?" "Are they given family members?" "What is a nurturer?" "What was fun to them? Was there no such thing as fun?" The more we read, the more we thought we understood. The more we thought we understood, the more questions we had. At the end of each period of reading and discussion, we glued these slips of paper onto three foot high letters cut from red bulletin board paper. Slowly we filled in letter by letter, beginning with "T" and spelling out the words "THE GIVER." As each letter was filled with slips representing our thoughts and our talk about the novel, we held a small ceremony, hanging the letter in the hallway alcove. It seemed as if these gigantic red letters covered with words upon words helped to organize the meanings we were making. As the letters on the wall grew into words, our own random thoughts and confusion grew into understanding. The letters were a visual representation of that understanding.

On the day we finished reading *The Giver* (Lowry, 1993), we hung the last letter in the hallway and stood together looking at the words. Spontaneously, the students began to read aloud slips from one letter and then another, talking about the changes in their thinking as they had experienced the novel—reading, questioning, talking, and constructing this visual representation of meaning making. "We should take a picture of this," remarked Chris. "I want to have a picture of me with the words," he added. Chris ran to get a chair and we took a picture of him crouched on the chair, his chin resting on his fist, as "The Thinker." There in the alcove, with the words, "THE GIVER" looming over our heads, I read an excerpt from Lois Lowry's (1994) acceptance speech for the Newbery Medal:

> The man that I named The Giver passed along to the boy knowledge, history, memories, color, pain, laughter, love, and truth. Every time you place a book in the hands of a child, you do the same thing. It is very risky. But each time a child opens a book, he pushes open the gate that separates him from Elsewhere. It gives him choices. It gives him freedom. Those are magnificent, wonderfully *unsafe* things. (p. 422)

Piecing Together a Survival Quilt

We spend a part of each year engaged in a study of historical fiction and related informational texts that I call "Survival Across Time." Our exploration centers on issues and events in which people have triumphed over conflict and seemingly insurmountable trials. During this study, small groups of students will choose and read one of a number of works of historical fiction. They will conduct research on the time period of the work, consulting a variety of materials. As a group or individually, the students will then propose and execute projects in which they present their responses to the texts and what they have learned.

Before we begin this unit of study, we spend some time talking about what it means to be confronted by adversity. Together, we read *Tar Beach* by Faith Ringgold (1991), the story of Cassie who dreams of being free to go where she wants. Ringgold's book is a "story quilt" which reflects her work as a visual artist, painting and constructing quilts, and as a writer, embellishing personal memoir and historical issues through storytelling. After reading, we talk about the power of having a dream or purpose in life. We talk about the quilt as a symbol of safety, security, and the histories of people.

I ask the students to think about a dream or a purpose they have and then to think of a way they might symbolize this dream or purpose. Each student then draws the symbol of his or her dream on the blank side of an index card. On the reverse side, I ask them to complete the following statement: "I survive because I have a dream. My dream is to . . . "

As you might imagine, the dreams of the students vary as they do. Some dream of becoming "famous singers," and others want to be rock stars or basketball players. Yalim symbolizes his dream to "be the first black president" with an election poster carrying his name. Deb dreams of becoming a veterinarian and helping animals. She symbolizes this dream with a brown puppy superimposed on a large red cross. Pete also dreams of working with animals. He symbolizes his dream with a drawing of a narwhal and writes:

> I survive because I have a dream. My dream is to become a world famous marine biologist and to earn my doctorate in marine mammals. The animal that I hope to study is the narwhal. It is a type of small, white whale with no dorsal fin and a long tusk. The purpose of the tusk is unknown. I intend to find out what its purpose is and how the narwhal is related to the legend of the unicorn.

Juanita symbolizes her dream with a heart, a sun, and a peace symbol, writing:

> My dream is to fight for my freedom because I deserve it just like everyone else in the world. I also dream to have the love from my family and from a family I haven't even met. All I want most is peace and happiness.

When the students have completed their cards, volunteers are assigned one of the titles of the picture books, novels, or informational texts we will be reading. On the face of a card, they write the title, repeating it again and again until the card is covered. These title cards will form the border of our "quilt." I then laminate all the cards and punch a hole in each of the four corners of every card. Together, before and after school, we construct the quilt. Students who want to work with me help cut yarn strips, arrange cards, or tie the cards together with the yarn. As we work, we talk about how to arrange the cards, alternating those with light and dark background or simple and detailed designs.

When the work is completed, we hang the "quilt" in our room. In the days that follow, students gather at the quilt searching for their card or the cards of their friends. They pull the quilt away from the wall so they can read the dream statements behind. As we continue our study, reading the stories of the lives of others, we return to our quilt searching for connections between these lives of the past and our own lives. Beginning and returning to their dreams provides the students with an added purpose for reading; they read in search of the dreams which sustained these people from the past.

Our survival quilt remains hanging in the room throughout the year until the last day of school when it is removed and carefully stored. In the years to come, it may be used to decorate a table where we will gather to eat and talk about books. The value of the quilt as a symbol of our community is reflected in the statements of students who notice its absence on the last day of school and lament, "Where is our quilt?" "Where are we?" "It seems so empty here without it."

Evaluation/Assessment

The evaluation/assessment of visual representations can be somewhat difficult. Our visual representations of meaning may be as varied as our responses to text. When we view art or visual images each of us may see something different. We may respond to color, shape, relationships, ideas, mood, and so forth. With this in mind, and with the knowledge that some of my students relate this aspect of literacy specifically to drawing and describe drawing as something they can not or do not want to do, I must think carefully about how to incorporate visual representation into the curriculum. It is interesting to note that many of the representations of meaning we have produced thus far have been group constructions comprised of individual pieces (Remember Quilt, Paper Characters, Ransom Note Mystery Poems, Spelling Out *The Giver*, and the Survival Quilt). As such, these pieces can be viewed and interpreted both individually and collectively. This engages us in a consideration of both individual and group meaning making. I am still in the early stages of searching for ways to integrate opportunities for my students to visually represent and extend the meaning of our literary experiences. Given this, our evaluation/ assessment of our products is also in the formative stage.

Our evaluation assessment of the visual product is frequently connected to the writing associated with the product. For example, when looking at the pieces of the Remember Quilt, we examine the poem as well as the quilt piece. We might create a rubric that focuses on the poem, the transfer of the poem to the individual strips of the fan, and the symbol of the writer placed upon the quilt piece. This is also true for the Survival Quilt. Here we look at the symbol of the dream on the front of the card and the written statement about the dream on the back of the card. Our Ransom Note Mystery poems are evaluated in much the same manner as we have evaluated other found poems.

At other times, when the emphasis lies solely with the visual representation, such as with the collage representing the main events, ideas, and theme of the novel *Journey* (MacLachlan, 1991), we must find a way to break down the elements of the piece. With this collage we might look at the overall construction, the reflection of an event from the novel, elements which relate to the details of this event, and elements which relate to the main idea of this event. With this experience I have also included a presentation in which the students display their collages and talk about the event they have chosen, the pictures they have included, their reasons for choosing these pictures, their processes in creating the collage, and their evaluation of the work.

I have included the planning sheet and rubric for Creating a Wallet for a Character from *The Outsiders'*(Hinton, 1989) and Writing a Letter to the Owner of the Wallet in the appendices (see appendices S and T). As I examine the wallets, I look for items that reflect both the literal details of the novel and the inferences students have made about the characters. The process is similar with the evaluation/assessment of the paper characters from *The Outsiders* (Hinton, 1989) and the Important Poem about the character (see appendix U). When I examine the paper characters constructed by the students, I look for the inclusion of details lifted from the descriptions of the character contained in the novel and inferences the students have made about the character which may be reflected in the character's posture or in the object(s) that he or she may be holding.

Conclusion

Our last days together each year fluctuate between periods of intense, frenzied activity and moments of quiet reflection. The students design covers for their portfolios or memory books and organize the contents. Anxious pleas such as "I need a pocket for my response notes," and "I lost my copy of the *Macbeth* script!" are interspersed with moments of quiet reflection. Students sit side-by-side, reading to one another something they have written and want to share once again. Others study the pages of their portfolios from front to back, evaluating their experiences and remarking, "Look at all I've done this year!" and "Look how I've changed!"

When the covers are completed and the portfolios are organized, I bind them into books using the school binding machine. The day that I complete this task is a day of celebration for us all. As I lift each book from the cardboard boxes I have used to carry them, I announce the full name of the author. Cheers and applause follow as each student walks forward to take his or her portfolio book. Some hold their books over their heads like trophies as they return to their desks. Others clutch them tightly to their chests. When everyone has a book, we pass the books around and blank pages inserted for this purpose are autographed by each member of our literacy community.

Finally, I hand out slips of paper and ask my students to write down one memory from the 7th grade. With music playing in the background, they write, smiling, whispering, and laughing. Without saying a word, they fold their slips of paper into tiny squares, dropping them into a glass jar passed from hand-to-hand. This jar I will keep until they reach the end of their 8th-grade year. Then, when they are saying their last good-byes to middle school, I will send the jar to their end-of-the-year party at a neighborhood park. I imagine them sitting together in the gathering dusk, opening the jar, and for a moment or two, remembering the 7th grade.

Appendix A

Teacher: Leigh Van Horn
Course: 7th-Grade Reading
Conference Period: Blue Day—First Period
Silver Day—Eighth Period

Course Syllabus

General Objectives
- Determine the meaning of words in a variety of written texts
- Identify supporting ideas in a variety of written texts
- Summarize a variety of written texts
- Perceive relationships and recognize outcomes in a variety of written texts
- Analyze information in a variety of written texts in order to make inferences and generalizations
- Recognize points of view, propaganda, and/or statements of fact and nonfact in a variety of written texts

Creating a Literary Community
- Short Stories and Excerpts from Novels
  - *The Conversation Club*—Diane Stanley
  - "The Reader of Books," excerpt, *Matilda*—Roald Dahl
  - *Aunt Chip and the Great Triple Creek Dam Affair*—Patricia Polacco
  - "Ethan Explains the B & B," excerpt, *The View From Saturday*—E. L. Konigsburg
  - *Walking the Log*—Bessie Nickens
- Poetry
  - "Remember"—Joy Harjo
- Novel
  - *The Van Gogh Café*—Cynthia Rylant
- Activities and Products
  - Define Reading, complete Reading and Writing Surveys, introduce and set up the process of keeping a Portfolio, Reader/Writer log, Word Bank, and Reader of the Day

- Read and respond to "Ethan Explains the B & B"
- Choral reading of the poem, "Remember"
- Read and respond to the novel *The Van Gogh Café* by Cynthia Rylant
- Create a life map to be used as an idea source for personal narrative/autobiographical writing and storytelling
- Write "I Used to Be, Now I Am" poem
- Class project—create a book based on our interpretation of *The Van Gogh Café*

The Outsiders

- Short Stories
  - *The Fourth of July*—Robin Brancato
  - *Priscilla and the Wimps*—Richard Peck
- Poetry
  - *Neighborhood Odes*—Gary Soto
  - "Book Lice"—Paul Fleischman
- Novel
  - *The Outsiders*—S. E. Hinton
- Activities and Products
  - Conduct character interrogations of the characters from short stories
  - Write an ode to your neighborhood
  - Read and respond to *The Outsiders* by S. E. Hinton
  - Create a scrapbook detailing the experiences of the Greasers and the Socs
  - Write a compare/contrast poem about the characters from *The Outsiders*
  - Write about a symbol from *The Outsiders*
  - Consider yourself in a new light through the writing of an "I Am" poem based upon *Poemcrazy: Freeing Your Life With Words* by Susan Wooldridge

Solving the Case

- Short Stories and Excerpts from Novels
  - "Mongoose," excerpt, *The Library Card*—Jerry Spinelli
  - *Turmoil in a Blue and Beige Bedroom*—Judie Angell
- Poetry
  - *Who Killed Mr. Chippendale?*—Mel Glenn
- Plays
  - *The Blue Carbuncle,* based on the story by A. C. Doyle

Appendix

- *The Monkey's Paw*, based on the story by W. W. Jacobs
- *The Invisible Man*, based on the story by H. G. Wells
- Novels (Individual Guided Reading—Student choice of one of the following mysteries to be read in class)
  - *Something Upstairs*—Avi
  - *Wolfrider*—Avi
  - *And Then There Were None*—Agatha Christie
  - *Driver's Ed*—Caroline Cooney
  - *Wanted*—Caroline Cooney
  - *Wilderness Peril*—Thomas Dygard
  - *The House of Dies Drear*—Virginia Hamilton
  - *Deadly Deception*—Betsy Haynes
  - *Candidate for Murder*—Joan Lowery Nixon
  - *The Kidnapping of Christina Lattimore*—Joan Lowery Nixon
  - *The Other Side of Dark*—Joan Lowery Nixon
  - *The Stalker*—Joan Lowery Nixon
  - *Whispers from the Dead*—Joan Lowery Nixon
  - *A Ghost in the House*—Betty Ren Wright
- Activities and Products
  - Read and respond to a mystery novel
  - Respond to a short story about a mysterious library card
  - Radio play readings of *Who Killed Mr. Chippendale?*, *The Blue Carbuncle*, *The Monkey's Paw*, and *The Invisible Man*
  - Make a detective notebook which will include photos and descriptions of characters, descriptions of setting and clues, sequence of events, notes of the detective. Use the detective notebook to write a short mystery from the point of view of the detective.
  - Create a Museum of Objects and Ideas
  - Write a narrative about an Object of Personal Significance

Shakespeare Lives On: Always Say Macbeth!

- Short Stories and Excerpts from Collections
  - *The Bard of Avon: The Story of William Shakespeare*—Diane Stanley
  - "Macbeth," excerpt, *Shakespeare Stories*—Leon Garfield and Michael Foreman
  - *Never Say Macbeth*—Sheila Front
- Play
  - *Macbeth*, Scholastic version based upon the play by William Shakespeare

- Activities and Products
  - Introduce William Shakespeare through a reading of a biography
  - Read and respond to a short story version of *Macbeth*
  - Draw the Globe Theater as we learn about it's history and purpose
  - Create theater signs, actor's company flags, and sets
  - Produce a film of our own reading of the play
  - Write a response to the class production and an analysis of the theme of *Macbeth*

Big Books and Book Reviews

- Students will read a Lone Star Award winning book and write a book review
- Readings include
  - Jackdaw Reproductions of primary source historical material
  - *Immigrant Kids*—Russell Freedman
- Big Books

  As part of an integrated 7th-grade experience, students use research and class readings on the topic of immigration as the basis for the creation of an original story or informational piece which will be written, illustrated, and bound. Topics include dedication, forward, cover art, end papers, binding, and author biography. Students will share their creations with the class. Students and teachers will vote on authors to receive "The Westbery Award." Award winning authors will share their books with 4th-grade students at area elementary schools.

Survival Across Time

- Short Stories and excerpts
  - *Sweet Clara and the Freedom Quilt*—Deborah Hopkinson
  - *Tar Beach*—Faith Ringgold
  - *A Weekend in September*—John Edward Weems
- Novels (Book Club—reading, responding, and discussing the novel in small groups) Student choice of one of the following historical fiction works to be read in class:
  - *I Am Regina*—Keehn
  - *Ruffles and Drums*—Cavanna
  - *Bull Run*—Fleishman
  - *Nightjohn*—Paulsen
  - *Across Five Aprils*—Hunt

- *The Silent Storm*—Garland
- *Number the Stars*—Lowry
- *The Devil's Arithmetic*—Yolen
- *Warriors Don't Cry*
- *Wild Timothy*—Blackwood
- *Shadow of the Dragon*—Garland
- Activities and Products
    - Create a piece of a survival quilt
    - Read and respond to historical fiction
    - Conduct related reading of articles, primary source materials and informational text
    - Propose a method of presenting the novel and the time period to the class (examples—timeline, diary, newspaper, play, book of poetry, etc.)
    - Execute and present your product to the class

The Future is in Your Hands
- Short Stories and Excerpts from Novels
    - Chapter 1, Part I, excerpt, *1984*—George Orwell
    - *User Friendly*—T. Ernesto Bethancourt
    - *Do You Want My Opinion?*—M. E. Kerr
    - *Future Tense*—Robert Lipsyte
    - *Examination Day*—Henry Slesar
    - Excerpts from *The Time Machine*—H. G. Wells
- Novels
    - *The Giver*—Lois Lowry
    - *Eva*—Peter Dickinson
    - *The Time Warp Trio*—Jon Scieska
- Additional Optional Readings
    - *Phoenix Rising*—Karen Hesse
    - *Invitation to the Game*—Monica Hughes
    - *The Girl Who Owned a City*—O. T. Nelson
    - *Z for Zachariah*—Robert O'Brien
- Activities and Products
    - Read excerpts from *1984* by George Orwell, consider and discuss the facets of his "future" that are now a part of our daily life
    - Create a context for future study by writing and illustrating a personal vision of the future
    - Read and discuss futuristic short stories

- Read and track questions, discoveries, and points of interest for discussion
- *The Giver* by Lois Lowry and *Eva* by Peter Dickinson
- Consider the issues addressed in *The Giver* and *Eva* through written response
- Read excerpts from Lois Lowry's Acceptance Speech for the Newbery Award
- Write a poem about a memory
- Interview a parent or grandparent about their view of the same event. Include these memories as a comparison
- Read *The Time Warp Trio* by Jon Scieska and excerpts from *The Time Machine* by H. G. Wells
- Predict outcomes, future actions, and draw conclusions by writing an epilogue to *The Giver*
- Small groups of students will be given the task of searching for an event from the past which may have altered the course of history. "Time Teams" will then create a journal in which they describe the world they have entered, the people and place in which the event occurs, why they believe this event changed the course of history, and how they, as explorers from the future, will alter that event. Maps of locations and interviews of inhabitants will be included.

Please note: Modifications may be made to the syllabus in order to address the needs of the students.

Appendix

APPENDIX B

MEETING OBJECTIVES

Week of: _____

Class Period: _____

Student Number	Student Name	SSR	R/W L	ROD	DIS	PRES	LIB	RP

Appendix C

Museum of Objects and Ideas
Planning Sheet

Step One:
Collect interesting words cut from magazines and newspapers. Glue your words onto the tickets provided and drop them into our fishbowl container.

Step Two:
Bring an object from home. The object may be of personal significance. Examples—a rock, a shell, a stuffed toy, a four leaf clover, a letter, a baseball, a pair of baby shoes, etc.

Step Three:
Listen to a demonstration of the process of labeling objects with words which make us think about the object and the words in a new way. For example—a map of the world with the words "abandon boundaries" placed on the map takes on a new significance. For some, the map becomes a political statement signifying that without boundaries we would become a world of one people, united in our goals. For others, it may signify giving up our individuality.

Step Four:
Draw five tickets at random from the bowl. Look up each word in the dictionary and write down the meaning which would be most applicable to your object. If none of the words apply, you may redraw.

Step Five:
Choose at least one word ticket that you could attach to your object in order to create an "idea."

Step Six:
You have been provided with two index cards. One card will be marked with the name of the object (what it is), the word or words you are using

to redefine your object, and the definitions you have chosen from the dictionary. This card will also contain a statement explaining your reasoning for choosing this (or these) particular word(s) for the object.

For example:

Object: Map of the World

Word(s): "Abandon"—To cease from maintaining, practicing, or using

"Boundary"—A bounding or separating line

Significance: I placed the words "abandon" and "boundary" on this map of the world in order to show my feelings that politics and political boundaries separate the people of the world. If we could abandon the boundaries which separate us, we might become united citizens of the world with common goals and aspirations.

The other card will state the name of the object (what it is) and describe it's personal significance to you.

For example:

Object: Map of the World

Personal Significance: For as long as I can remember, I have been fascinated by maps. I have even drawn some imaginary maps of places I have read about in books.

APPENDIX D

MUSEUM OF OBJECTS AND IDEAS

Rubric

Student Name:_____

Activity	Possible Points	Points Earned
Contribute at least 10 word tickets to the fishbowl.	10	_____
Bring an object of personal significance to class.	10	_____
Draw five tickets from the bowl, look up the words in the dictionary.	15	_____
Write the words and the meanings of the words you have chosen from the bowl in your reader/writer log.	15	_____
Choose at least one word ticket that may be attached to your object in order to create an "idea."	10	_____
Create Index Card One which includes:		
Name of the object	5	_____
Word(s) used and definitions of word(s) used	5	_____
Statement explaining your reasoning for choosing the word(s) to place on this particular object	10	_____
Create Index Card Two which includes:		
Name of the object	5	_____
Statement explaining the personal significance of the object	15	_____
Total Points:	100	_____

APPENDIX E

Essay About Object of Personal Significance

Rubric

Student Name: _____

Note: The elements of this rubric are based on the outline we created together in class after analyzing Lewis Nordan's essay.

Your essay should include the following:

	Possible Points	Points Earned
First:	20	_____

Describes where the object is located

Notes who sees the object

	Possible Points	Points Earned
Second:	20	_____

Describes the object in detail using words that allow the reader to see, hear, smell, touch, and/or taste the object. Description should be well organized. Example: top to bottom, inside to outside

	Possible Points	Points Earned
Third:	20	_____

Tells the history of the object—how it came into your hands, where it was before you had it, what has happened while it has belonged to you

	Possible Points	Points Earned
Fourth:	20	_____

Explains what the object cannot do and what the object can do

Fifth: 20 _____

Imagines what the person who gave you the object might have thought about as he or she acquired the object and/or as he or she gave the object to you

Total: 100 _____

Observations:

_____
_____
_____
_____
_____
_____
_____
_____
_____
_____
_____
_____
_____
_____
_____
_____
_____
_____
_____
_____

Appendix F

"I Am" Poem Planning Sheet

Use the following model to write a poem about yourself. You do not have to begin each line with the words, "I am." Be sure and include descriptive words so that the reader can "see," "hear," "touch," "feel," and "smell" what you are!

I am

What sound? _____

What animal? _____

What song? _____

What number? _____

What car? _____

What piece of furniture? _____

What food? _____

What musical instrument? _____

What place? _____

What element in nature? _____

What kind of tree? _____

What is something I am afraid of? _____

What is the world hiding behind my eyes? _____

APPENDIX G

QUESTIONS, COMMENTS, AND OBSERVATIONS

Double Trouble Squared—Kathryn Lasky
Period 5
1996–1997

Do you think the bust of Holmes is "alive"?

Is their house haunted?

Did the younger twins sense anything of a ghost? If they did, were they scared?

Sui Veritas Primo—Truth to Self—family motto.

Holmes is in Liberty's head?

Is their Aunt a vegetarian?

Are they really moving to London? (Crystal) dumb question—Note—written by Crystal

How long had they thought a ghost was in the house?

If Holmes is in Liberty's head, is that the ghost-like echo they've been hearing?

Can they secretly tell answers to each other in school?

Are the feet in the fireplace Holmes' feet? (Cover picture)

Had there been any deaths in that house?

Do the other twins, Molly and Charlie, send brain messages to each other?

Why couldn't the laughter be the younger twins?

Do Liberty's and July's parents know they're telepathic?

How long will Liberty and July not be able to talk telepathic? No, it will not last.

Who is the person talking with them when they talk telepathic?

Is the other person talking to them one of the twins? Or who?

Why were there ghosts mostly in the Tower of London?

Scarlet-red coat or jacket.

Appendix

What is the "tower green"?

Why was that guy so happy about those people losing their head?

Why do they use an ax and a sword to take off the heads?

What is a beefeater?

Is the beefeater the guy who was yellin' at them on their walk?

When they chopped off their head did they body keep moving or did it just drop onto the floor?

Did they chop off their heads publicly or privately?

Whey did the man grab them?

They had seen the man almost everywhere they had gone, had they seen him spying near their house or anything?

Who ate the other jelly beans that are missing?

Was their any history about that house?

Do their telepathic lines not work when one is asleep or is it working right now and they don't know it?

What's making the jellybeans glow?

Who said "Bravo, Bravo?" Will they ever find out?

Why did the author say Helen and Julia Stone were twins when they were not? (We have read "The Speckled Band")

Who said, "Don't leave me"?

Did they maybe see a little shadow or something that maybe the shadow could have been talking?

Is the thing in the room trying to scare them?

Where is that boy leading July?

When July is following that kid, was he alone?

Why is that boy trying to lead July?

Right now in London they can walk outside and not be scared, but back in the 1800's why did it change?

Can the voice be Watson's or Holmes' spirit?

Was there really Bakers Street Irregulars or is that just in the book?

Why don't they test that voice and see if its real!

I didn't know they had Reebok in London.

So, the house they are living in now was built in like the 1800s. Right?

Why are the twins so fascinated with Sherlock Holmes?

What is a beefeater?

Who is the boy?

Since Arthur Conan Doyle lived next door when he was alive could it be his spirit talking to them, happy that they are following his example of detectives?

Why does Liberty like reading about things so much? Is she just curious or is she scared something might happen to the twins?

Does their telepathy break up when it is bad weather?

What did they see?

What is that hissing sound that they heard?

Is there really a speckled band in the room?

What was the sound that she heard?

Is the thing they saw related to the thing in the room?

Is the piece of tape turning into the speckled band?

Where does the door lead to?

Who put the package there?

Did the doors mean the apartments were connected for some reason?

What was in the box?

Why are the jelly bean stains showing up all over? What does it mean?

Were the papers old writing by Sir Arthur Conan Doyle?

How did the door get there?

Why did July and Liberty get the papers instead of somebody else?

Perhaps when they heard "Bravo" it was Conan Doyle spirit happy that the twins might find some unknown writing of Holmes.

How did July and Liberty get so involved in Sherlock Holmes? And do they ever stop communicating?

Did the papers have any relation to the voice they heard?

Why was the book different because of the characters in the papers?

Were the papers they found the original version of the Sherlock Holmes mysteries?

How come they don't mention Watson in the story?

What made them have the guts to go through the door?

Shadrach Holmes is Sherlock's twin brother.

Those are Shadrach's feet in the secret door.

Why do you have to say the ghost's name before he comes alive?

Was Shadrach like going to be originally in the Sherlock Holmes story,

Appendix

but Doyle I guess decided to take Shadrach out?!

Why was Shadrach Holmes forgotten?

Shadrach Holmes is a ghost cause nobody remembers him. Sherlock is alive because his memory is alive.

Shadrach is very smart because he makes fun of the children. Is Shadrach a good detective like his twin brother Sherlock?

Shadrach has a very good vocabulary.

If Shadrach is alive since they said his name, shouldn't Sherlock and everyone else be alive too?

Maybe Doyle was writing his last book and Sherlock and Shadrach meet and do a mystery, but Doyle died.

Was Shadrach jealous of his brother?

Why was Shadrach taken out of the book by Sir Arthur Conan Doyle?

What is a bloak?

Was Microph as clever as Sherlock?

Did Shadrach like talking to the twins?

Were July and Liberty going to tell anybody about Shadrach?

Shadrach was eating the jelly beans all over.

If Sherlock isn't a ghost, where is he, did he die?

Does Shadrach like being a ghost?

Is Shadrack Jealous of Sherlock? Yes.

How did Sherlock get addicted to cocaine?

Why does Shadrach say all of the things about his brother?

Why don't the kids write about the man on Pinchen Lane so he will disappear?

Why did Sir Arthur Conan Doyle want to kill Sherlock Holmes?

Why did Sir A. C. Doyle name them the names? (Sherlock and Shadrach)

What does the manuscript say?

How does Shadrach know the kids will do what he wants?

Is Sherlock still addicted to cocaine or anything else?

What if nobody believes them when they bring the drafts into the public?

Why did the man want to take the twins?

Who took the twins?

Is Shadrach dead"

Who was speaking to them?

Do people in London believe that Sherlock Holmes is real?

Why can't women go to those meetings?

It is tradition?

So, now neither of them gets to go to the meeting?

Does Liberty like this kind of people?

I think they should make an exception for Liberty to go to the meeting.

Is Shadrach going to die again?

Is she going to prove to all the men that girls can do as much as guys?

Has Sherlock ever caught Moriarty?

Will they publish it or what?

Are the Blue Carbuncles obsessed with Sherlock?

Can Shadrach feel his pain?

Will Sherlock ever die?

Where is Sherlock in this story?

Is Sherlock taught in England schools?

What is wrong with Liberty when they walk in the house?

Is Shadrach taught in school?

Why did Simon come to Liberty's house?

Will the twins and Shadrach talk again?

Do the twins like Shadrach or Sherlock the best?

Is Shadrach going to be a fish forever?

Does Liberty live there for a long time?

Is Simon a ghost too?

Are the twins going to live in London?

Does Shadrach like being dead?

Shadrach and Holmes meet more of each other.

APPENDIX H

QUESTIONS, COMMENTS, AND OBSERVATIONS

Canyons—Gary Paulsen
Period 5
1996–1997

Why do some chapters have titles and some don't? What is the pattern?

Where does most of the story take place?

When there is a title it is in the past, when there isn't they are in the present day.

Why do they go from one time to another?

Why did he not know his father?

Is Brennan from Indian descent?

Why does he like running so much?

Why didn't he run?

Why did Brennan run and not get tired or exhausted?

Why does he wear headbands instead of a cap, does he want to be a girl?

Why didn't he try to stop her about telling his and her life?

Are the named chapters about Coyote Runs?

Why does he use tobacco so much?

Is Coyote Runs kind of like Brennan Cole, just in a different time period?

It seems that every time there is a title with a chapter, it is abut the Indians.

What a stupid idea to cut his head and let the light come in, and why?

Are the bluebellies like one of the Indian tribes that they are enemies with?

Who was grunting and who was nodding?

Why was he in such a rush to be a man?

Coyote Runs died in desert. In the story flashes back in forth in every other chapter.

What are tailormades?

Why didn't he go out and make more friends?

Why did he like to run so much?

Why is it so important that he doesn't cut the flower beds?

He sounds like a pretty NEAT kid. He sounds really mature for being able to run not be popular, but for his self. But, wouldn't you want to have some kind of friends?

Why dies he lie about his dad?

Why did Brennan's dad beat the snot out of him?

Does Brennan want to be popular since he has no friends?

Why doesn't Brennan go out and search for his father?

What did Coyote Runs thinking that was a waste?

What relationship do the Indians and Brennan have?

Did he ever think he led a hard life?

Why did Brennan work very hard at not being angry?

Why is he so upset about going camping? I'd be excited!

Why did he want to avoid everything his mom did?

Why didn't Brennan pick a different job instead of lawn mowing?

Why doesn't he like doing anything with his mom?

Why doesn't Brennan like Bill?

Was there something wrong with his mom that he didn't like?

Why did Brennan not want Bill to be nice?

Why had Bill been so nice to the little monsters, he should take control, or maybe he just wants to impress Brennan's mom.

Is something terrible going to happen while they are camping? What is going to happen, if anything?

Why doesn't Brennan like to exercise?

Is Brennan going to start to like Bill?

Why is Bill making it so hard on Brennan, his mom, and the little monsters? He's supposed to be nice.

Why don't the grownups do anything about the kids mooning each other.

What are bluebellies?

Who brings up Coyote Runs in the story?

Why did he think it was going to be such a loooong night?

Appendix

Why is like every other chapter they go t the past? Are they going to find Coyote Runs skull or someone elses?

About how old is Sancta?

Why did Coyote Runs think he was seeing things?

What does it mean when he saw Sancta rolling along?

You know Brennan liked to run. Well Coyote Runs just said that he could run as long as Sancta needed him to? Do Brennan and Coyote Runs have some connections?

Did Coyote Runs ever sleep on his boy to man trip?

Why does Gary Paulsen change chapters with Brennan and Coyote Runs? Is there some sort of relationship?

Why should they have to wear all of that heavy clothing, and what is it used for?

Why doesn't Sancta, Coyote Runs, and the raiding group raid the Mexicans camp now instead of wait forever to do so?

Is Brennan camping in the same place where Coyote Runs was once?

What is a low gully?

Why were the children so hyper? Why would they not come down? Was there nothing they could do to calm them down?

What was bothering Brennan?

Why was it hard for Brennan to sleep?

Is it really some kind of lion?

Is this book ever going to stop talking about Coyote Runs?

What made him go the wrong way?

So, are the bluebellies the Mexicans, or what?

What medicine is Coyote Runs talking about?

Is Coyote Runs medicine so strong that it can block a bullet?

Why did he want the straw colored horse so badly?

Why were the soldiers shooting at them? Was there something they wanted?

Why did they have to spit the water in the horse's mouth?

Is Coyote Runs' horse going to live and if so is Coyote Runs going to go back for him?

They spit in the horses mouths so they don't waste water.

How long will the raid last?

Why did the bluebellies keep chasing Coyote Runs?

Will the spirits help him?

Why did they kill him? Why were they laughing? Did they think something was funny?

Is he feeling perhaps the same pain Coyote Runs did when he was shot in the ankle?

Was his dream maybe of the raid?

Is Brennan in the same place where Coyote Runs was killed?

Is Brennan crazy or did someone haunt him for killing?

So, he's now found Coyote Runs skull from when he was shot?

Whose skull was it?

What will Brennan do with the skull?

Is the head in the back blown all the way out because they shot him sooo close!

Is the skull Coyote Runs?

The skull is Coyote Runs?

Is Coyote Runs saying "Take me spirit . . . " to Brennan?

If the skull is talking then maybe it will soon later give Brennan enough clues and then Brennan will find out it belonged to a boy named Coyote Runs.

Why did Brennan think it was a young boy's skull?

Was Coyote Runs after he died reborn as Brennan?

Is Coyote Runs trying to haunt Brennan or trying to help him?

Is Coyote Runs skull giving Brennan the dreams of his life?

Why did he want to see the girl so bad? Who was the girl? Was she important?

Is CR a ghost?

If it is the skull then should Brennan find out or try to talk to the skull and ask it why it is giving him dreams?

Is the reason Brennan won't call the police is because Coyote Runs won't allow him to?

Holmsley may be a biology teacher, but why is he obsessed with beetles?

Why did Brennan touch the beetle? Did he not think that it could hurt him?

Why did he bring beetles every day, did the whole class study them? Is that why he passed?

Is his favorite subject Biology now?

Appendix

Was studying the beetles extra credit?

Homesley is the kind of teacher that you go on your reunion and tell that he changed your life.

Will Homesley tell anyone about the skull?

Brennan must like and trust him a lot.

Will Homesley be able to solve the case of the skull?

Do you think Brennan should have showed the skull to a famous scientist or a biology teacher?

Did Homesley believe him at first?

What does pathology mean?

Is Holmesly going to convince Brennan to call the police if they find something about the skull?

How would he know what an Indian skull looks like?

Who was the body that got shot in the head with a bore rifle or bigger?

What is Brennan going to do with the skull?

Why is Brennan going crazy?

Are they going to figure out who killed that person?

Why would Brennan need to contact the army, how could they help him?

What is in the boxes from the archives?

Did he want to stay with Holmsley?

How long will it take Brennan to find the right box and letter to identify Coyote Runs?

Why would somebody want to drink horse's blood? It's kind of mean.

Did they drink the horse's blood because they were in the desert and perhaps there was a shortage of water.

Could they ranch in El Paso?

Is the book ever going to talk about the Indians, besides in the newspaper, like in their own chapter?

Will Homesley and Brennan find Coyote Runs' name in the papers?

Where is Hueco Flats?

Who is Captain John Bemis?

Is this happening during Coyote Runs' times?

Are they going to find something in the box?

Are they going to find important files about Coyote Runs?

Brennan won't know that the newspaper is wrong, will he?

Is he soooo into the reading that he is kind of in the Indian's place?

Is Brennan part Apache in his heritage?

How many articles were written about Coyote Runs and Magpie?

Does Brennan know that that is the article on what may have happened to Coyote Runs' skull?

How does Brennan know that the skull was Coyote Runs'? Has Brennan read the letter that Coyote Runs wrote?

Now that Brennan has an ideas of what happened to Coyote Runs will he understand how it has made him think and feel different?

Because he found out all of the information. How is it going to help, because all these guys are DEAD?

How many times has Brennan stayed up all night before? Is he used to that?

What made Brennan change?

Has Coyote Runs taken over Brennan's body?

Is Brennan sooo into it that he can feel everything that coyote Runs did. That is bizarre.

When Brennan gets closer to Coyote Runs death spot will Coyote Runs' spirit show up?

Will Brennan have enough guts to go toward the voices and put the skull back or will he wait?

Why did Brennan's mama show up? How did she know he was going to be there?

Are the cops going to catch Brennan before he puts Coyote Runs' skull in the sacred medicine place?

Who is Coyote Runs talking to if he died?

Is that Coyote Runs' voice in Brennan's head?

Is the Coyote Runs voice in italic?

Is Brennan's mom encouraging him to run to the canyon now?

Is she telling him to run because the cops are going to hurt him? Like arrest him?

Are the cops going to catch him?

Why was Brennan's mom worried?

When Brennan is getting closer to the canyon is he reacting what happened to Coyote Runs?

How did Coyote Runs act hurt?

Appendix 287

Whose bone did the soldiers break?

Why is Brennan living Coyote Runs' life? Is Coyote Runs causing that to happen?

When Brennan hears Coyote Runs in his mind saying "No two bluebellies will catch him" it could apply to Brennan because the cops also wear blue suits, so there is a sort of connection between the two because the ankle, bluebellies (cops), and he's running into the canyons in the same place Coyote Runs was.

Is Brennan going to have enough energy to make it to the canyon where the skull came from before the deputies catch him? Will his ankle effect if they catch him or not?

Since coyote Runs died and Brennan is acting that out, will Brennan also die or be seriously injured?

When Brennan gets to where he found the skull, what is he going to do?

What is a streambed and is it the same as a creek bed?

Why do the rescue men want Brennan and the skull?

What is a fissure?

Who are the two men funning for him?

Was Brennan or Coyote Runs saying that if Coyote Runs had made it to the fissures he may have survived?

Will Brennan take the skull home or not?

If he does will it give him bad luck?

Will fear overtake Brennan and will he give up?

Why does Coyote Runs always say "take me spirit"?

Since the skull has made his life become "smarter" or more into the world, will he stay like that or will he go back to his normal life before the skull came into his life? Did he like the skull in his life anyway? Why or why not?

What ever happened to the skull?

APPENDIX 1

QUESTIONS, COMMENTS, AND OBSERVATIONS

The Outsiders—S. E. Hinton
Period 5
1996–1997

Who's Paul Newman?

What kind of name is Soda?

Where did he get the name Soda?

Does he live in a bad neighborhood?

Did people back then hate the Greasers?

Why isn't Darry like Soda and Ponyboy? He's sort of strict unlike their father.

How many people are in their gang and who are they?

The Greasers make it sound like they're tough, but they seem kind of whimpy.

What is a Corvair?

What was so rough at his house?

Why don't the Socs pick on someone their own size?

Why was Darry near where his brother was at that time?

What does, "You're bleedin' like a stuck pig!" mean?

Why do they call him Ponyboy?

What is Ponyboy's real name?

Two-bit means 25 cents or a quarter.

What does "rarities" mean?

Did Dally lead a hard life?

What does "sagely" mean?

How can you tell the difference between tuff and tough? They both sound the same.

Are Evie and Sandy, Steve and Soda's girl friends?

Appendix

Why do all the people in this book have those weird nicknames?

Who came up with the word "tuff"?

Why are the first 3-4 words in the chapter in all caps?

Why were they so mean to those girls? They didn't do anything to them.

Why do they keep changing from Dally to Dallas?

Are Kools cigarettes?

Why is Ponyboy being so nice to Soc girls? He's supposed to like Greasers and hate Socs.

Why did Ponyboy and his friends go to the "Dingo" if they knew it was dangerous?

Why do they all have nicknames?

Isn't Dally a little crazy? Why would you still bother someone after they threw a coke in your face?

Is Johnny Dally's brother?

What do they mean when they say, "Shoot, you're 96 if you're a day!"?

When Johnny and Pony are with Marcia and Cherry, where is Dally?

Why won't they just say bruised, or is boozed easier to say? If you say bruised, are you not cool?

How come the Socs usually gang up on one person to where it's 1 vs. 4?

Why can't the Socs just leave the Greasers alone? What did they ever do to them?

Does Cherry like Ponyboy?

Are the people in the Mustang Socs? Cherry and Marcia are their girlfriends or something?

Will Sodapop ever get Micky Mouse back?

Is Sodapop like the responsible one? Like the parent.

Are the Socs following Two-bit Ponyboy, and someone else?

Do the Socs ever get in trouble for fighting? Do the Greasers get in trouble?

What city do they live in?

Did Ponyboy's Dad used to hit him like Darry did?

Reeling pickled means they were drunk.

Why don't they tell the police?

Are the Socs racist in a way because they don't think Greasers are good enough?

Why did the other Socs not help Bob out?

Did the Socs want to beat up Johnny?

Why is Ponyboy going with Johnny? He didn't kill the kid.

Are they going to get caught? I mean the cops are going to find the body, investigate, and someone like the other Socs is going to say something.

Why did the Socs jump Pony and Johnny?

How does Dally know about the house where Pony and Johnny are staying?

Is anybody else going to stay with Johnny and Ponyboy at the church?

Are Johnny and Ponyboy going to get in trouble with the cops?

What supplies was he going to get?

Who is older Johnny or Ponyboy? Johnny is acting older.

Why was Ponyboy so attached to his hair?

Can you imagine what Johnny feels about killing Bob?

Is anyone going to find them? Fifty dollars is not going to last long!

How did Ponyboy get a cigarette if when Johnny got back from getting groceries he didn't mention it?

I think "fuzz" is police.

What did Ponyboy do with the letter after he read it?

Where are Johnny and Ponyboy really?

They had a Dairy Queen back then? How old is DQ?

Is Cherry getting information from the Socs and telling the Greasers? Will she get to see Johnny and Ponyboy face to face and actually tell them what is going on?

Why do they call the Cops the fuzz?

Did he want attention when he bragged about jail?

I thought Darry hated Ponyboy.

If Ponyboy was burned, how did he just get up all of a sudden?

Is Sodapop happy that Ponyboy got caught so Sodapop could get all the attention?

Does anyone recognize Ponyboy and Johnny?

Is Johnny the only one still in the hospital?

If Johnny lives, will he still be a Greaser even though he can't walk or fight if he gets in trouble?

Will Johnny be scared of fire? Will he walk again?

Who's Kathi?

Wow! They're kind of starting to be friends!

Do they ever fight in Soc territory?

Is he going to be paralyzed?

Is he going to die?

Does it feel weird to Johnny that he had a feeling that one day he wanted to kill himself and his wish almost came true?

If Dally and Tim Shepard are friends, why do they beat each other up

Because of this stuff happening, they all got a lot closer friendship.

Are Ponyboy and Cherry still going to be friends?

I think that Ponyboy has a lot of manners towards people.

After Chapter 9 why would they have more chapters? That's like the perfect ending.

What more could happen? Dally could commit suicide.

These poor boys have had such a hard time. All this stuff. The death of Dally, the death of Johnny. I haven't had such a loss in my entire life! I guess I'm lucky, very lucky.

Is their gang slowly disappearing?

Are the Socs and Greasers going to become friends?

Why do they have to separate the Socs from the Greasers. They're just looking at clothing style, cars, and money. Why can't they get along by means of personality of what's on the inside?

Did Randy not like his father? He should feel lucky to have a father that cares for him.

Why is Pony saying he killed him? Why is he trying to convince himself that his friends aren't dead? He should move on.

When the Socs pulled up in the car, were they perhaps coming to apologize?

APPENDIX J

QUESTIONS, COMMENTS, AND OBSERVATIONS

The Giver—Lois Lowry
Period 5
1996–1997

When you look at the cover, what do you think the book will be about?

A guy looking back to his past—lonely old man thinking he could have changed his life.

Part of it will be a perfect world—this guy helps people.

He remembers a good past life; he is older having a hard time.

I think he might give stuff to people.

Was the aircraft a UFO?

Did the aircraft have anything to do with Jonas being frightened?

Is the beginning of this book futuristic?

Could the aircraft be from another country trying to warn them that something might happen and they better or need to be prepared for it?

Was Jonas the "Pilot in Training" that misread the navigational instructions?

Is Jonas a kid now and later becomes an old guy?

Is the beginning of the story the life of the old guy on the cover as a kid?

They have to say a standardized apology and response?

How old are Asher and Jonas?

Why was Jonas frightened?

Why was Jonas looking forward to this one December? Was something special going to happen?

Why didn't anybody know what "animals" meant? Were these people aliens because they didn't do stuff normally?

Who didn't obey the rules?

It seems like there kids never are bad or disobey. Rules are strict, but kids are kids. Why are they so perfect?

Is Jonas' and Lily's father a psychiatrist?

Appendix

When they say they "release" the elders and the new borns—is released like saying they die?

Are they given family members? They said none of the night crew had been given spouses.

What is a nurturer?

These kids are perfect. It seems like a TV show like on the Simpsons—their neighbors the Flanders who are perfect.

Why is there only two children in each family?

Is everyone's birthday in December or something?

What does it mean when it says "groups of eleven", "when I was seven" and "the ceremony of twelve"?

What was fun to them? Was there no such thing as fun hardly?

I think that ceremony of 12 means his 12th birthday.

What does the dad mean by "apprehensive"?

What do they do at a nurturing center?

At the ceremony held in December, was it like a big adoption convention? Were the "nurturers" like the foster parents?

What is a nurturing center?

Two children—one male, one female—to each family unit. It was written clearly in the rules. Why?

Why is it that the "parents" apply for a child and get one from somewhere? The kids aren't their parents' blood? Why?

Why do they rate people?

Is the "receiver" the man on the front of the book?

Is the ceremony for every kids' birthday?

You couldn't choose your job? Did the elders observe you so that they would know what assignment would fit you?

Who is Asher?

Why was Lily looking innocent towards Jonas?

Where does this story take place and when?

Are these people on another planet? Because this doesn't happen on Earth?

Were the comfort objects like stuffed teddies and bottles and stuff?

Why did they have to recycle their objects? Are they like in the future and trying to be resourceful?

If bears and elephants are imaginary creatures—then do they not have animals?

Are bicycles their only mode of transportation?

They have never heard of a hippo before? Where they live it must be weird.

They must not have animals, but how come only a few people know what they're called even if they don't exist?

The birthmothers can only have 3 children and then are laborers, but how many children can a family receive? Once all the birthmothers had 3 conceived, was a younger person sent to take their place, like Lily?

Dang! How old do you have to be to have a baby? Hopefully older than 10 or 12!

Why are people not allowed to have the freedom to have their own kids?

How do birthmothers become pregnant?

Asher said the apple jumped out of his hand. Is this true?

Why was Jonas testing his eyesight? Why was he squinting?

How old is the newchild?

Are those people monitored all the time with like an intercom system?

Why did he not like talking (Ben) about his skills?

Their whole lives are already chosen for them—their names, jobs, and even family members.

I agree totally! Their "laws" are so strict. They like have to be perfect, like they can't have fun—no life at all!!

Is the House of the Old like a nursing home?

If you are 12 years old are you considered an adult?

Is everyone in the same age group have the same birthday, or do they just celebrate and have the ceremony on the same day.

How can you bathe somebody without looking at them?

Do they (Jonas and his friends) like helping old people out?

How can you be 12 and be considered as an adult when you have to be 18 to be considered an adult in the U.S.?

If a baby has a problem with it, what do they do with it?

Is there a such thing as twins or triplets? Is every baby born single (one)?

Does Roberto want to keep it a secret where he went?

Do they have to tell their family "everything"?

Do they have any privacy?

Who was chastised (yelled at)?

Where do these people live?

Appendix

What kind of clothes do they wear? Do the clothes look like ours?

How can you tell your parents every thought you have?

I think that Jonas has problems. I mean he tells his parents every thought and some of the things he dreams about don't sound too good!

Does he have to tell every detail? Is it a rule?

I think that Jonas will be the beginning of something new, something like we have now. He believes that having to tell of the stirrings and other personal things is stupid. I think he'll begin acting like what we have today. Like anyone can become pregnant and laws can be broken!!

I also think that Jonas has problems but he can dream whatever he wants cause he's his own person and person and privacy and he doesn't have to be ashamed to dream that!

Does he always tell about these dreams?

Jonas surprised me when he told his parents about his dream. He sounded like a kid that wasn't like that!

This book is like a world that we haven't experienced yet. It may come in the future!

Why does everything have to be one hundred percent to be good for them?

They have to be eight years old to get a bike!

Do they have to wear hair ribbons until they are eight?

After they are 12, do they still live with their parents or do they have to get their own house?

Will he have to take the pill for the rest of his life?

When they appeal their jobs, does that mean they ask for another?

Why does Jonas have to take the pill?

How long do they have to work?

Does "released" from the community mean they kill them?

Do they have any other kinds of communication with other countries, like phones or something?

Is the nurture section some kind of an adoption place and do they release the children afterwards?

What does it mean to "apply" for a child? Do you have to?

If one of your first children dies, take Caleb for example, does your next child you apply have to be named the same as your first like Caleb?

Do they have a ceremony for every child that is born?

Why do they have just one person with a name and then when someone is released you can use the name again?

Let's say one of their friends is over. He sees something, he takes it. There is no way that world is perfect. Someone has to have a mean mind. What do you do if something comes missing and it's really been stolen? Are there security cameras in the houses?

It only says they get their haircut when they're ten. What about before? Do all younger kids have long hair?

Are there streets or is there just sidewalks for their bikes?

Does giving people things at certain ages control the community?

Are the other communities laws and rules the same?

When he crossed the river to the next community was it just like our time?Why weren't you allowed to pick your own match? That is stupid! I do not want to live in a world like that for sure!!!

Are you getting an Education while you work?

Do you have to have kids while you work—is that an option?

When Asher said "smack" instead of "snack" does that mean he has a talking disability?

That poor child. How would that lady like to be smacked for accidentally saying smack. He didn't mean to say that. Give him a break!

Why would being hit be funny?

What kind of jobs were they given?

When you say the wrong word you get smacked on the hand.

There wasn't any schools or anything to get jobs so how did they get education? (or where there schools?)

Do the adults get a new job every year?

Is the guy on the cover the guy who Jonas had never noticed before?

Does he teach Jonas and Jonas becomes really close to him? Does the man die and Jonas promises that he will never forget that man?

Do you have to have a bicycle or can you walk and do they not like cars or have they even heard of cars?

Had the old man been like or just like Jonas when he was young? Did he have the capacity to see beyond?

Is he a historian?

How did that lady know that Jonas was having dreams about the future?

Did the book say where Jonas worked and where Asher worked?

Boy!! What a job! How will Jonas do that? There's no time for play! How badly does he want the job now? Especially with no release!!

Appendix

Does this man have an attitude? Been alone most of his life so he's not used to children.

Is Jonas the next Giver?

Why does Gabe like only sleeping with Jonas and nobody else?

So when a receiver or a give dies, the whole community gets the memories.

Do they keep the bigger child or smaller child?

Why did he kill that new infant? He did not deserve to die? Do they kill babies born under six pounds?

Is Jonas going to hate his father? How long will he be mad at him?

So the Giver is going to pretend that he doesn't know what's really happened to Jonas?

The last Receiver, Rosemary, was Jonas' daughter!

How old is the Giver?

If they really want him for the memories, why don't they just give the memories to everyone?

Did Jonas have his eyes closed? Could he see coldness or snow?

Is the old man giving Jonas all the information he knows?

I think the old man is the giver because he is giving Jonas a lot of information?

Where is Jonas outdoors?

Is that old man's memories that are passing to Jonas a lesson?

What does a Giver do and what does the receiver do?

Jonas is following instructions. He is lying. Does the "Giver" mean he is giving something important to Jonas. He is giving him the memories of his life?

Now that he has lost some of his "memories" and "weight", is he becoming more loose, more energetic?

When you are a Giver you know everything.

When the Giver was receiving, did he call the person the Giver and when Jonas has to pass it on, will he be called the Giver?

Why don't they let them see colors? Why is it so controlled?

Who is Jonas?

I don't get the part about what they're going to do with the snow.

Well I don't understand the word consciousness.

In the book they kept saying the word consciousness to someone. Who was it?

Why does Jonas see red?

I think that Jonas will try to change the world to like it is now.

Is Jonas the only one that can see in color?

Can Jonas look back into his life and is that why they call themselves the giver and the receiver. Is a person in training to be a giver.

They never talk about stores. Where do they get their food and everything?

Is the Giver having a memory?

Once the Giver gives Jonas all his memories will he die?

Where has everything gone, the memories, colors, animals, life in general?

Appendix K

Transcript of Discussion of The Outsiders

The following is a transcript of a discussion of *The Outsiders*. My comments about the interactions are underlined. The initials "SS" refer to setting shifts. A setting shift occurs when one of us initiates a change in either the structure or the direction of the discussion and this is accepted by the others. The initials "MF" indicate possible meaning fields. Comments preceded by the initials "OC" (observer comment) refer to my immediate perceptions and interpretations.

Maria responds, writing, "I think that Johnny is going to die also".

I am walking around the room for a minute as I listen. Carolina is writing something in her Reader/Writer log and not reading along. When I go up to show her the page we are on, she covers what she is writing.

Van Horn: And a plan. Let's stop there where they are looking for a plan. I have a feeling that this is probably a time that you need to have a discussion. I'm looking at all the things that you have generated and thinking that it's time for us to get together and talk about what's happened so far. Can you believe that it's only been one day in his life and all this has already happened?

(SS): I make a bid to shift the setting from reading aloud and generating questions and comments to holding a discussion. My bid is accepted by the students and the setting shifts.)

Maria: Yes.

<u>(Maria indicates she will accept my statement used to indicate the opening of a setting shift.)</u>

Van Horn: Burton?

Burton: Oh, um. It's not like descriptive about all the bad things that happened. Everything is Darry's fault. If he wouldn't have slapped him, he wouldn't of ran out. And THAT started everything. Johnny wouldn't have... they wouldn't have taken a walk in the park, never run away. If they wouldn't have walked in the park, they wouldn't have ran away, they you know, none of this would of happened. It's ALL Darry's fault!

(Burton resists my question and answer bid and introduces an aspect of the novel that he wishes to discuss. Here I have the option of exercising a role of teacher as director of discussion or allowing Burton to continue in his bid to choose the topic of discussion. I choose to encourage Burton with a question to elicit further information.)

MF: "I've been thinking about this." (AND/OR) "Even though Darry is supposed to be the good guy, I don't agree."

11:34

As he speaks, Burton leans forward in his chair. His eyes are so wide they are almost popping out of the sockets. He pounds his fist against the flat of his other hand as he makes his point.

Van Horn: All Darry?

MF: "Are you sure you've thought it out?" (AND) "This is unusual, most students go with Hinton's description of Darry as the good guy, the caretaker." (OR) "I'm interested in this unique interpretation and I'd like to give you the opportunity to clarify and elaborate upon your thoughts."

Burton: He made it all. It's like... if it wasn't for him slapping Pony that night, none of it would have ever happened. They get him later...

MF: "I understand that you want me to elaborate on my initial statement." (AND) "Let me start at the beginning."

Van Horn: That's pretty scary when you think about that. Do you think that life could be like a chain of events and if we make the right choice everything could...

MF: "I want to encourage you to continue." (AND/OR) "I can hardly wait for you to conclude your explanation before I try to take you to the next step, comparing literature to life."

Burton: Yeah, cause...

(It appears that Burton is willing to continue with this rhythm wherein he makes the point and I question or comment in order to elicit further information.)

Appendix

Jake: It would change the chain of events.

MF: "I'd like to be a part of this conversation." (AND/OR) "I'm thinking about this in connection with my own life." OR "Burton's not the only one who has important thoughts."

(Jake makes a bid to enter the conversation, while at the same time using the term "chain of events" and thus building on the comments initiated by another student and the teacher.)

Jake says this thoughtfully, as if reflecting on the implications.

Burton: Yeah, cause Darry did everything. Darry slapped him. He ran and him and Johnny are about to run away. They go to the park and the Socs came and Johnny stabbed him . . .

MF: "Whatever, could everyone stop interrupting me and listen?" (OR) "I'm not going to be distracted by these comments on the side; I have a point to make." (AND/OR) "I will consider your comments later, I need to concentrate on where I was in making my point."

(Burton ignores the bid by Jake to enter the discussion, continuing with his thoughts.)

Van Horn: He wouldn't have done that if he hadn't been in that park.

MF: "You are pausing in your explanation, do you need my help?" (AND/OR) "I am beginning to see your point—Johnny wouldn't have been in the park if he hadn't gone there with Pony when Pony ran away because Darry slapped him." (AND) "This is a new way of looking at the sequence of events for me, I want to think about it with you."

Burton: No, he was mad, cause he got like slapped.

MF: "Right, you're getting it now." (AND) "See what I mean, I may be right about this?" (OR) "That's all there is too it—he was there in the park as a direct result of Darry slapping Pony."

Joe: If he hadn't fallen asleep in the lot, then Darry wouldn't have slapped him.

Joe speaks quietly from the corner of the room.

MF: "I have something to say." (AND) "Hold on a minute, have you people considered why Darry slapped Pony in the first place?" (AND) "It is possible that the chain of events or blame start with Pony."

(It appears that Joe is making a bid to enter the conversation by introducing a counterpoint or argument to what Burton has been saying. Should this become a rhythm it would be termed comment-counter comment.)

11:36

OC: Joe usually keeps to himself. This is the first time he has said anything in class. He is a voracious reader and a creative writer. I am elated that he has decided to participate.

Van Horn: Say that again . . .

MF: "Now we're getting somewhere; a difference of opinion could heat this discussion up!" (AND/OR) "Great, Joe's coming into the conversation for the first time." (AND) "I want to make sure that everyone heard that comment."

(Here I am returning to the comment-support rhythm as I ask Joe to repeat himself so that his bid to enter the discussion is emphasized.)

Joe: If Ponyboy hadn't fallen asleep in the lot, Darry wouldn't have slapped him.

MF: "Let's give this some thought." (AND/OR) "There may be more than one way to look at the issues."

Ted R.: If they'd never met the Socs, none of this would of happened.

MF: I hear what you are saying." (AND) "I have another idea."

OC: Ted is also very quiet in class. He seldom, if ever, makes comments to the class in general. This is a big moment. He is contributing, *and* he is making connections to the comments of Burton and Joe.

Van Horn: So it very well could have been Ponyboy's fault?

MF: "Let me clarify Joe's thought, before we think about what Ted has said."

Burton: I'd rather get in trouble, than you know . . .

Ted R.: If they'd never met the Socs, none of it probably would of happened.

MF: "Does anyone realize I've made a comment here?" (AND/OR) "I'm waiting for a response to my remark."

SS: Ted makes a bid to change the course of the conversation—to talk about the issues relating to the general differences in the characteristics of the Socs and the Greasers. His bid is rejected by Burton who wants to continue in his discussion of Darry.

Appendix

(Ted realizes his bid to enter the discussion may be negated as Burton interrupts with a new idea, unrelated to that proposed by Ted. In an effort to make it known that he has something to say and to renegotiate his entrance into the discussion, Ted repeats his original statement verbatim. This rhythm may be termed comment-repeat.) The class is spread out over the room. I am afraid that the microphone will not pick up all the new participants.

Van Horn: Nothing would have happened. Now I hate to stop you when you're fired up, but can you gather here in a circle and try talking one at a time.

MF: "I've got some new people participating in the discussion." (AND) "I can hear Joe and Ted, but is the microphone picking them up?"

(I respond to Ted, attempting to support his comment and then dilute the effort by making a comment about the logistics of the discussion. Because of this, Burton has an opportunity to reassert his leadership in directing the discussion.)

Burton: Darry sucks. He DOES.

When some of the students look shocked that Burton has used this term, he looks in my direction to see if I am offended. When I make no sign of disapproval. He lets his eyes sweep over the crowd and states emphatically, He DOES.

MF: "Mrs. Van Horn likes me." (AND) "I can say what I want to say in the way I want to say it."

(After several efforts to reassert his leadership role, Burton resorts to making a shocking comment or statement using language out of the accepted register. This assures him that he will regain the attention of the group. This may be termed as a comment-counter comment and it will either be accepted or rejected by the participants in the discussion. In this case it is accepted and encouraged as Bet whistles and urges the group to come in closer.)

Bet: (Whistles) Gather round, gather round.

MF: "Burton's cool." (AND/OR) "Wow, could have been a tricky situation there, but I'm cool with it, let's keep going."

SS: I attempt to reduce Burton's dominance of the conversation by reminding the students about the procedure within a discussion. I want others to join in the conversation. My bid to shift the discussion to other issues and to include other participants is recognized and moved forward by Anita.

<u>(At this point in the interactive sequence I revert to the teacher as director of the discussion role, reminding the participants of the methods for discussion and acknowledging Anita's bid to enter the discussion.)</u>

We have held one other discussion of an excerpt from *The View From Saturday*. I feel it may help to remind the students of our purpose, and that they can choose their method of operation.

> Van Horn: Now you remember when we did this before. This is only our second time. I want to see what you do when you're involved in a novel and you have 62 comments to talk about. Burton and Ted and Joe have already brought up some very controversial issues. Pause . . . How would you like to do it? Do you want to look at your comments and pick things or do you want to just start from where you were? Yeah, Anita . . .
>
> MF: "I need to get you restarted." (AND) "I want you to decide how to do this."
>
> OC: I almost lost them there with this talk about how to do talk. Sometimes it is difficult to get them to stop and listen to one another. They are so accustomed to listening to and learning from teachers, they don't seem to know how to listen to and learn from one another—yet.
>
> Anita: I think Johnny. Remember when Ponyboy said that Johnny had gotten really bad in that lot by the Socs. Since then he'd been keeping a knife, so he was like, well. Ponyboy was inside the water. Randy was probably pushing him in the water. He killed Bob with that pocket knife he had . . .
>
> MF: "I've been thinking about this from the sidelines and I have something to say." (AND/OR) "I have my opinion on this issue." (AND/OR) "You may have overlooked something in your argument—let me explain."

<u>(Anita is making a connection to the proposals made by the other students and building evidence for Travis' statement that it was all the Socs fault. She is attempting to change the rhythm from comment-support or comment-counter comment to one of comment-connect/build.)</u>

> Bet: So, you guys. He was like defending him. In a way. They would have killed either Ponyboy, or, or . . . Johnny. So it was kind of uh, self defense.
>
> 11:38
>
> OC: Bet is building on the comment made by Anita.

Appendix 305

MF: "I can expand on Anita's thought." (AND) "Good comment by Anita."

<u>(Bet picks up on the rhythm of comment-connect/build by clarifying and building on Anita's statement.)</u>

Burton: Either way . . .

MF: "Hey, I've lost control here." (AND/OR) "Whatever you guys want to think, my reasoning should have convinced you otherwise." (OR) "I can acknowledge opposing viewpoints."

<u>(It appears that Burton is going to make a statement which may suggest that the arguments proposed by the others are irrelevant to the point he is trying to make. He may be rejecting their efforts to engage in a comment-connect/build rhythm because he realizes that they are not building on his argument.)</u>

Van Horn: Is it self defense?

MF: "Good point." (AND) "I'm glad to see you building on the thoughts of others." (OR) "Can you explain yourself clearly so that others see the strength of your statement?"

<u>(I re-enter the conversation attempting to strengthen the input of Anita and Bet through the use of the comment-support rhythm.)</u>

Bet: Yeah.

MF: "I'm right."

Van Horn: Did we have any indication that he might do such a thing?

OC: A subtle reminder by me that sometimes the answer is in the text. In this case there was some foreshadowing which we had discussed in an earlier meeting.

Burton: Yeah.

MF: "Oh yeah, I remember what you're talking about."

All talk at once.

Van Horn: I mean Johnny. Did we have any clue that he might have done this?

Several say no.

<u>(The comment-support rhythm continues until one of the participants answers the question directly. Note that she makes use of my suggestion that we may find something in the text.)</u>

Anita: Yes, remember that he said that he would kill anybody else who would like bother him.

MF: "Let me try to help you understand." (AND/OR) "I hate to be bossy about this, but you have obviously missed something in the text."

SS: Sandy makes a bid to enrich the conversation by making comparisons to their own lives. This bid is not accepted at this time. It isn't until much later in the conversation that Bet will take up the challenge as she discusses her impressions of the Westbrook school dance.

Sandy: I would want to kill them.

OC: Sandy says this as if she knows what it feels like to be powerless.

MF: "If someone was hurting a friend of mine, I would take action." (AND/OR) "I will do whatever it takes to protect my friends." (OR) "If someone hurt Monica I would protect her."

(This type of comment usually introduces a monologue in which the student relates the text or his or her interpretation of the text to an event in their own life. It may be a singular event in which the student tells the story or it may serve as the impetus for a rhythm of interaction in which a student makes a personal connection and then other students react to this personal story or where the student makes a personal connection and other students react to this by telling their own personal stories. These rhythms might be termed personal connection-response or personal connection-personal connection.)

Appendix L

Evaluation Sheet

Mystery Suspense Theater Radio Show

Team Number and Member Names:

_____
_____
_____
_____

As you listen to the presentation, score the radio show. A score of one means that the item was missing, incomplete, confusing, or not effective. A score of five means the item was professionally created.

Was the introduction effective? Did it capture your attention? Did the opening convey a mysterious feeling?

                              1 2 3 4 5

Was the reading effective? Did the actors read with expression and feeling? Were they believable?

                              1 2 3 4 5

Did the team use sound effects to help you visualize the story? Were some other sound effects necessary?

                              1 2 3 4 5

Did the team design an effective commercial for the sponsor of their radio play? If you were the sponsor would you have approved the advertisement? If you were a consumer, would you have purchased the product?

                              1 2 3 4 5

Was the conclusion of the mystery suspense theater radio show effective? Did the team end the production with a piece of music, sound effect, or other device which extended the mood of the play?

                              1 2 3 4 5

Appendix M

Commercial for Mystery Suspense Theater Radio Show
Planning Sheet

You and your team must create a commercial for the sponsor of your mystery suspense theater radio show. Please use this sheet to help you plan your commercial.

Team Number and Member Names:

_____

_____

Name of the Play:

_____

Product Name:

_____

Description of the Product:

_____

_____

_____

Slogan for the Product:

_____

_____

_____

Who needs the product:

_____

Why do they need the product (Explain):

_____
_____
_____

What will the product do for its users:

_____

Where/how can someone who wants the product, purchase the product:

_____
_____
_____

Restate the name of the product and the slogan:

_____
_____
_____

Appendix N

Survival Across Time
Project Planning Sheet

You are currently reading a historical fiction novel about one of the following periods:

American Revolution
Civil War
Depression
World War II
Contemporary

You will be asked to create a product which will present information about this period in history. Examples of products you might propose are:

- Time Line with photocopies of key events of the period summarized
- Diary written from the point of view of someone who lived in this time
- Newspaper containing articles about the life and times of this period
- Collection of letters obtained by corresponding with people who lived in this time period
- Written and illustrated story about an event of this period (may be in historical fiction format)

Consider your unique talents and interests before you complete this proposal form. You may work with others who are reading the same book, but you must specify which part of the product you will be responsible for creating.

Student Name: _____

Historical Fiction Book: _____

Time Period: _____

Will you be working with others? _____

If you answered yes to the above question, who will you be working with?

_____

_____

Appendix 311

Describe your project in detail (What will you create and how will you go about the process?) For example: I am going to write to my relatives who fought in World War II. I will bind my letters to them along with their responses. I will also photocopy family photographs of these relatives and/or photographs contained in books about World War II which relate to the letters. The title of my book will be *Letters From Survivors of World War II.*

Please list any materials and/or information I can help you obtain:

APPENDIX O

RESPONSE OPTIONS/SPECIFICATIONS PLANNING SHEET

Canyons by Gary Paulsen

Please read the following response options/specifications and choose the one you would like to create. Consider your own unique talents and interests in choosing a project. You may write to me on this sheet if there are alternatives or adjustments you would like to propose. I have the supplies and will help you to make the books for both.

Response I

The writing of Gary Paulsen is full of descriptions which create "scenes" in our minds as we read. His words also evoke poetry.

Choose 10 quotations from *Canyons* which create a "picture" in your mind. You might choose one from several chapters. Copy these quotations and the page numbers in the novel where you found them.

Illustrate each quotation and place the illustration and the quote in the order that they occur in the novel. (You may use collage, markers, colored paper cut outs, etc.)

Write a poem to convey the mood or events depicted in each illustration. You may create "found poems" from the novel itself. If you do this, be sure to include the page numbers where you "found" the words.

Response II

Brennan has many thoughts and questions as he finds the skull and works to discover the story behind it.

Coyote Runs, too, wonders about going on a raid and becoming a man.

Pretend that you are either Brennan or Coyote Runs. Try to imagine what he is thinking and feeling. Keep a diary, including notes and sketches. For example, if you are Brennan, you could include notes and sketches about where you found the skull and your research into the event. If you are

Appendix

Coyote Runs, you could include a drawing of your horse or a map of the canyon where the raid took place. You might also include photographs and artifacts as in the example shown of Peter Beard's diary of his adventures in Africa. Try to use the same methods used by the author, Gary Paulsen, to let the reader "hear" the thoughts of Brennan as he experiences the adventure.

You must decide:
- Which moments in Brennan's or Coyote Runs' life you will write about. (You must have 20 entries.)
- What artifacts, sketches, or photos you will include in the journal. (You must have 10 artifacts.)

Appendix P

Paper Bag Mystery
Planning Sheet

Attention future mystery writers! Have you ever wished to follow in the footsteps of Arthur Conan Doyle or Agatha Christie, writing exciting, well-constructed mysteries for eager readers to enjoy? Here's your chance. The paper bag in front of you contains four clues that are vital to the solution of a mystery you are going to create. Follow these simple step-by-step instructions and you'll produce a story that is almost certain to fascinate mystery lovers.

I. Select a setting from the list below and underline it, or create your own setting and name or describe it.
- the desert
- the slopes of Mount Everest
- the basement of a rundown apartment house
- the turret of an abandoned castle
- an island in the Pacific Ocean
- a schoolroom
- other _____

II. Open your bag and list your four clues

Clues	Possible Meanings
1. _____	_____
2. _____	_____
3. _____	_____
4. _____	_____

III. What could each clue mean in the setting you have selected? Write one possible meaning for each clue.

IV. In what kind of crime might all four clues be involved?

Appendix

V. What was the motive for this crime? Chose a motive from the list below and underline it, or think up your own motive and name or describe it.

fame   love   power   greed
jealousy   revenge
Other _____

VI. You will need a cast of characters—a villain, a victim, and a hero (the detective who solves the crime). To cast your story, complete the area below. Use another sheet of paper if you need more space.

Villain

Name: _____
Physical Description: _____
_____
Personality Profile: _____
_____

Victim

Name: _____
Physical Description: _____
_____
Personality Profile: _____
_____

Detective

Name: _____
Physical Description: _____
_____
Personality Profile: _____
_____

VII. With one member of your group acting as scribe or secretary, involve the characters you have described and the clues you were given in a mystery that takes place in the setting you have selected to create a spellbinding story.

Appendix Q

YOU ARE THE DETECTIVE!!!
PLANNING SHEET

This is your detective notebook. You will use it to keep a record of the mystery you create. Included in your notebook will be the following:

1. Description of yourself as a detective (may include a photo).

2. Photographs and descriptions of the appearance and personality of three (3) characters in your mystery.

3. Photographs or drawings of at least three (3) clues to the mystery.

4. One to two page write-up by you, the detective, detailing your thoughts about the clues.

5. At least one sketch, map, or photo of the scene of the crime. (May include more than one, for example, the outside and inside of a building, or a car and the airport.)

6. One to two page write-up by you, the detective describing the scene of the crime and detailing your observations.

7. One to two page statement from *each* of the three (3) characters in your mystery. (Note, you may write this as an interview between you and the character.)

8. Your description of the crime and your conclusion (Who did it?)

9. Arrest Report with finger prints of the criminal.

10. Epilogue—What are the characters doing one year after you solved the mystery?

Appendix R

Detective Notebook

Rubric

Item Number	Complete	Points
1	_____	(10) _____
2	_____	(30) _____
3	_____	(15) _____
4	_____	(20) _____
5	_____	(15) _____
6	_____	(20) _____
7	_____	(30) _____
8	_____	(30) _____
9	_____	(15) _____
10	_____	(15) _____
		_____
Total		(200) _____

Appendix S

Character Sketch in a Wallet
Planning Sheet

You can tell a great deal about a person from the contents of his or her wallet. With this in mind, each of us is going to create a wallet for a character from *The Outsiders*.

Preparation

Choose a character from the novel
Note details about the character in your Reader/Writer Log:
- Favorite color
- Hobbies
- Friends
- Activities—does your character attend school, work, play sports?
- Lifestyle
- Values—what does your character value?

Activation

I will provide you with a set of blank cards that might be found in a wallet. You will decide which of these cards might be found in your character's wallet and design them accordingly.

I will provide you with the construction paper you will need to create the actual wallet. You will need to bring a glue stick to class.

You might want to put other items in your character's wallet. For example:
    Notes from a friend
    Detention hall slips
    Talisman—like a four leaf clover of a lucky coin
    Photographs of friends and family
    Paycheck
    Grocery list
I know you will think of other items specific to your character.

Evaluation

Your wallet should include at least 10 items that are relevant to the character you have chosen.

You will write a letter to your character, pretending that you have found his or her wallet and explaining what each item in the wallet tells you about the owner.

Appendix T

Letter to the Owner of Your Wallet
Rubric

Your letter to the owner of the wallet you have created should contain the following:

	Possible Points	Points Earned
Opening and closing salutation.	5	_____
Introductory statement about where you found the wallet. Note: This should be a place the character might have been (or was) in the novel.	5	_____
Statement introducing the idea that much can be learned about a person from the contents of his or her wallet.	5	_____
Description of each of the 10 items in the wallet. Note: Many of you have more than 10 items in your wallet. Choose 10 you want to write about in the letter. Note: As you write the description of each object refer to the next two items on the rubric.	20 (2ea.)	_____
The description of each item should be followed by a statement which tells the owner what you can infer from this item.	30 (3ea.)	_____
Following the above statement should be an additional statement in which you make a personal connection, telling the owner of the wallet something about yourself in relation to that particular item. For example, if you are talking about a movie ticket, you might write about your favorite movie or an experience you had at the movies.	30 (3ea.)	_____
Closing statement in which you form a plan or schedule a meeting where you can return the wallet to the owner.	5	_____

APPENDIX V

PAPER CHARACTERS AND CHARACTER PROFILE PLANNING SHEET

The Outsiders by S. E. Hinton

You will be working in a small group to create a paper character from *The Outsiders* and to write a character profile.

Here are some pages in the novel where you may find information about the following characters. There is much information throughout the novel, but this will get you started:

Character	Pages
Ponyboy Curtis	63, 64, 69, 72, 73
Darry Curtis	9, 18, 115
Sodapop Curtis	10, 37, 72, 73
Tim Shepard	120, 121
Steve Randle	11, 12
Two-Bit (Keith) Matthews	12, 29, 41
Dallas (Dally) Winston	12, 13, 16, 54, 55
Johnny Cade	13, 14, 31, 69
Sylvia, Evie, Sandy (Greaser Girls)	16
Cherry Valance	21, 25, 29, 30, 112
Marcia (Cherry's friend)	21, 29, 30
Robert (Bob) Sheldon	41, 50, 51, 140
Randy Adderson	41, 102, 103
Buck Merrill	53, 127
Blue Mustang	38, 41, 42, 101
The Fountain in the Park	49, 50, 51

You will also work with your group to write a profile of the character modeled after *The Important Book* by Margaret Wise Brown.

Use this poem as a model for your profile of character.

> The important thing
> about Johnny Cade is
> that he is gallant.
> He looks like a little dark puppy
> that has been kicked too many times.
> His the smallest and the youngest
> of the Greasers.
> He was beat up by the Socs
> and now carries a switchblade.
> He saved Pony's life,
> but killed a Soc named Bob
> in the process.
> He rescued children from a
> raging fire in an old abandoned
> church on Jay Mountain.
> He died soon after . . . his last
> words to Pony were
> "Stay gold"
> Johnny Cade was golden like the
> sunrise.
> But the important thing
> about Johnny Cade is
> that he is gallant.

You will choose one quote that exemplifies the character for you and include it with your profile. For example, the quote that I chose to go with my poem is as follows:

> "Listen, I don't mind dying now. It's worth it.
>
> It's worth saving those kids. Their lives are worth more than mine,
>
> they have more to live for." (p. 154)

References

Almasi, J. F., McKeown, M. G. & Beck,. I. L. (1996). The nature of engaged reading in classroom discussions of literature. *Journal of Literacy Research, 28* (1), 107–146.

Alvermann, D. E. (1981). The compensatory effect of graphic organizers on descriptive text. *Journal of Educational Research, 75* (1), 44–48.

Beck, L. (1995). *Reclaiming educational administration as a caring profession.* New York: Teachers College Press.

Bloome, D. (1986). Building literacy and the classroom community. *Theory into Practice, 25* (2), 71–76.

Calfee, R. C., Dunlap, K. L., & Wat, A. Y. (1994). Authentic discussion of texts in middle grade schooling: An analytic-narrative approach. *Journal of Reading, 37* (7), 546–556.

Calkins, L. M. (1994). *The art of teaching writing.* Portsmouth, NH: Heinemann.

Carlsen, W. S. (1991). Questioning in classrooms: A sociolinguistic perspective. *Review of Educational Research, 61* (2), 157–178.

Cazden, C. B. (1988). *Classroom discourse: The language of teaching and learning.* Portsmouth, NH: Heinemann.

Cherland, M. R. (1994). *Private practices: Girls reading fiction and constructing identity.* Bristol, PA: Taylor & Francis.

Cintorino, M. A. (1993). Getting together, getting along, getting to the business of teaching and learning. *English Journal, 82* (1), 23–32.

Cochran-Smith, M., & Lytle, S. (1993). *Inside/outside: Teacher research and knowledge.* New York: Teachers College Press.

Cole, M., John-Steiner, V., Scribner, S., & Souberman, E. (Eds.). (1978). *L. S. Vygotsky: Mind in society: The development of higher psychological processes.* Cambridge, MA: Harvard University Press.

Coleman, J. S. (1961). *The adolescent society: The social life of the teenager and its impact on education.* New York: The Free Press.

Collins, A., Brown, J. S., & Newman, S. E. (1989). Cognitive apprenticeship: Teaching the crafts of reading, writing, and mathematics. In L. Resnick (Ed.), *Knowing, learning, and instruction: Essays in honor of Robert Glaser,* pp. 453–494. Hillsdale, NJ: Erlbaum.

Cullinan, B. E. (Ed.). (1993). *Pen in hand: Children become writers.* Newark: DE: International Reading Association.

Dewey, J. (1944). *Democracy and education.* New York: Free Press.

Dillon, J. T. (1981). Duration of response to teacher questions and statements. *Contemporary Educational Psychology, 6* (1), 1–11.

Dixon-Krauss, L. (1996). *Vygotsky in the classroom: Mediated literacy instruction and assessment.* New York: Longman.

Eckert, P. (1989). *Jocks and burnouts: Social categories and identity in the high school.* New York: Teachers College Press.

Everhart, R. B. (1983). *Reading, writing and resistance: Adolescence and labor in a junior high school.* Boston: Routledge & Kegan Paul.

Fielding, L. G., & Pearson, P. D. (1994), February. Synthesis of research: Reading comprehension: What works. *Educational Leadership 51* (5), 62–68.

Finders, M. J. (1997) *Just girls: Hidden literacies and life in junior high.* New York: Teachers College Press.

Fletcher, R. (1993a). Roots and wings: Literature and children's writing. In B. E. Cullinan (Ed.), *Pen in hand: Children become writers* (pp. 7–17). Newark, DE: International Reading Association.

Fletcher, R. (1993b). *What a writer needs.* Portsmouth, NH: Heinemann.

Freire, P. (1985). *The politics of education: Culture, power, and liberation.* (D. Macedo, Trans.). Westport, CT: Bergin & Garvey.

Gallimore, R., & Goldenberg, C. N. (1993). Activity settings of early literacy: Home and school factors in children's emergent literacy. In E. Forman, N. Minick, & C. A. Stone (Eds.), *Contexts for learning: Sociocultural dynamics in children's development* (pp. 315–335). Oxford: Oxford University Press.

Goffman, E. (1973). *The presentation of self in everyday life.* Woodstock, NY: The Overlook Press.

Goodman, J. (1989). Education for critical democracy. *Journal of Education, 171* (2), 89–116.

Graves, D. H. (1994). *A fresh look at writing.* Portsmouth, NH: Heinemann.

Greene, M. (1988). *The dialectic of freedom.* New York: Teachers College Press.

Greene, M. (1992). The passions of pluralism: Multiculturalism and the expanding community. *Journal of Negro Education, 61* (3), 250–261.

Greene, M. (1995). *Releasing the imagination: Essays on education, the arts, and social change.* San Francisco: Jossey-Bass.

Griffin, P., Belyaeva, A., Soldatova, G., & the Velikhov-Hamburg Collective. (1993). Creating and reconstituting contexts for educational interactions, including a computer program. In E. A. Forman, N. Minick, and C. A. Stone (Eds.), *Contexts for learning: Sociocultural dynamics in children's development* (pp. 120–152). New York: Oxford University Press.

Guszak, F. J. (1967). Teacher questioning and reading. *The Reading Teacher, 21* (3), 227–234.

Harste, J. C., Short, K. G., & Burke, C. (1988). *Creating classrooms for authors: The reading-writing connection.* Portsmouth, NH: Heinemann.

Hollins, E. R. (1996). *Culture in school learning: Revealing the deep meaning.* Mahweh, NJ: Lawrence Erlbaum Associates.

Holquist, M. (Ed.). (1981). *The dialogic imagination: Four essays by M. M. Bakhtin.* (C. Emerson & M. Holquist, Trans.). Austin, TX: University of Texas Press. (Original work published in 1975)

hooks, b. (1994). *Teaching to transgress: Education as the practice of freedom.* New York: Routledge.

Hubbard, R. (1989). *Authors of pictures: Draughtsman of words.* Portsmouth, NH: Heinemann.

Hynds, S. (1990). Talking life and literature. In S. Hynds & D. L. Rubin (Eds.), *Perspectives on talk and learning* (pp. 163–178). Urbana, IL: National Council of Teachers of English.

Keene, E. O. & Zimmerman, S. (1997). *Mosaic of thought: Teaching comprehension in a reader's workshop.* Portsmouth, NH: Heinemann.

Kletzien, S. B. & Baloche, L. (1994). The shifting muffled sound of the pick: Facilitating student-to-student discussion. *Journal of Reading, 37* (7), 540–545.

Krogness, M. M. (1995). *Just teach me, Mrs. K.: Talking, reading, and writing with resistant adolescent learners.* Portsmouth, NH: Heinemann.

Langer, J. A. (1995). *Envisioning literature: Literary understanding and literature instruction.* New York: Teachers College Press.

Livdahl, B. S. (1993). To read it is to live it, different from just knowing it. *Journal of Reading, 37* (3), 192–200.

Lowry, L. (1994). Newbery medal acceptance. *The Horn Book Magazine,* July/August, pp. 414–422.

Metsala, J. L., Commeyras, M., & Sumner, G. (1996). Literature discussions based on student-posed questions. *The Reading Teacher, 50* (3), 262–265.

Mish, F. C., et al. (Eds.). (1998). *Merriam-Webster's collegiate dictionary* (10th ed.). Springfield, MA: Merriam-Webster.

Moffett, J. (1968). *Teaching the universe of discourse.* Boston: Houghton Mifflin.

Morrison, T. (1987). The site of memory. In W. Zinsser (Ed.), *Inventing the truth: The art and craft of memoir* (pp. 101–124). Boston: Houghton Mifflin.

Murray, D. M. (1996). *Crafting a life in essay, story, poem.* Portsmouth, NH: Boynton/Cook Publishers.

Myers, J. (1992). The social contexts of school and personal literacy. *Reading Research Quarterly, 27* (4), 297–334.

Palincsar, A. S. & Brown, A. L. (1984). Reciprocal teaching of comprehension-fostering and comprehension-monitoring activities. *Cognition and Instruction, 1* (2), 117–175.

Paris, S. C., Cross, D. R., & Lipson, M. Y. (1984). Informed strategies for learning: A program to improve children's reading awareness and comprehension.' *Journal of Educational Psychology, 76,* 1239–1252.

Patterson, L., & Hirtle, J. (1996). Bluebells, complexity, and teacher research: A system approach to classroom data. In D. J. Leu, C. K. Kinzer, & K. A. Hinchman (Eds.), *Literacies for the 21st century: Research and practice.* Forty-fifth yearbook of the National Reading Association (pp. 1–10). Chicago: National Reading Conference.

Probst, R. E. (1988). *Response and analysis: Teaching literature in junior and senior high school.* Portsmouth, NH: Boynton/Cook Publishers.

Purves, A. C. (1984). Teaching literature as an intellectual activity. *ADE Bulletin 78* (Summer), 17–19.

Purves, A. C., Rogers, T., & Soter, A. O. (1995). *How porcupines make love III: Readers, texts, cultures in the response based literature classroom.* White Plains, NY: Longman Publishers.

Raphael, T. E., & Pearson, P. D. (1985). Increasing student awareness of sources of information for answering questions. *American Educational Research Journal, 22* (2), 217–237.

Rosenblatt, L. (1995). *Literature as exploration.* New York: The Modern Language Association of America.

Rosenblatt, L. M. (1978). *The reader the text the poem: A transactional theory of the literary work.* Carbondale, IL: Southern Illinois University Press.

Rosenshine, B., Meister, C., & Chapman, S. (1996). Teaching students to generate questions: A review of the intervention studies. *Review of Educational Research, 66* (2), 181–221.

Routman, R. (1994). *Invitations: Changing as teachers and learners K–12.* Portsmouth, NH: Heinemann.

Searcy, B. (1988). Getting children into the literacy club—and keeping them there. *Childhood Education,* Winter, 74–77.

Shake, M. C., & Allington, R. L. (1985). Where do teachers' questions come from? *The Reading Teacher, 38* (4), 432–439.

Shor, I. (1992). *Empowering education: Critical teaching for social change.* Chicago: The University of Chicago Press.

Shor, I., & Freire, P. (1987). *A pedagogy for liberation: Dialogues on transforming education.* New York: Bergin & Garvey.

Short, K., Kaufman, G., Kaser, S., Kahn, L. H., & Crawford, K.M. (1999). "Teacher-watching": Examining teacher talk in literature circles. *Language Arts, 76* (5), 377–385.

Smith, F. (1981). Demonstrations, engagement, and sensitivity. *Language Arts, 58* (1), 103–112.

Smith, F. (1988). *Joining the literacy club: Further essays into education.* Portsmouth, NH: Heinemann.

Spencer, J. (1994, Fall). Drawing students into Shakespeare. *English in Texas,* pp. 30–34.

Sumara, D. J. (1996). *Private readings in public: Schooling the literary imagination.* New York: Peter Lang.

Wertsch, J. V., Tulviste, P., & Hagstrom, F. (1993). A sociocultural approach to agency. In E. A. Forman, N. Minick, & C. A. Stone (Eds.), *Contexts for learning: Sociocultural dynamics in children's development* (pp. 336–356). New York: Oxford University Press.

Wilhelm, J. D. (1997). *"You gotta be the book": Teaching engaged and reflective reading with adolescents.* New York: Teachers College Press.

Wooldridge, S. G. (1996). *Poemcrazy: Freeing your life with words.* New York: Clarkson N. Potter.

Zinsser, W. (Ed.). (1987). *Inventing the truth: The art and craft of memoir.* Boston: Houghton Mifflin.

Literature Used

Alphin, E. M. (1992). *Ghost cadet.* Madison, WI: Demco Media.

Angell, J. (1984). Turmoil in a blue and beige bedroom. In D. R. Gallo (Ed.), *Sixteen short stories by outstanding writers for young adults* (pp. 72–81). New York: Delacorte Press.

Anonymous. (1971). *A real diary: Go ask Alice.* New York: Prentice Hall.

Avi. (1990). *Something upstairs.* New York: Avon Books.

Avi. (1993). *Wolfrider: A tale of terror.* New York: Aladdin Paperbacks.

Barrett, A. (1998). *The voyage of the narwhal.* New York: W.W. Norton & Company.

Bitton-Jackson, Livia. (1997). *I have lived a thousand years: Growing up in the Holocaust.* New York: Scholastic.

Bowermaster, J. (1993). *The adventures and misadventures of Peter Beard in Africa.* New York: Little, Brown, and Company: A Bullfinch Press Book.

Brancato, R. F. (1984). Fourth of July. In D. R. Gallo (Ed.), *Sixteen short stories by outstanding writers for young adults* (pp. 102–111). New York: Delacorte Press.

Brown, M. W. (1949). *The important book.* New York: HarperCollins Publishers.

References

Canfield, J. Hansen, M. V., & Kirberger, K. (1997). *Chicken soup for the teenage soul: 101 stories of life, love and learning.* Deerfield Beach, FL: Health Communications.

Christie, A. (1991). *And then there were none.* New York: Berkley Books.

Cooney, C. B. (1994). *Driver's ed.* New York: Bantam Doubleday Dell Books for Young Readers.

Cooney, C. B. (1997). *Wanted.* New York: Scholastic.

Day, A. (1994). *Carl makes a scrapbook.* New York: Farrar, Straus and Giroux.

Dygard, T. J. (1991). *Wilderness Peril.* New York: Penguin Books.

Ensign, G. (1993). *Great beginnings: Opening lines of great novels.* New York: HarperCollins.

Fleischman, P. (1988). *Joyful noise: Poems for two voices.* New York: HarperTrophy.

Front, S. (1990). *Never say Macbeth.* New York: Doubleday.

Garfield, L. (1985). *Shakespeare stories.* New York: Houghton Mifflin.

Giovanni, N. (1993). A journey. In E. M. Aoki, A. S. Palincsar, W. H. Teale, V. R. Arnold, J. V. Tirajero, J. Flood, M. Priestley, J. V. Hoffman, N. Roser, A. W. Webb, D. Lapp, C. B. Smith, P. W. Williams, M. Martinez, & K. D. Wood (Eds.), *Become the Music* (p. 488). New York: Macmillan/McGraw Hill.

Glen, K. (1994). *Mystery in the spotlight.* New York: Scholastic.

Golding, W. (1954). *Lord of the flies.* New York: Perigee Books.

Hamilton, V. (1984). *The house of Dies Drear.* New York: Aladdin Paperbacks.

Haynes, B. (1994). *Deadly deception.* New York: Delacorte Press.

Hinton, S. E. (1989). *The outsiders.* New York: Dell.

Keehn, S. M. (1993). *I am Regina.* New York: Yearling Books.

Konigsburg, E. L. (1996). *The view from Saturday.* New York: Atheneum Books for Young Readers.

Lasky, K. (1991). *Double trouble squared: A Starbuck family adventure.* New York: Harcourt Brace Jovanovich.

Leitner, I. (1992). *The big lie: A true story.* New York: Scholastic.

Lowry, L. (1993). *The giver.* Boston: Houghton Mifflin.

MacLachlan, P. (1991). *Journey.* New York: Delacorte Press.

Morey, W. (1991). *Death walk.* Hillsboro, OR: Blue Heron.

Moss, M. (1995). *Amelia's notebook.* Berkeley, CA: Tricycle Press.

Nickens, B. (1994). *Walking the log: Memories of a southern childhood.* New York: Rizzoli.

Nixon, J. L. (1991). *A candidate for murder.* New York: Dell.

Nixon, J. L. (1992). *The kidnapping of Christina Lattimore.* New York: Bantam Doubleday Dell Books for Young Readers.

Nixon, J. L. (1992). *The other side of dark.* New York: Dell.

Nixon, J. L. (1992). *The stalker.* New York: Bantam Doubleday Dell Books for Young Readers.

Nixon, J. L. (1991). *Whispers from the dead.* New York: Bantam Doubleday Books for Young Readers.

Nordan, L. (1997). The dime store teapot. *House and Garden, 166* (10), 92–93.

Panzer, N. (Ed.). (1994). *Celebrate America in poetry and art.* New York: Hyperion Books for Children.

Paulsen, G. (1985). *Dogsong.* New York: Scholastic.

Paulsen, G. (1987). *Hatchet.* New York: Aladdin.

Paulsen, G. (1990). *Canyons.* New York: Dell Publishing.

Paulsen, G. (1993). *Nightjohn*. New York: Delacorte Press.

Pausewang, G. (1996). *The final journey*. (Patricia Crampton, Trans.). New York: Scholastic.(Original work published in 1992)

Pelzer, D. J. (1995). *A child called it*. Dearfield Beach, FL: Health Communications, Inc.

Polacco, P. (1996). *Aunt Chip and the great Triple Creek dam affair*. New York: Philomel Books.

Porter, C. (1993). *Meet Addy: An American girl*. New York: Scholastic.

Ringgold, F. (1991). *Tar beach*. New York: Scholastic.

Rylant, C. (1994). *Something permanent*. New York: Harcourt Brace.

Rylant, C. (1995). *The Van Gogh café*. New York: Harcourt Brace & Company.

Schoenbaum, S. (1991). *Shakespeare's lives*. Oxford: Clarendon Press.

Scholastic, Inc. (1994). *Shakespeare in the spotlight*. New York: Scholastic.

Soto, G. (1992). *Neighborhood odes*. New York: Harcourt Brace & Company.

Stanley, D. (1992). *Bard of Avon: The story of William Shakespeare*. New York: Morrow Books.

Stewart, S. (1995). *The library*. New York: Farrar, Straus and Giroux.

Taylor, T. (1994). *Sweet Friday island*. New York: Harcourt Brace.

Van Allsburg, C. (1985). *The polar express*. Boston: Houghton Mifflin.

White, E. B. (1952). *Charlotte's Web*. New York: HarperCollins.

Wright, B. R. (1991). *A ghost in the house*. New York: Scholastic.

Yolen, J. (1988). *The devil's arithmetic*. New York: Puffin Books.

INDEX

Author Index

Allington, R. L., 91
Almasi, J. F., 134
Alvermann, D. E., 91
Angell, J., 196, 197, 199, 200
Atwell, N., 16
Avi, 119, 123
Bakhtin, M. M., 192
Baloche, L., 135
Barrett, A., 251
Beck, I. L., 134
Beck, L., 25
Belyaeva, A., 3
Bloome, D., 6
Bowmaster, J., 208
Brancato, R. F., 174, 178, 190
Brown, J. S., 31, 91, 92, 255, 320
Burke, C., 45
Calfee, R. C., 135
Calkins, L., 72
Carlsen, W. S., 91
Cazden, C. B., 134
Chapman, S., 91
Cherland, M., 46
Christie, A., 119, 120, 121
Cintorino, M. A., 135
Cochran-Smith, M., xv
Cohen, R., 70, 71, 77
Cole, 137
Coleman, J., 52
Collins, A., 91
Cooney, C., 31, 63, 119, 125
Crawford, K. M., 138
Cross, D. R., 92
Cullinan, B., 68
Dewey, J., 22
Dillon, J. T., 134
Dunlap, K. L., 135
Dygard, T. J., 119
Eckert, P., 52, 58
Ensign, G., 224
Evans, E., 28
Everhart, R., 51
Fielding, L. G., 135
Finders, M. J., 250
Fleischman, P., 178, 179, 180, 182, 191
Fletcher, R., 70, 73, 202
Freire, P., 62, 90, 138
Gallimore, R., 46, 47, 53, 54
Garfield, L., 187, 233
Giovanni, N., 169, 178, 190
Glenn, K., 182, 183
Goffman, E., 54, 56
Goldenberg, C., 46, 47, 53, 54
Goodman, J., 38
Graves, D., 70, 201
Greene, M., xvii, 4, 42, 85, 87
Griffin, P., 3
Guszak, F. J., 91
Hagstrom, F., 6
Hamilton, V., 119
Harjo, J., 31, 247
Harste, J., 45
Haynes, B., 119
Hinton, S. E., 32, 40, 96, 98, 99, 108, 114, 129, 130, 174, 178, 190, 191, 215, 217, 219, 221, 251, 252, 255, 261
Hirtle, J., 95
Hollins, E., 60
hooks, b., 134
Hubbard, R., 246
Hynds, S., 134
John-Steiner, V., 137
Kahn, L. H., 138
Kaser, S., 138
Kaufman, G., 138
Keehn, S. M., 153
Kletzien, S. B., 135
Krogness, M. M., 70, 174
Langer, J., 14, 61
Lasky, K., 96, 98
Lipson, M. Y., 92
Livdahl, B.S., 20
Lowry, L., 96, 98, 257, 258
Lytle, S., xv
MacLachlan, P., 11, 27, 77, 93, 94, 95, 136, 141, 196, 250, 251, 260
Mallow, F., 95
McKeown, M. G., 134
Meister, C., 91
Moffett, J., 135

Morey, W., 31, 32
Morrison, T., 247
Murray, D., 68, 77
Myers, J., 63
Myers, W. D., 199
Newman, S. E., 91
Nickens, B.), 31, 327
Nixon, J. L., 119, 121
Nordan, L., 67, 68, 70, 71, 84
Palinscar, A. S., 92
Panzer, N., 31, 246, 247
Paris, S. C., 79, 92
Patterson, L., 95
Paulsen, G., 31, 50, 82, 96, 98, 156, 157, 205, 206, 208, 211, 212, 214, 233
Pausewang, G., 24, 127
Pearson, P. D., 92, 135
Probst, R., 166, 167, 178
Purves, A. C., 4, 167, 172
Raphael, T. E., 92
Ringgold, F., 258
Rogers, T., 167, 172, 252, 253
Rosenblatt, L., 13, 58, 61, 90
Rosenshine, B., 91
Routman, R., 68
Rylant, C., 27, 168, 170, 171, 173, 190, 200, 201, 203, 205
Scribner, S., 137
Searcy, B., 14
Shake, M. C., 91
Shakespeare, W., 167, 186, 187, 189, 190, 233, 236
Shor, I., 60
Short, K., 45, 138
Smith, F., 3, 4, 14, 44, 52, 137
Soldatova, G., 3
Soter, A. O., 167, 172
Soto, G., 219, 220, 221
Souberman, E., 137
Stanley, D., 186, 188
Sumara, D., 177
Taylor, T., 119, 120, 256
Tulviste, P., 6
Vygotsky, L. S., 90, 93, 137
Wat, A. Y., 135
Welty, E., 16, 77
Wertsch, J. V., 6
White, E. B., 66, 151, 328
Wilhelm, J. D., 167

Wooldridge, S., 38, 64, 78
Wright, B. R., 119
Zinsser, W., 42, 67

Subject Index

activating prior knowledge, 161, 215.
    See also schema
artifacts, xvi, 8, 10, 11, 162, 208, 209, 241, 313
Author's Chair
    comparison to Reader of the Day, 45
Canyons (Paulsen, 1990), 50, 98, 205, 206, 208, 211, 212, 214, 233
    connections between students, author, and characters, 206
    corresponding with the author, 214–215
    creating journals for the characters, 208–211
    evaluation and assessment, 241
    questions, comments, and observations, 281–287
    response options and specifications, 312
    summary of the novel, 205
    writing found poems based on, 211–214
character
    improvisation, 174, 177, 178, 190
    interrogation, 174–178, 190
choice
    in Reader of the Day activity, 45, 48, 62, 86, 87
    objects of personal significance, 87
    of curriculum. *See* collaborative curriculum
    of reading material, 118
    of seating, 35
    understanding of, 6
    written literary experiences, 195
choral reading, 168–169, 192
cognitive strategy
    defined, 91
collaboration
    cognitive, 135
    verbal, 135
collaborative curriculum, 60–61
community
    academic freedom, 6

Index

central ideas of, 112
classroom, 2, 4, 28, 34
collaborative role of teacher, 137
comparison of concept to freedom, 5
connection between language, 6
connections to communities in literary texts, 30–31
connections to the community of authors, 31–32
developing
physical context of the room, 8
sense of family, 5, 34
sense of freedom, 34
sense of identity, 58
sense of place, 58
sense of trust, 6
emotional psychological realm, 34–36
evaluation and assessment, 33–34
literacy, xiii, xv, xvi, xvii, 1, 2, 3, 4, 5, 8, 14, 17, 18, 23, 26, 27, 29, 30, 31, 33, 34, 35, 41, 42, 57, 63, 87, 112, 118, 129, 135, 156, 162, 163, 166, 170, 191, 261
academic, 62, 63
developing ideas about, 12–13
central ideas, 13
diversity, 35
equality, 35
making connections, 30, 147, 161, 302
personal, 62, 63
seating, 11–12
sustaining and developing, 17
network of, 27, 33
of learners, xv, 14, 17, 24, 36, 132, 149, 232, 260
of writers, 205
organizing, 9–11
peer influence, 20
physical context of, 8, 34, 35
power structure(s), xv, xvii
school, 7, 27
sense of empowerment, 114
sense of family, 6
ascriptive status, 57
sense of ownership, 113, 116, 117, 118
sense of trust, 99, 129
students define, 27
community of literary texts, 30

community of readers and writers. See community: of learners
complex adaptive system, 92, 95–99
stages of
comprehension, 95, 96
coupling (or information flow), 95, 96, 97, 98
differentiation, 95, 96, 97, 98
regularities (or patterns), 95, 97, 98, 129
examples, 95
self-organization (or learning accom-modation), 95, 96, 97, 98, 99, 129
conflict(s) in literature, 238
external conflict, 239
internal conflict, 238
person versus nature, 238
person versus person, 238
person versus self, 238
construct meaning. See meaning making
context
emergence of, 3
for educational interactions. See literacy community
conversations about literature
aspects of, 141
critical pedagogy, 46
defining selves
constructing life map(s), 42–44
developing ideas about the power of the individual, 37–42
evaluation and assessment, 83–84
through objects of personal significance, 63–77
through poetry, 77–83
through Reader of the Day, 44–63
dramatization. See performance
empowered, xvii, 26, 29, 40, 84, 85, 117, 130, 132, 146
empowerment, 1, 3, 6, 14, 36, 39, 49, 62, 83, 85, 88, 90, 91, 112, 114, 118, 128, 129, 132, 150, 164, 168
degenerative to, 129
form of agency, 6
evaluation and assessment
of activities for defining selves, 83–84
of generating questions, comments,

and observations, 128–129
of performance, 190–191
of talk, 161–162
of the literacy community, 33–34
of visual representation, 260–261
of writing, 240–242
found poems. See writing: found poems; poetry: found poems
genre, xviii, 118, 196, 221, 227
human agency
  defined, 6
identity, 36, 39, 40, 41, 57, 64, 78, 83, 85, 87, 130, 131, 206
  construction of, 87
  emergence of through reading, 57
  masks, 56
  reconceptualization of self, 78
  understanding of self, 83
individuation, 145, 149, 160, 162
  definition of, 145
inferential comprehension. See complex adaptive system: stages of: self-organization
interact, 12, 13, 19, 26, 35, 36, 41, 88, 95, 130, 132, 144, 147, 148, 179, 232
Journey (MacLachlan, 1991), 11
  constructing a collage, 250, 251, 260
  discussion of, 136, 141, 196
  reading of, 93
  summary of, 27
learning community. See community: of learners
life maps, 85
  construction, 42
  storytelling, 44
literacy club. See community:literacy
  Frank Smith description of, 3
literacy community. See community: literacy
literal comprehension. See complex adaptive system: stages of: regularities
Macbeth (Shakespeare)
  found poem(s), 233–236
  performance of, 166, 167, 185–190
  writing found poem(s), 242
  writing to draw conclusion(s), 236–240, 242
meaning making, xv, xvi, xvii, xviii, 17, 22, 34, 40, 85, 87, 88, 91, 99, 114, 129, 132, 144, 161, 164, 166, 167, 168, 169, 189, 190, 243, 246, 257, 258, 260
meeting objectives checklist, 33
meta-cognition. See reflection
Museum of Objects and Ideas, 64, 65, 84
  creation of, 65–67
  object(s) of personal significance, 64, 65, 68, 69, 70, 73, 76, 77, 84, 85, 87
  planning sheet, 270
mystery
  radio play(s). See radio play(s)
  reading of, 51, 63, 119, 121, 123
  writing of
    detective's notebook mystery, 227–233
    found poem(s), 256–257
    paper bag mystery, 221–227
note board, 9, 22
object(s) of personal significance. See Museum of Objects and Ideas
odes, 219, 220, 221
one-on-one student interview(s), xv, 2, 5, 39, 40, 46, 109, 114, 119, 127
Outsiders, The (Hinton, 1989), 30, 96, 98, 99, 215
  comparing and contrasting characters through poetry, 178, 180, 191
  creating a wallet exercise, 251–255
  creating paper characters, 32, 255–256
  writing about paper characters, 255
  defining the concepts, 215–219
  discussion of, 299
  questions, comments, and observations, 99–109, 288–291
  reading of, 32, 40, 99–109, 99, 108, 129, 130, 190, 221
  students' perspectives on writing questions, comments, and observations, 109–118
  summary of, 99
  writing neighborhood odes, 219–221
ownership, 52, 69, 83, 86, 89, 117, 192, 229
performance
  character interrogation, 174–178
  choral reading, 168–169

Index

developing ideas about, 165–168
evaluation and assessment, 190–191
Macbeth (Shakespeare), 185–190
radio plays, 182–185
Van Gogh Café (Rylant, 1995), 169–174
performance standards, xvii
picture books, 30
poetry
  based on photograph(s), 28, 29
  Book Lice (Fleischman, 1988), 179, 191
  Celebrate America in Poetry and Art (edited by Panzer, 1994), 246
  evaluation and assessment, 191, 241, 242
  found poem(s), 211, 214, 233, 256, 260, 312
  Journey (Giovanni, 1993), 168, 169, 178, 190
  Joyful Noise: Poems for Two Voices (Fleischman, 1988), 178
  Neighborhood Odes (Soto, 1992), 220
  Paintbrush (Canfield, Hansen, and Kirberger, 1997), 57
  performing, 180–182
  Pizza A Party and A Moonlight Ride, A (anonymous), 59
  Poemcrazy: Freeing Your Life With Words (Wooldridge, 1996), 64
  Poetry Cafe, 178–182
  Remember (Harjo, 1994), 31, 247
  Somebody Should Have Taught Him (Canfield, Hansen, and Kirberger, 1997), 56
  Something Permanent (Rylant, 1994), 27
  using to define selves, 77–83
power, 6, 7, 34. See empowerment
  defined, 6
  equalization of, 85, 88, 91, 112, 117, 132, 150
  of talk. See talk
  of the group, 1–6, 17, 26, 34, 35, 145, 162
  of the individual, 36, 37–42, 48, 85, 86, 87, 130, 145, 162, 164
  of visual representation. See visual representation
  of writing. See writing
  spiral of
    emotional-psychological elements, 34
    physical elements, 34
power structure(s). See community: power structure(s)
proximal development zone, 93
questioning
  of text. *See* text: questioning of
radio plays
  analyzing and performing, 182–183
  commercials, 184
  identifying aspects of a performance, 183
  Mystery in the Spotlight (Scholastic, Inc. 1994), 183
  The Adventure of the Blue Carbuncle, 183
  The Invisible Man (adaptation), 183
  The Monkey's Paw (adaptation), 183
  The Open Window (adaptation), 183
  The Specter Bridegroom, 183
read aloud(s), 94, 121, 205, 225
Reader of the Day, 10, 30, 33, 44, 45, 46, 47, 48, 49, 50, 51, 52, 53, 54, 57, 58, 59, 60, 61, 62, 63, 86, 102
  activity setting, 47
    interactive factors, 47
      cultural value(s), 47, 51
      operations and task demands, 47, 53
      participant(s), 47, 49, 61, 86, 303
      purpose(s) or motive(s), 47, 56, 59, 258
      script(s) for conduct, 47, 54, 55
  Author's Chair, comparison to, 46
  construction of identity, 87
  human need for expression, 62
  introducing, 46–47
  process defined, 47
  read aloud(s), 33, 41, 45, 47, 48, 55, 57, 58, 60, 61, 86, 130
  reader behavior, 55
  self directed learning, 60
  social context, 44, 46, 48, 49, 86, 87
  social pressure
    resistance to, 58
Reader/Writer log(s), 11, 13, 31, 33, 43, 64, 65, 111, 119, 120, 121, 123, 127, 150, 154, 241, 242

reading
  defining, 15–16
reading skill(s)
  analyzing information, xviii
  identifying supporting ideas, xviii
  meaning of words, xviii, 185
  perceiving relationships, xviii
  recognizing outcomes, xviii
  recognizing points of view, propaganda, and/or statement of fact and opinion, xviii
  summarizing, xviii, 255
reading/writing portfolio
  content, 9
  location, 9
  purpose, 9
reconceptualization of self. See identity: reconceptualization of self
reflection, 13, 36, 39, 85, 91, 97, 130, 132, 148, 149, 190, 193, 214, 260
regenerative knowledge, 51
  respect, 18, 19, 22, 23, 26, 35, 112, 122, 129, 150
  through caring, 23–26
  through honoring the products of learning, 22–23
  through learning from one another, 19–22
  through participation, 19
role, 18
rubric(s), 84, 183, 184, 190, 191, 228, 232, 241, 242, 260, 261
schema, 95, 98, 215
solidarity, 145, 149, 160, 162. See power: of the group
  definition of, 145
standardized test, xvii, xviii
surveys
  reading and writing, 16
Survival Across Time, 258
  survival quilt, 258–60
TAAS. See Texas Assessment of Academic Skills
talk
  developing ideas about, 133–136
  evaluation and assessment, 161–162
  in small groups, 150–161
  opening conversations, 136–144
  types of power in conversation, 144

  types of power within, 144–150
teacher generated questions, 116, 149
TEKS. See Texas Essential Knowledge and Skills
Texas Assessment of Academic Skills. See standardized test
Texas Essential Knowledge and Skills. See performance standard(s)
text
  questioning of, developing ideas about, 89–92
  questions, comments, and observations about
  as a complex adaptive system. See complex adaptive system
  evaluation and assessment, 128–129
  process, 92–95
  reading of a single text, 99–109
  student perspective(s), 109
  transferring to independent reading, 126–128
transaction
  defined, 90
transaction(s)
  in silent independent reading, 118–126
tour of classroom, 9–12
transacting with text. See text
Van Gogh Café, The (Rylant, 1995), 168, 190, 241
  performance of, 169–174
  writing alternate version, 200–205
word ticket(s), 11, 64, 66, 77, 84
writing
  about objects of personal significance, 67–76
  alternate versions of a text, 200–205
  character journal(s), 208–211, 208
  corresponding with an author. See *Canyons*: corresponding with the author
  defining selves through poetry, 77–83
  detective's notebook, 227–233
  developing ideas, 193
  drawing as an aid to, 246
  evaluation and assessment, 83–84, 190–191, 240–242, 260–261
  found poem(s). See *Canyons*: found

poems
  in response to photographs, 196–200
    process described, 197
    student examples, 198
  inner dialogue, 196, 197, 200, 241
  letter to a character, 251–255
  mystery poem(s), 256–257
  odes, 219
  paper bag mystery, 221–227
  personal essay, 68, 69, 77
    selection of topic, 70
  the important thing about a character, 255–256
  to compare and contrast characters, 178–182
  to define concepts, 215–219
  to develop an understanding of Shakespeare, 233–236
  to draw conclusions, 236–240
  to express meaning, 193

Title Index

Adventures and Misadventures of Peter Beard in Africa, The (Bowmaster, 1993), 208
Always Return Your Phone Calls, (Canfield, Hansen, and Kirberger, 1997, p. 55–56), 51
Amelia's Notebook (Moss, 1995), 31
And Then There Were None (Christie, 1991), 119, 120
Aunt Chip and the Great Triple Creek Dam Affair (Polacco, 1996), 31
Bard of Avon, The (Stanley, 1992), 186, 188
Bible, The (Canfield, Hansen, and Kirberger, 1997, p. 78), 50
Big Lie: A True Story, The (Leitner, 1992), 24
Book Lice (Fleischman, 1988), 179, 191
Candidate for Murder, A (Nixon, 1991), 119
Canyons (Paulsen, 1990), 50, 98, 205, 206, 208, 211, 212, 214, 233
  connections between students, author, and characters, 206
  corresponding with the author, 214–215
  creating journals for the characters, 208–211
  evaluation and assessment, 241
  questions, comments, and observations, 281–287
  response options and specifications, 312
  summary of the novel, 205
  writing found poems based on, 211–214
Carl Makes a Scrapbook (Day, 1994), 31
Celebrate America in Poetry and Art (edited by Panzer, 1994), 31, 246
Charlotte's Web (White, 1952), 66, 328
Chicken Soup for the Teenage Soul (Canfield, Hansen, and Kirberger, 1997), 30, 50, 55, 57, 60, 62
Child Called It, A (Pelzer, 1995), 41, 50, 61
Deadly Deception (Haynes, 1994), 119
Death Walk (Morey, 1991), 31
Devil's Arithmetic, The (Yolen, 1988), 24
Dimestore Teapot, The (Nordan, 1997), 67, 68, 77
Dogsong (Paulsen, 1985), 206
Double Trouble Squared (Lasky, 1991), 96, 98, 99, 129
  questions, comments, and observations, 276–280
Driver's Ed (Cooney, 1994), 119
Final Journey, The (Pausewang, 1996), 24, 127
Fourth of July (Brancato, 1984), 174, 190
Ghost Cadet (Alphin, 1992), 21
Ghost in the House, A (Wright, 1991), 119
Giver, The (Lowry, 1993), 96, 98, 129, 257, 258
  questions, comments, and observations, 292–298
Great Beginnings: Opening Lines of Great Novels (Ensign, 1993), 224
Hatchet (Paulsen, 1987), 206
House of Dies Drear, The (Hamilton, 1984), 119
I Am Regina (Keehn, 1993), 153
I Have Lived a Thousand Years (Bitton-Jackson, 1997), 150

Important Book, The (Brown, 1949), 255, 320
Inventing the Truth: The Art and Craft of a Memoir (ed. Zinsser, 1987), 67
Journey (Giovanni, 1993), 168, 169, 178, 190
Journey (MacLachlan, 1991), 11
  constructing a collage, 250, 251, 260
  discussion of, 136, 141, 196
  reading of, 93
  summary of, 27
Kidnapping of Christina Lattimore, The (Nixon, 1992), 119
Library, The (Stewart, 1995), 31
Lord of the Flies (Golding, 1954), 58
Macbeth (Shakespeare)
  found poem(s), 233–36
  performance of, 166, 167, 185–190
  writing found poem(s), 242
  writing to draw conclusion(s), 236–240, 242
Meet Addy: An American Girl (Porter, 1993), 53
Neighborhood Odes (Soto, 1992), 219, 220
Nightjohn (Paulsen, 1993), 82, 156, 157
Other Side of Dark, The (Nixon, 1992), 119, 121
Outsiders, The (Hinton, 1989), 30, 96, 98, 99, 215
  comparing and contrasting characters through poetry, 178, 180, 191
  creating a wallet exercise, 251–255
  creating paper characters, 32, 255–256
  writing about paper characters, 255
  defining the concepts, 215–219
  discussion of, 299
  questions, comments, and observations, 99–109, 288–291
  reading of, 32, 40, 99–109, 99, 108, 129, 130, 190, 221
  students' perspectives on writing questions, comments, and observations, 109–118
  summary of, 99
  writing neighborhood odes, 219–221

Pizza A Party and A Moonlight Ride, A (anonymous), 51, 55
Poemcrazy: Freeing Your Life With Words (Wooldridge, 1996), 64
Polar Express (Allsburg, 1985), 58
Mystery in the Spotlight (Scholastic, Inc. 1994), 183
Real Diary: Go Ask Alice, A (anonymous, 1971), 53
Remember (Harjo, 1994), 31, 247, 260
Somebody Should Have Taught Him (Canfield, Hansen, and Kirberger, 1997), 56
Something Permanent (1994), 27
Something Upstairs (Avi, 1990), 119
Stalker, The (Nixon, 1992), 187
Sweet Friday Island (Taylor, 1994), 119, 120, 256
Tar Beach (Ringgold, 1991), 258
Van Gogh Café, The (Rylant, 1995), 168, 190, 241
View From Saturday, The (Konigsburg, 1996), 27, 69, 77
Walking the Log: Memories of a Southern Childhood (Nickens, 1994), 31
Wanted (Cooney, 1997), 63, 119, 125
Whispers from the Dead (Nixon, 1991), 119
Wilderness Peril (Dygard, 1991), 119

About the Author

Leigh Van Horn is currently assistant professor of Reading and Language Arts in the Department of Urban Education at the University of Houston—Downtown. Van Horn teaches field and university based courses in reading and language arts theory and methodology and works with pre-service and in-service teachers as well as students in urban elementary and middle schools in efforts to identify, describe, and expand upon the methodologies which will best serve the needs of a diverse cultural population. Her research focuses upon issues related to literacy, empowerment, and urban education.

CALLAHAN LIBRARY
ST JOSEPH'S COLLEGE
25 Audubon Avenue
Patchogue, NY 11772-2399